N. Riche   21-

Aesthetic Computing

LEONARDO

Roger F. Malina, series editor

Aesthetic Computing

edited by Paul Fishwick

The MIT Press
Cambridge, Massachusetts
London, England

MIT Press books may be purchased at special quantity discounts for business or sales promotional use. For information, please email special_sales@mitpress.mit.edu or write to Special Sales Department, The MIT Press, 55 Hayward Street, Cambridge, MA 02142.

This book was set in Garamond 3 and Bell Gothic on 3B2 by Asco Typesetters, Hong Kong. Printed and bound in the United States of America.

Library of Congress Cataloging-in-Publication Data

Aesthetic computing / edited by Paul Fishwick.
    p.   cm.
Includes bibliographical references and index.
ISBN 0-262-06250-X (alk. paper)
1. Computer science. 2. Aesthetics. I. Fishwick, Paul A.
QA76.5.A3393   2006
004—dc22   2005054458

10 9 8 7 6 5 4 3 2 1

To Barbara Jean Fishwick

Contents

Contents

The cultural convergence of art, science, and technology provides ample opportunity for artists to challenge the very notion of how art is produced and to call into question its subject matter and its function in society. The mission of the Leonardo book series, published by The MIT Press, is to publish texts by artists, scientists, researchers, and scholars that present innovative discourse on the convergence of art, science, and technology.

Envisioned as a catalyst for enterprise, research, and creative and scholarly experimentation, the book series enables diverse intellectual communities to explore common grounds of expertise. The Leonardo book series provides a context for the discussion of contemporary practice, ideas, and frameworks in this rapidly evolving arena where art and science connect.

To find more information about Leonardo/ISAST and to order our publications, go to Leonardo Online at ⟨http://lbs.mit.edu⟩ or send e-mail to ⟨leonardobooks@mitpress.mit.edu⟩.

Joel Slayton
Chair, Leonardo Book Series

Book Series Advisory Committee: Annick Bureaud, Pamela Grant Ryan, Michael Punt, Douglas Sery

Leonardo/International Society for the Arts, Sciences, and Technology (ISAST)

Leonardo, the International Society for the Arts, Sciences, and Technology, and the affiliated French organization Association Leonardo have two very simple goals:

1. to document and make known the work of artists, researchers, and scholars interested in the ways that the contemporary arts interact with science and technology, and
2. to create a forum and meeting places where artists, scientists, and engineers can meet, exchange ideas, and, where appropriate, collaborate.

When the journal *Leonardo* was started some thirty-five years ago, these creative disciplines existed in segregated institutional and social networks, a situation dramatized at that time by the "Two Cultures" debates initiated by C. P. Snow. Today we live in a different time of cross-disciplinary ferment, collaboration and intellectual confrontation enabled by new hybrid organizations, new funding sponsors, and the shared tools of computers and the Internet. Above all, new generations of artist-researchers and researcher-artists are now at work individually and in collaborative teams bridging the art, science, and technology disciplines. Perhaps in our lifetime we will see the emergence of "new Leonardos," creative individuals or teams who will not only develop a meaningful art for our times but also drive new agendas in science and stimulate technological innovation that addresses today's human needs.

For more information on the activities of the Leonardo organizations and networks, please visit our Web site at ⟨http://www.leonardo.info⟩.

Roger F. Malina
Chair, Leonardo/ISAST

Preface

This book concerns *aesthetics* and *computing* with an emphasis on how the former affects the latter. *Aesthetics* is defined as sense perception and the associated cognitive state of a person who is under the influence of the *aesthetic experience*. One speaks of a "beautiful sunset" or an artist's painting. Most would agree that the experience of nature is part of aesthetics, whereas art is a subset delimited by intentional and creative acts. The line between aesthetics and art may be blurred, however, if one imagines that the organic state of the brain during the aesthetic experience would actually be a *form of creation on the part of the recipient*, if only we possessed sufficiently advanced technology capable of rendering cognitive state (i.e., art through brain activity). Nevertheless, we use the term *aesthetic* rather than art to define the broadest possible array of effects of art and design on the field of computer science, or *computing*.

We are entering a remarkable period of time when advances in technology—3D displays, tangible and pervasive computing, and the ability to extend computing to the realm of other senses (i.e., sound, touch, smell)—have the potential to radically alter computer science, and possibly its formal foundation: mathematics. We have the aesthetics of the arts on one hand, and the criteria for optimality in mathematics and computing, on the other. Could aesthetics in mathematics and computing be more than a search for the optimal condition, and art rather than simply a client of computing, actually be contributing to it? The authors in this volume write about such possibilities, and in this sense, this volume is groundbreaking in its attempt to redefine aesthetics in computing and art simultaneously. Familiar objects such as automobiles and houses are true blends of design, art, and utility. Is it surprising, then, that the artifacts of mathematics and computing would be any different?

The book is divided into four sections: (1) philosophy and representation, (2) art and design, (3) mathematics and computing, and (4) interface and interaction. Aside from the observation that *the general* usually precedes *the specific* in an explanation, the sections have no particular ordering. The first section deals with the raw concepts of aesthetics, computing, semiotics, and representation. Fishwick espouses the need *to expand* the definition of aesthetics in computing to borrow from design and the arts in an attempt to progress beyond the idea that aesthetics is primarily about optimality. Lee employs Goodman's theory of art-as-symbol-system, as a way to successfully critique symbol use in aesthetic computing. Malina covers a wide swath of art and computing within the context of the history of the *Leonardo* foundation. He defines the *weak* and *strong* claims for aesthetic computing. Nake and Grabowski make the striking observation that, ultimately, aesthetic computing brings *subjectivity* and *quality* into an area that has traditionally known mostly perceived objectivity and quantity. Paton tells us that *metaphor* is at the heart of aesthetic computing in the way representations are used as interfaces between human and computer.

The second section covers how artists are shaping and expanding the field of computer science. Cox emphasizes the importance of metaphor in visualization as the primary vehicle by which we make sense of data, and she stresses the importance of the social fabric of aesthetic computing—*renaissance teams*. Fleischmann and Strauss bring about new interactive spaces as both artistic exhibits and progenitors of new ways of doing human-computer interaction (HCI). Huff has created a series of artworks that emphasize deeply mathematical concepts within an elaborate visual space that pays special attention to color and texture at many levels of detail. Mignonneau and Sommerer reinforce the notion of artist as inventor *of interfaces*, pointing out that both types of aesthetics (optimal condition as found traditionally in programming and visual and sensory, as found in art) can coexist. That is to say—we can do both in aesthetic computing, without sacrificing one type of aesthetic for the other. Prophet and d'Inverno define what it means, in a way consistent with Cox, to have effective *transdisciplinary* teams composed of artists, designers, and scientists. She points out that the effects of such collaboration are manifold—affecting the fields of computing and art, as well as the way in which team participants view their own work. Reas and Fry invented *Processing*, which is an open source code effort with a vibrant community. Processing has the distinct potential to do two things: give designers and artists new ways of communicating, and give computer scientists new ways of attracting people to their field through design as a catalyst. The *code* becomes the artist's material.

The third section represents the core of mathematics and computing, and how aesthetics are interpreted. While aesthetics and mathematics have been covered within the same context before, there is significant room for elaboration on exactly how aesthetics are defined, and these authors provide seminal views for these definitions. Diehl and

Görg describe how the visualization of software and data amount to defining computer scientists view attributes in software such as beauty and elegance. Emmer walks us through the entire history of aesthetics of mathematics, with descriptions on how mathematicians view the aesthetics of their field. Leymarie exposes us to the beauty of shape to discover why we find certain forms pleasing and others displeasing. He introduces the *shock scaffold* as a means to that end. Leyton boldly defines a view of aesthetics in terms of two new geometrically grounded principles: *maximization of transfer* and *recoverability*. Quigley makes a detailed and comprehensive statement of how aesthetics are defined within information visualization, a topic of significance in computer science. Vickers and Alty introduce the relatively new modality of sound and music to computing. They inject music into the task of programming as a way to improve debugging and analysis.

The fourth section emphasizes that the task of aesthetic computing confronts the computer-human interface—the ways in which humans interact with computers. Bertelsen creates a view of the interface as a study of *primary* and *secondary artifacts*, and of *tertiary artifacts* that stress HCI as an *aesthetic discipline*. Bolter and Gromala use the optical metaphors of *transparency* and *reflectivity* to define how we view the human-computer interface. For a particular task in computing are we attempting to see beyond (i.e., see through) the interface or reflect on it? Löwgren illustrates how our current view of human-computer interaction is lacking unless we take into account a new set of qualities. He defines nineteen new "use qualities" that go beyond the traditional utilitarian HCI perspective. Tractinsky and Zmiri present an empirical study of skins (i.e., used to design the "look and feel" of actual and virtual control devices). They note that HCI, while traditionally focused on task efficiency, plays a significant role in evaluating the importance of emotion and aesthetics in the interface.

To form a new area, many people are required both to define the area and to enable it to flourish. There are numerous acknowledgments to be made, so I'll begin with thanking the people at MIT Press for their encouragement and making this book possible. In particular, I would like to thank both Doug Sery and Valerie Geary, as well as Roger Malina who directs the *Leonardo* foundation, and its associated journals and activities. The topic of aesthetic computing had its beginnings at a small workshop in southwest Germany: Dagstuhl, which is directed by Reinhard Wilhelm. This event, Dagstuhl Seminar 02291, served as a landmark occurrence for fleshing out core issues in aesthetic computing. I would like to thank my workshop co-organizers, Roger Malina and Christa Sommerer, as well as all workshop participants listed in alphabetical order by last name: Olav Bertelsen, Jay Bolter, Willi Bruns, Annick Bureaud, Stephan Diehl, Florian Dombois, Achim Ebert, Ernest Edmonds, Karl Entacher, Susanne Grabowski, Hans Hagen, Volker Höhing, Kristiina Karvonen, John Lee, Jonas Löwgren, Jon McCormack, Richard Merritt, Boris

Müller, Jörg Müller, Frieder Nake, Daniela-Alina Plewe, Jane Prophet, Rhonda Roland Shearer, Steven Schkolne, Angelika Schulz, Neora Berger Shem-Shaul, and Noam Tractinsky. Without their active participation, there would be neither an area nor a book. This work was sponsored in part by the National Science Foundation under grant EIA-0119532 (Anita LaSalle) and the Air Force Research Laboratory under contract F30602-01-1-05920119532 (Alex Sisti). Our research group is grateful for their financial support. I would also like to thank all of my students for the past four years in the Aesthetic Computing classes at the University of Florida: they have helped validate this area, and contributed their combined computing and artistic craft. In particular, Kristian Damkjer, John Hopkins, Taewoo Kim, Hyunju Shim, Minho Park, and Jinho Lee were active graduate students who contributed to concepts in dynamic model representation during the editing of this book.

While this book answers many questions on how aesthetics can be applied to computing, it also raises some key questions that will need further elaboration by the community. We must carefully address these in the years to come:

- To what extent can the traditional definitions of aesthetics in computing and art be interrelated and connected, with each informing the other?
- What roles can quality, subjectivity, and emotion play in mathematics and computing as ways to achieve a balance between form and function?
- What are effective social frameworks in which artists, designers, mathematicians, and computer scientists can collaborate in teams or in distributed networks?

Aesthetic Computing

I

Philosophy and Representation

An Introduction to Aesthetic Computing

Paul Fishwick

In this brief introduction to a new area of study, *aesthetic computing*, we first define the terminology, then position the area in the context of related fields that combine art, mathematics, and computing. Aesthetic computing is concerned with the impact and effects of aesthetics on the *field of computing*. This text is divided into two primary sections. The first section we discuss aesthetics, art, and the motivation for defining another hybrid phrase. The attempt here is to capture the field by historical context, definition, and a graphical illustration. The close relationship between aesthetics and art (i.e., aesthetics being the philosophy of art) is justified with citations to recent literature, to the point we can use the two words interchangeably. In the second section, we describe research on novel representations created locally at the University of Florida, in the aesthetic computing class and the simulation and modeling research laboratory.

To help spur a discussion in aesthetic computing, an attempt to bring several key researchers and practitioners to the same table prompted a meeting in Dagstuhl, Germany (Dagstuhl), in mid-July 2002. We held a week-long workshop, organized by Roger Malina, Christa Sommerer, and myself. More than thirty representatives of art, design, computer science, and mathematics attended the workshop, which was cosponsored by Dagstuhl and Leonardo (*Leonardo*). The purpose of the workshop was to carve out an area, or at least to see whether this was possible, based on the notion that aesthetics and art could play a role in computing disciplines. A manifesto was created on the last day of the workshop as a preliminary definition for the area, and was recently published in *Leonardo* (Fishwick 2003).

Aesthetics and Art

Aesthetic computing is the application of aesthetics to computing. The goal of aesthetic computing is to affect areas within *computing*, which for our purposes, will be defined broadly as the area of *computer science*. With respect to aesthetics, this goal also includes the idea that the application of aesthetics to computing and mathematics, the formal foundations for computing, can extend beyond classic concepts such as symmetry and invariance to encompass the wide range of aesthetic definitions and categories normally associated with making art. One might, for example, represent structures in computing using the style of Gaudi or the Bauhaus school. The words *aesthetics* and *computing* need further discussion before we proceed. "Aesthetics" stems from the Greek αισθητική *aisthitiki*, derived from *aisthesis* (i.e., perceived by the senses). Plato's aesthetics revolved around his *forms*, and Greek society stressed mimesis (i.e., imitation, mimicry) as central to art's purpose. Within the continuing history of aesthetics, prior to Kant's *Critique* (1790) and including Baumgarten's (1750) introduction of aesthetics as the *science of the beautiful*, art and aesthetics have not been well connected. Art was generally not associated with aesthetics, and aesthetics as an area within philosophy was not focused on art. Since Kant's treatise, aesthetics has been expanded to encompass both the logical and the perceptual. The Oxford English Dictionary (2003) contains the following two definitions for aesthetics: (1) the science that treats the conditions of sensuous perception; and (2) the philosophy or theory of taste, or of the perception of the beautiful in nature and art. In the *Encyclopedia of Aesthetics*, one of the most comprehensive references on the subject, spanning four volumes, Kelly (1998, p. 11) in his preface, states

Ask contemporary aestheticians what they do, however, and they are likely to respond that aesthetics is the philosophical analysis of the beliefs, concepts, and theories implicit in the creation, experience, interpretation, or critique of art.

Kelly proceeds to highlight the goal of the encyclopedia, which is "to trace the genealogy of aesthetics" in such a way as to integrate both its philosophical and its cultural roles. The word "art," in the sense in which Kelly discusses aesthetics, is defined broadly enough to combine logical as well as material aspects, or computing and art. Thus, an elegant computer program and a sculpture are both forms of art. Furthermore, one may speak generally of aesthetics in terms of symmetry and harmony or, more singularly, in terms of the aesthetics of the artist Dali, for example, or the surrealist movement as a whole. Other definitions of aesthetics, as found in Bredin and Santoro-Brienza (2000) and Osborne (1970), also emphasize the close relationships between aesthetics and art. In summary, aesthetics provides a philosophical foundation for art in theory and practice.

While the previous discussion provides close connections between aesthetics and art, the term *art* has yet to be defined. There is a huge literature base for those wishing to define what art is; however, we will refer to Dorn's overview (1999) in which he characterizes art in two dimensions. First, philosophically, art can be defined as an idea, form, or language. Second, psychologically, one can define art with top-down and bottom-up conceptions. Art may also be characterized in terms of alternative perspectives, which tend to be highly correlated with specific historical and cultural contexts. Adams (1996) and Freeland (2001) take a more categorical approach to art theory. For example, Adams emphasizes the following contemporary interpretations: formalism, iconography, Marxism, feminism, biography, semiotics, and psychoanalysis. In terms of art practice, Wilson (2002) presents a large number of areas, examples, and contemporary issues that affect the artist. Edwards (1986) and Edmonds and Candy (2002) advocate a pragmatic role for art, seated in creativity.

Computing

While attempting to define aesthetics and art can provoke numerous debates, defining computing may be a little easier. Within the academy, computing is referred to by an assortment of names such as computer science, computer and information science, and computer engineering. Each of these subareas may have a slightly different strategy, but we will associate computing with computer science without sacrificing clarity or scope. Computer science incorporates a large number of areas, some of which are evolving fairly rapidly. In general, the Association for Computing Machinery (ACM) and the IEEE Computer Society (IEEE-CS) have numerous special interest groups and technical committees that give us a handle on the breadth of the discipline. Subareas include discrete mathematics, theory of computing, programming languages, data structures, artificial intelligence, computer–human interaction (also known as human–computer interaction or HCI), operating systems, computer graphics, computer simulation, and computer vision. When we speak of aesthetic computing, we therefore apply aesthetics to one or more of these subareas.

Recently, Denning (2003) suggests a new high-level taxonomy based on application domains, core technologies, design principles, and computing mechanics. While on the subject of computing, it is important to stress the relationship between mathematics and computing. Computer science is founded on core elements of *discrete mathematics*; thus, we can view aesthetic computing as encompassing a number of mathematical concepts, especially areas involving formal grammar, language notation, geometry, and topology. Discrete mathematics forms the early core of most computer science curricula, along with the algebraic extension to automata theory, which is generally studied in one's senior year at university. The importance of mathematics to computing cannot be overemphasized; it establishes the formal infrastructure in which mathematical concepts and abstractions can be related to basic computing concepts. Thus, much of aesthetic computing corresponds naturally with mathematical formalism.

Aesthetic Computing: An Overview

We are now in a position to combine two words *aesthetic* and *computing*. We define aesthetic computing as *the application of the theory and practice of art to the field of computing*. While this definition lacks the nuances and scope of Kelly's earlier definition of aesthetics, it defines it more concisely for our purposes. Aesthetic computing relates to the following sorts of sample activities: (1) representing programs and data structures with customized, culturally specific notations; (2) incorporating artistic methods in typically computing-intensive activities, such as scientific visualization; (3) improving the emotional and cultural level of interaction with the computer.

Generally, aesthetic computing involves one of two types of aesthetics applications: *analysis* and *synthesis*. Analytic applications tend to evaluate artifacts of computing and mathematics from the perspective of classical aesthetic *qualities* such as mimesis, symmetry, parsimony, and beauty. Synthetic applications tend to employ aesthetics as a means of *representation* of the artifacts. The word "representation" is broadly defined to encompass the concepts of interaction and interface, rather than simply static presentation.

Aesthetics and computing are therefore rich in both practical and theoretical taxonomy, categories, and encyclopedic knowledge. One aspect of aesthetics that may at first seem tangential is considered central to aesthetic computing: *plurality* (Goodman 1978). Most references to art cover aesthetics from a multitude of cultural aspects, genres, and historical episodes. Plurality therefore appears to be a critical component of aesthetics as it applies to computing, lest we imagine that only traditional aesthetics associated with mathematics (Plotnitsky 1998)—parsimony, symmetry, and so forth—are relevant. In fact, one of the goals of aesthetic computing is to facilitate the expanding role of aesthetics in mathematics, and by extension, computing. This plurality must encompass both body and mind, the material as well as the mental. This suggests *aesthetic diversity* (Fishwick 2002a), and perhaps that more traditional aesthetics of mathematics and computing are subsets of those found in art (e.g., minimalism, symmetry, the harmony of the golden ratio in architecture).

Reviewing the numerous historical approaches to art, and the contemporary categories for facilitating critiques, one generalizes about aesthetics' concern with cultural perspective—that is, the idea that an object can be viewed and considered from many

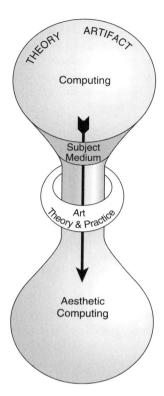

Figure 1.1 Aesthetic computing process architecture.

angles, through numerous *lenses*. This multiperspectivism is an important concept in aesthetic computing, serving as a bridge between the two areas. Certainly, art has the potential to create new ways of looking, listening, and touching things that are relevant to computing: interfaces, programs, data, and models. The pluralistic heart of aesthetics encourages multiple representations. Computing supports plurality in many of its subdisciplines, but in aesthetics and art practice, it is virtually a defining criterion.

The architectural diagram for aesthetic computing shown in figure 1.1 defines it as a unique area. In the hourglass-shaped figure, imaginary sand particles flow from top to bottom "spheres." The particles are modulated by a "Subject/Medium" filter. The diagram allows us to discuss a variety of approaches, beginning with a computing discipline identified by one of its objects (i.e., an artifact), its theory, or its practice (i.e., how the discipline proceeds within the computing field).

The "Subject/Medium" filter suggests that we are not using the computing discipline strictly to generate tools, but rather to provide a *raw medium* or the *subject material* for art.

Various media theorists (Manovich 2001; Coyne 1999) have discussed the concept of materialism at length; however, we use the word in its dictionary definition of *embodiment*, in contrast to *mind*. Thus, virtual reality, as discussed within the art literature (Grau 2003), is materialistic because it is consistent with embodiment and immersion in an enhanced sensory experience, regardless of whether this experience is *real* or *illusory*. Mental constructs, on the other hand, are nonsensory and so have no material existence. Continuing HCI and visualization research extends such materialistic qualities as presence, engagement, and immersion which facilitate human sensory connection to otherwise *invisible information*, or information that has minimal sensory qualities.

Returning to the filter in figure 1.1, when a program is used for its "tool-worthiness," there is little or no reflection on the essence of computing (i.e., the internals of the program or data structures, their underlying mathematical structures) or the practices of computing. However, art created using the medium of programming (i.e., as in the emerging area of *software art*) involves greater reflection and emphasis on the computing (i.e., the programming, as a subarea of computing, in this case). Likewise, when artistic approaches or styles are used in representation, the elements of computing are treated as the subject material—the focal point of the artwork. An important part of the figure diagram is the flow terminus in the bottom sphere; the result may be usable or unusable in the strict sense of performance-based interface usability (Nielsen 1993). It could be seen as art to be displayed or an interface to be used, or as some combination of these two. The word "usability," in a more general sense, can be quite complex; for example, improving a user's emotional state is also a valid *use* (Picard 1997; Jordan 2000; Brave and Nass 2002; Norman 2004). The concept of *use* can also extend beyond human performance.

Some examples are in order to understand this flow from top to bottom in figure 1.1. First, let's refer to a recent paper written by four coauthors (Fishwick et al. 2004), two computer scientists, one interaction designer (HCI), and one artist. Other examples will be delineated as subsequent items.

The two computer scientists (Diehl and Fishwick) apply aesthetics to the *representation* of formal structures in computing, such as computer programs and mathematical models. Thus, artifacts at the top of figure 1.1 flow through to the bottom sphere of aesthetic influence. The resulting artifacts are meant to be usable, and the focus is on representing the computing artifacts as *subject material* for art. Prophet (the artist) works closely in a team that includes, among others, a computer scientist whose expertise is scientific visualization. Her involvement in the *Cell project* stems from affecting the *practice* of computing. While this work was aimed at producing a usable visualization product, she and her collaborators will produce subsequent artifacts relevant to their individual disciplines. Löwgren, the interaction design specialist, enumerated several key qualities HCI designs must have to address the aesthetic requirements of future interfaces, including *pliability*, *fluency*, and *seductivity*.

Focusing on subject material for art, the area of "software art" recently highlighted within the 2003 Ars Electronica conference (ARS 2003) used computer code as *raw material* (i.e., a medium) for art. The *Processing* language (Processing) developed by Fry and Reas is a good example of this activity within the art world. Based on Java, *Processing* is a language oriented toward designers and artists. Interestingly, some of the programming examples at the *Processing* web site stretch the boundaries between surfacing computing artifacts as medium and subject. For example, some Processing Java applets such as *distance_2d*, directly represent and surface underlying computational structures. In *distance_2d*, the essence of what it means to be a matrix is surfaced, making the computing artifact (i.e., a matrix) the subject material of the piece.

Since the *theory* of computing is founded on mathematics, the architecture in figure 1.1 provides room for representing mathematical structures through aesthetic filters. The focus is usually on representing the solution space for mathematical structures (i.e., manifolds, surfaces, tessellations) (Emmer 1993); however, other visualizations based on problem spaces (i.e., representing the notation) are also possible (Fishwick 2002a). Leyton (Leyton 2001) provides a group-theoretic approach for generating of art and music, whereas Ferguson is a hybrid artist-mathematician who specializes in building mathematical artifacts in "stone and bronze" (Ferguson and Ferguson 1994). Lakoff and Núñez (2000)—though not explicitly indicating a role for art—provide strong evidence that metaphor lies at the root of mathematics. Extending this argument, if art plays a key role in embodying metaphor, then aesthetics and art should play increasingly significant roles in all aspects of mathematics from its cognitive roots to its material notation.

The use of the word "aesthetics" related to computing deserves some discussion. Recognizing that the core specifications for computing theory are mathematical, we note that Hadamard (1945) introduced and documented the psychology inherent to mathematics. The classic Platonic definition of mathematical aesthetics describes mental pleasures associated with specifying theorems and deriving proofs. More generally, the mathematician's aesthetics involves concepts such as invariance, symmetry, parsimony, proportion, and harmony. Hadamard's studies of famous mathematicians points out that the vast majority of them perform mental visualizations both in posing a problem and in solving it. Describing the proof involving an infinity of primes, Hadamard (1945, p. 75) refers to "strange and cloudy imagery" and relative physical distances. In one of the study's better known quotes (Hadamard 1945, Appendix II), Einstein wrote to Hadamard that "The words or the language, as they are written or spoken, do not seem to play any role in my mechanism of thought. The psychical entities which seem to serve as elements in thought are certain signs and more or less clear images which can be 'voluntarily' reproduced and combined."

One wonders, after reading Hadamard's treatise, whether these mental visualizations are a sheer economic necessity based on the relative expense of exercising other types of notations, or whether mathematics is forever constrained to the mind. The mind is the fount for mathematics, but it serves the same function for all human activity. Descartes' binding of algebra and geometry and contemporary "math-art" activities (Emmer 1993; BRIDGES) provide interesting revelations on aesthetics, and mathematics. A strong foundation has been laid for ongoing research in the field. In the domain of computer programming, Petre and Blackwell (1999) document a significant number of visual and aural effects imagined by programmers as they perform their craft. One programmer describes such effects moving "in my head ... like dancing symbols.... I can see the strings [of symbols] assemble and transform, like luminous characters suspended behind my eyelids. . . ."

Petre and Blackwell caution against leaping to prematurely positive conclusions about the benefits of visual programming for all situations. However, any empirical test of the efficacy of visual paradigms seems to be necessarily bound by technological limitations of graphics, sound, and interaction hardware devices. Until these environments become commonplace, affordable, and efficient, nontext–based representation will always be biased by less than adequate technology. Moreover, all new interface modalities suffer from a cultural bias against adopting new interfaces when existing modalities are familiar and still function. What would empirical studies show if we had an ideal user-friendly environment like the immersive holodeck of "Star Trek" (Paramount)? Unfortunately, further design, engineering, and empirical studies are needed to answer this question.

Early on in the history of computing, Donald Knuth showed himself to be a strong advocate of aesthetics in programming (Knuth 1997; 2003). As Knuth points out in his discussion of Metafont (Knuth 1986), which underlies his TeX typesetting system, "Type design can be hazardous to your other interests. Once you get hooked, you will develop intense feelings about letterforms." More generally, Knuth directly addresses the issue of aesthetics as more than purely cognitive, beyond the Platonic mental *ideals*. A textual section of a computer program has both denotative and connotative signifiers, and it is easy to imagine the program aligning with the goals of art, stretching the traditional boundaries of what may be considered a usable computer program representation. Nake (1974) explores the idea of aesthetics *as* information processing. More recently, Gelernter (Gelernter 1998a; 1998b) has provided significant justification for aesthetics in computing. Defending the vital role of attributes such as emotion, style, and aesthetics in all aspects of computing, Gelernter illustrates with a case study of how the Macintosh interface and style has revolutionized the industry, though it was first viewed as strictly for novices.

Mathematics has historically emphasized *solution* spaces, and not notational spaces (i.e., for framing *problems*), but visualization in computer science is playing an increasing role in visualizing structures and data (Stasko et al. 1998; Card et al. 1999; Diehl 2001).

The Novelty of Aesthetic Computing

Every discipline should have to justify its existence or, at the very least, include formal critiques to put its subject matter in the proper context. Is aesthetic computing a new field, or simply rehashed old material? It has not yet survived the test of time or the rigors of comprehensive criticism; to date, only a single workshop has been held on the subject.

Aesthetic computing combines two key areas: art and computing. One might object that aesthetic computing appears to be about design, and that art and design have different agendas. Their goals merit alternative approaches and philosophies, but aesthetic computing can have either purely artistic or design goals, depending on the practitioners involved. Its goals may also produce usable or nonusable results, if we adopt a strict definition of usability. Traditional design and illustration research involving computing tends to be rather sparse for several reasons. The design of web pages and operating system interfaces (i.e., the desktop metaphor) is a small subset within the field of computing. Significantly greater *diversity and depth* of aesthetics needs to be applied to all areas of computing, from notations to formal structures. We must analyze the subarea lists of the Association for Computing Machinery (ACM) and the Institute for Electrical and Electronics, Engineers Computer Society (IEEE-CS), which define the breadth of computing. A recent National Academy study on computing (CSTB 2003, chap. 4) recommends considering the effects of the arts within the computing field.

The richness of work in digital design and arts, or the *information arts* (Wilson 2002), suggests relations to aesthetic computing, but the goals of each area are quite different. For one thing, aesthetic computing is not meant to be an all-encompassing "bridging term" between aesthetics and computing. It is about surfacing the core components of computer science, its areas of study, and its methodologies. One of its core goals is to modify computer science through the catalysis of aesthetics. This is not the same as using artificial intelligence to create designs or algorithms to effect new forms of artificial life, as exciting as these enterprises may be. The goal of work done to date in applying digital methods to art is the *converse* goal to that of Aesthetic Computing.

Visualization, specifically scientific, information, and software visualization, lacks the sort of personalization or customization aesthetic computing makes potentially viable.

These areas play vital roles in combining aesthetics and computing, but to date, designs have tended to be visually minimalistic and oriented toward a generic concept of *user*.

The assumed roles of aesthetics as applied to computing are too limiting. First, we are not limited to traditional concepts such as symmetry and harmony when defining computing aesthetics. Instead, we are free to choose, say, the aesthetics of a particular artist or art movement. Second, formal constructs within computing are sometimes bypassed in considering aesthetics. One can interpret "aesthetic algorithm" (Nadin 1991), for example, in several ways—assuming the algorithm has aesthetics traditionally associated with mathematics (i.e., as in the first example), or referring to the artistic phenomena resulting from executing the algorithm code. But these interpretations differ from one in which the *algorithm itself* has an artistic manifestation. The structure and representation of algorithms are part of *computing*, whereas the aesthetics of the algorithm's execution is more closely aligned with the visual arts.

Exploring design, art, and computing, we hope to carve a niche for aesthetic computing enriching these other disciplines in the process.

Applying Aesthetics: The Artistic Influence

For as long as mathematics and technology have existed, artists have used them for their own purposes, *applying* these tools to create new works of art. Examples include the use of Euclidean geometry in perspective drawing and painting (Kemp 1992), Vermeer's postulated use of the camera obscura for his paintings (Steadman 2002), the influence of multidimensional space and non-Euclidean geometry on the art of Duchamp (Henderson 1983; Robbin 1992; Schlain 1993) and Escher (Schattschneider 2004), mechanization and mass production trends in modern art, and more recently, computing trends (i.e., artificial life, genetic algorithms, chaos theory) on new media (Wilson 2002). The literature is rife with examples of artists applying mathematics, technology, and most recently, computing to the creation of art.

In studying the converse situation, however, we must ask why no corresponding history of artistic practice affecting computing exists. Also, what aspects of aesthetics can be applied? On the whole, it is clear that both mathematicians and computer scientists have been deeply affected by aesthetic qualities such as beauty, symmetry, and abstraction. However, one does not normally see the same level of artistic theory and practice applied mathematics and computing. Why is this? One hypothesis is that, with advanced computing technologies, we are only now beginning to see the effect of art on computing. Let's begin with what it means *to apply aesthetics to computing*, dividing aesthetics into three broad groups: modality, quality, and culture.

Modality refers to the ways in which we interface and interact with objects. Art practices encourage things like pluralism in representation (see Deem 1993 for an unusually precise example), interaction, dynamism, and materiality (i.e., embodiment). One might ascribe these concepts to fields such as human–computer interaction, when in actuality, these are part and parcel of the arts. Exploring one or more modalities in the interface is what artists do, therefore, any aspect of computing that stresses this approach owes a significant debt to the arts. However, fields such as HCI, ubiquitous computing, augmented reality, virtual reality, and tangible computing are made possible only by rapid advances in computer-related technology. We have had to wait for the technology to become available to leverage the arts. This same requirement for advanced technology to apply art to computing is present for the next group.

Culture in the arts is manifested in many ways—specific artists, art movements, and genres. Genres range from impressionism to romanticism and modernism to feminism and postmodernism. Aspects of these movements, sensory styles, or their philosophies can be applied within computing. Modalities for such representation is evolving slowly due to economic constraints. Subjectivism is expensive; a single standardized objective interface is cheaper. Multiple representations are more costly; however, technologies such as XML (e.g., with its pronounced content-presentation capability) and mass customization are making it possible to *apply* multiple styles and representations to computing. As the subjectivist hallmark of the arts becomes less expensive, representations in computing will change.

Quality refers to aesthetics before Kant's blending of *mind and body*, that is, general aesthetic qualities. These are not so much applied from as made consistent with some of the arts. Qualities such as mimesis, symmetry, complexity, parsimony, minimalism, and beauty, for example, could be said to be present in the arts.

To apply aesthetics to computing, we draw on a long history of the arts in which modality, culture, and quality have played significant roles. Only fairly recently have we begun to think about concrete ways in which the arts play an increasingly critical role in computing.

Mathematical Modeling: Research at the University of Florida

At the University of Florida, our primary emphasis has been on artifacts in computing best termed *mathematical models*, to represent the dynamics of systems (Fishwick 1995). Dynamical models represent how system attributes change over time. The "aesthetic filter" is applied, noting that our software framework emphasizes the ability to easily change model representations, thus enabling customization and culturally diverse notations. Thus, we take the *synthetic approach*, described earlier, to applying aesthetics to computing.

Our work can be seen as being a type of three-dimensional (3D) design for these notations. Customization appeals directly to the concept of plurality discussed earlier in the context of aesthetics. A simple example is illustrated and described in (Fishwick et al. 2004).

In applying aesthetics to computing, we need to confine ourselves to some aspect of computing, or one of its subfields such as automata theory, HCI, visualization, or discrete structures, to name a few. Potentially, any of the subfields can be enhanced with a more thorough investigation of aesthetic *application*. For the RUBE Project (Kim et al. 2002; Hopkins and Fishwick 2001; 2003), we have focused primarily on representations, informed through an artistic sensibility, in mathematics and computing notation, from the notation of algebraic and differential equations to that of program and data structures. Our basic approach is to build a system that allows construction of a multiplicity of notations to reveal the same underlying formalism in numerous ways. Not only do different people and cultural entities enjoy working with different metaphors, but the same person or group can benefit from exposure to diverse presentations.

The RUBE software system we have constructed allows us to apply different representations to a select number of formal dynamic model specifications. Using RUBE, it is possible to change the way formal models look and sound. By formal models, we refer to a large class of models used to specify systems incorporating time for analysis and simulation: finite state machines, Petri networks, Markov models, queuing models, System Dynamics graphs, as well as ordinary and partial differential equations. RUBE uses XML (eXtensible Markup Language), which separates content from presentation while allowing arbitrary style-defined bindings to unite them. In XML parlance, *content* refers to an abstract specification defined as a document tree, and *presentation* refers to how the tree is presented to the user, its look and sound. Thus, using RUBE and guided by the XML philosophy, one may specify an equation, but then present it as linear text, a network, or a 3D structure. Choosing which presentation to employ can be guided by XML style sheets and their associated transformations. These transformations bind the presentation to the content.

Based on open source software, RUBE's architecture begins with authoring toolkits: *SodiPodi* for 2D vector drawing, and *Blender* for 3D modeling. Let's consider the 3D pipeline beginning with Blender. Creating a 3D model in Blender, the artist then uses a Python scripting interface that allows attributions to be made regarding semantics. For example, one might identify an object as a *state* or a *function*. After the semantic assignment, the artist creates an X3D (eXtensible 3D) file for the presentation, and a special XML file for specifying the formal model. After some XML transformations, this XML file is translated into Javascript or Java, to reincorporate it into the X3D/VRML file, resulting in an interactive Virtual Reality Modeling Language (VRML) world. The 2D transformations are similar, except that scalable vector graphics (SVG) are used for presentation.

Let's begin with a formal definition of a finite state machine (FSM) M (Fishwick 1995). These machines have states interconnected through transitions that are activated by an input to the machine of a particular value. M is formally defined in traditional notation as

$$M = \langle Q, I, 0, \delta, \lambda \rangle$$

$$Q = \{S1, S2, S3\}, \quad \delta : Q \times I \rightarrow Q$$

$$\delta(S1, 0) = S1; \quad \delta(S2, 0) = S2; \quad \delta(S3, 0) = S3;$$

$$\delta(S1, 1) = S2; \quad \delta(S2, 1) = S3; \quad \delta(S3, 1) = S2$$

$$I = \{0, 1\}, \quad \lambda : Q \rightarrow 0$$

This text might seem to be the formal specification for M, but it is actually one of many ways to look at the underlying formalism encoded in XML. It is one type of presentation among many. In general, all presentations require additional natural language semantics if we are to make sense of them. Q is the state set for M; I the input set, O the output set, δ the transition function from one state to another, and λ the output function. Figure 1.2 illustrates our second presentation for the FSM. The iconic presentation of a circle for the S2 state encodes the concept of a boundary and that which it encompasses. This iconicity

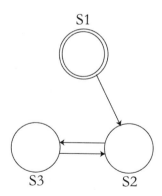

Figure 1.2   A 2D static snapshot of an interactive diagrammatic FSM interface constructed with SodiPodi, a 2D vector package based on scalable vector graphics (SVG).

is similar to that noted by Shin (2002) in her discussion of Peirce's logic diagrams. That is, the graphical depiction of S2 is consistent with the underlying metaphors of set theory, whereas the purely textual presentation does not capture these metaphors. Moreover, as represented on a noninteractive medium such as paper, figure 1.2 is incomplete since the additional information (such as the input values needed to effect a change of state) encoded in the text representation is equally present during interaction with the figure. The arrows convey the notion of transition from one state to another. The figure's metaphors dramatically improve our understanding of the machine semantics, leading to the possibility that using presentations with alternative aesthetics might strengthen these metaphors' impact. The underlying assumption is that material aspects of levels of representation are based largely on what is available, affordable, and materially efficient.

Consider figure 1.3 as a representation that has only recently become possible through computer graphics and the ability to employ 3D components. The metaphor, encouraged by the iconicity of diagrams (Shin 2002), of the circle as a *boundary* has been replaced by a set of tanks (on the left), and small gazebolike structures (on the right). The arrows in figure 1.2 are replaced by either a pipe filled with water (left) or a red-clothed woman walking from one state to another along a lamp-lit walkway (right). These examples provide different metaphors for understanding the formal structure. Even with something as basic as a circle in iconic mapping, one can imagine beyond what's "inside the circle" and conceptualize moving from one circle to another. The 3D metaphors strengthen this feeling of immersion, more clearly envisioning being inside the gazebo, like the woman, or watching fluid move from one position (i.e., state) to another.

A host of philosophical issues come into play here. Isn't there a need to enforce visual minimalism within this sort of structure? What cultural barriers might prevent the adoption of models like figure 1.3 for science and engineering? Regarding minimalism, we should note that is quite possible to preserve abstraction without requiring visual minimalism. Within the context of the art community, this can be seen when we compare and contrast the genres of abstract expressionism and surrealism. Both genres contain a wide variety of works that employ symbolism, iconography, and the richness of semiotics even though the visual presentations are strikingly different. Consequently, abstraction as a one-to-many mapping has nothing to do with how we visually or aurally represent notations; the circle in figure 1.2 and the gazebo in figure 1.3 are both at the same level of abstraction regarding notating a state. Both require the same number of bits from an information theoretic perspective of recording that the entity is a state, although the bits to record the alternative presentations are different. Deriving the idea of an abstract state in an FSM, for example, need not imply that the state be presented *visually in a minimalist*

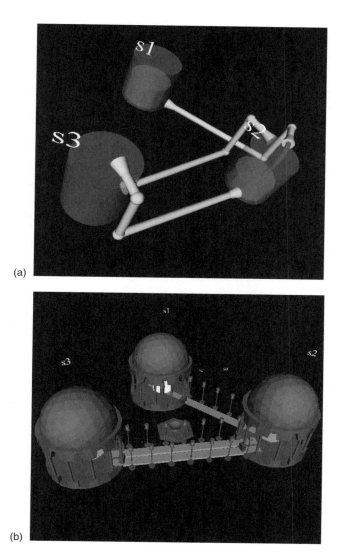

(a)

(b)

Figure 1.3 Two 3D models representing the diagram in figure 1.2: (a) a set of three transparent, cylindrical tanks that transfer water (representing a change in state), and (b) three gazebos with adjoining walkways, and an agent walking from state to state. Both FSMs were constructed with the Virtual Reality Modeling Language (VRML).

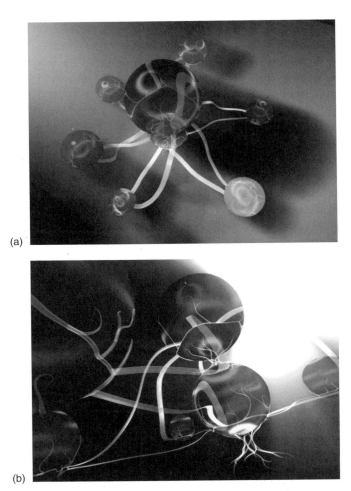

(a)

(b)

Figure 1.4 Four views of a network of nodes, with feedback, for modeling a banded waveguide physical model for sound (Joella Walz). Modeled with Maya.

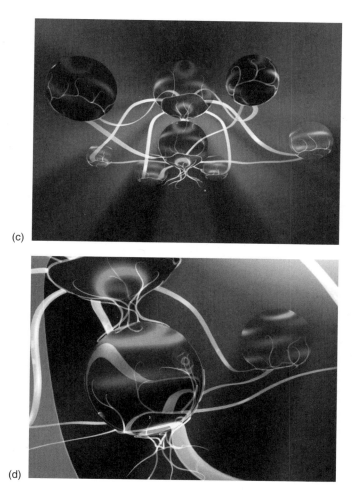

(c)

(d)

Figure 1.4 (continued)

fashion. The key objective is to strengthen the metaphor underlying what it means *to be a state,* and the corresponding metaphorical elements of *boundary.* The abstraction afforded by states suggests a one-to-many mapping in which one FSM may map to a large number of different applications.

The second question about cultural barriers may be at the heart of the aesthetic computing challenge. Educated with minimalist figures and text, computer scientists may be shocked to realize our representations for formal objects are not as constrained as originally thought. Until the era of computer graphics and fast computers, we had little need to

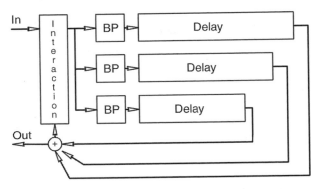

Figure 1.5 A 2D diagrammatic rendition of the banded waveguide model in figure 1.4.

inquire about what initially appeared to be exotic ways to encode formal knowledge. This is a challenge not only for computer scientists, however, but also for artists, who should be encouraged to consider the computer, and computing practices, as *subject material* as well as raw material. This suggestion may strike some artists as a modernist era agenda; however, as a tool or a subject, the computer with its mathematical foundation creates significantly higher complexity than paint, palette knife, or chisel ever could.

The following two examples were created in the author's aesthetic computing class (AC) at the University of Florida. The class includes both artists and computer scientists who work individually and on group projects to represent mathematical models found in mathematics, program and data structures, and computer simulation.

Figure 1.4, based on a virtual model created by an artist (Joella Walz), represents a functional feedback data flow network, whose purpose is to physically model sound. One type of modeled instrument, with the appropriate parameter settings, is of a Tibetan Prayer Bowl, which gives off a resonant bell sound.

Figure 1.5 shows the equivalent 2D diagram (Essl 2002) for the structure shown in figure 1.4. The first thing one notices is that the diagram has more complete information, since it is specifically made for print media, whereas the structure in figure 1.4 requires a highly interactive environment to determine which nodes are the delays, the band pass filters, and the primary interaction node. For figure 1.4 to be as useful as figure 1.5, barring issues of aesthetics and customization, the necessary *interaction environment* must be in place to easily determine node roles and connections.

Figure 1.7, created by a computer scientist (John Campbell), shows a physical model of the Taylor series (figure 1.6), found in most introductory calculus books. The Taylor series is an infinite sum resulting in a polynomial approximation to function F(x).

$$F(x) = \sum_{N=0}^{\infty} \frac{F'^{(N)}(A)}{N!} (x-A)^{\wedge}N$$

Figure 1.6 Textual presentation of Taylor series expansion.

Summary

As in any new field, many issues are bound to stand out, and they often cluster around a discipline. Each discipline involved with aesthetic computing is assumed to have its own interests at stake. For art, the issues will likely center on the need to do new, contemporary work rather than retread what has already been tried. The same can be said for design and computing. For computing, art is seen in all of its history, not just its current leading edge; thus, the application of aesthetics to mathematics and computing can take on a wide range of art genres. Artists and computer scientists are similar, then, in that they select from the whole history of the other area, while focusing mainly on the newer research in their own field. While we may promote their interconnection, each field must explore its own potential, according to its own concept of advancement.

To progress, we need to take up the key challenges in each field. For art, the reflection on computing naturally has a utilitarian component—computers are used to achieve specific results. This is not to suggest that artists working in aesthetic computing must always yield to utility, but the goal should be to fully explore the range of utility from "useless" art to art with a specific technological purpose. The very word "use" is fraught with complexity, of course, since one could argue that a nonuseful work of art showing the attributes of a matrix actually has an *aesthetic* or *educational* use. Usability should not be limited to the very strict definition of performing a task in a robotic fashion. If the challenge for art is learning to live with utility as almost a revisiting of the Greek concept of techné, the challenge for computing is to recognize that the interface should be as much about quality as it is about quantitative performance. This quality includes attributes such as emotion and aesthetics, and it reflects the fairly new wave of human-centered activities saturating the computing discipline. Computing is not just about mental formalisms and algorithmic complexity; it is also about how to more effectively interface along the lines of tangible, augmented, and ubiquitous computing. Computing professionals need to pay more attention to these areas and observe the critical role art plays in promoting novel representational techniques.

Usability is further complicated by the fact that the newer generations of computer interfaces are expensive and more difficult to operate. All figures in this text serve as static

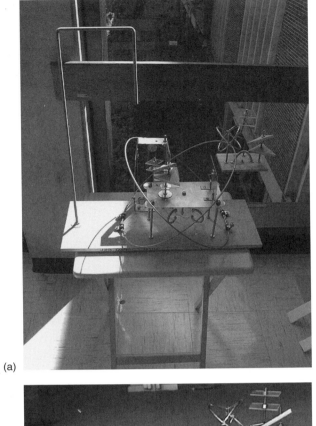

(a)

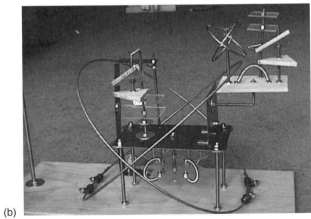

(b)

Figure 1.7 Two views of a metal, Plexiglas, and wood representation of the Taylor series expansion (John Campbell).

presentations of potentially interactive, immersive, and engaging artifacts. Unfortunately, because media such as paper do not capture these qualities, information-dense diagrams appear to be the only valid representations. Time, effort, and progress in both art and computing are needed to engender the sort of environment that aesthetic computing promises. Along the way, artists and computer scientists should design new environments, evaluate them, and interact with each other.

Acknowledgments

The author would like to thank his graduate students in the RUBE Project (Minho Park, Jinho Lee, and Hyunju Shim), as well as all students of the aesthetic computing class, and with special thanks to Joella Walz and John Campbell for their final virtual and physical projects. Also, special thanks to Mihai Nadin for his constructive comments on an earlier draft of this chapter. This work would not have been possible without grants from the National Science Foundation (EIA-0119532) and the Air Force Research Laboratory (F30602-01-1-05920119532).

References

ACM. Association for Computing Machinery (ACM). Accessed at http://www.acm.org.

AC. Aesthetic Computing Class, University of Florida. Accessed at http://www.cise.ufl.edu/~fishwick/aescomputing.

Adams, Laurie Schneider. 1996. *The Methodologies of Art: An Introduction*. Boulder, CO: Westview Press.

ARS2003. ARS Electronica Conference, "CODE—The Language of Our Time," 2003. Accessed at http://www.aec.at.

Baumgarten, Alexander Gottlieb [1750] 1961. *Aesthetica*. Hildesheim: G. Olms.

Bloom, Allan. 1968. *The Republic of Plato*. 2nd ed. New York: Basic Books.

Brave, Scott, and Nass, Clifford. 2002. "Emotion in Human-Computer Interaction." In *The Human-Computer Interaction Handbook: Fundamentals, Evolving Technologies and Emerging Applications*. Jacko, Julie A. and Sears, Andrew, eds. Mahwah, NJ: Lawrence Erlbaum Assoc.

Bredin, Hugh, and Santoro-Brienza, Liberato. 2000. *Philosophies of Art and Beauty: Introducing Aesthetics*. Edinburgh: Edinburgh University Press.

BRIDGES: Mathematical connections in art, music, and science. Accessed at http://www.sckans .edu/~bridges/.

Card, Stuart, Mackinlay, Jock, and Shneiderman, Ben, eds. 1999. *Readings in Information Visualization: Using Vision to Think*. St. Louis, MO: Morgan Kaufman Publishers.

Coyne, R. 1999. *Technoromanticism: Digital Narrative, Holism, and the Romance of the Real*. Cambridge, MA: MIT Press.

CSTB. 2003. *Beyond Productivity: Information Technology, Innovation, and Creativity*. Washington, DC: National Academies Press, Computer Science and Telecommunications Board.

Dagstuhl Seminar (Aesthetic Computing) 02291. 2002. Accessed at http://www.dagstuhl.de/ 02291, July.

Deem, George. 1993. *Art School*. Thames and Hudson.

Denning, Peter J. November 2003. "Great Principles of Computing." *Communications of the ACM*, 46(11): 15–20.

Diehl, Stephan, ed. 2001. *Software Visualization*. New York: Springer Verlag, LNCS 2269.

Dorn, Charles M. 1999. *Mind in Art: Cognitive Foundations in Art Education*. Mahwah, NJ: Lawrence Erlbaum Associates, Inc.

Edmonds, Ernest, and Candy, Linda. October 2002. "Creativity, Art Practice, and Knowledge." *Communications of the ACM* 45(10): 91–95.

Edwards, Betty. 1986. *Drawing on the Artist Within*. New York: Simon and Schuster, Inc.

Emmer, Michele, ed. 1993. *The Visual Mind: Art and Mathematics*. Cambridge, MA: MIT Press.

Essl, Georg. 2002. "Physical Wave Propagation Modeling for Real-Time Synthesis of Natural Sounds." PhD dissertation, Princeton, NJ: Princeton University.

Ferguson, Claire, and Ferguson, Helaman. 1994. *Mathematics in Stone and Bronze*. Meridian Creative Group.

Fishwick, Paul. 1995. *Simulation Model Design and Execution: Building Digital Worlds*. Prentice Hall.

Fishwick, Paul. 2002a. "Aesthetic Programming: Crafting Personalized Software." *Leonardo* 35(4): 383–90. MIT Press.

Fishwick, Paul. September–October 2002b. "Aesthetic Computing: Making Artistic Mathematics and Software." *YLEM Journal*, Special issue on Art and Programming. 10(22): 6–11.

Fishwick, Paul. 2003. "Aesthetic Computing Manifesto." *Leonardo* 36(4): 255–56. MIT Press.

Fishwick, Paul, Diehl, Stephan, Prophet, Jane, and Lowgren, Jonas. 2005. "Perspectives on Aesthetic Computing." *Leonardo* 38(2): 133–41.

Freeland, Cynthia. 2001. *But Is It Art?* New York: Oxford University Press.

Gelernter, David. 1998a. *Machine Beauty: Elegance and the Heart of Technology.* New York: Basic Books.

Gelernter, David. 1998b. *The Aesthetics of Computing.* Detroit: Phoenix Press.

Goodman, Nelson. 1978. *Ways of Worldmaking.* Indianapolis: Hackett Publishing Company.

Grau, Oliver. 2003. *Virtual Art: From Illusion to Immersion.* Cambridge, MA: MIT Press.

Hadamard, Jacques. 1945. *The Psychology of Invention in the Mathematical Field.* Princeton, NJ: Princeton University Press.

Henderson, Linda D. 1983. *The Fourth Dimension and Non-Euclidean Geometry in Modern Art.* Princeton, NJ: Princeton University Press.

Hopkins, John, and Fishwick, Paul. 2001. "Synthetic Human Agents for Modeling and Simulation." *Proceedings of the IEEE* 89(2): 131–47.

Hopkins, John, and Fishwick, Paul. 2003. "Exploiting the Agent-Based Metaphor in Software Visualization using the RUBE System." *Journal of Visual Languages and Computing* 14(1): 97–117.

IEEE-CS, Institute for Electrical and Electronics Engineers Computer Society. Accessed at http://www.ieee.org and http://www.computer.org.

Jordan, Patrick W. 2000. *Designing Pleasurable Products: An Introduction to the New Human Factors.* New York: Taylor and Francis.

Kant, Immanuel [1790]. 1952. *The Critique of Judgement*, trans. James Creed Meredith. Oxford: Clarendon Press.

Kelly, Michael, ed. 1998. *Preface to Encyclopedia of Aesthetics*. New York: Oxford University Press, Vol. 1, pp. 9–17.

Kemp, Martin. 1992. *The Science of Art: Optical Themes in Western Art from Brunelleschi to Seurat*. New Haven, CT: Yale University Press.

Kim, Taewoo, Jinho, Jinho, and Fishwick, Paul. July 2002. "A Two-Stage Modeling and Simulation Process for Web-Based Modeling and Simulation." *ACM Trans. on Modeling and Simulation* 12(3): 230–48.

Knuth, Donald. 1986. *The METAFont Book*. Addison-Wesley Publishing Co.

Knuth, Donald. 1997. *The Art of Computer Programming*. 3rd ed. Addison-Wesley. In 3 volumes (Fundamental Algorithms, Seminumerical Algorithms, and Sorting and Searching), with the fourth volume in preparation.

Knuth, Donald. 2003. *Things a Computer Scientist Rarely Talks About*. Stanford, CA: CSLI Publications.

Lakoff, George, and Núñez, Rafel E. 2000. *Where Mathematics Comes From: How the Embodied Mind Brings Mathematics into Being*. New York: Basic Books.

Leonardo. Accessed at http://mitpress2.mit.edu/e-journals/Leonardo/.

Leyton, Michael. 2001. *A Generative Theory of Shape*. New York: Springer Verlag.

Manovich, Lev. 2001. *The Language of New Media*. Cambridge, MA: MIT Press.

Nadin, Mihai. 1991. "Science and Beauty: Aesthetic Structuring of Knowledge." *Leonardo* 24(1): 67–72.

Nake, Frieder. 1974. *Ästhetik als Informationsverarbeitung*. Vienna/New York: Springer-Verlag.

Nielsen, Jakob. 1993. *Usability Engineering*. Morgan Kaufmann.

Norman, Donald A. 2004. *Emotional Design: Why We Love (or Hate) Everyday Things*. New York: Basic Books.

Osborne, Harold. 1970. *Aesthetics and Art Theory: An Historical Introduction*. New York: E. P. Dutton and Co.

Oxford English Dictionary. 2003. Accessed at http://www.oed.com.

Paramount Pictures, Star Trek Series. Accessed at http://www.paramount.com.

Petre, Marian, and Blackwell, Alan F. 1999. "Mental Imagery in Program Design and Visual Programming." *International Journal of Human-Computer Studies* 51(1): 7–30.

Picard, Rosalind W. 1997. *Affective Computing*. Cambridge, MA: MIT Press.

Plotnitsky, Arkady. 1998. "Mathematics and Aesthetics." In *Encyclopedia of Aesthetics*. Michael Kelly, ed. vol. 3. New York: Oxford University Press, pp. 191–98.

Processing Language. Accessed at http://www.proce55ing.net.

Robbin, Tony. 1992. *Fourfield: Computers, Art and the 4th Dimension*. Bulfinch Press.

Schattschneider, Doris. 2004. *M.C. Escher: Visions of Symmetry: Notebooks, Periodic Drawings, and Related Works*, 2nd ed. Harry N. Abrams Publishing.

Schlain, Leonard. 1993. *Art and Physics*. Quill Publishing.

Shin, Sun-Joo. 2002. *The Iconic Logic of Peirce's Graphs*. Cambridge, MA: MIT Press.

Stasko, John, Domingue, John, Brown, Marc, and Price, Blaine, eds. 1998. *Software Visualization: Programming as a Multimedia Experience*. Cambridge, MA: MIT Press.

Steadman, Philip. 2002. *Vermeer's Camera: Uncovering the Truth Behind the Masterpieces*. New York: Oxford University Press.

Tractinsky, Noam, Katz, A. S., and Ikar, D. 2000. "What Is Beautiful Is Usable." *Interacting with Computers* 13(2): 127–45.

Wilson, Stephen. 2002. *Information Arts: Intersections of Art, Science, and Technology*. Cambridge, MA: MIT Press.

2

Goodman's Aesthetics and the Languages of Computing

John Lee

Why discuss the philosophy of Nelson Goodman in the context of this book? The wider project is to investigate the notion of "aesthetic computing," what it might be, and what its significance and uses are. This raises questions such as how computing might compare with any other area in which aesthetics could be discussed. Is there anything about computing in itself that opens new aesthetic possibilities or suggests any particular theoretical treatment? Does computing offer a fundamentally distinct kind of medium? Or does its apparent self-active capacity introduce new issues about agency or intention in art?

Goodman is relevant here because of his extraordinary, wide-ranging, and intensely original approach to the philosophy of art. His focus on symbol systems and languages gives him a natural affinity with computing; still, in introducing his theory in 1968, Goodman wrote a chapter section entitled "Analogs and Digits" only mentioning computing in passing, nor does he discuss it much in his later work. We explore his work, then, in the hope of finding clues to the nature of computing as a topic for aesthetic treatment. Although our objective is by no means to definitively establish Goodman's precise views, but rather to use his writings as a starting point, it will be useful to sketch his position as clearly as we can at the outset.

Goodman and the Aesthetic

Goodman comes from a line of philosophers sometimes known as "linguistic," because of their close focus on examining the uses of language as a means of investigating concepts. His seminal work, *Languages of Art* (1968),[1] analyzes not only the language used in theoretical discussions of art and everyday conversation about art, but art itself as a sphere of linguistic activity. Goodman regards, languages as symbol systems. Symbol systems are what people use to communicate, and art is fundamentally about communication; in Goodman's view, art in general is a collection of symbol systems.

Languages of Art is not the easiest of books. Goodman's language is apt to be fairly technical and his discussions complex. Perhaps because of this, aspects of his views are elaborated and developed in a number of later works, often in a more accessible style. His full analysis of his position is highly sophisticated. He devotes a good deal of his discussion to issues that are traditional fare for the philosophy of art, for instance, the nature of pictures as a form of representation. In itself this may not be central to the present context, but it does lead directly to an understanding of the key points in his view of symbols and the range and nature of symbol systems.

Goodman takes great pains to point out that a number of traditional views on pictorial representation fail to stand up to scrutiny. In particular, pictures do not represent whatever they depict through resemblance, because the relation of resemblance has a number of features that pictorial representation does not share, such as *symmetry*. Resemblance is symmetrical, hence the depicted object resembles the picture; but it does not represent it. In fact, Goodman claims, pictures are a language no less than is English, and the nature of their capacity to refer to or represent things in the world is essentially the same. They are used, according to systems of rules, by people who agree that certain symbols will stand for certain things.

Nonetheless, pictures are clearly a different kind of symbol system from some others, and Goodman approaches this subject by distinguishing *notational* symbol systems from those that are not, in somewhat technical terms. According to Goodman, five basic conditions are required for a symbol system to be notational, the first two syntactic, and the rest semantic:

1. The system must consist of symbols (utterances, inscriptions, marks) that form equivalence classes (*characters*), which can be exchanged without syntactical effect. Alphabets are a prototypical example—any "a" is as good as any other; they are "character-indifferent." The characters have to be disjoint, so that no mark qualifies as an instance of more than one character. In general, Goodman takes compound inscriptions (e.g., sentences) to be characters as well.
2. Characters have to be "finitely differentiable" (or "articulate") in the sense that their disjointness is feasibly testable; this rules out, in particular, "dense" systems in which any two (ordered) characters have another between them.
3. Notational systems must be *unambiguous*, so that the extension (i.e., what is referred to, which Goodman calls the "compliance-class") of an inscription is invariant with respect to time, context, and so on.

4. The compliance-classes of all characters must be disjoint. (Also, the system will ideally be nonredundant.)

5. Compliance-classes must also be finitely differentiable. Thus, for example, any system that is "semantically dense," in that its compliants form an ordering such that any two have another between them, is excluded.

Goodman illustrates these points in relation to clocks and pressure gauges, which measure infinitely variable quantities. Here, the semantic domain can always be seen as dense, and without marks on the dial there is no syntactic differentiation of characters, so the representation system is clearly non-notational. It becomes syntactically notational if, say, dots are distributed around the dial, each taken to be the center of a disjoint region so that the pointer appearing anywhere within that region counts as an inscription of a certain character. If the ranges of pressure correlated with these regions are also disjoint (and articulate), then the system meets the semantic requirements as well, and hence is simply a notation. On a clock face, the hour hand is typically notational in this way, whereas the minute hand may be seen as marking the absolute elapsed time since a particular mark was passed, and hence is used non-notationally.

Goodman observes that many kinds of diagrams are in fact essentially notational, and others mixed, such as many drawings used in architecture and design and road maps, which may be non-notational impressions of form or layout, but measurements and the use of drawings may be partly or largely notational. To address the difference between non-notational diagrams and *pictures*, Goodman introduces a further notion of "repleteness." A symbol is relatively replete if a relatively large number of its properties are involved in its identity as a symbol; a drawing is more a picture and less a mere diagram if less about it can be changed without making it into a different picture. Whereas, you can perhaps change the line thickness or color in a diagram without changing its identity, according to Goodman, changing any aspect of a picture might change its identity. Goodman summarizes the matter of the pictorial as follows:

Descriptions are distinguished from depictions not through being more arbitrary but through belonging to articulate rather than to dense schemes; and words are more conventional than pictures only if convention is construed in terms of differentiation rather than of artificiality. (RP 230–31)

These considerations may seem obscure and beside the point, but we begin to sense their importance to our current concerns when Goodman more generally elaborates a number of what he calls "symptoms of the aesthetic" (LA 252–55). The aesthetic, in his view, is not something that one can simply define. Goodman, in any case, is opposed to the kind of realism that treats anything as having a specific definitive essence. The aesthetic, like everything else, is a product of human activity and human understanding. But some features are typically shared by situations in which we are inclined to use the term "aesthetic." Symptoms are neither necessary nor sufficient to define whatever conditions they are symptomatic of, symptoms somehow characterize its typical presentation. Strikingly, Goodman identifies *syntactic and semantic density* as symptoms of the aesthetic, and also *relative repleteness*.

We now develop Goodman's ideas of "exemplification" and "expression." The former arises technically in contrast to "denotation." In standard usage, denotation is the relation of reference; a word, for example, denotes what it refers to. A common noun such as "dog" refers to dogs in general; one says that the set of dogs is its "extension," or in Goodman's curious terminology its "compliance-class." Similarly the extension of "red" is all red things. Exemplification, according to Goodman, is a form of reference just as denotation is, though one often unnoticed by philosophers. In fact, it is simply the converse of denotation: what is denoted by a term exemplifies that term. Thus, red things all exemplify "red." Goodman's best known example of this is the swatch exemplifying the properties of a bolt of cloth; in general, a sample exemplifies. The story is somewhat more complex, however, since the swatch does not exemplify incidental properties of the bolt such as "being made on a Tuesday." We *use* samples to exemplify (or represent) certain properties, but not others. Exemplification is, again, a common feature of pictorial representation: pictures exemplify properties of what they denote, which is unusual among words (though sometimes observed in words that describe words, e.g. "polysyllabic" and "sesquipedalian"). Goodman gives *expression* a special significance. In his usage, expression is bound up with metaphor; it is a sort of nonliteral exemplification. A symphony does not actually exemplify, say, feelings of tragic loss (MM 61), because it does not have any feelings; but it can metaphorically express these feelings through the properties it does exemplify (tempo *lento* in a minor mode, perhaps). Of course, not all that is exemplified is expressive.

Exemplification is expressly identified as a symptom of the aesthetic. In WW, Goodman adds a fifth symptom: *multiple and complex reference*. Whereas scientific and other kinds of discourse not usually thought of as aesthetic are often at pains to achieve precision and simplicity, aesthetic domains often revel in ambiguity, seeking to develop complexity.

It may seem suspicious that these symptoms of the aesthetic derive so clearly from, and align so well with, the properties of pictorial representation. To those concerned only with the art found in traditional galleries this is perhaps not disturbing, but otherwise the approach is surely too narrow. Not so, according to Goodman, who is actually very concerned to extend an account of the term "aesthetic" to all areas where it might apply. He suggests (emphasising it is only a suggestion) that his symptoms are "disjunctively necessary and conjunctively sufficient" for something to be aesthetic. Clearly many aesthetic products do not exhibit syntactic and semantic density, such as novels, but they always seem to have at least one of the symptoms—and it is important to stress again that these are symptoms, not defining characteristics. In an illuminating account of his own multimedia performance presentation, *Hockey Seen* (MM 69–70), Goodman points to the rich interplay of its various aspects; how, for example, it represents (via dance movements) hockey, which itself exemplifies ferocity of competition, which in turn expresses violence, frustration, and the struggle between aggression and authority.

Finally, it is important to note here that Goodman is not concerned to offer any means of evaluating aesthetic *quality*. Whether or not a work of art is *good* is not his target, only when something is susceptible to such evaluation. Bad art may well exhibit the symptoms of the aesthetic just as fully as good art; whatever can be labeled "hideous" exhibits such symptoms.

The Notion of the Work

It is useful to trace further Goodman's interest in the notion of a *work* (of art). He wants to characterize the identity of a work, because he is interested in the various classes works fall into. For example, he thinks there are important distinctions between notational and non-notational types of works. Consider a painting such as the *Mona Lisa*: the work is unique and its identity is completely bound up with the question of who produced it; a faithful reproduction can be illicitly presented as the original, thus constituting a forgery. Novels, by contrast, cannot be forged; any sequence of letters that corresponds with the original text is a genuine instance of the novel.

According to Goodman, when Pierre Menard happens to write a novel identical to Cervantes' *Don Quixote*, in Borges's story,[2] Menard's novel just *is* the *Quixote*—who wrote it, and where or when it was written, are irrelevant to its identity as a work (RP 62). Goodman calls paintings an "autographic" type of work, whereas notational or literary works are "allographic." Music, of the typical Western kind, is notated, and the creation of the notation Goodman calls the "execution" of the work, but it still needs to be "implemented" through performance to properly exist. This idea of implementation is given considerable prominence. A novel is implemented by being printed, published, promoted, circulated, and ultimately read. A play is implemented through performance before an audience in a theater, an etching by the taking of impressions, a painting perhaps by being framed and hung. A work is somehow incomplete until it has fulfilled its communicational destiny: execution is the making of a work, but implementation is what makes it work (MM 142–45; recapitulating Goodman 1982).

These ideas require, and are given, a complex and sustained defense, far too extensive to be discussed in detail here. Nonetheless, Goodman sometimes misleads by overemphasizing the specific nature of implementation in some cases. Once a play, for example, is written, it has a certain completeness: one can read it, envision possible performances, and so on. These modes of apprehension, we might say, are different from the apprehension by an engaged audience in a crowded, atmospheric theater. We might even hold that a play, enjoyed by an audience is apprehended *as a different work* from that experienced by merely reading the play. This is in keeping with Goodman's notion that something is not a work of art once and for all, but can *function* as a work of art at different times and in different contexts. Anything has the potential to be artwork, as Duchamp's urinal demonstrates. Though Goodman somewhat underemphasises the fact that the function of a work (as of any communicational device) depends as much on those who react to it as on its creator—a community, set of practices, and cultural context need to emerge for the work to be *recognized* as art.

The question Goodman usually prefers to ask is not "What is art?," but "*When* is art?"—so one may be tempted to say a given text is a work of performance theater only when performed. This comes close to tautology, but it is not clear how we should individuate the types or genres of artworks to make this a more informative categorization (nor whether this would be useful). Something can function as a range of different works, of different types, and in different circumstances, in which the nature of implementation and its role in defining the work are also different.

In contrasting, Goodman insists that the text is definitive of a literary work, admitting there may be diverse "interpretations" of the text, but countenancing differences of implementation that could affect the identity of the work only if they change the text, as in translation (RP 49–65). It is not entirely clear how this applies to a text such as a play, but Goodman seems adamant that the unperformed play or sonata, the unbuilt building design, the unexhibited picture, and the unpublished novel are incomplete, have not "fulfilled their function" (MM 142). This merely points out one kind of function they have not fulfilled, however, surely among many. Clearly they often fulfill other functions entirely satisfactorily. The question "*Does it work?*" may have many answers—a point we return to later.

The Languages of Computing

Computing is notoriously linguistic. It is formal and syntactic, consisting at some level entirely of strings of numbers. We program computers with specialized languages, which are reduced to strings of numbers in the end. Even at the more abstract levels, we normally specify algorithms linguistically, perhaps in some logical formalism. And the linguistic tokens involved—numbers or symbols—are generally completely discrete and differentiable. Computation, it seems, is paradigmatically notational in syntactic terms.

Semantically, computational representations can of course relate to undifferentiated domains, as a number can represent a particular value of a continuous quantity. Hence representations in a computer need not be wholly notational, but can be more like the hour hand on the clock, which records the continuous passage of time in discrete segments (or the number on the digital clock, a less obvious but isomorphic instance of the same relationship).

However, clocks, even analog clocks, are not by nature aesthetic objects. Of course, many are, but arguably become so by exceeding the simplest functional idea of a clock. They may be ornamented, minimalized, made of interesting materials or have an unusual size or shape. Plausibly, such developments on the idea of a clock endow the clock with at least one of the symptoms Goodman identified if aesthetically successful. How the clock represents, since unlike a picture it represents only unidimensional time, may be largely irrelevant, but it may exemplify simplicity, express the loving care of the craftsman, and so on. In the right context, the cheap, plastic mass-produced clock may also function as art, expressing perhaps an ironic tribute to kitsch or retro: the exemplified properties can themselves be time- and context-dependent.

These points relate to the physical nature of a clock. The aesthetics of computing is hardly concerned with this: Apple Computers may be clearly intended to be attractive, but such judgments fall into the realm of product design. The interesting question is how something that by nature is primarily notational can acquire an aesthetic function. A better example may be the literary medium. According to Goodman, novels, poetry, and other productions in "discursive" languages such as English are syntactically notational, though they tend to fail the semantic criteria (LA 178); they are also likely to be weak in exemplification. However, they do at least commonly show the symptom of multiple and complex reference. The language used is often ambiguous, superfluous, and metaphorical. Literature, in fact, departs from strict notationality in all these ways. However, computer languages generally lack these qualities; generally they are specifically designed without them.

This is the common view, but the situation with computer languages is not straightforward. Clearly there are many varieties, to some extent because of functional differences and developments. Modern languages such as Java have benefited from the development of object-oriented structures and related notions of data typing and data hiding. This may actually make them easier to use, but sometimes also more complex, with the benefit in producing a functionally equivalent program that is more elegant in structure. Here an obvious relationship to familiar notions of aesthetic value exists in mathematics and science, which put a premium on elegance in terms of such properties as efficiency, minimal use of resources, and economy of expression. Often these properties might be most persuasively ascribed to the abstract algorithm instantiated by a program, rather than anything specific to a programming language. Other properties of a program, however, are clearly describable at the level of the notation itself. Some of these may have to do with layout, for example, the arrangements of white space, characters, and line breaks that create indentations and other features of the screen display that improve readability for programmers. In many languages, these aspects will be ignored by the computer processing the language, and thus have no semantic import related to the interpretation of the language, though for the programmer they are an inherent part of appreciating the meaning of the program. They are also often associated with strong views about appearance that are clearly detachable from functionality.

There is a relationship here to an idea of "secondary notation," originally developed by Petre and Green (1992) to describe how expert users of a computer-aided design system for electronic chips would make use of the design's visible features, such as grouping of components, that had no significance for the system. This could sometimes improve the understandability of the display; but it often seems to impose features such as symmetry of layout that have no clear functional correlate. Lee (1998) proposed that this amounts to increasing the "repleteness" of the symbolic scheme—which for Goodman implies reducing its notationality—and something similar is at work in the layout phenomena alluded to earlier. In such cases, "secondary notation" can be seen in technical terms as one way in which programming languages starts to evince symptoms of the aesthetic. However, this is a somewhat rarefied and specialized symptom, likely only to be appreciated by programmers. We can perhaps yet find a more general way of articulating a notion of aesthetic computing in relation to Goodman's theory.

Execution and Implementation Again

In works such as novels, Goodman locates the nature of the work in the text. The text defines the work, and the writing of the text is its execution. The text is then implemented by dissemination to readers. Music (of the traditional Western kind) similarly rests on a text. A performance of a work is a performance of *that* work only if it corresponds with the text. Musical notation is, in Goodman's view, the closest thing in practical use to a notation as defined in his theory, though even this has various aspects of "secondary notation," such as in the ways notes are grouped. Perhaps it will be fruitful to consider a computer program in a similar way, as a highly notational text that forms the basis of some kind of implementation.

As an aside, we should beware of confusion with the familiar use of the terms "execution" and "implementation" in computing contexts. At best, this is likely to be misleading. The words seem to be used almost in the opposite sense: the programmer writes a program as an implementation of some algorithm; the computer then executes it. Using the music analogy, we might want to interpret this in Goodman's terms by saying that the programmer executes a work (the program) by writing it, and the program is then implemented by the computer to produce some result that (at least in part) "fulfils its function." This function could well be an aesthetic function, though of course it need not be.

It's worth noting here that there is nothing incongruous about artistic implementation, in this sense, being a mechanized procedure. Printing and publication are often that, and ever more so. In Goodman's view, the contribution of the artist may be confined entirely to the execution stage. But there may be a problem in this, with the kind of work we are considering here. A musical text is an essentially notational object, apparently therefore lacking aesthetic symptoms. Is Goodman hence committed to the view that a musical score is not in itself an aesthetic product? This is apparently absurd, since the score is all the composer produces. Goodman does not appear to have addressed this question head-on, but his response is clearly along the lines that the score is the necessary core of the work—which he latter holds to consist of the set of all performances—and is thus generative of the aesthetic product, even though it is not that product itself. The performances may be good or bad, and clearly contribute greatly to the nature of the product, but in principle they must all *comply* precisely with the score. *How* they are produced is immaterial: anything that complies will be a performance of the work, although the score can constrain compliance to an arbitrary degree (e.g., what instruments are used is typically a requirement but, as in Bach's *Art of the Fugue*, can be left unspecified). Hence, although the production of the work is "two-stage" and requires the contribution of an intermediary whose efforts may critically determine the *quality* of the outcome, the production of an aesthetic outcome as such could be entirely mechanical (as, indeed, Mozart composed works for a mechanical organ). Some might hold that a purely mechanical process can add no significant aesthetic content to the result, but Goodman's position must be that it can fulfill an aesthetic function that is otherwise only potential. If unimplemented, the work does not exist; in that case, therefore, there is no aesthetic product.

Again, it seems clear that an aesthetic function could be fulfilled by implementation in ways other than conventional performance (e.g., by reading the score and appreciating its musical qualities directly), which indicates that a score can be generative of a range of different though related works, understood as deriving from distinct classes of implementations. Goodman's reluctance to admit this emerges especially in his discussion of literature

(RP 49–65), in which he holds that a text defines exactly one work, and thus sidelines implementation. This is comparatively plausible for novels, but less so for plays and other texts for which more than one kind of implementation seems normal. This is at least partly because something like a play can be seen as two kinds of text: on the one hand, it describes, denotes, and hence has as its compliants, events in a world, and in this sense is like a novel; on the other hand it prescribes a series of events on a stage, a performance, and is in this sense like a musical score. The former type of text is more discursive, the latter perhaps more notational. It would be gratuitous to insist that the distinct *syntax* of plays defines performance as the canonical mode of implementation (for then why not also Plato's dialogs), but it's hard to see what other options Goodman has left open.[3] Goodman would certainly want to claim that for highly notational texts such as musical scores there can be only one compliance class (hence only one kind of compliant performance), but even, this is only with an interpretation of the text as notational.

The position of the composer, then, does seem to closely parallel that of the computer programmer. A notational work is produced, which the computer implements. The result of the implementation could be any of the things normally associated with computer art: images, texts, multimedia experiences, or music. Examples of computer art produced by such means (and systems designed to produce them; see examples at http://www .processing.org) are abundant. In such cases, we can say that Goodman's ideas extend directly to art in the context of computing in the same way they apply to art in other contexts. But, of course, a good deal of work with computers (by artists and others) is not done by writing programs. We use programs that already exist, such things as word processors, but also diverse drawing and painting programs that allow us to produce digital images with the same manual gestures as a pencil. How does the preceding account apply here?

Any computer system can be described at a number of levels. The account one gives at each of these levels is different in both syntactic and semantic terms, though one has neither of these at the lowest possible level, since only the physical fact of a mechanism in which electronic charges move around exists. To achieve even the first level above this requires an act of *interpretation*. The charges are interpreted as representing binary digits, 1s and 0s. Their organized movements represent arithmetical procedures such as addition. Nothing about the physical level requires or defines this interpretation, but of course, the machine is designed expressly so that the interpretation will always succeed.[4] "Above" this level are indefinitely many others, at each of which a formalism is syntactically and semantically defined so that various operations can be coherently interpreted in terms of some domain. Examples are typical programming languages, but also drawing and painting systems. Input is mapped to output in a coherent way: in a spell-checking system, errors are mapped to correct spellings (we hope); in the paint program, perhaps stylus pressure is mapped to line width, or movement to line development. These mappings can be varied, for example, stylus pressure to color, or movement to rotation of the whole image; this is unproblematic, in that input "semantics" is defined in terms of manipulation of the expressive medium.

It becomes much more complex, of course, if the semantics of the input are defined in terms of the semantics of the expression. This can be intuitively captured in the idea of a "meaning-checker," or a paint program that manipulates images depending on what they depict. Such a program is not normally available, and (currently) at best only for very specialized domains, as in computer-aided design systems. Assuming, then, that our semantics are defined in terms of the medium, we have a system for manipulating the medium that in principle seems to be similar, from the artist's perspective, to using paint or other means of manipulating color on surfaces. The computer paint program is therefore seen here as part of a system for execution of a one-stage autographic work. There will be gray areas, for example, if the paint system supports scripting for special effects; but in general it is unhelpful to think of the computer as carrying out implementation, in Goodman's sense, as it might for an algorithmically programmed two-stage allographic composition of the kind considered earlier. Goodman has perhaps provided us with some terminology to sharpen an intuitive, but commonly obscure, distinction in this area.

The computer is a tool to assist execution in the case just addressed, and to assist implementation in the previous case. What if the computer itself carries out execution in a self-active way? Can the computer *be an artist*? This question is at least as controversial, and as unlikely to be answered in short compass, as the question of computer intelligence. One way of side-stepping it, however, might be to exploit further Goodman's execution-implementation distinction. We already noted that Goodman allows for arbitrary objects (his example is a pebble on a beach) to be implemented as works of art, and we applied the same reasoning to Duchamp's urinal. In these cases, the role of the artist is entirely in implementation, since the execution is foregone. Perhaps the situation is similar with computer-generated art: the computer provides the execution, which an artist then implements, by exhibiting it, explaining it, perhaps further manipulating it, and so on. Of course, in many cases the artist is the programmer, and it is then a moot point whether the computer is actually only subserving implementation, no matter how elaborate its contribution. But if we reach a position where, say, the computer is thought to have altered its own program to the point that the original programmer no longer clearly has control over the result, then we might treat the outcome as *sui generis*—not an aesthetic product in itself, but something that can be made to work as art by the artist's further contribution.[5] (The same trivially applies in any case in which the programmer, albeit human, acts entirely independently of the implementer.)

This case emphasizes Goodman's insistence on regarding the executed item, whether a text or score or found item, as a formal object with a role completely divorced from any issue about its origin. It does not matter how or why a text is produced: it remains the same text, and anything syntactically identical to it, however produced, is an instance of the same text (RP 64–65). Similarly, a computer program or system will have the same status, regarding its possible aesthetic uses, whether it is produced by a programmer or by another computer system. In this sense, a computer can take the role of an artist. We have noted there is also nothing necessarily odd about the computer implementing a work, so at least cannot rule out the possibility of genuinely aesthetic works that are both executed and implemented by computer. Notice, however, that these are all two-stage allographic works. Much less clear is whether one can make sense of the idea of a computer producing a one-stage autographic work, similar to a painting.

Again we are in threatening proximity to the deep waters of intelligence, agency, and responsibility, but we can make one observation. Any process that can be computed must meet certain criteria, such as having a completely explicit "effective procedure." This is plausible for publishing a book or performing music; but it is much less clearly so for writing a book, and is certainly not the case for turning a beach pebble into art. For non-notational work, implementation can be a wide range of things; but for notational work it must be possible to take the text as a *specification* of any implementation. A notational text, as such, has no qualities relevant to its use that do not play a direct role in determining its compliance class—anything else would be a metanotational addition, such as "secondary notation." Any implementation must be the creation or identification of a compliant; otherwise it would have no coherent relation to the text as notation. The text could be implemented as something else, such as calligraphy, but this would be irrelevant to its notational nature and highly underspecified by the text. All notation has this in common with computer programs.

It remains unclear (notwithstanding the preceding remarks) whether we would ever agree in practice that a computer that wrote music, say, had not simply functioned as a tool of its programmer. The issue of "creativity," shunned by Goodman (MM 154, 198), appears on the horizon. We will not pursue this here, except to reiterate that the discussion has been about identifying rather than evaluating aesthetic phenomena. Though computers may produce creations exhibiting some of the symptoms of the aesthetic, we have certainly not shown they could ever produce good art.

Conclusion

This chapter has attempted to offer a case study of applying an existing and relatively well-developed philosophical theory to limited aspects of this new domain of aesthetic computing. The reader must judge how successful or useful an exercise this has been. Perhaps it will have opened up some new ways of thinking about fundamental issues.

Doubtless some will question the possibility of such an exercise being useful, being skeptical of the whole theoretical orientation. On the one hand, retrorealists still cling to the notions of absolute truth and beauty memorably expressed by Keats; on the other hand, the neonihilists take aesthetic judgment to be wholly arbitrary and relative, devoid of any intelligible structure. Goodman places himself between these extremes as "a relativist who nevertheless maintains that there is a distinction between right and wrong theories, interpretations and works of art" (MM, *Preface*). This is a position that at least deserves to be taken seriously.

In closing, it may be interesting to apply some of the notions discussed here to a specific example. Fishwick (2002; also this volume) describes an approach to programming whereby one selects some arbitrary model from a range of architectural styles and others inspired by art or other aesthetic domains. Various features of the style are exploited to construct models that allow representation of the programming task. In principle, these may be constructed physically from various materials, or by using a computer modeling system. The models may help achieve a clearer understanding of the program or the problem it relates to, be directly available for the machine to run (if computer-based), and have their own inherent aesthetic interest.

Goodman views models as a complex topic (since they can be "almost anything from a naked blonde to a quadratic equation"; LA 171), but in this case they seem to fall within a large class that are formally similar to diagrams, elevated to three or even four dimensions. Fishwick's models represent algorithms, which seem inevitably to constitute a differentiated, discrete semantic domain. The models themselves, of course, are not (or not necessarily) syntactically differentiated, hence they do not necessarily form a notation system. However, one might say they augment a notational system, in the sense that a notational system is the basis of their usability; one could strip them down to their most minimal usable form, very like a notational diagram. They thus evoke the notion of "secondary notation" discussed earlier: the notation is augmented with features that are more "replete," not entirely semantically arbitrary (i.e., are not like calligraphy), but dependent on exemplification for their value. They therefore do show symptoms of the aesthetic.

How, though, can the diagnosis be confirmed? Only by being implemented as works of art. And this comes down to their *users*. The emphasis here indicates that such implementation is an aspect of the models' use: if used only as formal notation (possible in principle), they would not be fulfilling their function as artworks. As ever, we require a rich environment of practice to nurture that use. Aesthetic computing, though it may not yet constitute such an environment, is surely headed in that direction.

Notes

1. In keeping with Goodman's own habit, his books are hereinafter designated by initials: LA (*Languages of Art*), MM (*Of Mind and Other Matters*, 1984), WW (*Ways of Worldmaking*, 1978), RP (*Reconceptions in Philosophy*, Goodman and Elgin 1988).

2. Jorge Luis Borges, "Pierre Menard, the Author of the Quixote," in Borges (1964).

3. Concerning certain aspects of the compliants of texts, Goodman has a subtle argument based on his theory of "projectibility"; but this does not seem to apply here. (See also discussion in Elgin 1983, 111, 113–20.)

4. Goodman briefly discusses a similar point in relation to Fodor's theory of mind (RP 106–07).

5. Bear in mind the earlier point, that nothing entirely *sui generis* will succeed as art, whatever implementation is attempted, in the absence of a cultural context that allows for it.

References

Borges, J. L. 1964. *Labyrinths*. New York: New Directions.

Elgin, C. Z. 1983. *With Reference to Reference*. Indianapolis: Hackett Publishing Co.

Fishwick, P. 2002. "Aesthetic Programming: Crafting Personalised Software." *Leonardo* 35(4): 383–390. MIT Press.

Goodman, N. 1968. *Languages of Art*, 1st ed. Indianapolis: Bobbs-Merrill.

Goodman, N. 1978. *Ways of Worldmaking*. Indianapolis: Hackett Publishing Co.

Goodman, N. 1982. "Implementation of the Arts." *Journal of Aesthetics and Art Criticism* 40: 281–283.

Goodman, N. 1984. *Of Mind and Other Matters*. Cambridge, MA: Harvard University Press.

Goodman, N., and Elgin, C. Z. 1988. *Reconceptions in Philosophy*. New York: Routledge.

Lee, J. R. 1998. "Words and Pictures—Goodman Revisited." In R. Paton and I. Neilson, eds. *Visual Representations and Interpretations*. Pp. 21–31. New York: Springer-Verlag.

Petre, M., and Green, T. R. G. 1992. "Requirements of Graphical Notations for Professional Users: Electronics CAD Systems as a Case Study." *Le Travail Humain* 55: 47–70.

3

A Forty-Year Perspective on Aesthetic Computing in the *Leonardo* Journal

Roger F. Malina

When the Leonardo organization first started publishing the work of pioneering computer artists in the late 1960s,[1] it was far from obvious that computer art would become the powerful means for contemporary expression that it has today. Little did those pioneers suspect that industries would grow up around their early work in computer graphics, animation, and interactive systems.

Most new technologies do not prove to be suitable for artmaking, or are used only during transitional periods, as occurred, for instance, with copier art or fax art. Today, we see pervasive use of computers in a wide range of art forms that are beginning to shape how we organize and respond to visual and sound information, by both restructuring perceptual processes and modifying cognition. The designed environment, from clothing to cities, is beginning to be reshaped to respond to the new lived experience of distant and distributed communication and computation. The expectation is that over the long term we can expect the nature and expression of human consciousness to evolve through the extension of the human senses and the creation of synthetic senses; we can anticipate that these changes will be as profound as those provoked by the cultural appropriation of technologies of print and perspective underlying the developments now known as humanism.

The change in the situation of computer artists, as seen from the point of view of the *Leonardo* journal editorial office, has been dramatic. The first issue of *Leonardo*, in 1968, featured an article by Roy Ascott entitled "The Cybernetic Stance: My Process and Purpose" (Ascott 1968); the third issue included Robert Mallary's essay "Notes on Jack Burnham's Concepts of a Software Exhibition" (Mallary 1969). Nearly a thousand articles dealing with computer-mediated art have now been published in the Leonardo journals, books, and web publications. The early texts laid out many of the conceptual issues that have now been explored for 40 years. Our first book related to the use of computers in art, *Visual Art, Mathematics and Computers* (Malina 1979), found a small but receptive audience. At this time, intense debates were challenging the very notion that significant art, art that would be inconceivable without their use, could be made using computers.

Forty years later, this debate is closed and the computer has both been widely adopted in such earlier art forms as photography, film, and animation, and led to the emergence of distinctive new art modes, from interactive to net to software art. The Leonardo Book Series now includes several books a year dealing with the use of computers in the arts, including Lev Manovitch's *Language of New Media* (Manovich 2001), Judy Malloy's *Women, Art and Technology* (Malloy 2003), and Jay Bolter and Diane Gromala's *Windows and Mirrors* (Bolter and Gromala 2003). This latter book tackles head-on the dichotomous view opposing computers as transparent "information appliances" to computers as a medium for reshaping perception and cognition. The term "aesthetic computing" encapsulates not only this dichotomy, but the richness of this emerging field of inquiry and practice. A critical mass of work now being conducted is having a major impact in the nature of the "information society."

Pioneers in the field confronted widespread opposition to their experimentation with computer science and technology in the arts, and this book documents the efforts of pioneers to transfer ideas and techniques from the arts to computer science and engineering in the face of similar opposition and skepticism. There is now strong evidence for the emergence of this new field of aesthetic computing.

The Stone Age of the Digital Arts

Yet we must emphasize that the computer remains a very primitive device whose cultural appropriation has barely begun. At an early International Symposium on Electronic Arts (ISEA) conference, William Buxton, then of Xerox PARC, made an impassioned plea for reimagining what computers could be. He compared the human–machine interface of the computer keyboard or mouse with the machine–human interface of the trombone or trumpet. A trumpet player uses eyes, ears, breath, saliva, body movement, and touch to such an extent that the trumpet truly becomes a seamless extension of the artist's will. A jazz ensemble achieves a level of interactive creation that remains unmatched by any computer-mediated system. Even today's handheld and wearable devices are essentially foreign objects to the body and mind of the user.

A number of experimental computer-machine interfaces and immersive environments, many developed by artists, now exist, but none is in large-scale production, nor do any yet achieve the jazz ensemble's seamless integration of human and tool in group work. The deep desire to achieve this kind of seamless and multimodal integration can be seen in various initiatives in ubiquitous, pervasive, and wearable computing; clearly the computer is only just beginning to enter the biological age. In addition, as Alex Galloway (Galloway 2004) argues in his book *Protocol*, we are only beginning to understand how the very design structures and protocols underlying computers and networks predetermine the kind of cultural behaviors and artifacts that we can imagine or realize with computer systems. Computer protocols and standards are now the terrain of artistic experimentation.

In photography and film, for instance, the technology stabilized relatively early, leading to a proliferation of artistic creation, but computer media are still in a state of rapid development and mutation. As a result, artists often find themselves on the cutting edge of technical development, as evidenced by the numerous patents now being filed by artists.

The rapid mutation of terminology indicates that the heart of the matter has not yet been identified. The early practitioners of machine, algorithmic, electronic, interactive, computer, digital, web or net, software, and new media art[2] have shared few things other than the use of the computer itself; their goals and practices differ widely, and they do not share a common aesthetic. In addition, many new media artists also make use of many other technologies that are not computer based and only incidentally digital. Steve Wilson, in his Leonardo book *Information Arts* (Wilson 2002), has documented the growing array of scientific and technology areas where artists now occupy aesthetic territory. These range through all the physical, chemical, cognitive, and biological sciences, from nano- to macrotechnologies. If the computer-based arts are still in their infancy, these other art forms are just at the point of conception. Wilson argues that "digital" or "computer-based" may no longer be a coherent aesthetic category, and a broader approach of "information" arts is warranted. Thus, we can anticipate that aesthetic computing will eventually be embedded within the broader field of information science aesthetics.

The Institutional Setting

In the 1960s and 1970s, few art schools had programs addressing the use of computers in artmaking, and only such visionary centers as Gyorgy Kepes's Center for Advanced Visual Studies at MIT provided environments where artists could access the latest tools and devices. A few initiatives, such as Experiments in Art and Technology, brought together artists and engineers on common projects. And a few exhibitions such as Reichardt's "Cybernetic Serendipity" (Reichardt 1968) began the process within the public sphere of cultural appropriation of the new technologies for artistic expression.

All major universities now have, or are starting, new programs in art and technology or art and new media. Some schools are dedicated to the new art forms, such as the School for New Media in Cologne, Germany. There are research and exhibition venues such as

Ars Electronica in Linz, Austria, and IRCAM in Paris, France. Although initially new institutional frameworks were created mostly in North America and Western Europe, programs are now available internationally from the Philippines to Bulgaria, from Argentina and Brazil to India and Australia. Recently UNESCO started a major initiative called DIGIARTS, which has accelerated the institutional process within international structures and organizations.[3]

A striking feature of the institutional developments is the wide variety of settings within which such programs have evolved. These settings range from art and music schools to engineering and science departments, schools of architecture, film, and design, as well as independent new institutions. This pedagogical diversity indicates that the computer arts are not merely additions to a list of cultural technologies such as photography, film, and video or even forms such as painting and sculpture, theater, or poetry. The assertion of the Aesthetic Computing Manifesto (Fishwick et al. 2003) is that an emerging body of work lays the basis for a new discipline and not just for a need to encourage inter- or transdisciplinarity.

Within the industrial and corporate world, a number of programs such as the Art and Entertainment Research Council Committee at Intel[4] have emerged. Yet to some extent, the explosion of the web and development of a viable associated graphic design and game industry have diverted attention and obscured the needed underlying restructuring of the disciplinary approaches. There is a danger of creating new disciplinary barriers around the computer arts. Still in their infancy, the institutional frameworks that foster interdisciplinary work often need to bridge the nonprofit/for-profit societal systems.

Unfortunately, early programs such as Xerox Parc's PAIR program established by Rich Gold (Harris 1999) and Interval Research Inc. no longer exist; their demise coincided with the contraction of research and development funding when the Internet "bubble" burst. Leonardo has published "Arts Lab" (Naimark 2003), a study under the leadership of Michael Naimark, and supported by the Rockefeller Foundation. The study sought to learn lessons from the last 40 years of institutional experiments, ranging from the early Experiments in Art and Technology (EAT) program to today's leading institutions such as ZKM, Ars Electronica, Banff Center for the Arts, and ICC as well as the demise of the innovative programs at Xerox Parc and Interval Research. The study also articulated the need to develop hybrid institutions bridging the nonprofit educational and for-profit corporate research and development sectors, covering a range of activities from the arts to applied and industrial design.

Naimark argued that such an environment, with twin targets in the computer arts and aesthetic computing, could be made self-sustainable by drawing on a variety of financing sources from patent and intellectual property to traditional grants, philanthropic donations, art market sales, and the commercial arts. A recent report from the U.S. National Research Council (Mitchell 2003) articulates a comprehensive case for art and technology interaction as a source of economic growth and innovation through organizational clusters promoting new uses of information technologies in the creative industries, within geographic regions.

Aesthetic Computing Methodologies

Aesthetic computing requires the establishment of methodologies to migrate relevant ideas from the theory and practice of the arts to computer science and engineering. A number of well-established methodologies have been used successfully in different fields. These can be broken down into at least five approaches, all of which are documented in this book:

1. The migration of ideas and concepts developed in one discipline to another, often through indirect social channels, or appropriation of metaphorical systems.
2. Artists collaborating with a scientist or engineer who implements the artist's concept (or vice versa).
3. Artists, scientists, and engineers working together in a team on a common project.
4. Consortia of artists, scientists, and engineers working on different projects but pooling resources to enable access to a technological platform. In the process, they develop new tools or approaches that can be applied to diverse objectives.
5. Artists who are sufficiently well trained in science and technology to develop the new technologies needed for their projects; these "new Leonardos" contribute directly to innovation in computer science and engineering. Conversely, scientists and engineers are found who engage directly in artistic practice.

The Strong and Weak Claims for Aesthetic Computing

We again find ourselves in one of those special times in cultural history when artists, scientists, and engineers using the same tool or medium (in this case the computer) can share experiences and vocabularies and develop common views regarding interesting problems to solve or exciting and successful solutions. Inevitably shared epistemologies, aesthetics, and ethical systems emerge from this process. The benefits of these developments can be articulated through a weak and a strong claim for aesthetic computing.

The weak claim is that by stimulating the flow of ideas and methods from the arts to computing, computer scientists and engineers will achieve their objectives more easily, quickly, or elegantly. Artists are, in a sense, domain experts representing the users of the technologies, and by including them in the process of developing computing, one can anticipate more rapid or successful social adoption of new devices. This responds to the perceived problem that large investments in new consumer computing devices are often unproductive, and corporate developers often fail to anticipate new social patterns of use. Multidisciplinary teams involving artists can be productive approaches to finding innovative and elegant solutions to preestablished research problems. Studies in creativity and innovation theory support these claims.

The strong claim for aesthetic computing is that by introducing ideas and methods from art and design into computing, new practices and approaches will emerge responding to new objectives that would not naturally have evolved within the computer sciences and engineering. The interplay of aesthetic and ethical consideration with the drivers that motivate individual inventors in developing new technologies is complicated, but the aphorism "what one person can imagine, another can invent," often attributed to Jules Verne, reflects an underlying truism about the cultural contingency of technological and scientific development. The artists Rabinowitz and Galloway have expressed this idea with their statement that artists "must create on the same scale as they can destroy" (Rabinowitz and Galloway 1984). Early interactive telecommunications and virtual community projects (Ascott and Loeffler 1991) by pioneering artists in the 1970s reflect deep underlying social dreams and desires only subsequently adopted within commercial and entertainment sectors. Scientists and engineers often argue that science and technology are culturally and ethically neutral, yet these activities are structurally embedded in cultural, political, and economic systems that predetermine the priority of research problems and what kinds of solutions are deemed acceptable.

It is interesting to note that the size of research and development budgets in the computer games, special effects, and computer animation industries are now large enough to set research agendas and fund both basic computer science research and applications in universities and industry. When Leonardo published the work of computer graphics and interactive art pioneers, they often had to adapt their ideas to available hardware and software systems. Today's computer game and animation artists patent their inventions, driving the development of new hardware systems.

If C. P. Snow (Snow 1993) were rewriting his essay today, he might argue that the disciplinary problem has become significantly more complex because of the closer coupling of the arts to the entertainment industry, science to government, and engineering to the corporate world. In a real sense, the two-culture problem has become a multicultural problem; art-science-technology interaction now confronts new issues of diversity of cultural imperatives based on ethnic, language, or geographic origin as well as spiritual, metaphysical, and religious world views of human purpose and destiny. The strong claim for aesthetic computing is that the emerging computer science and technology will have radically different objectives and methodologies.

Experiment, Theory, Simulation, and Visualization

Scientists and engineers now work in realms that are almost totally outside direct human sensory experience. Astronomers work with forms of energy, such as gravity waves and neutrinos, that are not directly accessible to the human nervous system. Physicists and biologists work on such small scales that quantum effects and group phenomena emerge that are unknown on the scale humans can experience directly. Chemists and nanoscientists can now design materials with properties that are totally foreign to natural systems. In zero gravity, astronauts experience behaviors that are totally new to human sensory and locomotive experience. And, of course, computer scientists and engineers have created a globally linked Internet system providing such rapid feedback and diffusion of human interaction, Howard Rheingold (Rheingold 2002) argues, that we are entering a space of new social phenomena and behaviors.

The human cognitive system did not develop with these extensions of the human nervous system in place or interacting with these new environments and phenomena. So how do we develop our intuition about worlds and phenomena it is physically impossible for our human senses to experience directly? How do we build systems of values and meanings, of ethics and aesthetics, in this new epistemological landscape? Ken Goldberg, in his Leonardo book *The Robot in the Garden* (Goldberg 2000), elaborates on these issues in his exploration of "telepistemology"; the crucial question is no longer the location of the "ghost in the machine," but whether humans, as primitive hybrid human-robots in this new foreign landscape, can find a new orientation and vision for the human condition.

It is not often understood that, to reflect this new epistemological and ontological landscape, the scientific method itself has evolved and adapted to confront situations outside daily experience that are not amenable to the usual confrontation of direct observation and experiment with hypothesis and theory. The twin methodologies of scientific visualization and computer simulation have emerged as essential approaches in dealing with phenomena accessible to the human senses only through their extension, amplification, or augmentation.

Scientific visualization provides tools and methodologies for interacting with large volumes of data that cannot be absorbed or analyzed without such tools, but also allows simultaneous confrontation with very heterogeneous forms of information. This has led to new developments in distributed computing such as the GRID methods being developed by physicists or virtual observatories by astronomers. Many scientific investigations can now be carried out without intervening on the physical world, by analyzing large volumes of existing data in the public domain.

Computer simulation provides numerical approaches for emulating complex nonlinear systems that cannot be described in closed mathematical form. In many fields, the only way to create testable hypotheses is by creating such simulations of "virtual worlds."

Such problems range from understanding the evolution of the large-scale structure of the universe in cosmology, the behavior of networks of chemical interaction within living cells, and the modeling of complex systems such as planetary climate.

Scientific visualization and computer simulation are methodological areas in which artists have been very active, as described in this book, and are likely to be particularly fertile fields for new work in aesthetic computing.

Conclusion

Over the 40 years of the journal *Leonardo's* publication, the field of computer arts has developed in a multifaceted variety of institutional and interdisciplinary contexts. The computer arts have now established themselves as a vital field of theory and practice. Today, the inverse process of aesthetic computing is emerging with the introduction of art and design ideas and methods into computer science and engineering. There are at least two reasons for encouraging the interaction of artists, scientists, and engineers—the weak and strong claims for aesthetic computing.

The weak claim instrumentalizes the necessary process of acculturation of new pervasive computer and information technologies affecting our social organization and perceptual and cognitive processes; it is a possible source for innovation. The strong claim for aesthetic computing is that by introducing ideas and methods from the arts to computing science and engineering, new objectives and methodologies can be established to redirect the future development of computing, provoking new developments and inventions that would otherwise have been impossible. A different computer science and engineering may emerge.

Acknowledgments

I would like to thank the Rockefeller, Ford, and Langlois Foundations for their support of the Leonardo/the International Society for the Arts, Sciences and Technology over the period during which Leonardo cosponsored the Aesthetic Computing workshop at Dagstuhl.

Notes

1. Leonardo/ISAST is a professional organization that seeks to document and promote the work of artists whose work involves contemporary science and technology, and to stimulate collaboration among artists, scientists, and engineers. The Leonardo publications can be accessed at http://www/leonardo.info. These publications include the *Leonardo* journal, *Leonardo Music Journal*, the Leonardo Book Series, and the electronic publications LEA and Leonardo On Line.

2. See, for example, the New Media Dictionary project, at http://www.comm.uqam.ca/GRAM/Accueil.html. A number of researchers have been documenting the rapid mutation of terminology. No good comprehensive cross-linguistic thesauruses exist.

3. See http://portal.unesco.org/digiarts. The UNESCO DIGIARTS program supports a number of regional initiatives, as well as work in schools, through the young digital creators program.

4. See Intel Art and Entertainment Research Committee at http://www.intel.com/research/university/aim/arts.htm.

References

Ascott, R. 1968. "The Cybernetic Stance: My Process and Purpose." *Leonardo* 1(2): 105–12.

Ascott, R., and Loeffler, C. 1991. "Connectivity: Art and Interactive Telecommunications." *Leonardo* 24(2): 1–85.

Bolter, J., and Gromala, D. 2003. *Windows and Mirrors*. Cambridge, MA: MIT Press.

Fishwick, P., et al. 2003. "Aesthetic Computing Manifesto." *Leonardo* 36(4): 255.

Galloway, A. 2004. *Protocol*. Cambridge, MA: MIT Press.

Goldberg, K. 2000. *The Robot in the Garden: Telerobotics and Telepistemology in the Age of the Internet*. Cambridge, MA: MIT Press.

Harris, C., ed. 1999. *Art and Innovation*. Cambridge, MA: MIT Press.

Malina, F., ed. 1979. *Visual Art, Mathematics and Computers: Selections from the Journal Leonardo*. Oxford, UK: Pergamon Press.

Mallary, R. 1969. "Notes on Jack Burnham's Concepts of a Software Exhibition." *Leonardo* 3(2): 189–90.

Malloy, J. 2003. *Women, Art and Technology*. Cambridge, MA: MIT Press.

Manovich, L. 2001. *The Language of New Media*. Cambridge, MA: MIT Press.

Mitchell, W., ed. 2003. *Beyond Productivity: Information Technology, Innovation and Creativity*. Washington, DC: National Academy Press.

Naimark, M. 2003. Truth, Beauty, Freedom, and Money: Technology-Based Art and the Dynamics of Sustainability. Accessed at http://www.artslab.net.

Rabinowitz, S., and Galloway, E. 1984. Café Manifesto. Accessed at http://main.ecafe.com.

Reichardt, J., ed. 1968. "Cybernetic Serendipity: The Computer and the Arts." *Studio International* special issue. London: Studio International.

Rheingold, H. 2002. *Smart Mobs: The Next Social Revolution*. Cambridge, MA: Perseus Publishing.

Snow, C. P. 1993. *The Two Cultures*. Cambridge: Cambridge University Press.

Wilson, S. 2002. *Information Arts: Intersections of Art, Science, and Technology*. Cambridge, MA: MIT Press.

4

The Interface as Sign and as Aesthetic Event

Frieder Nake and Susanne Grabowski

What kind of artifacts should *aesthetic computing* be concerned with? How would they differ from artifacts of ordinary computing?

As Paul Fishwick tells us in his introduction to this volume, computing deals with models, programs, data, and interfaces. Software systems developers invent abstract *models*, which are rendered in computable form, that is, in *programs* and *data*. Users apply such programs to their contexts, which may, to some extent, be represented in the form of data. The use situation is called human–computer interaction. The *interface*, where the two interacting systems, human and computer, meet is the topic of this chapter.

Changing the state of a computable system almost exclusively involves using an *interactive* system. Communication plays a central role, and interactive software interfaces are designed with the goal of successful communication. These interfaces must therefore be functionally effective and aesthetically attractive. This is what visual design is about (Mullet and Sano 1995). No contradiction seems to exist between function and aesthetics when communication is the goal. Interaction design, which is gradually replacing interface ergonomics (i.e., human computer interaction, HCI), appears as a first case of aesthetic computing. We intend to analyze it a bit deeper.

The days of the ever-present graphic user interface may be numbered, as skimming the yearly HCI conference proceedings reveals the growing tendency to go beyond the desktop. Not many have realized that a crossover of computing and aesthetics is happening. Computer users are triggering computational processes on semiotic machines, which they gain access to only through layers of signs. Whenever signs are involved, our perceptive capacities are required. This is to say that the situation is an aesthetic one. Aesthetic computing is viewed too narrowly if we take it as the application, or addition, of some vaguely understood aesthetic rules to the usual computing situation. *Aesthetics* are rather an *inherent*, but until recently largely hidden, aspect of computing. We need to pull this aspect into the open for investigation, interpretation, and construction.

Whatever the term "aesthetics" may be narrowly defined, as, we all have some preconception of its meaning. Its first, and most important, aspect is sensual perception; its second aspect is beauty. "Aesthetic computing" deliberately introduces subjectivism into computing, with all its consequences. The most important of these is that much of what computing science and software development are concerned with must be reconsidered and, quite likely, transformed into terms less precise than an engineering discipline would usually accept. We should be prepared to accept a certain degree of vagueness that comes with the idea of aesthetic computing.

In recent years, a number of authors have pointed out the need to turn from quantity and measurement to quality and judgment in scientific work. Singling out only four from many wonderful studies on this topic, we refer to Winograd (1996), Ehn (1998), Raskin (2000), and Löwgren (2004, chapter 20 in this volume). The ACM magazine, *interactions*, also carries many discussions of the subject.

Engineering comprises construction and evaluation. In the arts, these are two separate activities performed by artists and critics, respectively. Höök and colleagues (2003) have raised the question of how user testing and art criticism could combine in new ways of sense-making sensibility. Aesthetic computing involves criticism of a kind that is still largely unknown in computing.

To put it frankly, the concerns of aesthetic computing are quality rather than quantity, style rather than truth (Wiesing 1991). Not all of our readers may be ready to accept such a formula. We hope to show why a gradual shift from truth and efficiency to style and joy is at the heart of this endeavor.

A Bit More on Aesthetic Computing

Aesthetic computing is certainly not about art. If it were, its proponents would not want it to be. Despite current attempts to create cross-fertilization between two fields of design so far apart yet so close to each other as art and computing, it remains to be shown what lies hidden behind the term, *aesthetic computing*. Conspicuously, the terms *aesthetics* and *art* are used interchangeably in some early publications. To many artists, this is a terrifying idea.

The distinction we draw here between art and aesthetics may sound strange to some readers. Roughly, art is a realm of social activity, an institution of modern society concerned with a certain kind of artifacts. Aesthetics, on the other hand, is the theory of sensual perception. The concepts are related, but are not the same. You may be a great artist without paying any attention to the theoretical field of aesthetics. Or you may excell in aesthetics without having much sensitivity for art.

Syntactically, "aesthetic computing" must be a special kind of application of aesthetics, much as "electrical engineering" could be considered an application of James Clark Maxwell's theory of electromagnetism to engineering. Putting it that way reveals the asymmetry of the two words: If we could say that "electrical engineering" was the application of engineering principles to the realm of electricity, by analogy, aesthetic computing could be an application of computing principles to the realm of aesthetics (as, e.g., in Georg Nees's very early doctoral dissertation on generative aesthetics, 1969).

Though this would be closer to computer art, aesthetic computing would still not be a matter of art. It would, however, definitely border on the activity called "art." Interesting as the general relation of art and computing and complicated as the relationship of aesthetics and art are, our concern here is more specific. We want to look at the interface between human and computer artifact. This will be largely determined by semiotics, the theory of signs.

The relation of three human activities—aesthetics, computing, and semiotics—determines the context of our discussion. We use the human–computer interface to raise, from a semiotic perspective, such questions as What can aesthetics offer to the design of good interfaces? How can we better understand the design and use of an interface if we approach it aesthetically? Is pleasingness of an interface more relevant than usefulness? Should joy of use replace ease of use? Should we play with the interface, rather than the interface function for us?

The remainder of this chapter falls into six sections. First, we describe a particular application of computing to art and that program's interface. The example serves as reference for a more general discussion. We then take three views of the example: the objective and formal view (from computing), the subjective and emotional view (from aesthetics), and the connecting and medial view (from semiotics). The next two sections generalize our case to the situation of interactive software. We offer semiotic fundamentals of interactivity, pointing out how important an aesthetic perspective is for understanding and designing interaction.

Before we continue, we would like to add one more introductory comment. It has often been deplored that works of art presented in galleries and museums usually reach only a tiny percentage of the population. True, some shows nowadays make a tremendous national and international impact, for example, the Venice Biennual, the Documenta at Kassel, Germany, or the Ars Electronica Festival at Linz, Austria. But even these are far inferior in global impact to such commercial aesthetic enterprises as major movie (*Jurassic*

Figure 4.1 The Apple iMac computer. All the hardware, except keyboard and mouse, are contained in one case.

Park or the *Matrix* series) or book releases (*Harry Potter*). Sports events are also mass culture aesthetics that greatly outperform the aesthetics of fine art.

The computer has become as popular and ubiquitous a medium as the telephone, radio, or television. One important aspect of this ubiquity is the graphic user interface (GUI) as a mass culture aesthetic phenomenon of, perhaps, unparalleled significance for global culture. Computers used in work situations as well as computer games rely on these graphic interfaces.

Digital media are increasingly pervasive in modern society. It is impossible to use them without being familiar with their interface. The actual computing processes almost disappear behind the interface. Take the beautifully designed little colored Apple iMac computer as it appeared in shopping centers in 1998 (figure 4.1). The computer as a *machine* was less significant than the interface design. The debut of the original iMac (already off the market) was an aesthetic event, though no technological breakthrough. One of its successors from Apple, the far-out design of the *Cube* (again no commercial success), became the first computer in history to be displayed in the New York Museum of Modern Art Design section.

Much more could be said about the relationship of aesthetics and computing in general. A good deal has recently been published on the theory, history, and practice of digital media. At times, it may seem more attention is being paid to the origins of digital media than was given the origins of computing. The reader can consult Bolter and Grusin (2000), Lunenfeld (1999), Manovich (2003), and Packer and Jordan (2001), to name a few examples.

To justify aesthetic computing, we must look deeper into the essence of computing and interaction. Interfaces are considered as signs, but signs may gain such power that they replace the thing they represent. Now we embark on a journey that will return us to this message.

An Example of Computing and Art

As mentioned before, aesthetic computing is not the same as computer art. We define computer art as the use of software (and, of course, other means and materials) to generate aesthetic objects relevant to the social process of art.

On the other hand, Paul Fishwick defines *aesthetic computing* as "the application of the theory and practice of art to computing" (in this volume). Both of these concepts apply aspects, techniques, or results of one kind of human activity (computing or art) to another (art or computing). But limiting our view in this way will not get us very far. We want to adopt the position that aesthetics and computing have entered a dialectic relationship. What does that entail?

Any phenomenon in the world may be studied dialectically (some would claim they *must* be studied dialectically). To do so, we try to identify forces within the phenomenon that are responsible for change, development, and evolution. In principle, it suffices to identify two such forces that contradict each other. Their contradiction drives change. Dialectics is really about mutual change, influence, and evolution. The *abstract* dialectics of aesthetics and computing involves only conceptual differences between the two. Two more or less opposing forces of reality have a *concrete* dialectic relationship when we observe actual change in our environment influenced by the two forces. Something like this appears to be happening with the use of software.

Computing is totally tied to computability, that is a range of formalism, generality, prediction, and certainty (even if undeterministic). Aesthetics, on the other hand, is tied up with perceivability—a range of vagueness, exemplarity, interpretation, and randomness. Both have rules, but rules are very different in aesthetics and algorithmics. An algorithmic rule is general and requests to be followed. An aesthetic rule is singular and only states that something could be done this way.

The dialectics of aesthetics and computing involves the tension between the capacities of the human mind and human creation. Art, for example, appears as a movement between those contradictory poles.

To illustrate, we chose an example from an artist working with computers. Manfred Mohr is a New York artist who began writing programs to generate his paintings by the end of the 1960s. For about 30 years he had used the cube in three or more dimensions as the basis of his paintings. Until the end of the twentieth century, he had created his very personal style of concrete, constructivist art. His canvases stand out with strong black lines on white ground (occasionally, he allowed for some shades of gray or silver). He never accepted the term "computer art" for his work. If he used any identification other than just *art*, he called it "algorithmic art."

Figure 4.2 Manfred Mohr: P-707/F, 2001. Endura Chrome on canvas and wood, 140 × 143 cm. By permission of the artist. The rendition in black and white is for reference only. It misses much of the aesthetic quality of the work.

Recently, Mohr reintroduced color. He has totally changed the appeal of his paintings except for one thing: they still possess a clear algorithmic foundation. Mohr's paintings are now geometric structures of bright colored areas. The reason for the color is to visually express the complexity of some process happening to the six-dimensional hypercube. Figure 4.2 is a black-and-white reproduction of one of Mohr's recent works (Museum für Konkrete Kunst 2001).

Contrary to what we might expect, Manfred Mohr is not interested in "making the invisible visible." He knows there is no way to visually gain in*sight* into six dimensions. His interest is not didactics but art. His mental jump into the sixth dimension is to create an algorithmic background of high complexity, which he uses to generate surprising two-dimensional events of color and form.

Up to here, this case is not significant to aesthetic computing. It is not different from similar models that are formally described and transformed into some visual form on the display screen. We have introduced Mohr's art to illustrate an algorithmic interface to this kind of art, which may show an aesthetic quality that could be taken as a case of aesthetic computing.

We take the algorithmic situation as the starting point for a different consideration. Figure 4.3 shows the interface of a program, which Matthias Krauß, then a graduate student of computing science at the University of Bremen, wrote overnight after we had

Figure 4.3 Interface of DeviceX (the original is in colors). Left: graphic rendition of the geometry; right: graphics of the topology; top: slider to be moved by interactive physical device.

discussed Manfred Mohr's art. The focus of the discussion had been how to use inherent features of digital media to create new approaches to works of art. We felt that the dual existence of the work on screen and in computer memory must become the source for possible new encounters with the work. We started to look for presentations located between canvas and Internet. We wanted literally to *enter* into the picture.

Figure 4.3, to the lower left, shows a picture typical for Mohr's new genre. Although reproduced here in black and white only, you can easily identify polygonal shapes of different shades of gray. You can also see black lines, some of which are wider than others.

On top of the screen shot, a small version of the same picture is repeated. Further to the right, is a regularly sized pattern of small squares separated by strong horizontal and thin vertical lines.

Users of the program move the cursor about with the mouse to find out what they can do. They soon discover (no hint given!) that they can "grab" the small picture on top and drag it across the screen, from left to right, and back again. As they move it, its content changes (figure 4.4). The sliding image coincides with the large picture to the left when it reaches its left-most position, and shows the large picture on the right when moved there.

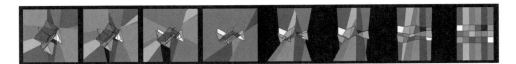

Figure 4.4 DeviceX: Eight consecutive states of the transition from geometry (left) to topology (right).

We have observed students playing with this device (we call it *DeviceX*). They soon discover that the slider continuously transforms the left into the right picture. There must be a rule governing the relation of the two pictures. The right-hand side displays each of the colored areas by equal shape and size. Some, though not necessarily all, are also visible on the left. The transformation suggests that the areas are reduced to standard size and shape without losing their color. Also, their neighborhood is preserved. Indeed, the reduction of shape complexity allows for an improved visualization of relations of neighborhood. The left and right parts appear as twins, although they look totally different.

The idea behind this arrangement is to invite people to play with the slider and, in doing so, derive hypotheses about neighborhoods. The painting (in digital form) reveals part of its algorithmic background. The object of art and its interpretation are united. In the usual art situation, the two are canvas and catalog. In our case, both object and interpretation exist as invisible software and visible graphics. The graphic appearance—most important to the artist—becomes the face of the software.

Before leaving the example, we briefly mention that the actual software is a bit richer than described here. Clicking on the lines between areas, or on areas themselves, causes those parts of the object to flicker in each of the three presentations. By moving the device, users can observe what the fate of the flickering element is.

Incidentally, *DeviceX* may be used with (hyper)cubes of any dimension from three upwards. Playing with it may, by way of analogy, add to one's insight. Also available is a wireframe projection of the rotating hypercube. These renditions will at some later time be brought closer to the *DeviceX* presentation, thereby enhancing functionality and interface features simultaneously.

In the following sections, we interpret the example from three perspectives: the computational, the aesthetic, and the semiotic.

The Computational View

In a first step, we look at the example from the perspective of computing. Computers are machines for evaluating computable functions. Anything in the world, objects or processes, for which a formal model can be made in terms of computable functions can be evaluated by computer. Processor and memory swallow and chew computable objects and processes. These reside inside the computer. They may be transformed, generate all sorts of offspring, and generally lead a "life" unnoticed, but rich and rapid.

In our example, the external object or process is Manfred Mohr's idea of generating some specific and well-defined event in the world of the six-dimensional hypercube and projecting it down to the two dimensions of the image plane.

Once this process has been described in general terms, it is transformed into a program, complete with input and output routines. The input is needed to tell the operating system at which point in parameter space the computable function (program) is to be evaluated. The output gives us perceptible results.

The program in our example presents a model of the 6D hypercube. It randomly selects one vertex (identified by a 6-bit binary code), and determines its opposing vertex (as the end of a spatial diagonal). The idea is to move from the first vertex to the opposite one along edges. Such a "diagonal path" consists of a sequence of six connected edges. Four diagonal paths are randomly selected. Vertices along each are numbered, and vertices with the same number are connected. This procedure generates quadrilaterals, which are projected onto the image plane.

The quadrilaterals are colored randomly from a color pallet. Provision is taken to wrap areas around between the first and fourth diagonal path. Colorization in the image plane is done in the sequence of projection. Edges of quadrilaterals may therefore cut through color areas, and shapes may turn out to look different.

The example illustrates a remarkable fact distinguishing computing from other kinds of manipulating subject matter. What we have described is an *idea* that exists mentally. Describing it may become so complex and complicated we need pen and paper to fix its details exactly. Experience tells us that we are often fully convinced of the absolute precision of an idea, only to realize later that it was not all that clear. What was clear as a mental construct may be vague or even flawed when it is externalized.

The ultimate test for precision and clarity of a program text is the explicitness it requires. In programming language, we must spell out everything related to its expressive power. Programming turns mental constructs into executable descriptions to instruct the computer. Programming is the ultimate answer to Peirce's question of "How to make our ideas clear" (Peirce 1940).

A description is linguistic in nature; as such it is a sign. However, its executability on the computer metaphorically turns it into a machine. We say "the program runs"— invisibly, perhaps, filling up memory space with its results. To monitor its performance, we need a perceptible presentation of the result.

Aesthetic Aspects of the Example

Aesthetics is concerned with the sensual dimension of perception. The question of whether or not we like what we perceive, that is, the question of beauty, is secondary. Sensual perception of the program in our example is bound to the visual output appearing on the screen.

The program becomes invisible once it enters computer storage. Equally invisible are the objects to which it is applied. Output routines transform *internal representations* of computable objects and processes into *external presentations*. Internal representations are invisible to us, but they can be manipulated by the computer. External presentations are visible, but not manipulable by the computer.

Let us call the objects and processes that become subject matter of computations "algorithmic objects." Algorithmic objects exist as pairs of an internal representation and an external presentation. Our human interest is focused on the external presentation since we want to see it, point to it, talk about it, and so on. If computation did not enter the game, this would be the end.

But computation changes things insofar as their visible aspect is pealed away from their manipulable aspect. The computer does not directly operate on the pixels on the screen. It operates on their representations in the display buffer, and further down on this scale of manipulability are representations of other entities that form the real stuff of programs. In a very real sense, what is important for us with our contextualized and situational interest is but a side effect for the computer, with its decontextualized and desituated operations, and vice versa.

The human's interest in having a machine do the computation is to eliminate something that we are not particularly good at. In principle, we could perform these tasks ourselves, but in reality no one will, because we have the machine. This distinction is a decisive and telling one.

Most of the organization of computable processes rests on our ability to divide complex tasks into groups, networks, or hierarchies of simpler tasks down to the point of triviality. Whenever this point is reached, the machine takes over.

However, parts that cannot be turned into algorithms, or even be made explicit, always remain. Not only do such parts "remain" as leftovers of mechanization; they emerge as new implicit tasks and skills. They are all ours to carry out. The machine's part of a joint activity is local, free of context, and independent of situation. The human's part is global, rich in context, and dependent on situation.

The latter part is where aesthetics enter. For interactive use of software, we need sensual access to whatever the machine does. Such access is bound to our bodily existence. Otherwise, the objects, processes, or relations that exist inside the computer don't immediately exist for us. Without sensual perception of the situation, we remain blind and deaf, literally untouched.

Returning to the results of the program's operations in the Mohr example, the program has determined an internal representation as indicated. It continues to produce the two (or even three) views on the screen (see figure 4.3).

We call the left part of the screen image a presentation of the *geometry*, whereas the right part graphically presents the *topology* of the 6D situation. To be sure, neither geometry nor topology can be *seen*. They are abstract mathematics. Interestingly, the program now appears closer to our mental efforts (though still infinitely away). It is closer insofar as it also cannot see anything. The algorithmic events behind Manfred Mohr's canvas are, however, so complex that *thinking* of them alone does not help much.

The aesthetics of the interface give us access to the algorithmic side of the program. Don't expect the visual quality to be breathtaking. Figure 4.3 shows two important aspects: (1) We need the possibility to compare the *difference* between two distinct aspects to gain insight, as with the presentation of geometry and topology in the example; (2) we need continuous change or movement, preferably our bodily movement. The slider of *DeviceX* helps us get closer to this.

The coupling of a bodily operation with a sensual perception is important because it creates a nonsymbolic level of experience, a sense of immediacy, that appears to be important in many processes of cognition and insight.

As we see it, the important aesthetic dimension of computing is not primarily some sort of visualization. Of course, we need the visual presentation to see rather than listen to the algorithmic object. Visualization, therefore, is but a trivial aspect of aesthetic computing. Mathematicians, medical doctors, and all kinds of scientists have always known about the advantages of visualizations.

If aesthetic computing is to make use of the tremendous depth of the aesthetic dimension, the external presentations of algorithmic objects must themselves be the focus of art and research. Such presentations may not be allowed to be separated from their internal representations. Aesthetic computing must take up sensual facets of mental constructs. Isn't this another dialectic?

The previous example suggests the appearance of difference, and continuous transformation caused by manual operation, are two components of the dialectics of aesthetics and computing.

The Semiotic View

Our third, and last, look at Manfred Mohr's art using the *DeviceX* is the most abstract—the semiotic perspective. We maintain that the computational objects and processes are semiotic, and their semiotic nature is even more obvious when we view computing from the aesthetic perspective.

The internal representations of algorithmic objects are semiotic, and so are the external presentations. This claim must be substantiated. If we succeed in this, semiotics would offer a common ground to aesthetics and computing alike.

Observe what happens when the user grabs the slider (with the mouse) and drags it along the top row of the display, from left to right and back. As she does this, the image "in" the slider changes instantaneously even when the dragging is done quickly. This indicates an interpolation is taking place between the left-most and right-most images. The image's appearance depends on the current position of the slider. We will be using some terminology of semiotics as founded by Charles Sanders Peirce (Peirce 1992; 1998).

What does the slider's position stand for? The data provided by that position are taken as the representamen (Peirce's term) of a sign. Call that data x and assume x is a value between 0 and 1. The program then calculates a new external presentation, $P(x) = (1 - x)P(0) + xP(1)$, where $P(0)$ and $P(1)$ are the left and right extremes.

The semiotics of the situation is that movement of the mouse/slider pair creates, in every moment, a number x, which becomes the *representamen* of a sign. This sign is created by the program's interpolating computation. The result of this computation becomes the *object* of the sign. Since this operation is determined with no freedom of interpretation, the sign's *interpretant* (its meaning) coincides with its object.

The newly constructed object is displayed, that is, externalized. Technically speaking, the new appearance of the little image is stored in the display buffer, partially replacing the old buffer contents. The display processor, of course, immediately creates the new screen image.

For the human observer, the internal sign *object* becomes a new external *representamen*. It is what she perceives. She reinterpretes what she sees immediately—in fact, permanently. Chances are that the object of the sign, as the user constitutes it, remains almost invariant, at least after some first interaction. But her construction of an *interpretant*, the most important component of the sign, changes under the influence of the newly appearing image.

We thus conclude that the process of observing *DeviceX* (and, through it, the work of Manfred Mohr) involves a complex relationship between the human's interpretation and the program's determination of a semiotic process. The human continually observes the screen image. She must gain the impression that it is she who directly causes the image's changes. The visible appearance on the screen largely determines her perception.

The computer, in the meantime, is constantly active. Without its activities, nothing would happen. It permanently produces internal representations and immediately displays them. This immediacy, enhanced by the coupling of manual operation and mental cognition, convinces the user that she is generating all the changes.

Interactive Use of Software: The Interface as Sign

We now attempt to draw some generalizations from our example. We first restate the situation described in the preceding section, in which we observe two autonomous systems. One of those systems is the human user. The other is the computer controlled by the currently active program. The two systems are autonomous only in our analysis. There is good reason to claim some sort of autonomy even on behalf of the machine (which is, of course, not autonomous in any stricter sense of the word). We do not want to consider this argument in greater detail. Pragmatically, we maintain a relative autonomy for both systems. From the point of view of the typical nonexpert user, such a perspective seems well justified.

The two relatively autonomous systems are engaged in their respective activities. In the case of the human, these activities may become arbitrarily complex. For the computer, they may be as restricted as running the operating system to control all of the user's operations.

Obviously, the two systems coordinate their mutual operation, so there must be some coupling between them. This coupling is primarily semiotic: output of one system is perceived and interpreted by the other system. Insofar as the two systems coordinate their operation, they are engaged in semiotic processes. The user is observing the screen and taking new measures according to her interpretation and interest. The screen appears to her as a complex sign (the *representamen* of a sign, to be more precise). Figure 4.5 shows a typical example. That complex sign (fully created only in the user's head) causes her to execute certain operations that end in signals as inputs to the program. The program (or some part of it) reacts by updating the screen according to the user's external moves (feedback), and executing an internal operation triggered by the input signal. We have described this in more detail elsewhere (Nake 1994).

For the current purpose, it should suffice to say that a genuine and restricted sign process are coupled during interactive use of the computer. The genuine sign process is the one the user is carrying out, which we will simply call the *sign process*. The restricted sign process is the one the computer is performing. It is restricted insofar as the machine can treat only signals, not full signs (signals are signs with a trivial interpretant; the interpretant is equal to the sign's object). We call this the *signal process*.

So human–computer interaction turns out to be the *coupling of a sign process and a signal process*. The interface between human and machine is the location of their coupling. It appears to the user as a complex compound sign that is easy to interpret and change. The

Figure 4.5 Typical graphic user interface in times of ubiquity. This GUI is the face of the Apple operating system OS X.

pliability Jonas Löwgren cites as an important criterion of use quality appears as the ease of semiotic change.

The interface appears as the representamen of a sign of great dynamics. Simple operations on behalf of the user—for example, moving the cursor sign by moving the mouse, or clicking on an item from a menu list to select it—may be carried out "inside" that interface sign. Any such operation results in an immediate change of the representamen of the sign. This means that the interface acts like a permanently changing billboard onto which both systems draw and write.

Interactive Use of Software: An Aesthetic Event

The common perception of a work of art, by one person standing in front of a painting in a gallery, is clearly no mass event. The work of art requires a delicate response from the admirer in the gallery, which is likely to be totally different from the response of an addict to Internet surfing or gaming in a private home. Yet their experiences have common ground. Different as their sensations and emotions may be, it is aesthetics that attracts or repells our two friends. Reaction to film, video, or GUI may be very elegant and delicately intellectual. In contrast to much of the aesthetics of art, interface aesthetics inspires mass reaction. It may be comparable to the aesthetics of advertising and consumer product packaging of mediocre quality.

Interface aesthetics is different from the aesthetics of packaging, however, in that the interface to software *belongs* to the software. Software never appears without its interface. The human–computer *inter*face is, first of all, the *face* of its software. In fact, the semiotic analysis emphasizes the tendency of the interface, considered as something *between* two systems, to disappear. If we assume the interface is an important, but in some way separate component of computing potentials, we render software faceless. But software cannot exist without face. The face of software is its appearance at the periphery of the computer; without its face, it does not exist at all.

This has not always been the situation, nor will it necessarily remain so. In the days when computers filled rooms, you fed a stack of punched cards into the machine, and waited for another machine to print out results. It was not totally wrong to say the stack *was* your program. By that time, the program was still a tangible, local, and individual *thing*. Only gradually it revealed its *media* qualities. They now appear as the program's face. "Interface," we tend to believe, is a concept better akin to the world of machines than to that of media.

Recognizing that software always possesses a face provides a fruitful approach to software design. Design of software artifacts, then, includes design of its face. The interface between human beings and software artifacts disappears as a separate, material thing and reappears as a semiotic process that is deeply entangled in aesthetics. The aesthetics of computing appears as *part of*, not an addition to, *the design* of software.

Like any other human activity beyond pure survival, computing allows for two sociotechnical relations: designing and producing artifacts for others to use; and using artifacts designed by others.

Computing relies on two kinds of artifact, hardware and software. Our discussion focuses only on the software. From the user's point of view, the situation is not so different from that of the gallery visitor. The gallery visitor enters a room, casually walks to one of several paintings, and takes a position favorable for staring at the painting.

The software user also casually moves to the desk and positions herself favorably for her task. Sitting down, she generates a few mouse clicks, waits for a moment or two, and then stares at the screen.

But at this point, similarities between the two use-of-an-artifact situations end. The art lover may be thrilled by what she stares at. She approaches the canvas for a closer look, reads a sticker close by the picture, talks to someone, steps back again, scans the canvas with her eyes, engages in a lot of physical and cognitive actions before she moves on, but never touches the artifact.

The software user, to the contrary, remains relatively stable in her chair. She grabs the mouse, moves it around, clicks, hits some of the keys in front of her, but most likely does not touch the artifact (except for keys and mouse). Her distance from the object, the screen, is much shorter than the gallery visitor's. Her eye movements may be fewer, and extend over shorter distances. Both viewers may be deeply involved and challenged but let's identify the differences between the two experiences.

The painting in the gallery remains invariant, no matter how many people stare at it. The mental images, or ideas, visitors may carry away, however, change and are different in each case. On the other hand, the screen image on the display changes almost constantly. Its changes influence the mental images of users. However, an advanced or expert user will have quite a stable idea of the software, its appearance, and its functions. Even though she does not usually physically touch the screen, metaphorically she does. She "opens" some icon (representing a "folder," or a data file). She "pulls down" a menu (again, representing some function). She redefines the value of some parameter, and does all sorts of other things. Each of these operations has a double effect: changing the state of the hardware and changing the visual appearance (or sound) of the display, if only temporarily.

Both of these spectator situations are blatant cases of aesthetics. Our subjects are confronted with a framed image of something and if they don't make sense of it, they get lost. Not many will fail to see the gallery situation as one of aesthetic relevance. Perhaps not many will immediately accept the idea that the software case is aesthetically relevant as well. But it is insofar as we cannot even take notice of the object of our interest unless we concentrate (perhaps subconsciously) on the aesthetics of its appearance.

When the cultural impact of computers was still limited to complex or voluminous calculations in places like research laboratories, universities, and some administrative offices, computers could still be taken as machines of a special kind. Their aesthetics was absolutely irrelevant, at best, of only superficial interest. This applied to both hardware and software.

The situation has changed dramatically. With the advent of the personal computer in the early 1980s, the characterization of software as a *tool* gained a material basis beyond mere metaphor. The tool period did not last long, but created a tremendous wealth of research results in the field of HCI before giving way to the *media* period. As the globally connected computer took the world by storm, its hidden media qualities were revealed. Its digital nature, in our view, is not the decisive feature of digital media, but rather its dual quality of *instrumental* and *medial* properties. The term *instrumental medium* reflects this fact (Schelhowe 1997).

As instrumental media, hardware/software systems are driven by their inherent dialectic. They can no longer be understood nor designed as two (or even more) separate components: function and interface. Digital media, the means of computing, have gained their *eigen*aesthetics. To acknowledge this in all consequence is what aesthetic computing may be about.

It is hard to imagine that aesthetic computing could spread and thrive without taking notice of Walter Benjamin's seminal essay, *The Work of Art in the Age of Mechanical Reproduction*. Nadin (1997), referring to Benjamin's central notion of *aura*, draws our attention to the shift away from the artifact itself to the process of art. Something similar occurs with signs and media: they are determined as processes more than as objects.

The artifacts themselves, which aesthetic computing may be concerned with, do not appear different from those with which computing is generally concerned, though we expect they will be treated differently. Aesthetic computing sounds like the call for a shift in attitude toward the distinction between hard and soft science. Truth would no longer be expected to come from strict formalism only but also from vague aspects of style, dissolving, at least in part, what computing stands for.

Acknowledgment

We happily acknowledge the continued exchange with, and thrilling ideas of, Matthias Krauß. He has contributed *DeviceX*, but much more, to our joint project, compArt. Without Manfred Mohr's friendship, we would not have had access to such a beautiful example for our argument. We have benefitted from concerns raised by reviewers though we may not have resolved these issues to their full satisfaction.

References

Bolter, Jay David, and Grusin, Richard. 2000. *Remediation. Understanding New Media.* Cambridge, MA: MIT Press.

Ehn, Pelle. 1998. "Manifesto for a Digital Bauhaus." *Digital Creativity* 9: 207–17.

Höök, Kristina, Sengers, Phoebe, and Andersson, Gerd. 2003. "Sense and Sensibility: Evaluation and Interactive Art." *CHI 2003 Conference Proc.* New York: ACM Press, pp. 241–48.

Lunenfeld, Peter, ed. 1999. *The Digital Dialectic. New Essays on New Media.* Cambridge, MA: MIT Press.

Manovich, Lev. 2003. "New Media from Borges to HTML." In Noah Wardrip-Fruin and Nick Montfort, eds. 2003. *The New Media Reader.* Cambridge, MA: MIT Press, pp. 13–25.

Mullet, Kevin, and Sano, Darrell. 1995. *Designing Visual Interfaces*. Englewood Cliffs, NJ: Prentice Hall.

Museum für Konkrete Kunst, ed. 2001. *Manfred Mohr Space. Color.* [Catalogue to the exhibition. Texts, in German and English, by Manfred Mohr and Frieder Nake.] Ingolstadt: Museum für Konkrete Kunst.

Nadin, Mihai. 1997. *The Civilization of Illiteracy*. Dresden: University Press.

Nake, Frieder. 1994. "Human–Computer Interaction: Sign and Signals Interfacing." *Languages of Design* 2: 193–205.

Nees, Georg. 1969. *Generative Computergrafik*. München: Siemens.

Packer, Randall, and Jordan, Ken, eds. 2001. *Multimedia. From Wagner to Virtual Reality*. New York: W.W. Norton.

Peirce, Charles S. 1940. "How to Make Our Ideas Clear." In Justus Buchler, ed. *Philosophical Writings of Peirce*. New York: Dover Publishing, pp. 23–41 (originally published in 1878).

Peirce, Charles S. 1992, 1998. *The Essential Peirce. Selected Philosophical Writings*. 2 vols. Nathan Houser, Christian Kloesel, and the Peirce Edition Project, eds. Bloomington: Indiana University Press.

Raskin, Jef. 2000. *The Humane Interface. New Directions for Designing Interactive Systems*. Reading, MA: Addison Wesley.

Schelhowe, Heidi. 1997. *Das Medium aus der Maschine. Zur Metamorphose des Computers*. Frankfurt, New York: Campus.

Wiesing, Lambert. 1991. *Stil statt Wahrheit. Kurt Schwitters und Ludwig Wittgenstein über ästhetische Lebensformen*. Munich: Finke.

Winograd, Terry, ed. 1996. *Bringing Design to Software*. Reading, MA: Addison Wesley.

5

Metaphorical Dimensions of Diagrammatic Graph Representations

Ray Paton

Aesthetic issues impact on computational thinking and practice in diverse ways. Issues associated with abstract properties of human cognitive constructions can have aesthetic qualities, for example, with regard to patterns, symmetries, and transformations in algebras, topologies, and categories. Some deal with aesthetic properties of computational outputs such as graphics, images, data, sound, and music. There are also aesthetic dimensions to how we think about and develop human-centric computing. It is especially (though not totally) in this latter context that this chapter examines aspects of language, metaphor, and hermeneutics applied to the use of diagrammatic graphs for modeling knowledge. Knowledge models allow people to present or represent knowledge for the purposes of communication, explanation, and exploration (Paton 2004). We now make explicit two underlying assumptions to this work: first, knowledge is embodied in, but not identical with, words and the relations between them,[1] and second, aesthetic qualities of graphs (such as symmetry, form, pattern, and closure) contribute significantly to their construction and interpretation.

A diagrammatic graph is a graph in the mathematical sense, constructed to fulfil a number of possibly nonoverlapping roles or functions including modeling, summarization, communication, and memorization of domain knowledge, and to model systems and knowledge for exploring domains (e.g., Paton 2001; 2002). In this chapter they are mostly equated with different types of semantic or conceptual structures. A large number of diagrammatic graph approaches to modeling knowledge and concepts have been developed. Contemporary methods range from representations for learning and understanding (e.g., Novak 1998) to formalisms for dealing with logic and ontology (e.g., Sowa 2000).

Many approaches relate to mediating representations or languages between people and computers (e.g., Sowa 2000; Lehman 1992).

The term "diagrammatic graph" has been chosen because the individual meanings of "diagram" and "graph" are not always transparent across disciplines. To provide some appreciation of the usage of graph-related terms with regard to concepts and knowledge, we conducted a simple Google™ search of websites for these terms. Each paired combination was searched (e.g., concept network, semantic lattice, etc.) for the following terms: concept, semantic, knowledge, and cognitive combined with network, web, mesh, map, frame, lattice, grid, and graph (i.e., 32 pairs). Of all these, the only combination not found was "cognitive lattice" (with only one occurrence of "semantic mesh"). So for the present purposes, "diagrammatic graph" replaces the terms such as network and lattice (which collectively we call "reticulations"; e.g., Paton 2002).

The goals of producing the diagrammatic graphs described here are to represent and articulate conceptual, semantic, and linguistic structures emerging from a dialogue or an individual's self-reflection. These structures (frameworks, lattices, diagrams) are not static; they evolve as a domain is explored and knowledge is made explicit. Their purpose is not to attempt to represent what is "in someone's head," nor provide a visual way of engineering computer code. The primary focus in the present discussion is on people's articulated (discursive) knowledge, which we describe as knowledge models (Paton 2002).

Graph usage is broad and crosses many centuries, cultures, and disciplines. Kruja and colleagues (2002) reviewed examples of how graph drawings have been used in Western cultures as instruments for presenting and solving problems, and in visual representation, since at least the Middle Ages. For example, graphs have also been used to represent or calculate combinations of or permutations between components such as squares of opposition in logic and music, and in certain games (see also, Gardner 1983). There is also evidence of graph use in other cultures (e.g., Ascher 1988). Within a contemporary setting, diagrammatic graphs appear in many disciplines and forms such as ball-and-stick molecular model, food webs, lineage trees, decision trees, state transition networks, ER models, semantic networks, life cycles, circuit diagrams, Forrester diagrams, flow diagrams, Feynman diagrams, and social networks. We concur with Miller (2001, p 237), when he notes, "At the creative moment boundaries between disciplines dissolve. Aesthetics becomes paramount."

Toward a Hermeneutics of Diagramming

We apply hermeneutic thinking to the sharing of common perspectives on domain knowledge (Meyer and Paton 2002). Diagrammatic graphs can greatly assist dialogue when explanation, articulation, and a need for shared understanding are required. They can be used to help characterize tacit knowledge, explore metacognitive knowledge, and provide a context for mobilizing knowledge in multidisciplinary domains (e.g., Meyer and Paton 2002; Paton 2004).

Hermeneutics, derived from the Greek word ερμηνεύω, conveys the meanings of both "explain" and "interpret." Two aspects of hermeneutic investigations should be distinguished, namely, the study of the principles on which a text is to be understood and the interpretation of a text into a message that is understandable to the listener or reader. Partly based on the writings of Ricoeur (1981), the approach incorporates the dynamic between interpreting text in terms of metaphor and explaining metaphor in terms of text. Within the current discussion, we exploit this dynamic in two ways: associating a number of metaphors with graphing and its products, and using metaphor to help explain and interpret certain graphs (and subgraphs). Metaphor is the language used to talk about one thing in terms of something else. We use conceptual metaphors, as they preserve inference structures between source and target domains (e.g., Lakoff and Johnson 1981). To clarify usage, metaphors used in this way are presented in UPPER CASE letters.

Within this hermeneutic approach, the construction of a graph involves a finished product, processes for producing the artifact, and adherence to certain composition rules (guidelines) for production and interpretation. A diagrammatic form can be used to summarize a process (such as a problem-solving process, algorithm, or protocol). A degree of approximation is used in producing the graphs described here. A person using them need not learn formal logic or linguistics to apply them. The advantage is that there is no need to "shoe-horn" or apply a "Procrustean axe" to a person's knowledge to make it fit a formalism. The method encourages experimentation with and exploration of the knowledge in a domain. This facilitates appreciation of knowledge in process (rather than as a fixed entity), and the importance of a diversity of representations, dialogues, and viewpoints.

To emphasize their descriptive nature and avoid using any single type of formalism, models operating in a domain of discourse are called informal models (e.g., Paton et al. 1994). Within an evolving dialogue and domain description, a plurality of such models is required. The formality–informality distinction is made explicit to anticipate potential misunderstandings by people who wish to immediately transform models into computer code, mathematical symbols, logic, or particular diagramming conventions. Emphasis is placed on building informal models to clarify understanding and enhance dialogue.

To illustrate some of the interpretive dimensions of diagramming we consider a simple example from ecology (figure 5.1). We use this example partly because it is easily appreciated by many readers and also because a number of helpful insights from ecology relate to diagramming and interpretation. The sharing of meaning through dialogue in this example highlights a number of important issues for the rest of this chapter. Dialogue about

Figure 5.1 Sharing meanings.

the real world involves several domains of interaction such as objects and relations of reference, cognitive objects (including modeling relations) and the domain of discourse (including diagrams). In figure 5.1 the two people figures share a similar perspective on the system and can enter into dialogue about it (double-headed arrow). In this case they are also parts of the system to which they refer (technically we are presenting an endosystem). The cognitive models the people separately access may be very different, and these could be reflected in the language and diagrams, which they use as representations of (aspects of) the system. In this case, there is a tetrahedron graph (upper right) and a much-idealized diagram (lower right). The hermeneutic transition toward a sharing of perspective relies on the multimodal interactions between explanation and interpretation.

Metaphors for Diagramming

It is necessary to remind the reader that deconstructing a metaphor is not necessarily a criticism of the practice of using it. Science would be nothing without the metaphors by means of which theories are constructed, new concepts are built, models are conceived and their structures are worked out.
—HARRÉ 2002

It has already been noted that aesthetic qualities of diagrammatic graphs contribute to their construction and interpretation. In this section we explore the diagramming process and its products (both interim and final) in terms of a number of metaphors that help articulate these models. The diagrammatic graphs discussed here and used for mobilizing and modeling knowledge are fundamentally pictures. As Picasso noted in 1935 (quoted by Miller 1996, p 432), "A picture is not thought out or settled beforehand.... An idea is a starting point and nothing more." This is the sense of exploration that diagramming brings. Indeed, I concur with Miller (1996) and many others, both art and science at their most fundamental are adventures into the unknown.

Personal theoretical frameworks are involved in building domain knowledge. We take these frameworks to be embodied cognitive objects constructed to enable us to access models, form hypotheses, explain, predict, and classify (Paton et al. 1994; Meyer and Paton 2001). An individual's sharing of domain knowledge and self-reflection of regarding experience, practice, and dialogue takes place within the setting of a domain of discourse. Personal (idiosyncratic) knowledge is in process or flux. A part of knowledge domain construction involves importing, transferring, or displacing language, concepts, and theoretical frameworks from heterogeneous sources. In discussing the displacement and representation of one thing in terms of something else, we may say we are making use of metaphor. Scientific metaphors can fulfil three roles, concerned with catechresis (supplying new terms to the theoretical vocabulary), ontology (involvement in formulating hypothetical entities) and teaching/learning (facilitating dialogue between a teacher and student).

Table 5.1 provides a summary of some metaphorical dimensions related to the diagrammatic graph concept. It is not a complete list. The words in the two rightmost columns communicate aspects of diagrammatic graphs in terms of both process and product. Different metaphor sharing terms indicates that there are many, diverse possible displacements of language and meanings. For example, they all share family resemblances as things people make and use, so some common lexical items involve design, some construction, and some application.

TEXT and ART share language and ideas such as form, composition, and interpretation. MAPPING is a relational activity that projects items from one domain to another (e.g., from a 3D space to a 2D plane) and locates things in relation to each other. MAPS, TEXTS, and ART share ideas about FRAME or CONTAINER such as context, and also about JOURNEY such as composition as a JOURNEY by an author. To different extents, BRIDGE, GATEWAY, and WINDOW convey ideas of mediation, a portal, and a conduit between places. Language associated with BRIDGE, GATEWAY, and WINDOW can be used to talk about modeling analogical (metaphorical) displacements. BRIDGE and GATEWAY also share ideas about a JOURNEY, and GATEWAY and WINDOW about a FRAME. GATEWAY can mediate conceptual displacements between the other two.

Table 5.1 Some metaphors associated with diagrams and diagramming

Metaphor	Some Associated Objects and Properties	Some Associated Relations and Processes
TEXT	Form, meaning, texture, story, script, narrative, plot, theme, subject, character, topic, word, sentence, paragraph, texture, context, perspective, layout, passage, container, dialogue, . . .	Read, write, interpret, understand, portray, represent, edit, inform, review, draft, annotate, sketch (out), illustrate, illumine, document, imagine, draft, reveal, communicate, clarify, compose, . . .
MAP	Landscape, surface, contour, chart, topography, space, relationship, location, displacement, territory, position, navigation, context, viewpoint, symbol, meaning, layout, . . .	Survey, plan, chart, order, sketch, simplify, project, model, locate, interpret, read, design, navigate, scope, represent, triangulate, map, coordinate, inform, relate, arrange, . . .
JOURNEY	Displacement, story, passage, narrative, history, trace, location, destination, path, target, goal, voyage, pilgrim, track, duration, span, route, landmark, map, bearing, trace, trip, course, . . .	Walk, travel, visit, embark, navigate, move, start, stop, wander, journey, triangulate, roam, stray, hike, sail, fly, convey, locate, relocate, displace, guide, trek, sojourn, commute, go, stay, . . .
ART	Form, meaning, structure, symmetry, image, icon, pattern, texture, context, design, viewpoint, perspective, character, composition, . . .	View, interpret, compose, represent, present, illustrate, illumine, look, draw, paint, sketch, sculpt, imagine, create, communicate, . . .
BRIDGE	Conduit, mediator, route, path, obstacle, construction, separation, passage, route, layout, framework, device, purpose, . . .	Join, span, connect, carry, mediate, convey, transfer, relate, displace, build, design, pass, cross, enable, travel, link, . . .
GATEWAY	Opening, path, journey, opportunity, door, doorway, passage, portal, entrance, interface, doorway, threshold, bridge, . . .	Open, close, move, transfer, pass (through), travel, displace, access, exchange, enter, block, connect, link, . . .
WINDOW	Barrier, container, gateway, frame, opening, opportunity, closure, perspective, local, portal, interface, . . .	View, picture, peer, look, focus, frame, bound, interface, relate, open, illumine, reveal, expose, disclose, clarify, close, . . .

Table 5.1 (continued)

Metaphor	Some Associated Objects and Properties	Some Associated Relations and Processes
CONTAINER	Boundary, containment, closure, barrier, frame, inside, outside, bag, set, wall, instrument, function, class, . . .	Enclose, include, exclude, contain, hide, store, incorporate, comprise, hold, carry, bear, encapsulate, embody, . . .
FRAME	Skeleton, plan, container, contained, structure, outline, framework, form, lattice, structure, order, arrangement, . . .	Locate, juxtapose, place, position, enclose, border, redact, outline, arrange, order, organize, compose, link, relate, . . .
SCHEMA	Outline, plan, order, script, method, skeleton, inside-outside, boundary, net(work), framework, interface, . . .	Organize, plan, order, represent, sketch, script, arrange, outline, relate, link, combine, . . .
INSTRUMENT	Device, tool, machine, useability, efficiency, role, function, equipment, utensil, purpose, design, . . .	Manipulate, modify, arrange, transform, simplify, ease, assist, reveal, expose, enhance, enable, use, analyse, detect, . . .

The triplet of CONTAINER, FRAME, and SCHEMA could be treated as a single metaphorical context. However, as the associated terms in table 5.1 indicate, although there are many common words and ideas, they also have subtle and important differences. This triplet could have been collected under CONTAINER, with FRAME and SCHEMA also, in different ways, indicating internal structure. The presence of internal structure can be used to separate a class concept from a collection concept. Collective nouns allow the components of a whole to be collected together. They include terms such as family, army, and forest as well as more anonymous terms such as group, pile, stack, and system. Compared with class terms, collective nouns are relatively rare. Collections can have rich internal organizational features. They may be organized to produce hierarchies or networks using many verb types. The value of internal structure is that it provides insights into how the whole is organized or integrated with respect to the interaction patterns between the parts. We return to this in the final section, in which we discuss the idea of the colimit of a pattern.

We may consider a general SCHEMA in which to place the metaphors, noting that this is but one of many possible types. Within a reflective mode of operation a graph can provide a WINDOW or GATEWAY to the associated ideas and is a MAP to begin setting out and relating terms. In the context of a dialogue, it is also a BRIDGE between the two interpretive parties. A graph can be used as a FRAME on which to CONTAIN other terms.

A single diagram may afford a number of roles depending on the context and who is interpreting the figure. Within a hermeneutic dialogue, it is possible that any given graph can be interpreted in many ways and for more than one purpose. A number of other metaphors may be accessed when describing diagramming, especially in wider cultural contexts (not discussed here). For example, the ORGANISMIC metaphor can be used, accessing ideas such as life cycle, evolution, adaptation, migration, and functioning. Thus, Garland (1994) quotes Beck, the designer of the London Underground diagram, who notes "Surely the Underground Diagram ... must be thought of as a living and changing thing, with schematic and spare-part osteopathy going on all the time" (Beck, quoted by Garland 1994, p 23).

Table 5.2 summarizes some features of the roles a diagram plays as an INSTRUMENT and how these can be related to some of the metaphors in table 5.1. Clearly, instrumentality is a major descriptive dimension for examining what diagrams afford. We examine

Table 5.2 Some relationships among functionalities, activities, and metaphors

Functionality	Some Associated Activites	METAPHOR
Explanation	Explain, communicate, inform, illustrate, interpret, describe, clarify, understand, . . .	TEXT, ART, BRIDGE
Exploration	Explore, investigate, navigate, map, survey, chart, imagine, direct, relate, open, . . .	MAP, JOURNEY, WINDOW, GATEWAY
Memorization	Remember, imagine, image, visualize, order, direct, arrange, link, carry, . . .	FRAME, SCHEMA, CONTAINER
Representation	Structure, frame, order, organize, relate, link, plan, direct, locate, outline, . . .	MAP, FRAME, ART, CONTAINER, SCHEMA
Computation	Calculate, permute, predict, trace, order, transform, locate, coordinate, commute, . . .	SCHEMA, MAP, JOURNEY
Simplification	Model, simplify, idealize, explicate, explain, outline, inform, access, mediate, . . .	MAP, GATEWAY, BRIDGE

this functional, rather than structural, aspect of diagrams in more detail in the next section.

Interactions Between Diagrammatic Graphs

In Picasso's *Guernica* painting he comments that paintings are "but research and experiment" (cited by Miller 1996, p 433). Composing diagrammatic graphs is investigation, combining instrumentality and experiment. In this section we explore the multifunctionality of graphical instrumentality by examining the functions and metaphors summarized in table 5.2. We will illustrate this with diagramming techniques. Specifically, we consider the applications and interactions between three diagrammatic graphs: star graph, star complex, and C-graph.

The "star" graph is a tree with a uniform depth of 1. This form is also described across disciplines as a spider diagram, SO (significant other) gram, and pattern notes. These graphs are very easy to sketch. In one sense, they are little more than lists of associated terms. However, their graphical presentation can be exploited in a number of helpful ways. In constructing the graph, we may anticipate a certain number of peripheral terms, which generate more as the structure is being populated. Regions of the graph may relate to thematic or categorical ideas, as in the sense of MAPPING. The FRAME holds the whole together. The simple nature of these graphs allows them to be used as a visual summary to aid memory.

Star graphs can fulfill a number of exploratory functions. We have shown that these graphs are useful in the initial stages of knowledge modeling projects (e.g., Meyer and Paton 2002; Wilson and Keller-McNulty 2000; Leishman and McNamara 2004). At its first iteration (i.e., figure 5.2 (a)), we see a tree of 16 leaves. The tree could be made deeper if leaves form the root nodes for other star graphs. As the graph forms it becomes clear that some of the peripheral terms are also connectable to each other. At this stage, the star graph ceases to be a tree and a "star complex" forms. In figure 5.2 (b), we see certain relational patterns emerging among the verbs, for example: explore → model → frame → organize → relate, and organize → explain → communicate → teach. These relational patterns can convey narrative and thematic meanings.

Each of the verbs in figure 5.2 could be used to seed a diagrammatic graph composed of verb associations and their interrelations. We call these C-graphs (Paton 2002; 2004). Figure 5.3 gives an example using one of the verbs from figure 5.2 ("organize"). C-graphs may begin looking like star graphs but can also evolve into networks of links. The diagram in figure 5.3 began as a star graph, but soon developed into a network structure. Usually the C-graph arcs are labeled with an index of when they appeared. This provides

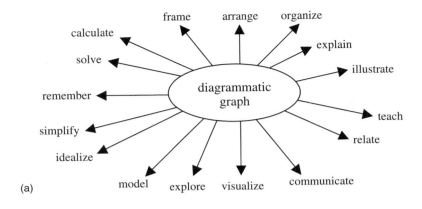

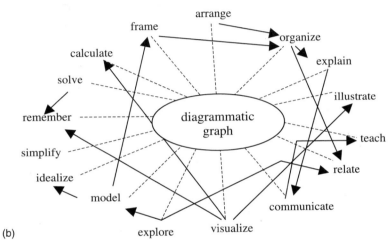

Figure 5.2 Star graph (a) and star complex (b) for verbs associated with "diagrammatic graph."

an historical trace and an index for labeling arcs. However, to preserve readability of figure 5.3, arc labels are not included.

Many graphs deal with objects and relations; C-graphs deal with relations and relations between relations. Inspection of the form a C-graph takes shows that some verbs are linked to many others, some are members of longer open paths, and some are part of closed paths or loops. The arc meanings in the C-graph reveal a number of patterns of association including

themes   concerned with sequences of processes;
nestings   dealing with one process that is a part of another; and
clusters   often concerned with similar processes.

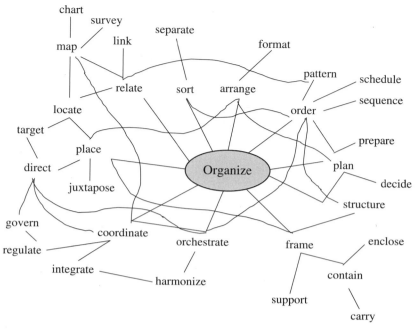

Figure 5.3 A C-graph for "organize."

These subgraphs may be localized to regions of the graph or more widely distributed. Themes in C-graphs can MAP JOURNEYS onto LANDSCAPES. Nestings and clusters relate to FRAMES and SCHEMATA within CONTAINERS.

The process of building a diagrammatic graph can have as much value related to explanation and exploration as the product related to representation and memorization. The different forms and roles that graphs may take, their interrelationships in modeling knowledge (in process and as a product), and the various metaphors that can be used to assist understanding lead to the idea of a "society of graphs" (Paton 2002). These societies have many internal interactions, a rich internal (organizational) structure, division of labor, and components that may be heterogeneous.

Consider now how this idea of a society of graphs can be applied to help our appreciation of the richness of concepts associated with the processes or activities of diagramming. Some aspects were summarized in table 5.2. Taking each of the six processes as the root of a star graph produces a tree in which the internal nodes are these verbs. It is important to note that the graph has not evolved from the top down. The six subgraphs (star graphs) were constructed semi-independently, and then the lateral connections were made. In figure 5.4 we find a rich and diverse picture of many activities associated with

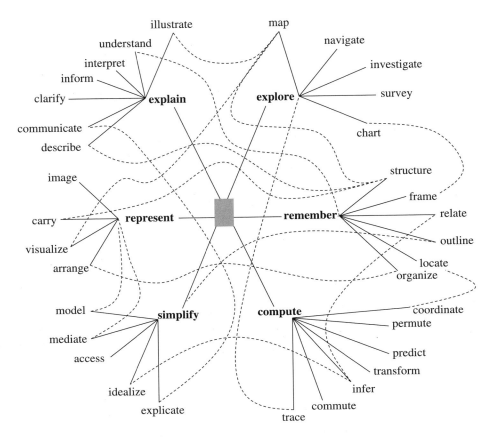

Figure 5.4 C-graph of star graphs.

diagramming. The MAP provides many ways of exploring the multiplicities of diagrammatic graphs and their interactions.

Enriching the Metaphorical Picture

> Our meddling intellect
> Mishapes the beauteous forms of things:—
> We murder to dissect
> —WORDSWORTH: "AN EVENING SCENE ON THE SAME SUBJECT"

The diagrams discussed so far have been multifunctional and contributed to a society of interactions. They were "seeded" with a word (or start term or idea) and then "grew" as

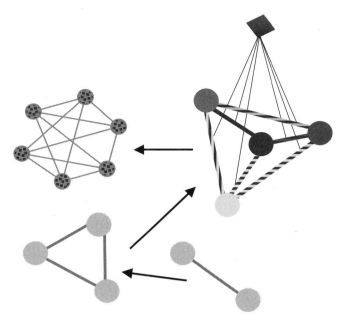

Figure 5.5 Some relations between graphs.

the domain unfolded. It is hoped that the examples have reflected a synthetic approach within an interpretive-explanatory (diagramming) FRAME that produces ART and TEXT. The illustrative examples have focussed on verbs and processes rather than objects and nouns. We now consider how we can explore these general metaphors for diagrammatic graphs to understand their functionality. Clearly the displacements between the conceptual metaphors are pertinent not only to diagrammatic graphs but to any collections of ideas that share such properties. The graph in figure 5.5 consists of four component subgraphs. The (2 node, 1 arc) graph (bottom right) denotes two metaphors (nodes) and their shared displacements (labeled arc). The simplex (triangular face of a polyhedron) and the tetrahedron (4 simplices) denote further organization of metaphors and displacements. The triads of metaphors discussed earlier form simplices that can be combined into polyhedra. Each of these is a possible CONTAINER for displaceable meanings. For example, the phrase "walking through a text to survey an author's plan" combines language related to TEXT, MAP, and JOURNEY. The introduction of a fourth metaphor, such as GATEWAY, then moves from the simplex to the tetrahedron. We may now wish to explore aspects of the functionality of our understanding of the patterns of interaction between the four metaphors.

In the case of the tetrahedron graph shown in figure 5.5, it is possible to describe the coherent patterns of interaction between the parts (the metaphorical sources or contexts) as the colimit (represented as the diamond-shaped node) of the pattern. It is also possible to take the arcs of the tetrahedron graph and map them to nodes in its line graph. In this case, the arcs in the line graph denote relations between relations in the source graph. This kind of thinking about the graphical relations uses abstract properties of graphs that can provide a richer picture of the diagramming process and its products. This graph is itself a FRAME within which we may explore metaphorical relations.

Conclusion

Diagramming is a common activity in many domains of inquiry. It shares aesthetic features that break down (misplaced) barriers between artistic and scientific activity. It also highlights the problematic distinctions made between process and product. A number of metaphors used to articulate knowledge about the process and the product (diagrammatic graphs) have been discussed, and we described some illustrative ways in which the graph production can be reflected in these metaphors. Different graphs have different forms and can serve different purposes. This leads to the idea of a "society of graphs," a diverse range from simple constructs such as a star graph and star complex to abstract mathematical constructs such as colimits and line graphs.

Acknowledgments

This work has grown out of numerous multidisciplinary dialogues and collaborations. I wish to acknowledge the importance of discussions with Andree Ehresmann, Ronnie Brown, and Mary Meyer. My thanks also go to John Lee, Frieder Nake, and an anonymous reviewer for their helpful comments on an earlier version of this chapter.

Note

1. My thanks to Frieder Nake for this comment.

References

Ascher, M. 1988. "Graphs in Cultures: A Study in Ethnomathematics." *Historia Mathematica* 15: 201–27.

Gardner, M. 1983. *Logic Machines and Diagrams*, 2nd ed., Brighton: Harvester.

Garland, K. 1994. "Mr Beck's Underground Map." Harrow Weald, Middlesex: Capital Transport Publishing.

Harré, R. 2002. "The Memory Machine." *Theoria et Historia Scientiarum* 6(2): 271–91.

Kruja, E., Marks, J., Blair, A., and Waters, R. J. 2002. "A Short Note on the History of Graph Drawing." In P. Mutzel, M. Jünger, and S. Leipert, eds. *Graph Drawing 2001 LNCS*. Berlin: Springer-Verlag, pp. 272–86.

Lakoff, G., and Johnson, M. 1981. *Metaphors We Live By*. Chicago: University of Chicago Press.

Lehman, F. 1992. "Semantic Networks." *Computers Math, Applic.* 23(2–5): 1–50.

Leishman, D., and McNamara, L. 2004. "Interlopers, Translators, Scribes and Seers: Anthropology, knowledge representation and Bayesian statistics for predictive modeling in multidisciplinary science and engineering projects." In G. Malcolm, ed. *Multidisciplinary Approaches to Visual Representations and Interpretations*. Amsterdam: Elsevier.

Meyer, M., and Paton, R. C. 2002. "Interpreting, Representing and Integrating Knowledge from Interdisciplinary Projects." *Theoria et Historia Scientiarum* 6(2): 323–56.

Miller, A. I. 1996. *Insights of Genius Imagery and Creativity in Science and Art*. New York: Copernicus/ Springer-Verlag.

Miller, A. I. 2001. *Einstein, Picasso Space, Time, and the Beauty that Causes Havoc*. New York: Basic Books.

Novak, J. D. 1998. *Learning, Creating and Using Knowledge*. Mahwah, NJ: Lawrence Erlbaum Associates.

Paton, R. C. 2001. "Conceptual and Descriptive Displacements for the Mobilisation of Multiple Models." Unpublished report, LA-UR-01-0019, Los Alamos National Lab.

Paton, R. C. 2002. "Diagrammatic Representations for Modelling Biological Knowledge." *BioSystems* 66: 43–53.

Paton, R. C. 2004. "Mobilising Knowledge Models Using Societies of Graphs." In Malcolm, G., ed. *Multidisciplinary Approaches to Visual Representations and Interpretations*. Amsterdam: Elsevier.

Paton, R. C., Lynch, S., Jones, D., Nwana, H. S., Bench-Capon, T. J. M., and Shave, M. J. R. 1994. "Domain Characterisation for Knowledge Based Systems." Proceedings of A.I. 94—Fourteenth International Avignon Conference, Volume 1, pp. 41–54.

Ricoeur, P. 1981. *Hermeneutics and the Human Sciences*. Cambridge: Cambridge University Press.

Sowa, J. 2000. *Knowledge Representation Logical, Philosophical, and Computational Foundations*. Pacific Grove, CA: Brooks/Cole.

Wilson, A., and Keller-McNulty, S. 2000. "Statistical Representations for Information Integration." Unpublished report, LA-UR-00-4850, Los Alamos National Lab.

II

Art and Design

6

Metaphoric Mappings: The Art of Visualization

Donna Cox

In its broadest sense, visualization is the process of making the invisible visible. It has been a human endeavor for tens of thousands of years. From cave paintings to virtual CAVE™ environments, the process of making the cognitive imagination visual using available and culturally dominant technologies is one of the most consistent behaviors of humankind. The power of visualization can be demonstrated in diverse areas such as religion, commerce, science, and popular culture (Brown 1990; McCormick et al. 1987).

Modern data visualization is a broad term that includes both scientific and information visualization. Data visualization is the process of using computer-mediated technologies to transform numerical data into a digital visual model. Data is typically defined as a system of numbers that provides measurable, quantitative information. Data can also include computational and scientific models; sensored output from instruments; and geographic, statistical, and contextual information. Scientific data is the primary focus here. To be consistent in the following discussion, I use the term data-viz to specify data-driven visualization and distinguish it from other types of nondata-driven visualization such as hand-drawn scientific illustrations or digital nondata-driven virtual artwork.

I argue that there is a direct relationship between data-viz and the cognitive, creative mapping process discussed in metaphor theory. Linguistic and visual metaphors are defined as mappings from one domain of information (the source) into another domain (the target). Likewise, data-viz maps numbers into pictures, resulting in visaphors, digital visual metaphors.

Visaphors can be interactive software applications or digital animations. They can be displayed using a variety of technologies, from stereo rear-screen projected CAVE™ to QuickTime movies. In this chapter, virtual reality and other mixed realities are considered as alternative physical display systems for presenting visaphors. Other physical displays include large-scale digital projection domes, IMAX theaters, passive stereo theaters, digital reality theaters, television screens, and printed media. These varieties of display media provide an experiential substrate and context for visaphors; however, the primary focus here is on the creation of visaphors in the art of visualization and their relationship to contemporary metaphor theory.

Metaphor Theory and Cultural Contingency

Metaphor is not just a linguistic trick or cultural trope. Discourse on metaphor and culture has engendered a paradigm shift in the way we understand creativity and acquisition of knowledge. Over the last five decades, researchers have generated more than 10,000 articles and books on metaphor and related studies. Most of these writings have concentrated on linguistic metaphor and the connection to cognitive processes.

George Lakoff and Mark Johnson (Lakoff and Johnson 1980) recontextualize metaphor as being more about how people think than about linguistics. Metaphor involves the cognitive process of understanding one domain of information in terms of another domain. For example, "man is a wolf" is an English metaphor that generates a new understanding of "man" by associating characteristics about "wolf" (e.g., voracious, predator, beastly, runs in packs) with the concept of "man." The source domain is wolf, and characteristics from the source domain are mapped onto the target domain, "man." This cognitive mapping is not an arbitrary process. Some characteristics will be cognitively mapped from "wolf" onto "man," and other characteristics are ignored, such as "four legged" or "furry."

man (target domain) is a wolf (source domain)
man ← wolf (beastly, voracious, hungry, runs in packs)

The domain of information about "man" is presented and understood in terms of information concerning "wolf." It is within this transdomain mapping process that new meaning is generated (Black 1961). The process of mapping is important to understanding how metaphors create new meaning and how this mapping relates to data-viz. Each domain constitutes a system of beliefs, also called a concept network (Indurkhya 1992). For example, "man" constitutes a concept network of ideas, beliefs, and assumptions about the collective imaginary of "man." Likewise "wolf" constitutes a domain or concept network including beliefs, facts, and folklore. The verbal metaphor creates a new association, thus expanding the concept network of "man."

Lakoff and Johnson analyzed a plethora of linguistic metaphors (Lakoff and Johnson 1999). They define "conventional" metaphors as those that have evolved into literal language through common use and familiarity. From their analysis, they have provided cognitive linguistic proof that much of our conceptualization and linguistic metaphoric representations of the world have evolved from our physical embodied experiences.

Conventional metaphors are embedded in our culture to the point that we literally interpret their meaning. The example, "time is money" is a conventional metaphor that has become embedded in American culture. We understand "time" in terms of money and conceptualize "time" as being "spent," "saved," or "wasted." Such basic conventional metaphors help structure our everyday thinking. We interpret these metaphors literally as a conventional part of speech, and this common language further influences how we conceptualize and behave. For example, "argument is war" formulates how we think about arguing. We "defend," "strategize," "attack," and "defeat" arguments. If our culture had adopted "argument is illness," then an "argument" would be "diagnosed" and "treated." Likewise, metaphoric usage can affect politics (Lakoff 2002).

Creative thinking is measured in the novelty of a metaphor. Indurkhya defined the metaphoric content continuum as a range across a spectrum from the most familiar, literal conventional metaphors to novel, figurative metaphors (Indurkhya 1992). For example, verbal metaphors such as "books are fresh fruit" are more figurative and novel than "time was well spent," which is interpreted as literal language. Most theorists agree that novel verbal metaphors can eventually evolve into conventional language as a culture accommodates the metaphor and reduces novelty to literality.

While extensive research has focused on verbal metaphors, fewer researchers have analyzed the visual counterparts. Charles Forceville (Forceville 1994; 1996) analyzed pictorial metaphors in advertising. Focusing on figurative metaphors in static public billboards, he compared structural similarities to linguistic metaphors. In visual terms, he analyzed the mapping of characteristics from the visual source domain onto the visual target domain. For example, an advertisement shows a person with a pair of earphones that look like bricks. The text of this advertisement and the visual juxtaposition imply that most earphones are heavy and the earphone product being advertised is light. We cognitively select characteristics from the concept network about bricks (source domain) and map these characteristics onto the concept network about earphones (target domain). This mapping process is partial and nonarbitrary. We do not map the "bricks" characteristics of being clay baked or rectilinear. Rather, we gain a new understanding of "earphones" in terms of bricks by mapping "heavy," "hard," and "uncomfortable."

Target Domain ← Source Domain
Concept Network about Earphones ← Concept Network about Bricks
earphones ← bricks (heavy, hard, uncomfortable)

Another example shows beer engulfed in an iced champagne bucket. This juxtaposition maps champagne attributes onto the beer product. Some attributes are mapped and some are not. For example, champagne is "high class and quality, special, and refined." An unmapped characteristic is that the beer is a wine that ferments in French barrels. Forceville identifies the target and source, demonstrates the mapping process, and discusses the communication and cultural issues involved with visual metaphors.

Target Domain ← Source Domain
Concept Network about beer ← Concept Network about champagne
beer product ← champagne (high class and quality, special, refined taste)

Visual metaphors impact our cultural understanding of everyday reality much as linguistic metaphors. Through implication and juxtaposition, visual metaphors impact the public psychologically and socially. Modern culture is glutted with images, graphics, and high-tech visual effects. In addition, science is in a golden age of the visual. Data-viz is an important part of our culture and science. The following section provides a description of data-viz and relates this process to metaphor theory. From studies in linguistic and visual metaphor, I have adapted a framework within which to understand visaphor characteristics:

1.   Visaphor is defined by having two parts: target domain and source domain.
2.   Visaphor provides understanding of the target domain in terms of the source domain.
3.   The target and source domains each represent an implication or conceptual system, also called a concept network.
4.   A concept network includes collections of beliefs, concepts, symbols, technologies, cultural biases, assumptions, other metaphors, personal impressions, other property systems, and other worlds.
5.   Properties or characteristics from the source domain are mapped onto the target domain.
6.   This is not a one-to-one mapping; some characteristics get mapped, others do not.
7.   This is not an arbitrary mapping; it has to make sense.
8.   In this mapping, new meaning arises through novel association and contributes to target domain concept network.
9.   Some visaphors have become embedded in culture so that we no longer recognize their metaphorical nature; they are interpreted as literal or conventional.
10.   The metaphoric-content continuum ranges from conventional everyday visaphors to the novel, figurative visaphors.

11. Aesthetics and creativity influence the position of visaphors on the metaphoric-content continuum.

12. The audience interpretation depends on the context and the communication setting.

Data-Viz: Mapping Numbers into Pictures

Dealing with Data: What Is It and Where Does It Come From?

In general, the two primary sources of scientific numerical data are observational and computational. Observational sources include instruments or sensor data such as telescopes or computed-axial tomography (CAT). Other observational data include collected data such as census statistics. Modeled computational data result from the digital scientific and mathematical models that solve physical equations using approximation methods (Kaufmann and Smarr 1993).

The concept of "raw" data is misleading because it suggests the numbers offer clean, pure immediacy. One can argue that all data are mediated and filtered in some fashion. This mediation is part of the design and assumptions in the computational mathematical models as well as in the particular physical design of data-gathering instruments and sensors. Most scientific data sets are complex and large. Data generated by supercomputers and large-scale sensors result in multiple-terabyte multidimensional data sets that preclude a visual one-to-one mapping to digital screen space. Data are almost always filtered using mathematical or visualization methods. One of the greatest challenges to the future of visualization is the integration of data from many different sources.

Transformation of Data into Visual Models

Data-viz is a way of organizing the incoming kaleidoscopic flood of quantitative information. Quantity is a concept we use daily, and quantifying physical experience for insight is important to organizing our conscious world. We want to understand what proportion of people die at our age, how many calories we consume, how much gas costs, and how much liquid fills your cup. Motivation for understanding information in visual form goes beyond academic inquiry. The graphical display of quantitative information is important to the culture and the individual. Visaphors permeate our visual culture and influence people.

Data-viz provides insight by transforming numerical information into a visual model. More specifically, scientific visualization is the process of transforming a system of numbers, mathematical and scientific models, observations, statistics, assumptions, instrument recordings, and other data into animated and interactive visuals rendered through two- and three-dimensional computer graphics. "Rendering" is defined as the process of creating the onscreen digital appearance. Data-viz is a mapping process.

Visual model ← Data attributes

Here, the data are the source domain concept network. The target and source domains are concept networks. Creating visaphors requires the cognitive mapping process described in the preceding eleven-point framework.

Target domain (Concept network) ← Source domain (Concept network)
Visual model (Target concept network) ← Data (Source concept network)

The Science of Visualization

The science of visualization is an approach based on the analysis of human visual and perceptual systems. Researchers have developed a system of guidelines or principles that promises to enable people to understand more visual information (Ware and Beatty 1988; Ware 2000). This system includes what colors to use (Ware and Beatty 1988; Gershon 1990, 1994), how shape forms present information (Beck 1966), and what affects human perception of visual information. However, visualization is more than perception; it is also a process of visual and cognitive interpretation (Gregory 1990). People see, use, and interpret images according to their experience, cultural understandings, habits, and discipline-specific preferences (Berger 1977; Berlin and Kay 1969; Varela et al. 1997; Rosch and Lloyd 1978; Mulaik 1995; Lakoff and Johnson 1980). Choice in the representation and mapping of data affects the interpretation as well as final quality and aesthetics of the visualization.

The Art of Visualization

Consider what must take place at a higher cognitive level when addressing the most important question in making a visaphor: how can the numbers and correlated facts be designed and transformed into a visual model that makes sense? The art of visualization is the creative translation of data into visual representations. This process relates to use of signs in semiology (Hawkes 1977; Bertin 1983) and involves the invention of symbolic icons or visual metaphors that are directly bound to data and designed within the constraints of the computer graphics technology. This is a difficult task, and some argue this process often requires the expertise of many people (Cox 1988, 1990, 1991, 2001, 2003a; Brown 1990; Foley and Ribarsky 1994). Research on automating this design process has been limited (Robertson 1991; MaCKinlay 1986; Ribarsky et al. 1993).

This is a very simple example of binding data to a visual element. The three numbers below are being mapped to the colors red, green, and blue.

Red, green, blue $\leftarrow$ 1, 2, 3

Most of the time the data are large and complex beyond simple mapping. Thousands of spatial and temporal numbers are mapped in data-viz. The creator has the opportunity to choose various visual techniques to render the data. One technique is the use of glyphs, data-driven symbolic, iconic, graphical objects that are bound to the data with attributes such as shape, color, size, position, and orientation. They are useful for showing features of the data. A feature is defined as anything interesting in the data. Glyphs are effective visual objects and have become an essential part of many visualization environments (Treinish 1993; Foley and Ribarsky 1994; Schroeder et al. 1998). Glyphs have evolved in 3D computer graphics and are part of the literal, visual language of visualization. Most people understand them in terms of a literal translation of the data; however, they had novel origins. A Kodak research scientist and I developed the first glyphs in 1988 (Ellson and Cox 1988; Keller and Keller 1993).

Figures 6.1 and 6.2 exemplify the use of glyphs in understanding turbulent and complicated air flow in an atmospheric simulation of a tornado (Mead 2003). This simulation is an idealized model. The original large-scale data set is a 3D cubic volume of gridded cells (418 × 418 × 80). Each of these 14 million cells has seven associated dependent variables of microphysical data such as ice and rain.

Visual model $\leftarrow$ Volume of data (98 million numbers)
Glyph $\leftarrow$ Subset of the data

The colored spherical balls and stream tubes in figure 6.1 and the upper part of figure 6.2 are glyphs representing vertical velocity in the time-evolving severe thunderstorm. A typical method for understanding complicated flow processes, where salient features may be hidden by turbulent clutter, is to release particles within the flow field and trace the arrangements of the particles. Imagine that clusters of leaves are released into a dust devil in your yard. These imaginary leaves have no friction or weight. They simply follow the air flow and trace the pattern of the invisible wind. Visualizing tracer particles as glyphs provides understanding and correlation of flow features within the associated microphysical data.

The spherical glyphs are like the imaginary leaves and indicate positions in the flow of the air currents. The stream tube glyphs provide flow geometry. In figure 6.1, the stream tubes trace a short history of motion in the life of individual particles during the time evolution of the simulation. In contrast, the stream tubes at the top of figure 6.2 trace a long

Figure 6.1 High-resolution storm and tornado supercomputer simulation: the animation reveals a swirling tornado to the right that will strengthen as it merges with the larger rotating updraft to the left. The upper part of the figure is animation Frame 7100. A sheet of particles released and traced within the flow field is represented by spherical and stream tube glyphs. The stream tubes represent a short history of selected particles to show flow geometry. When glyphs flow in positive direction, they are colored red to yellow, with yellow being the highest velocity. Negative velocities are blue to cyan. The lower part of the figure shows frame 7200 in the time evolution of the simulation. Both upper and lower parts show a transparent gray isosurface, a component scalar field of water droplet and ice. Scientific lead: Robert Wilhelmson (NCSA/UIUC); simulation by Lou Wicker (National Severe Storms Laboratory, NOAA), Matt Gilmore, and Lee Cronce (Department of Atmospheric Sciences, UIUC); visualization by Robert Patterson, Stuart Levy, Matt Hall, Alex Betts, all of NCSA's experimental technologies division, and Donna Cox, the division's director. Copyright NCSA/UIUC.

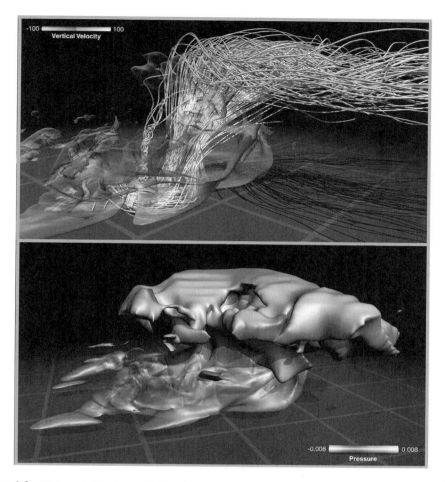

Figure 6.2 High-resolution storm and tornado supercomputer simulations: upper figure is Frame 7200 from an animated visualization. The stream tube glyphs represent the flow geometry from frame 5600 to 7200, an extended period of the simulation. The transparent gray isosurface in the upper figure shows the component microphysical scalar fields of water droplet and ice. Lower part of the figure shows two component isosurfaces. The pressure-colored component isosurface was constructed from two dependent microphysical fields: cloud droplets and ice. This isosurface has been color mapped with the pressure field sampled on the structured 3D grid. The gray transparent isosurface in the lower figure is a component of three dependent variables in the 3D grid: rain, snow, and graupel (soft hail). Scientific lead: Robert Wilhelmson (NCSA/UIUC); simulation by Lou Wicker (National Severe Storms Laboratory, NOAA), Matt Gilmore, and Lee Cronce (Department of Atmospheric Sciences, UIUC); visualization by Robert Patterson, Stuart Levy, Matt Hall, Alex Betts, all of NCSA's experimental technologies division, and Donna Cox, the division's director. Copyright NCSA/UIUC 2003.

history in the life of tracer particles, providing a more complete view of flow geometry. The glyphs have been colored to indicate when they are flowing upward (positive vertical velocity) and downward (negative vertical velocity).

In figure 6.1 and upper figure 6.2, the derivative particle trajectories are computed by integrating the velocity field using a fourth-order Runge-Kutta algorithm (Davis and Rabinowitz 1984). Velocities between grid cells are interpolated and registered with other dependent variables. This approximation algorithm calculates the trajectories of the vertical velocity showing updrafts and downdrafts of air.

Glyph position-orientation ← Flow of air traced in space-time
Orange-blue spherical glyphs ← Flow of air up-down

The surfaces in figures 6.1 and 6.2 were derived from the 3D grid data using a marching cubes algorithm (Lorensen and Cline 1987), which is an approximation method for extracting surfaces from a volume. These approximation methods involve sampling choices and testing of various thresholds. Not all of the data can possibly be shown at once. For example, at each grid cell in the 3D volume there are seven associated microphysical variables.

Gray surface ← Threshold boundary of a microphysical variable (e.g., rain and cloud)

Aesthetic and other editorial decisions are mapping processes. For example, selections of the transparency, color, camera choreography, shape of glyph, and other devices such as shadows and lighting are all aesthetic decisions. In addition, approximation and filtering methods are used in many steps along the way from the idealized simulation to the final rendering. Data are mediated in the many steps toward being visual.

Data-viz requires editorial decisions in both the mathematical and graphic presentation of data. Interactive techniques have been developed to show as much of the multidimensions as possible. However, a one-to-one mapping is never possible in complex, large data sets. We simply cannot see all of the variables at once.

This is not an arbitrary process. Great effort is made to hone the data and present it with as much accuracy and aesthetics as possible. However, one must remember that the visaphor is a visual model. The target visaphor and source data are concept networks that have inherent implications, beliefs, assumptions, approximations, aesthetic decisions, and the adaptation of other conventional visaphors such as glyphs. People learn how to read the image from familiarity with the conceptual network. The visaphor is understood in terms of the data, but information is lost.

Visualization of the tornado has been an iterative process working with scientists. These animated visualizations will be shown on television to a large public audience. However, it is not apparent to the lay viewer that the visaphor comprises layers of approximations and editorial decisions. Most people believe the visaphor is a literal fact, on a particular day when these visualizations are displayed in mainstream media.

I provide an example of popular visualization that displays cultural bias. Figure 6.3 shows one of the first visualizations of the Internet, a visualization study of the NSFnet. On the upper part of figure 6.3, the partial boundary around the United States is skirted by a 300-foot virtual cliff made possible through 3D computer graphics; it drops into blackness without Mexico, Canada, or water. This cyberspace map ignores its international neighbors and is America-centric. On the lower part of figure 6.3, the conventional earth map is used as a background for the backbone (white) and client networks. The color map indicates flow of network traffic measured in millions of bytes. Modern technology-aware people visually learn to read this cyberspace map with its quantifiable color scale as a literal translation of data. When the network was first being built, technologists called the primary connections the "backbone." The white backbone is itself metaphorical, connoting human physical attributes: the structure that holds up and connects other things.

What is not apparent to a general audience in either of these visaphors is that the nonpresent source data concept network has its assumptions, cultural biases, technological beliefs, geographical and mapping conventions, unintentional errors, approximations, misspelled words, hand-corrected routing information, classified military networks, wireless satellite connections on mobile trucks, and an entire evolving technology and political system we simplify into the term "data." The target visaphor concept network also has its assumptions, editing methods, geographical biases, and mapping conventions.

Finally, visaphors can be measured creatively and aesthetically by their position along the metaphoric-content continuum (Indurkhya). I will use the IntelliBadge project to show visaphors that span the metaphoric-content continuum. The two parts of figure 6.4, show identical data represented using two different visaphor schemas. The source data domain for both visaphors is a real-time changing numerical database that tracks the movement of people in a convention center via radiofrequency signals, and their aggregates show these people's professional interests (see IntelliBadge™). The dynamic multicolored bar chart (upper figure 6.4) shows the distribution of aggregate professional interests of people moving through six areas at a convention center: ballroom, four technical sessions, and the exhibition hall. The colors correspond to these areas of interest such as visualization (blue) and applications (magenta). The same tracking data are mapped to a visaphor called "How Does Your Conference Grow" (lower figure 6.4). Each room is a flower, and the colored petals shrink and grow according to the flow of people entering and leaving the rooms.

Byte traffic into the NSFNET T1 backbone (Sept. '91)

0   1 billion

Byte traffic into the ANS/NSFNET T3 backbone (Dec. '94)

0   1 trillion

Copyright 1996 Donna Cox and Robert Patterson

Figure 6.3 Visualization study of the NSFnet 1991, 1994: the first data-driven visualization studies of the NSFnet and the beginning of the emerging Internet. Copyright Donna Cox and Robert Patterson, 1991, 1994.

Length of yellow in bar graph ← Total aggregate professional interests in "data"
Size of yellow petal in flower ← Total aggregate professional interests in "data"

The dynamic, digital bar chart (upper figure 6.4) is a conventional visaphor. Bar charts have been used in our visual culture for so many years they constitute a conventional data representation, though they were once novel. This visaphor is considered a literal translation of data. In contrast, the garden iconic representation is a figurative, novel visaphor. Quantifying information is common and many visualizations have become conventional as they became familiar. Visual devices of charts, graphs, and maps were novel originally (Tufte 1983).

Alternative Mappings and Postcolonialism

Geographic maps are excellent examples of how literal, conventional visual metaphors have developed into coherent and consistent systems. Their novel origins have been lost over time due to familiarity and cultural accommodation. In the history of maps, texts before the 1960s show a cultural bias toward Western Europe (Bagrow and Skelton 1964). The projection systems, lines on maps, and legends can be traced back to a disciple of Aristotle. We interpret such conventions literally today, though their origins reveal that our modern maps have evolved from a biased set of devices for representing maps.

Indigenous peoples navigated land and sea with competency and accuracy; but they used a different variety of materials and visual idioms. Early cartographer's criticisms "that these savages couldn't draw in perspective" are unfounded. For example, the Marshall Islanders designed intricate patterns from palm fiber and shells to represent wave-crests, navigation sites, and mariner's direction. These accurate and useful maps provided alternative visual metaphors for navigating land and water. Likewise, the Aztec and Mayan maps were accurate though they employed different projections and icons than Western European maps. Cortez conquered the great Aztec civilization using their indigenous maps painted on cloth. Afterwards, the invaders systematically destroyed these early meso-American maps and replaced them with Spanish, Western European maps.

Map-making has primarily been dominated by Western European thinking (Black 1997). We can locate a variety of visual methods that enabled different groups of people to navigate their terrain, find locations in the land they explored, and mark territories with alternative measuring devices. Diamond argues that indigenous peoples are as intelligent as technology-dominant peoples though they have different ways of describing the world and the motivations of their cultures (Diamond 1999). Today's methods for spatially

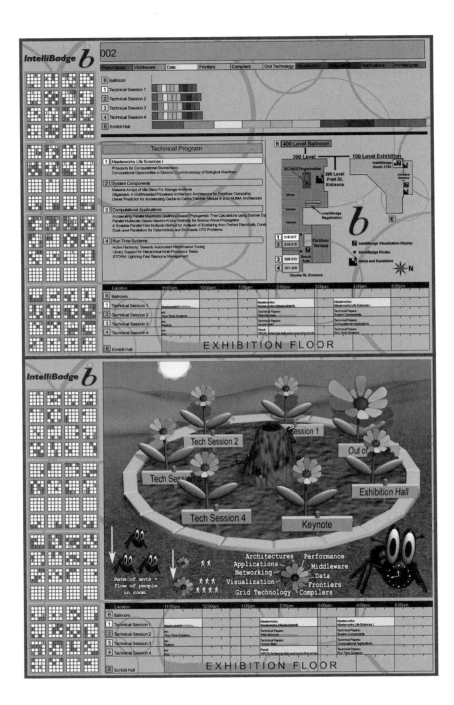

Donna Cox

quantifying information have roots in civilizations that are not more intelligent, but more dominant. Navigating the highways of life would involve very different visual icons, projections, and embodied experiences if Aboriginal peoples had colonized the world instead of Europeans (Said 1985).

Contemporary astronomy and astrophysical maps of the universe fit into this idea that maps have evolved from conventions, but reflect the dominant cultural biases. For example, the Milky Way model in figure 6.5 has been developed from star catalogs, perspective projection, and data according to the latest scientific research. Yet telescopic images are mediated approximations and have inherent error ranges. Most visaphors fail to show these approximations. These visual models help us understand one domain of information in terms of another, but these are not one-to-one mappings. Information is often edited or lost. Visaphors are aids, but taking the metaphoric relationships too seriously undermines our creative possibilities.

That being said, visaphors cannot be arbitrary; they have to work in a physical dimension or people will not use them. Maps have to enable us to navigate space in a way that helps we get to where we want to go, and maps have to be consistent with our physical explorations. However, alternative approaches to map-making may have been abandoned for consistency and dominant conventions. We need to recognize data-viz is a culturally contingent process and information is filtered through our technological media. I contend that the process of data-viz is metaphorical in nature, and recognition of this will lead to more complete and creative visual models of our understanding of the universe.

Varieties of Visualization Experiences: Case Studies

The following describes the invention of visaphor and development of its technology through continuous visualization projects since 1983.

Figure 6.4 IntelliBadge™: upper figure shows a "Conference at a Glance" schema. At the top is a dynamic multicolored bar chart that shows the relative number of people from each interest category at each current activity/location. This visualization was done by Paul Rajlich, NCSA Visualization Group; lower figure shows the same data as the interest profile bar chart. The size of the flowers corresponds to the number of people present at each tracked location at any given time. Flowers have ten different colored petals that correspond to ten interest profile categories, and the same coloring scheme used in the dynamic bar chart. The size of each petal is proportional to the cumulative interest level for a given category based on the user profiles of the attendees present at each location. The rate at which attendees go in and out of rooms is visualized by the ants going in and out of their nest. This garden visaphor was created by Donna Cox, Tony Kaap, and Lorne Leonard. Copyright NCSA/UIUC 2002.

Figure 6.5 Milky Way galaxy model. Since we live in the Milky Way galaxy and no technology can provide a view of it from the outside, other probabilistic methods have been used to develop a visual model. This visualization was based on a high-resolution photograph by David Malin, Anglo-Australian observatory, of M83, a galaxy that is thought to be like the Milky Way. The background galaxies are based on data from Brent Tully's galaxy catalog. This 3D model is used as a framework to embed other astronomical simulation and observed data and enables a virtual camera to traverse and move about the galaxy. Other start catalogs include Hipparcos, Princeton, and Frei/Gunn Galaxy Catalog, Princeton. Visualization by Robert Patterson, Stuart Levy, and Donna Cox, NCSA/UIUC. Copyright 2002 NCSA/UIUC.

Compulages: Computer Collages and Algorithmic Art

I began investigating the aesthetics of computing in 1983 when exploring algorithms to make interactive computer images and prints for art exhibitions. These early investigations involved writing C++ software that warped and colored the digital values of pixel screen space according to a mathematical and algorithmic specification. I generated a 2D statistical function that calculated the normal distribution curve on a 2D axis, and then mapped these curves perpendicular to screen space with the apex of the curve being the height of a 3D hill of graduated pixel values. The 2D to 3D mapping algorithm enabled the hills and valleys of the projected 3D normal distribution curves to overlap and wrap around, numerically, until they segmented into aesthetically interesting forms. In conjunction with this 2D to 3D statistical algorithm, I developed an interactive computer-assisted RGB editor (ICARE) that enabled a user to specify trigonometric functions to control red, green, and blue color-indexed values that mapped into the digital values of the statistical algorithm. From there, I algorithmically divided the computer screen into a matrix, zoomed into each segment of the matrix, and shot photographs of the screen with a camera. At that time, I did not have access to very expensive digital scanners. I printed each of the color photographic sections in a darkroom. After sandwiching the prints between ultraviolet protective glass and archival board, I recomposed the prints back on the wall as a matrix. I coined the term "Compulage" in 1983 to describe these computer collages. The typical size of a compulage was about 6 feet by 6 feet.

Renaissance Teams and Scientific Collaborations

Since 1985, I have collaborated with scientists and computer technologists to visualize scientific data from supercomputer simulations at the National Center for Supercomputing Applications (NCSA) at the University of Illinois, Urbana-Champaign. "Renaissance Teams" are teams of specialists including artists and designers collaborating to solve problems in the visualization of data (Ellson and Cox 1988). As an artist and designer working in this high-technology environment, I have participated in and focused on these collaborations in several ways, including the production, direction, design, color, and editing of the visuals.

In 1994, I was associate director for Scientific Visualization and art director for the PIXAR/NCSA segment of a large-scale film project. "Cosmic Voyage," an IMAX movie about the relative scale of things in the universe, was nominated for an Academy Award in 1996. Over 6 million people have seen this IMAX film. A typical IMAX screen is about 70 feet across; the film is more than 10 times the film emulsion area of a regular Hollywood 35-millimeter movie. An IMAX theater is an immersive space because the audience is totally surrounded with image and audio. Computational science and visualization was an important part of the making of "Cosmic Voyage." The advanced technologies of supercomputing and visualization were employed to artistically render images of galaxies colliding in swirling paintlike effects. I collaborated with artists, scientists, and technologists to realize an unprecedented number of data-driven visualizations for the scientific educational film. In addition, we were developing new technologies to help create animations for the IMAX film (Cox 1996, 2000ab, 2003a). The following is a description of Virtual Director.™

Aesthetics of the Virtual Choreography: Virtual Director™

This section describes a new technology and relates metaphorical relationships in its construction. In 1996, Robert Patterson (NCSA), Marcus Thiébaux, then a student at University of Illinois, and I created Virtual Director™, a software framework that operates in the CAVE, a room-size, virtual environment with a rear-screen projection system that allows one to see in 3D stereo. Virtual Director™ is a "choreography" and "navigation" system that enables the user to control the virtual camera, record frames, and see the recording on a virtual television screen in the CAVE. Virtual Director™ also enables users to collaborate over the Internet and interact even though they may be geographically located at great distances from each other. Initially, we used Virtual Director™ to create scenes for "Cosmic Voyage"; however, we have further developed and expanded this software (Cox et al. 2000).

We also used Virtual Director™ to work interactively with scientists at the Hayden Planetarium. Each user has an independent point of view and can navigate independently while creating and sharing camera paths. Users share the same visual "space" and see the same environment, and they can fly to different locations within that space. When users meet in cyberspace, they see their collaborators as Avatars, that is, visual metaphors for humans in cyberspace. The original Eastern meaning of Avatar was the incarnation of god on earth. In virtual reality, an Avatar is the incarnation of the human in virtual space. With Virtual Director™ software, a user is represented over the network as an Avatar and can see other Avatars floating and flying in cyberspace. Terms such as "navigation," "flying," "choreography," and "Avatars" have metaphorical associations. We understand new technology by appropriating such understandings from other concept networks.

We used Virtual Director's™ remote virtual collaborative capabilities over the Internet, from our CAVE at the University of Illinois to the New York City Hayden Planetarium digital dome. My team worked from Illinois and collaborated in real time with the Hayden Planetarium staff to design and choreograph camera paths through the synthetic astrophysical space. The Hayden Planetarium is using the interactive Virtual Director™ for evening public interactive shows in which the audience can control the digital dome and the Milky Way galaxy model. This virtual reality technology has provided a method to create animations for many visualization projects since 1993.

Digital Domes and Virtual Tours through the Universe

Visaphors can be displayed on a variety of media and alternative display devices. This section provides examples of a variety of environments in which visaphors have been displayed. Various media provide a communication context for visaphors that can strongly influence audiences (e.g., museum, planetarium).

We collaborated with the Hayden Planetarium, at the American Museum of Natural History, in New York City, to produce two "space" shows for their large digital dome theater as well as their Big Bang Theatre exhibit. A "space" show is here defined as digital image playback with audio and music. The first show, "Passport to the Universe," narrated by actor Tom Hanks, opened at the Millennium 2000 New Year's donor celebration.

The second show, "The Search for Life," narrated by actor Harrison Ford, opened February 2002. Both of these high-resolution, digital shows are exhibited in the upper hemisphere of a large digital dome (over 9 million pixels), which provides an immersive experience to 440 people during each 17-minute show. We created digital visualizations of the large-scale structure of the universe as well as the local galactic structure near the Milky Way galaxy. Brent Tully, an astronomer from University of Hawaii, provided mapped locations of galaxies from telescopic data. My NCSA team and I created digital images of a voyage through the cosmos arriving at the large-scale structure of the universe. Over 2.5 million people have seen this exhibit in the last couple of years.

The "Big Bang" is a scientific metaphor for the modern story of the first instant of the universe. We also collaborated with Hayden Planetarium to provide imagery for their Big Bang Theatre exhibit, which occupies the lower hemisphere of the digital dome structure. Modern Big Bang theorists believe that the universe formed over 15 billion years ago and hot, dense gas formed stars and protogalaxies that congregated along filaments. Astronomers view today's galactic filamentary structure of the universe through telescopes. Choreographer Robert Patterson, software developer Stuart Levy, and I worked with astrophysicist Dr. Michael Norman to visualize over 500 gigabytes of simulation data to show the evolution of the universe following the Big Bang (see figure 6.6). The audience of 200 people can peer over a railing into a large bowl-shaped digital display to view the animations, reminiscent of a boiling caldron of hot gases producing strings of galaxies. Poet Maya Angelou narrates as the audience watches the formation of the universe. This scientific narrative of creation draws on the latest technology and scientific theory.

In addition to visaphors for museums and planetariums, we have also developed them for television shows. Many visaphors developed for one medium can also be used for another. We produced high-definition (over 2 million pixels) visualizations for Public Broadcasting System's (PBS) NOVA/WGBH show, "Runaway Universe." I was producer and art director for the NCSA visualizations for this 1-hour special describing how scientists use visualizations to map the universe. Patterson, Levy, and I visualized scientific and astronomical data for this program that was aired in November 2000 and again in July 2001. The show takes us on a virtual voyage from the early universe (figure 6.6), to the formation of our galaxy, out of the Milky Way (figure 6.5) to the Virgo Cluster of galaxies. This journey is made possible through the use of digital computer graphics images, telescopic star catalog data, and supercomputer simulations. In addition, we also produced visualizations for the Discovery Channel's "Unfolding Universe," which premiered June 2002 (Cox 2003b; Kahler et al. 2002). We created more than 17 scenes using data from five scientists and involving several rendering software applications. These visualizations included a boiling red giant star, tours of super clusters of galaxies, colliding galaxies,

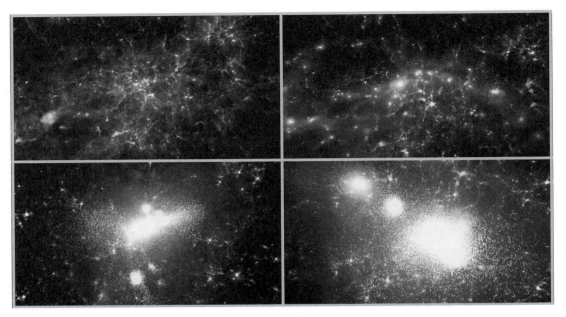

Figure 6.6 Large-scale to small-scale structure of the universe. Four frames (upper left, upper right, lower left, lower right) from visualization of the evolution of the universe; Adaptive Mesh Refinement (AMR) simulation used 200,000 CPU hours on Origin 2000 and resolves the formation of individual galaxies as well as their weblike, large-scale distribution in space. Color is used to differentiate gas density, dark matter, birthing stars, and other small-scale features. One continuous camera move from 300 million light years scale of cosmic web formation (upper left) down to a scale of 30 thousand light years of interacting galaxies and star formation (lower right). Simulation by Michael Norman, NCSA, Greg Bryon, Princeton, and Brian O'Shea, UIUC; visualization by Donna Cox, Stuart Levy, and Robert Patterson, NCSA. Copyright NCSA/UIUC 2000.

and the first star born. All of these visaphors require the same data-driven digital mapping process described earlier.

IntelliBadge™: Visaphors to Show People-Tracking

This section provides the context for the development of visaphors described earlier, "How does your conference grow?" and the Dynamic Bar graph.

IntelliBadge™, an NCSA experimental technology, is an academic experiment that uses smart technology to track participants at major public events. It was first publicly showcased at SC2002, the world's premier supercomputing conference, in the Baltimore Convention Center, November 16–21, 2002. The IntelliBadge™ project involved real-time data-viz (Cox et al. 2003ab). About one thousand conference attendees volunteered to carry radiofrequency identification (RFID) tags during the events. Our team developed an entire system to provide attendees with value-added services and real-time visualizations of their flow patterns during the conference. This system included a real-time database, interactive and playback visualization software, and a web application. It gathers radiofrequency data, tracks the movement of people in conference events, provides conference statistics, and aggregates people's professional interests. Participants were able to log into the system to check statistics and gather information, either at kiosks or remotely through the IntelliBadge™ website. Concerned about the privacy of individuals, we assured attendees the database was protected.

Two visaphors were used to show the flow of people and their aggregate interests at the conference. The first was a dynamic bar chart (upper figure 6.4). The second visaphor, "How does your conference grow?" (lower figure 6.4), visualizes the conference as a garden with each flower representing a separate event room. The flowers are scaled according to the number of people in the room. The flower petals grow or shrink as people entered or exited the rooms, according to their professional interests. The rate at which people flow in and out of the rooms is represented by ants entering and leaving the flowers. The real-time visualization of people moving throughout the physical space employed techniques similar to other data-driven visualizations. Poetic and playful, the garden visaphor was a delight to those who viewed it at various locations throughout the convention center.

Conclusion

The popularity of data-viz and its public presentation has increased dramatically since the advance of computer graphics, supercomputing, and the Internet. Millions of people flock to view visaphors that enhance scientific narratives. They view these images in large-display, general audience, immersive environments. Visaphors shape our cultural beliefs and provide people with a scientific view of reality. Because they carry the "weight of scientific accuracy," most people believe that visaphors represent the "true" view of reality. However, data are not sacred, and visaphors are approximation models, not reality. We must never forget that the map is not the territory and recognize that data are culturally contingent and there may be alternative ways of viewing the universe. In the process of creating consistency and organizing information, we may have abandoned alternative creative approaches to scientific visualization.

Data-viz is a metaphorical interaction. It provides beautiful images and supports our cultural narratives. Sitting in a digital dome and taking virtual voyages through stars and galaxies is a magical experience. To create these visaphors, visualization artists incorporate aesthetics as an inherent part of a very complex process in which data have been mediated and filtered and used to communicate scientific theories. While data are not sacred, data mapping cannot be arbitrary. Creativity is the awareness that alternatives might work, but need to be tested. "Thinking outside the box" requires new perspectives that are practical and visual and make things work. Thinking out of the box is really "thinking out of the metaphor."

References

Bagrow, Leo, and Skelton, R. A. 1964. *History of Cartography*. Cambridge, MA: Harvard University Press.

Beck, J. 1966. "Effect of Orientation and of Shape Similarity on Perceptual Grouping." *Perception and Psychophysics* 1: 300–02.

Berger, J. 1977. *Ways of Seeing*. New York: Penguin Books.

Berlin, B., and Kay, P. 1969. *Basic Color Terms: Their Universality and Evolution*. Berkeley: University of California Press.

Bertin, J. 1983. *Semiology of Graphics*. Madison, WI: The University of Wisconsin Press.

Black, Jeremy. 1997. *Maps and History Constructing Images of the Past*. New Haven, CT: Yale University Press.

Black, Max. 1961. *Models and Metaphors*. Ithaca, NY: Cornell University Press.

Brown, Maxine. 1990. "History of Visualization." Unpublished article from the National Center for Supercomputer Applications (NCSA).

Cox, Donna J. 1988. "Using the Supercomputer to Visualize Higher Dimensions: An Artist's Contribution to Scientific Visualization." *Leonardo* 21: 233–42.

———. 1989. The Tao of Postmodernism: "Computer Art, Scientific Visualization, and Other Paradoxes. ACM SIGGRAPH '89 Art Show Catalogue, Computer Art in Context." *Leonardo* (Supplemental Issue): 7–12.

———. 1990. "Scientific Visualization: Mapping Information." *AUSGRAPH '90 Proceedings*, Australia: Australian Computer Graphics Association: 101–6.

———. 1991. "Collaborations in Art/Science: Renaissance Teams." *The Journal of Biocommunications* 18(2): 10–15.

———. 1992. "Caricature, Readymades, and Metamorphosis: Visual Mathematics in the Context of Art." *Leonardo* 25(3/4): 295–302.

———. 1996. "Cosmic Voyage: Scientific Visualization for Imax Film." In *Siggraph 96 Visual Proceedings.* P. 129. New York: ACM Press.

———. 2000a. "Creating the Cosmos: Visualization & Remote Virtual Collaboration." *Consciousness Reframed.*

———. 2000b. Myth Information. *Toward a Science of Consciousness (Abstract). The Journal of Consciousness Studies.*

———. 2001. The Art of Scientific Visualization, Data Representation, and Renaissance Teams. University of Illinois at Chicago, Informatics Seminar. Arrowsmith Project.

———. 2003a. "Algorithmic Art, Scientific Visualization, and Tele-Immersion: An Evolving Dialogue with the Universe." In *Art, Women and Technology.* Cambridge, MA: MIT Press.

———. 2003b. *Unfolding Universe.* Producer and NCSA Team Leader for scientific visualizations. New York: Discovery Communications, Inc.

Cox, Donna, Patterson, Robert, and Thiebaux, Marcus, inventors. November 28, 2000. "Virtual Reality 3D Interface System for Data Creation, Viewing and Editing." USA 6154723.

Cox, D., Kindratenko, Volodymyr, and Pointer, David. 2003. IntelliBadge(™). In *First International Workshop on Ubiquitous Systems for Supporting Social Interaction and Face-to-Face Communication in Public Spaces: UbiComp 2003,* pp. 41–47.

Cox, D., Kindratenko, Volodymyr, and Pointer, David. 2003. IntelliBadge(™): Towards Providing Location-Aware Value-Added Services at Academic Conferences. In *UbiComp 2003: Ubiquitous Computing.* A. Dey, A. Schmidt, and J. McCarthy. Pp. 264–80. Berlin: Springer.

Davis, Philip J., and Rabinowitz, Philip. 1984. Methods of Numerical Integration. New York: Academic Press.

Diamond, Jared. 1999. *Guns, Germs, and Steel: The Fates of Human Societies.* New York: W. W. Norton and Company.

Ellson, Richard, and Cox, Donna. 1988. "Visualization of Injection Molding." *Simulation: Journal of the Society for Computer Simulation* 51(5): 184–88.

Foley, Jim, and Ribarsky, Bill. 1994. "Next-generation Data Visualization Tools." In *Scientific Visualization Advances and Challenges*. L. Rosenblum et al., eds. Pp. 103–27. London: Academic Press Limited.

Forceville, Charles. 1994. "Pictorial Metaphor in Advertisements." *Metaphor and Symbolic Activity* 9(1): 1–29.

———. 1996. *Pictorial Metaphor in Advertising*. London: Routledge.

———. 2002. "The Identification of Target and Source in Pictorial Metaphors." *Journal of Pragmatics* 34: 1–14.

Gershon, N. D. 1990. "Visualization of Three-Dimensional Image Processing of Positron Emission Tomography (PET) Images." *Proceedings of IEEE Visualization '90 Conference*. Computer Society Press.

Gershon, Nahum. 1994. "From Perception to Visualization." In *Scientific Visualization Advances and Challenges*. L. Rosenblum et al., eds. Pp. 129–39. London: Academic Press Limited.

Gregory, R. L. 1990. *Eye and Brain. The Psychology of Seeing*. Princeton, NJ: Princeton University Press.

Hawkes, Terence. 1977. *Structuralism and Semiotics*. Berkeley: University of California Press.

Indurkhya, Bipin. 1992. *Metaphor and Cognition An Interactionist Approach*. Dordrecht: Kluwer Academic Publishers.

Kahler, Ralf, Cox, Donna, Patterson, Robert, Levy, Stuart, Hege, Hans-Christian, and Abel, Tom. 2002. "Rendering the First Star in the Universe—A Case Study." In *Proceedings Visualization 2002*. Pp. 537–39. Washington, DC: IEEE.

Kaufmann III, W., and Smarr, Larry. 1993. *Supercomputing and the Transformation of Science*. Washington, DC, Scientific American Library, New York: W. H. Freeman.

Keller, P. R. and Keller, M. M. 1993. *Visual Cues: Practical Data Visualization*. Los Alamitos, CA: IEEE Society Press, Manning Publication.

Lakoff, George. 2002. *Moral Politics: What Conservatives Know that Liberals Don't*. Chicago: The University of Chicago Press.

Lakoff, George, and Johnson, Mark. 1999. *Philosophy in the Flesh: The Embodied Mind and Its Challenge to Western Thought*. New York: Basic Books.

Lakoff, George, and Johnson, Mark. 1980. *Metaphors We Live By*. Chicago: The University of Chicago Press.

Lakoff, George, and Nunez, Rafael E. 2000. *Where Mathematics Comes From: How the Embodied Mind Brings Mathematics into Being*. New York: Basic Books.

Lorensen, W. E., and Cline, H. E. 1987. "Marching Cubes: A High Resolution 3D Surface Construction Algorithm." *Computer Graphics* 21(3): 163–69.

MaCKinlay, J. 1986. "Automating the Design of Graphical Presentations of Relational Information." *ACM Transactions on Graphics* 5(2): 110–41.

McCormick, B. H., DeFanti, Thomas A., and Brown, Maxine D. 1987. "Visualization in Scientific Computing." *Computer Graphics* 21(6).

MEAD. "Modeling Environment for Atmospheric Discovery (MEAD)." Last accessed 2003 at http://www.ncsa.uiuc.edu/expeditions/MEAD/.

Mulaik, Stanley A. 1995. "The Metaphoric Origins of Objectivity, Subjectivity, and Consciousness in the Direct Perception of Reality." *Philosophy of Science* 62(2): 283–303.

Ribarsky, M. W., Ayers, E. J., and Mukherjea, S. 1993. "Using Glyphmaker to Create Customized Visualizations of Complex Data." GIT GVU-93-25.

Robertson, P. K. 1991. "A Methodology for Choosing Data Representations." *IEEE Computer Graphics and Applications* 11(3): 56–67.

Rosch, Eleanor, and Lloyd, Barbara. 1978. *Cognition and Categorization*. New York: John Wiley & Sons.

Said, Edward W. 1985. *Beginnings Intention & Method*. New York: Columbia University Press.

Schroeder, Will, Martin, Kenneth M., and Lorensen, William E. 1998. "The Visualization Toolkit: An Object-Oriented Approach to 3D Graphics." Upper Saddle River, NJ: Prentice Hall.

Treinish, L. 1993. "Inside Multidimensional Data." *Byte* 18(4): 132–33.

Tufte, Edward R. 1983. *The Visual Display of Quantitative Information*. Cheshire, CT: Graphics Press.

Varela, Francisco J., Thompson, Evan, and Rosch, Eleanor. 1997. *The Embodied Mind: Cognitive Science and Human Experience*. Cambridge, MA: MIT Press.

Ware, C., and Beatty, J. 1988. "Using Color Dimensions to Display Data Dimensions." *Human Factors* 20(2): 127–42.

Ware, Colin. 2000. *Information Visualization: Perception for Design*. New York: Academic Press.

7

Public Space of Knowledge: Artistic Practice in Aesthetic Computing

Monika Fleischmann and Wolfgang Strauss

It is probably not enough to ask that only media authors and especially media artists should investigate the structure of the programmable machine. Much rather, the question is how artists can today still stand before a canvas at all or still work on a block of stone at all without understanding the cultural history of the programmable machine—with its all-pervasive influences on contemporary society and our existence—as a conscious background to their own work and to their own life.
—TROGEMANN 2004

This chapter places our culturally and aesthetically motivated research and development of new interfaces and interactive systems within the context of *aesthetic computing*, a concept put forward by Paul Fishwick. As media artists and researchers at the Fraunhofer Institute for Media Communication (IMK), we investigate the influence of digital transformations through computers and networks on society. In doing so, we make use of public space on site and on the Internet as a field for experimentally testing and evaluating new forms of communication. Our interest is in creating new accesses to space and the public with a view to enabling expanded horizons of perception and experience. Our objective is to build up exemplary action spaces that can be physically experienced so as to visibly demonstrate the effect of the technologies on the informed body. In this way we put the concept of visualization familiar in computer science into a sensory and cognitive context, since showing how we understand what we see and perceive is an important role of media art.

For us, the notion of *aesthetic computing* implies giving computing a meaning and shape, and also investing the process of interaction with diverse and unforeseeable forms. In the process of producing and exhibiting interactive works, the relationship between imagination and information, between language (code) and material (interface), is the fundamental basis of the artistic or applied development in question.

It is beyond the bounds of this text to discuss in detail *aesthetics* as a concept. But as the philosopher Wolfgang Welsch has stated, the notion, traditionally understood as the philosophy of art, has changed with the effects of the New Media on visual culture and our perceptual system:

Vision was traditionally favored because of its hallmarks of distance, precision and universality, because of its capacity for determination and its proximity to cognition. [Today] other senses have attracted new attention. Hearing, for example, is being appreciated . . . because of its essentially social character in contrast to the individualistic execution of vision, and because of its link with emotional elements as opposed to the emotionless mastery of phenomena through vision. Touch has found its advocates in the same way, due both to new developments in media technology and to its emphatically corporal character—this again in contrast to the "pure," uninvolved character of vision. (Welsch 1997)

We suggest that some further concepts should be added to this expanded perceptual system: immediacy and real time, presence and tele-presence, navigation and control.

These days, almost all distances have been eliminated. The impact of the terrorist attack on New York City's World Trade Center on September 11, 2001, and the catastrophic December 26, 2004, tsunami, caused by a massive earthquake in the Indian Ocean, are immediately apparent, as television and the Internet bring their horror into every living room almost in real time. Both tragedies unleashed a flood of images, making it impossible not to be involved. All that preserves a certain distance are the missing smell of the place, the composed cropping of the images, and the possibility of switching off the TV or PC. On the other hand, the break-up of the (extended) family, and the "anonymization" of both society and the working environment give rise to an increased desire to participate in events that can be shared with others. The yearning for presence and being in the world results from the lack of social communication. The communication media, themselves part of the cause of this loss, are supposed to help bring us together and trigger a renewed flood of information that calls for new control and navigation systems to help provide orientation. The interaction of an expanded, complex, and contradictory perceptual system is the starting point of our own position, interests, and questions.

Our work, therefore, involves investigating perception and its transformation by communication technologies. Our artistic works are mirrors for the viewer, who observes himself. One of our first interactive artworks, "Liquid Views" (Fleischmann, Bohn, and Strauss

Figure 7.1 Silicon senses—a multimodal interface allows access to a digital system in many different ways.

1993), addresses the story of Narcissus and the psychology of self-recognition and identity as they are discussed in various theories of perception. "Energy_Passages" (Fleischmann and Strauss 2004) reflects a medially constructed reality. "Home of the Brain" (Fleischmann and Strauss 1992), like our "knowledge discovery tools" (Strauss, Fleischmann, et al. 2002), presents digital navigation systems. Body-related interfaces, such as the motion platform "Virtual Balance" (Strauss and Fleischmann 1996), the "PointScreen" system with the "Info-Jukebox," which works without being touched through the body's electrostatic energy field (Strauss, Fleischmann, et al. 2003), or the performative installation "Murmuring Fields" and the eMuse system (Strauss, Fleischmann, et al. 1999a), deal with information that is directly inscribed into the body (figure 7.1).

Our current research topic, "Knowledge Media—Knowledge Arts," is concerned with developing systems and presenting data spaces as new forms of access to information and knowledge. As *research artists*, we see ourselves at the interface between art, technology, and society, where architecture, design, computer science, art, and society intersect. Under the subject of "mixed realities," we are working on concepts connected with the layering and penetration of real and digital spaces, which we call "knowledge spaces."

Space of Knowledge

Our concept of *space of knowledge* refers to a hyperdatabase-supported architectural space, in which both explicit and implicit knowledge is present (Fleischmann, Strauss, et al. 2002). The aim is to lay the foundations for integrating our memory into the architectonic space in a multimodally perceptible form, to discover new forms of accessing knowledge and enable greater use of the architectonic space in the context of sensory memory. Our motivation to build *space of knowledge* is grounded in new media art, architecture, and design and relates to the notion of mnemotechnique (Matussek 2004). Building on our current research and development of digitized architectural space, we outline three interferential layers of *space of knowledge*:

1. The "information space" is primarily where the infrastructural network of a digital archive is created.
2. The "explorative space" offers online knowledge tools such as *Semantic Map*[1] and *Timeline*,[2] which support the intuitive discovery of information.
3. The "participation space" is where nonmaterial and performative interfaces provide experimental access to mixed reality space.

Interconnecting these layers gives rise to a new understanding of the term "mixed realities" as space fused or furnished with data (Strauss and Fleischmann 2001).

Information Space: A Digital Archive—The Hyperdatabase

In this section we discuss the archivist's role in building an online archive and information space. We present "netzspannung.org," an online archive for media art.

The age-old idea of a comprehensive information and knowledge space can be realized today through graphical interfaces on the monitor screen. The educational platform "netzspannung.org" puts media art in the context of topical questions and issues in theory and research. Among other things, the platform presents a comprehensive text and video Internet archive of material from the fields of cultural history, media theory, and computer science in a distributed system that can be personalized and that reacts automatically to new information (Paal 2001). It contains lecture series and text compendia such as *Iconic Turn 2002–03* and *Digital Transformations* (Fleischmann and Reinhard 2004). Published in two languages—English and German—and targeting both national and international audiences, the online archive contributes significantly to the continuing education and training of teachers and students.

Our motive in creating netzspannung.org[3] was to build a lasting information space on the development of media art and digital culture. Very quickly we realized we were getting ensnared in a vast, bewildering network of information sources. An information space with an unlimited number of information points and links must draw on more than one powerful database. The development of distributed applications—hyperdatabases[4]—is, therefore, central to our platform's infrastructure, which should react to changes in the information space. For example, when new information is being registered, it should be supplied automatically to each relevant information unit. In developing the platform in this way, we were mindful of Marvin Minsky's "future forecast" in the 1980s, sketching out the future of the information space with a fictional conversation between two readers in a library: "Can you imagine that they used to have libraries where the books didn't talk to each other?" (Kurzweil 1991).

New technologies in man-machine communication, invisible computers, mobility and sensor data will have to be more thoroughly incorporated into existing research with information systems, giving rise to a series of new, personalized, applications. After all, the question of relevant information always depends on the person, the situation, and their spatial and temporal context. Normally, information on the Internet is based on hypertext structures, extended by links referring to further information already defined by the initial authors. In addition, the knowledge tools of netzspannung.org can be used to edit information, to introduce or depict information from the Internet in another context and thus create new knowledge, supported by our cross-platform application environment (Paal et al. 2005). Only information that can be personalized in this way introduces the concept of interactivity for online archives.

Unlike approaches to personalization in commercial applications, geared mainly to observing and monitoring the (buying) behavior of users, personalization with netzspannung .org means primarily providing community members with individual virtual workspace on an educational platform that can be accessed free of charge (Hirsh et al. 2000).

Developing the concept of and implementing the Internet platform netzspannung.org, based on the needs of a diverse community and within an interdisciplinary team of artists, theorists, and computer scientists was not an easy task. Software philosopher Ted Nelson opened our mind to the requirements of database people versus the needs of artists: "you need to decide in advance what all of your fields are going to be. That is how it is in the database world, you have to decide all of that in advance.... For some of us, ideas keep changing. You have to be able to change those fields all the time. That is where the database guys get off the boat" (see Engelbart 2000). This is why we had to define a system able to adapt the infrastructure to the ongoing input of members online. Nelson was one of the first to suggest the potential of distributed networks of individually powerful computers for creating social forms directed by the individual members. His concepts of interconnections and parallelism of structure inspired Tim Berners-Lee and others for the World Wide Web. What Nelson is talking about is not just a technology, but a community of network culture. Howard Rheingold writes in *Tools for Thought*:

Ted Nelson is voicing what a few people have known for a while, from the technical side—that the intersection of communication and computer technologies will create a new communication medium with great possibilities. But he notes that the art of showing us those possibilities might belong to a different breed of thinker, people with different kinds of motivations and skills than the people who invented the technology. (Rheingold 2000)

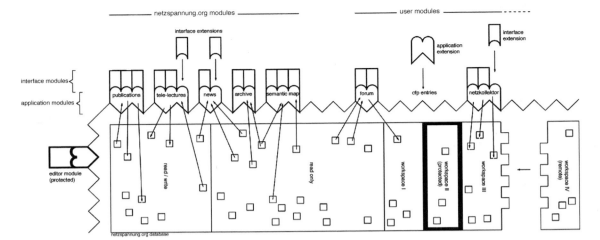

Figure 7.2 Schematic drawing of netzspannung.org platform architecture.

With this in mind, the netzspannung.org team developed a three-layer model platform architecture as a "distributed community engine," representing the open, documented interfaces that allow users to implement their own projects. The architecture can be understood as a "network operating system." The base is an "Internet hard disk" that allows storage of standard formats such as XML but also self-defined data models. The base interface connects to an "application layer," on top of which is an "interface layer" for creating individual interfaces. The architecture (figure 7.2) supports various well-known database-system protocols, offering flexibility and different layers of complexity (Paal 2001). The netzspannung.org community of artists and scientists have used the platform technology as an underlying technical infrastructure for their individual projects in the last few years (see MARS artists).[5]

Our vision was to build the netzspannung.org online archive to interconnect different people and disciplines so that they could learn and acquire knowledge about the intersection of art, science, technology, and communication. Today the Internet platform not only comprises a high-quality collection of information on digital culture and media arts, but also links this information, sets it in various contexts, and makes it available online as a constantly expanding information space, accessible via knowledge discovery tools (Novak et al. 2003).

Large volumes of data have to be broken down into a wealth of individual elements, isolated, grouped, put into context and constituted into complete entities. The "knowledge discovery tools" of netzspannung.org do precisely this, demonstrating visual database exploration techniques online.

Monika Fleischmann and Wolfgang Strauss

Explorative Space: Knowledge Discovery Tools

Just as large telescopes help astronomers see the stars, digital cultures need new instruments to be able to see, survey, and evaluate the rapidly growing volumes of data. The problem of finding information in large-scale digital archives, which have highly heterogeneous content, has hitherto been solved by entering specific queries in search engines. But how can you find information whose existence you can only guess at? What do you do if you don't know exactly what you are looking for? How can you see what is available in an archive? How can you be inspired by what is there?

Our knowledge discovery tools, derived from the vision of Tim Berners-Lee, filter relevant content from the flood of information and interlink a network of meanings. "I know what you are looking for," these tools tell us. In his article "The Semantic Web" (Berners-Lee et al. 2001) on the future of the Internet, the inventor of the World Wide Web assumes that without the help of software assistants, the potential of the Internet and online archives is unminable for the individual. Development regarding the network of meanings is based on the interaction of three technologies: (1) software agents, which unlike the present-day search engine trawl through information in line with our interests; (2) a machine-readable language capable of representing the semantic content of documents; and (3) ontologies, that is, semantic networks, which based on the standardization of meaning, but only where standardization brings more benefits than it brings about disadvantages.

The netzspannung.org archive provides content from a whole range of disciplines such as media art, IT, design, and theory. The aim of netzspannung.org is, therefore, to develop cross-disciplinary forms of contextualization and visualization by using techniques for finding patterns and trends in large data sets. Knowledge discovery tools are user interfaces for mining data, which permit a "dynamic zoom" on large volumes of data and facilitate the visualization of heterogeneous data resources displayed in semantic context.

Here we describe the knowledge discovery tools, based on pattern recognition and machine learning, which have been developed at the MARS lab. So far three different interface techniques have been implemented:

1. The *Semantic Map* compiles content into clusters and facilitates an explorative navigation of interdisciplinary relationships based on semantic interrelations.
2. The *Timeline* interface arranges content in parallel into various categories and times (x-, y-grid) to identify chronological relationships between different fields of content.
3. The *Knowledge Explorer* is a more complex tool for communities of experts. Experts can use it to structure data pools, but also create personal knowledge maps and share them with other members of the community, who can then tap into uncharted pools of information (Novak 2002).

Later we describe the *Semantic Map* in more detail as an example of the knowledge discovery tools. The *Semantic Map* is a tool that evaluates, structures, and visualizes semantic links between individual documents in the netzspannung.org database. During the first stage of data processing, the brief descriptions of all netzspannung.org's database entries are analyzed in terms of both the words used and their absolute as well as relative frequency, filtering out very frequent words that are irrelevant to the content (e.g. "the," "with," etc.). This process generates, among other things, a list of the most important words. These words are weighted by our editorial staff and used for the graphical visualization: they form the titles of the clusters. The database entries are graphically arranged in a map by using a neural network. With the help of the so-called Kohonen Map (Kohonen 2001), the system allocates each database entry to a cluster on the basis of the text analysis at the same time relating it to all the other database entries in accordance with their semantic proximity (figure 7.3).

The Semantic Map, therefore, allocates netzspannung.org's database entries to the clusters that are closest in content, and indicates the interrelations among the database entries. This form of contextualization and visualization provides users with different access points

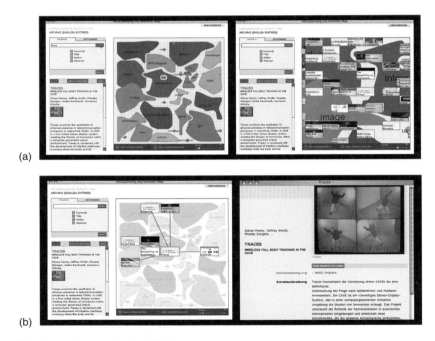

(a)

(b)

Figure 7.3 Semantic map interface (GUI).

Monika Fleischmann and Wolfgang Strauss

for "rummaging through" the content of netzspannung.org's database and discovering new content. The Semantic Map offers surprising perspectives on individual works of media art by creating connections between individual projects, which are combined into different clusters, constantly rearranged by key concepts.

Participation Space: Mixed Reality Architecture to Enter

We approach the question of how online archives can be implemented on both metaphoric-virtual and physical-real levels as accessible and tangible space of knowledge through our Mixed Reality methods for permeating and layering physical and electronic spaces.

We are pursuing the idea of creating networked spaces of knowledge constructed by overlapping the physical and electronic domains. These are places and spaces that are accessed via experimental interfaces linking real and virtual space. We therefore extend the notion of Mixed Reality, which Paul Milgram (Milgram et al. 1994) defined as a spectrum extending from real to virtual experiences, with augmented reality and augmented virtuality bridging the two. In our Mixed Reality approach, physical space and data space are layered onto each other, resulting in a dynamic, spatial database that can be entered.

The term underlying this, Mixed Reality, describes the overlayering of real and virtual spaces to integrate multilayered levels of reality. It denotes a situation in which the user's action space is composed of elements from different existential categories (material, electronic, natural, artificial, etc.). This Mixed Reality combines real spaces, objects, or people with electronic illusion spaces and enables interaction with digital representations. Space, spatial memory, and the relation of body to space are the bases for a body- and space-oriented interface.

The interactive Mixed Reality space appears as a room furnished with data. The room stands for physical interaction space. Data-furniture is both physical objects networked with computer systems and digital artifacts linked to the physical environment. The notion of data-furniture connects experience of mnemotechnics and cognitive science for the interface. It is a spatially organized information architecture, in which data are revealed through users' movement and action in the combined real-virtual space and interaction with other users. Data-furniture depicts digital information as visible, audible, tangible, and touchless interface objects integrated in architectural space.

A production system for the real-time processing of the most diverse data formats was developed: eMUSE, the electronic multiuser stage environment (Strauss et al. 1999a,b). It enables the creation of a mixed-reality space continuum in which an enterable audio archive—the *Murmuring Fields* installation[6]—as an interactive sound space for multiple users can create the impression of a concert space (Fleischmann et al. 2000). eMUSE not

Figure 7.4 Staging the space of mixed reality.

only integrates several people, live in a shared space, representing them in a virtual environment, but it also allows the collaboration of spatially remote users via the Internet. Related scientific or artistic works include MIT's *KidsRoom* (Bobick et al. 1999) and David Rockeby's *Very Nervous System* (1986–90[7]; see figure 7.4).

With *Murmuring Fields*, we developed a performative audio archive and a sound space for the Mixed Reality stage. Data space and action space are interconnected by an optical tracking system. Performers experience and compose the sound space through movement. The performer's body becomes a musical instrument. In *Murmuring Fields* the virtual space is structured in four zones with statements from the scientists and philosophers Vilém

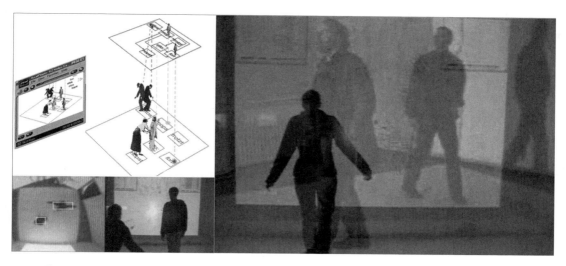

Figure 7.5 Interaction and movement on the mixed reality stage: watching oneself from the outside.

Flusser, Marvin Minsky, Joseph Weizenbaum, and Paul Virilio in different languages such as English, German, and French. By moving around, performers trigger the spatially arranged soundscape. Depending on speed and direction of movement, new meaning is created as the temporal structure of sentences, words, and syllables appear in a different way. Sound follows movement and generates a dynamic circuit based on mnemonics as a spatial dramaturgy (figure 7.5).

Theater scholar Ulrike Hass referred to her observation as "shifting the limits of the narrative": "The Mixed Reality stage turns everybody more or less into an actor and, at the same time, reduces the difference between the theatre and everyday life." Hass believes that a similar change is taking place in the theatrical narrative. She observes an expansion of the theatrical space, of the physical action, and of perception. "This Mixed Reality stage is so special because it is relatively free from images. Here, the sound experience turns into the object of interaction." This is also a difficulty for the audience as long as it has only an observing position. Hass mentions three important points, which single out the Murmuring Fields: (1) The relation between digital and virtual space; (2) the increased status of space compared to image; and (3) the Mixed Reality space as an expansion of physical action and perception (Strauss and Fleischmann 1999b).

The body is the location for all experiences. From a performative perspective, the body, materiality, mediality, and interactivity are at the heart of man's observations. The body is the interface, the link to everything in the world. In this respect, we are pursuing the view that sensory experiences and conceptual reflection come together in the "sensory thought process of the body," a view epistemologist George Lakoff, among others, discusses in *Philosophy in the Flesh. The Embodied Mind* (Lakoff 1999). Maurice Merleau-Ponty talked about the body as "flesh," made of the same flesh as the world, and it is because of this that we can know and understand the world (Merleau-Ponty 1968). For Merleau-Ponty, consciousness is not just something that goes on in our heads. Merleau-Ponty's concept of the lived body eliminates Descartes' mind-body dualism. Rather, our intentional consciousness is experienced in and through our bodies.

Public Art: Spaces of Knowledge on the Road

The project *Energy-Passages* (Fleischmann and Strauss 2004) is a participative mixed-reality installation in public space. Here we investigate questions of knowledge discovery, using specially developed software tools to enable the theme of information the visitor experiences. The urban staging of an "information flow" confronts the visitor in front of Munich's House of Literature with the medially mediated communication of a mass medium—the daily newspaper, which we characterize as public linguistic space (figure 7.6).

In the tradition of the open-air summer cinema, the large projection in the street creates a cheerful space for verbal communication and gestures—and this in Munich in the midst of winter, November 2004. Things are made public and discussed publicly by the passersby. With *Energy_Passages*, we present the city as a linguistic space, which is measured as an invisible urban architecture. An automated computer program analyses the news provided in the daily newspaper, reducing it to catchwords. The 27,000 words contained in current news are reduced to 500 that are relevant—that is, the 500 most used words. The words filtered in this process appear in a large projection as information flow, representing a spectrum of information that usually accompanies us unnoticed throughout the day and forms our cultural conscience. The words mentioned most frequently in November 2004 in Munich, Germany, are "percent" and "million"—one day it is "Arafat"—whereas words such as truth, friendship, and love are quite rare. Before the installation, the audience discusses the influence mass media exert and how they impact on our vision of the world (figure 7.7).

Visitors to the installation can select individual terms from the information flow via microphone or touchscreen. A network of terms then appears that were linked to the chosen terms by content in the newspaper. We created a computer-based linguistic tool, which is turned into an information browser by machine-made "cross-reading." Computer voices directly react to their selection and accompany these terms in the form of a polyphonic echo. By selecting specific terms, passersby "rewrite" the newspaper, developing a

Figure 7.6 Energy_Passages: information flow.

Figure 7.7 Semantic network of terms linked to the chosen term "Kunst" (arts).

"living newspaper." Their selected catchwords also lead to the retrieval of the corresponding passages from the daily press. The information cube displays a world map, indicating the geographical origin of each individual message. This highlights the city's partnership links with another city but also those that do not appear on the map. Whereas some terms contained in the information flow allow for associational links, the fragmented enumeration of individual pieces of text, as they appear in the living newspaper, refer to the loss of context we experience due to the acceleration and mass of information (figure 7.8).

Especially children, elderly people, artists, and female passersby walked enthusiastically through the flow, as if it were a shower of light and energy. We conducted informal usability studies on people who experienced the exhibit. By watching on site as well as

Figure 7.8 The Living Newspaper and the world view created by the visitors.

through a webcam online, and talking to the "performing" visitors, we improved in the first days, for example, the graphics of the touchscreen interface, the colors of the selected word in the information flow, the setting of the microphones, and the information on the screens in and on the cube. Not only during the 4 weeks of the exhibition, but still today we receive feedback, on the basis of our online documentation and video, from renowned experts in Germany and abroad.

Sherry Turkle, Professor of Sociology at the MIT, sent the following statement:

The notion of a spatial experience of the discourse of the news within a city space and the possibility of deconstructing the newspaper captures the fragmentation of how media is experienced by citizens in a culture of simulation. It thus mirrors and concretizes an important cultural and political moment, turning it into an object for reflection. (Turkle 2004)

Christiane Paul, New Media art curator at the Whitney Museum in New York, wrote that "Energy_Passages literally reinscribes the passages of energy that inform our daily life onto the street, allowing passers-by to 'perform' the events of the day in their multiple semantic connections" (Paul 2004).

The technical carrier constructions for Energy_Passages are the installation's architecture, which forms an ensemble of external buildings, an electronic front garden in an urban space. Together with the existing furniture in the form of stone tables and benches by Jenny Holzer, this reading garden has developed into an external space for the House of Literature, which specifically relates to it (figure 7.9).

"Ortstermine 2004—Kunst im öffentlichen Raum" (Local appointments 2004—The arts in public space), a virtual, sensory, and cognitively perceivable urban space, was developed in Munich, created mainly by algorithms, visualization, and a new type of ontological interface. This new urban space is clearly understood to be different from spaces existing in the world of goods, with its advertising messages and images. The theme of the flow, in the form of a large image, creates a public and media space designed by text, language, and light that is directly on one's way and can be entered as a materialized archive.[8]

Conclusion

In presenting some of our approaches and concepts, we hope that the perspectives of *aesthetic computing*, as initiated by Paul Fishwick and others, will lead to a theory and practice that produces program structures as universal principles and archetypical thought. These can be combined with contemporary art and aesthetics theories, as Georg Trogemann, professor of computer science at Cologne's Academy of Media Arts, calls for in his article

Figure 7.9 Energy_Passages: overlaying and highlighting the carved words from artist Jenny Holzer.

"Müssen Medienkünstler programmieren können?" (Trogemann 2004). Such discourse on aesthetic computing could eliminate the still prevalent distinction in developing digital culture between practical engagement (computing) and critical media, or art, theoretical reflection (aesthetics). As Trogemann writes, "generative information aesthetics" already provided a theoretical underpinning in Germany in the 1960s and 1970s, combining algorithmics and aesthetics and being substantially molded by the physicist, semiotician, and philosopher Max Bense and his pupils. Bense offers a joint perspective of the natural sciences, art, and philosophy to define existential rationalism so as to overcome the division between science and arts.[9]

For media artists, the basis of the theory and practice of *aesthetic computing* must be an investigation of the medium of the computer and its *special medial sense* (Schiesser

2004). The concept of the *special sense* of the media, shaped by the Zurich cultural historian Giaco Schiesser, assumes that all media have some special character and not only transmit messages, but are also—as *Friedrich Nietzsche*[10] and *Herbert Marshall McLuhan*[11] already recognized—involved in the content of the message. Thus, they not only convey meaning, but are also involved in creating meaning. Accordingly, artistic works in the area of *aesthetic computing* must lead to a synthesis of sensory perception and cognitive insight, yielding new ways of thinking and models of experience such as new cartographic and navigational instruments, thus creating the basis for innovations.

Alongside the genuine task areas of the individual disciplines of media art and computer science, specific research collaboration should be defined between the natural sciences and the arts, and specific support instruments designed for this.

Notes

1. Semantic Map—Knowledge Discovery Tool, at http://netzspannung.org/about/tools/semantic-map/.

2. Timeline—Knowledge Discovery Tool, at http://netzspannung.org/about/tools/timeline/?lang=en.

3. netzspannung.org—online archive on media art and digital culture, at http://netzspannung.org.

4. Hyperdatabase: the concept of the hyperdatabase was outlined by Prof. Hans-Jörg Schek of the Swiss Federal Institute of Technology (ETH), Zurich. At http://www-dbs.inf.ethz.ch/.

5. MARS artists: Shu Lea Cheang realized: "Carry On," at http://netzspannung.org/carryon/; http://netzspannung.org/about/mars/projects/.

6. Murmuring Fields—Mixed Reality Installation, 1999. Available at http://www.erena.kth.se/murmur.html; also refer to http://www.medienkunstnetz.de/works/murmuring-fields/.

7. Very Nervous System, at http://homepage.mac.com/davidrokeby/vns.html.

8. Energy_Passages: Refer to the project description and technical explanation: http://www.energie-passagen.de/projekt.htm; video: http://www.energie-passagen.de/bilder/energiepassagen.mpg.

9. Bense, Max: http://www.medienkunstnetz.de/artist/bense/biography/.

10. The half-blind Friedrich Nietzsche saw that the medium of the typewriter, itself, "plays a part in writing our thoughts."

11. Marshall McLuhan, "the medium is the message."

References

Berners-Lee, Tim, Hendler, James, and Lassila, Ora. 2001. "The Semantic Web. A New Form of Web Content that Is Meaningful to Computers Will Unleash a Revolution of New Possibilities." *Scientific American.* May 2001. Available at http://www.sciam.com/article.cfm?articleID=00048144-10D2-1C70-84A9809EC588EF21.

Bobick, Aaron, and Intille, S., Davis, J., et al. "The KidsRoom: A Perceptually-Based Interactive Immersive Story Environment." *PRESENCE: Teleoperators and Virtual Environments* 8; 4 (August 1999).

Engelbart's Colloquium. 2000. "The Unfinished Revolution," Held at Stanford University. Session 9: "Where Our Hyper-Media Really Should Go!" Ted Nelson. Available at http://www.bootstrap .org/colloquium/session_09/session_09_nelson.html.

Fleischmann, Monika, and Reinhard, Ulrike, eds. 2004. *Digitale Transformationen.* Heidelberg. Available at http://netzspannung.org/positions/digital-transformations/.

Fleischmann, Monika, and Strauss, W. 1992. Home of the Brain; Golden Nica for Interactive Art; Prix Ars Electronica, Katalog Ars Electronica 92, Linz. Available at http://www.aec.at/en/archives/ prix_archive/prix_projekt.asp?iProjectID=2479.

Fleischmann, Monika, and Strauss, Wolfgang. 2004. "Kunst an der Schnittstelle von Technik, Forschung und Gesellschaft." In *Digitale Transformationen.* Heidelberg. Available at http://netzspannung .org/positions/digital-transformations/artists/.

Fleischmann, Monika, Bohn, Christian, and Strauss, Wolfgang. 1993. "Rigid Waves—Liquid Views." *Visual Proceedings: Machine Culture;* Siggraph '93, Anaheim.

Fleischmann, Monika, Strauss, Wolfgang, Blome, Gabriele, Novak, Jasminko, and Paal, Stefan. 2002. "netzspannung.org—A Collaborative Knowledge Space for Media Art and Technology." In *Proceedings of Ichim02,* International Cultural Heritage Informatics Meeting, Museums and the Web conference, Boston, 2002.

Fleischmann, Monika, Strauss, Wolfgang, Novak, Jasminko, et al. 2001. "netzspannung.org—An Internet Media Lab for Knowledge Discovery in Mixed Realities." In *Proceedings of Cast01*, Living in Mixed Realities. September 21–22, 2001. Schloß Birlinghoven, Sankt Augustin, Germany, pp. 121–29.

Fleischmann, Monika, Strauss, Wolfgang, and Novak, Jasminko. 2000. "Murmuring Fields Rehearsals—Building up the Mixed Reality Stage." In *Proceedings of KES*, Brighton, UK, 2000. Available at http://www.erena.kth.se/murmur.html.

Hirsh, Haym, Basu, Chumki, and Davison, Brian D. 2000. "Learning to Personalize." In *Communications of the ACM* (August 2000). 43 (8).

"Iconic Turn" lecture series, organized by the Burda Academy for the Third Millennium in collaboration with the Human Sciences Centre of Ludwig Maximilian's University (LMU), Munich, Germany. [In its role as cooperation partner, netzspannung.org recorded the individual contributions to the "Iconic Turn" lecture cycle at Ludwig Maximilian's University, Munich, and streamed them live. The event took place from summer semester 2002 to summer semester 2003.] Available at http://netzspannung.org/positions/lectures/iconic-turn/.

The Fraunhofer Institute for Media Communication (IMK). [IMK undertakes research and development in all facets of new digital media, including content design, production, distribution, and interaction. Its key objectives are to expand the range and functionality of digital media, to examine their creative and social possibilities, to develop innovative solutions, and to open up new fields of application.] Available at http://www.imk.fraunhofer.de/.

Kohonen, Teuvo. 2001. *Self-Organizing Maps*. 3rd ed. New York: Springer.

Kurzweil, Raymond. 1991. *The Age of Knowledge*. [An illustration of the second industrial revolution written for "The Futurecast," a monthly column in the *Library Journal*. September 1991.] Published on KurzweilAI.net, August 6, 2001, at http://www.kurzweilai.net/articles/art0246.html?printable=1.

Lakoff, George. 1999. *Philosophy in the Flesh. The Embodied Mind and Its Challenge to Western Thought*. New York: Basic Books.

MARS, The Fraunhofer IMK Research Group, Media Arts and Research Studies (MARS) [Established in 1997, MARS' approach focuses on the generation of artistic strategies for the development of media technologies and the productive employment of media technological research in the arts and related fields.] Available at http://www.imk.fraunhofer.de/mars.

Matussek, Peter. 2004. "Der Performative Turn: Wissen als Schauspiel." In *Digitale Transformationen*. Monika Fleischmann and Ulrike Reinhard, eds. Heidelberg, Available at http://netzspannung.org/positions/digital-transformations/theory/.

Merleau-Ponty, Maurice. 1968. *The Visible and the Invisible*, trans. Lingis. Evanston: Northwestern University Press.

Milgram, Paul, Takemura, Haruo, Utsumi, Akira, and Kishin, Fumio. 1994. "Augmented Reality: A Class of Displays on the Reality-Virtuality Continuum." In *Proceedings SPIE: Telemanipulator and Telepresence Technologies*. Vol. 2351, Society of Photo-Optical Instrumentation Engineers, Bellingham, Washington, 1994, pp. 282–92.

Novak, Jasminko. 2002. "Augmenting the Knowledge Bandwidth and Connecting Heterogeneous Expert Communities through Uncovering Tacit Knowledge." In *Proceedings of IEEE*, 4th International Workshop on Knowledge Media Networking, IEEE Computer Society Press, CRL, Kyoto, Japan, July 2002.

Novak, Jasminko, Wurst, Michael, Schneider, Martin, Fleischmann, Monika, and Strauss, Wolfgang. 2003. *Discovering, Visualizing and Sharing Knowledge through Personalized Learning Knowledge Maps—An Agent-Based Approach*. AAAI Spring Symposium on Agent-mediated Knowledge Management (AMKM03). Stanford University, California, 2003.

Paal, Stefan. 2001. "Distributed Extension of Internet Information Systems." In *Proceedings of 13th IASTED International Conference on Parallel and Distributed Computing and Systems* (PDCS 2001), August 21–24, 2001. Anaheim, California.

Paal, Stefan, Kammüller, Reiner, and Freisleben, Bernd. 2005. "Crossware: Integration Middleware for Autonomic Cross-Platform Internet Application Environments." *Journal of Integrated Computer-Aided Engineering*. IOS Press.

Paul, Christiane. 2004. Adjunct Curator of New Media Arts at the Whitney Museum of American Art. December 5, 2004. email from New York. Full quote at http://www.energie-passagen.de/presse2.html.

Rheingold, Howard. 2000. *Tools for Thought. The History and Future of Mind-Expanding Technology*. Cambridge, MA: The MIT Press. Available at http://www.rheingold.com/texts/tft/14.html.

Schiesser, Giaco. 2004. "Arbeit am und mit EigenSinn. Medien—Kunst—Ausbildung." In *Digitale Transformationen*. Monika Fleischmann and Ulrike Reinhard, eds. Heidelberg. Available at http://netzspannung.org/positions/digital-transformations/theory/.

Strauss, Wolfgang, and Fleischmann, Monika. 1996. "The Role of Design and the Mediation of Contents." *Proceedings CADEX '96 IEEE, Computergraphics.*

Strauss, Wolfgang, and Fleischmann, Monika. 2001. "Imagine Space Fused with Data." In *Proceedings of Cast01—Living in Mixed Realities.* September 21–22. Schloß Birlinghoven, Sankt Augustin, Germany 2001, pp. 41–45. Available at http://www.netzspannung.org/version1/extensions/cast01-proceedings/pdf/by_name/Strauss.pdf.

Strauss, Wolfgang, Fleischmann, Monika, et al. 1999a. "Staging the Space of Mixed Reality—Reconsidering the Concept of a Multi-user Environment." *Proceedings VRML 99—Fourth Symposium on the Virtual Reality Modeling Language*, pp. 93–98. Paderborn, Germany. Available at http://www.nada.kth.se/erena/emuse.html.

Strauss, Wolfgang, Fleischmann, Monika, et al. 1999b. *The eRENA Report: Linking between Real and Virtual Spaces.* Available at http://www.imk.fraunhofer.de/images/mars/erena99_D6_2.pdf.

Strauss, Wolfgang, Fleischmann, Monika, et al. 2002. "Knowledge Discovery and Memory Space as Asymmetric Information." In *IEEE Proceedings CA 2002 Computer Animation.* Geneva, Switzerland.

Strauss, Wolfgang, Fleischmann, Monika, Denzinger, Jochen, et al. 2003. "Information Jukebox—A Semi-Public Device for Presenting Multimedia Information Content." In *Personal and Ubiquitous Computing.* Vol. 7. Springer. London. Available at http://www.springerlink.com/app/home/contribution.asp?wasp=gaf8yjqqlq5qy7hp9g7t&referrer=parent&backto=searcharticlesresults,4,6;.

Trogemann, Georg. 2004. Müssen Medienkünstler programmieren können? In *Digitale Transformationen.* Heidelberg: Verlagsgesellschaft. Available at http://netzspannung.org/positions/digital-transformations/theory/.

Turkle, Sherry. 2004. Professor of the Social Studies of Science and Technology and Director, MIT Initiative on Technology and Self Program in Science, Technology, and Society. Statement sent from Boston. November 11, 2004. Full quote at http://www.energie-passagen.de/presse2.html.

Welsch, Wolfgang. 1997. "Aesthetics Beyond Aesthetics." *Proceedings of the XIIIth International Congress of Aesthetics, Lahti 1995.* Vol. III: *Practical Aesthetics in Practice and Theory.* Martti Honkanen, ed. Helsinki, pp. 18–37.

8

Visually Encoding Numbers Utilizing Prime Factors

Kenneth A. Huff

From the first time our fingers trace the spiral of a seashell, our lives are permeated with the joy of discovery. Forms, patterns, and experiences are layered in our memories and become part of the fundamental cognitive framework through which we identify and classify the world. Tapping into these primal connections, this work evokes a desire to understand and makes possible the thrill of discovering something new.

The creations are abstract, organic, three-dimensional (3D) constructions and while the subject matter is entirely imagined, the works are highly detailed, photorealistic.

Inspiration is drawn from a variety of natural patterns and forms, combining ideas from a number of sources rather than creating literal reconstructions. Overarching themes based on ideas from mathematics and the sciences also weave through the body of work. The arches, loops, and whorls of a fingerprint might be translated into arrangements of a multitude of small objects, which in turn are inspired by electron micrographs of sintered ceramic powders. The iridescence of a beetle might be applied to forms inspired by the twisting surfaces of a wilting leaf or the spiral forms of a fossilized mollusk shell. A monolithic form based on a mathematical knot may be constructed from materials reminiscent of geological sedimentation patterns.

Especially intriguing have been patterns found within groups of similar objects, such as the leaves on a tree. When examining two leaves from a given tree, the similarities make it readily apparent that they are from the same tree or type of tree. Even though they share these many similarities, each leaf is unique in its fine details.

Touching on many of these ideas, a recent theme in the body of work explores the use of many similar forms with unique variations created by using the prime factorizations of positive integers as the genetic construction codes. This theme is the basis for the *Encoding with Prime Factors* series.

To explain this new theme, some of the many specific sources of inspiration and some previous work that led to this series are shown. After describing the reason for focusing on prime numbers and defining terms used in conjunction with this work, illustrations and completed works exemplify the concepts.

In the context of *aesthetic computing*, this work can be seen as an example of the potentially infinite representations of a given idea.

Inspiration

There are many and varied sources of inspiration for this new theme of encoding numbers into virtual objects based on the numbers' prime factors. The two most important are naturally occurring patterns of variation and methods of visually encoding information.

Variation in Nature

The thorns and leaves of the succulent in figure 8.1 are arranged in a twisted grid pattern, with obvious similarity between the individual elements. While the thorns all have the same basic structure, each is unique in its details. The angle at which each emerges from

Figure 8.1   A close-up photograph of a succulent.

the surface, the lengths of and variations in surface texture and color are all examples of these unique details. The variations in the heart-shaped leaves are more pronounced. Placement, proportions, and angles are some of these leaves' varying attributes.

Similarly, the dark lines on the underside of the fern leaf in figure 8.2 show an ordered structure along with a great deal of individual variation.

Visually Encoded Information

The flag-bearing, dancing figures of Sir Arthur Conan Doyle's *The Adventure of the Dancing Men* from *The Return of Sherlock Holmes*; the dots and dashes of Samuel Morse's telegraph code; the bars and spaces of barcodes appearing on everything from books to bath toys— all are examples of visually encoded language or numbers. Each of these visual systems presents in different form information normally experienced in one way; these systems sometimes obscure the information content from immediate or intuitive interpretation, but all are decipherable if we know the system used to encode the original information.

Previous Work

A major theme explored in previous works is the creation of pattern and form in multitudes of similar, yet unique objects. The black tubular form in the foreground of *2002.1*

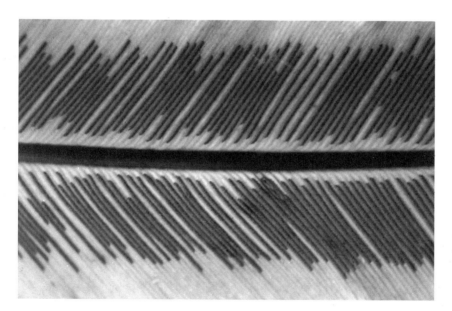

Figure 8.2 A close-up photograph of the underside of a fern leaf.

Figure 8.3   *2002.1,* a virtual 3D construction by the author.

(figures 8.3 and 8.4) is constructed of hundreds of small, layered plates. Each plate has a unique form (variations in thickness and proportion; conformation to the underlying visible or implied forms) and unique surface details (pits, ridges, and color).

The software system in which the work is created, *Maya* from Alias Systems, includes a programming language used to develop new tools to help implement ideas. Most often, these tools deal with the construction or modeling of surfaces or objects and incorporate random, yet controlled, variation. These tools have allowed a dramatic increase in the complexity of the final imagery while maintaining an appropriate level of control over the results. The plates in *2002.1* are examples of the use of such tools. The thickness, proportions, and exact placement of individual plates are based on random numerical values within specified ranges.

Figure 8.4 A detailed close-up of *2002.1.*

An early work incorporating the idea of similar forms with variation is *960810.01* (figure 8.5, completed in 1996). While the grid of sixteen objects is very orderly and structured, each of the objects is unique in its particular configuration.

This work also exemplifies the usefulness of the custom-developed tools. It was created with an earlier generation of the software environment that did not include a programming language. Each of the wires extending from the discs was individually constructed, including placement of the terminating spheres. With current techniques, the mechanics of constructing the forms could have been automated after the initial guiding curves were created.

In *99.13* (figure 8.6, created in 1999), the number of individual objects has increased. Procedural tools were used to create the variations in surface texture, as shown in the detail

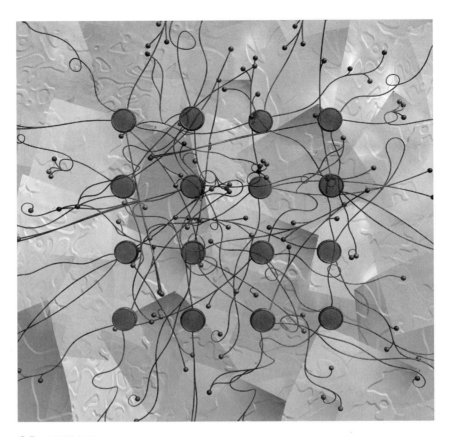

Figure 8.5 *960810.01.*

in figure 8.7. The unique patterning on each of the disc surfaces is based on interference between two simpler grid-based patterns (Huff 1999).

Earlier Work Incorporating Prime Numbers

As a direct predecessor to the *Encoding with Prime Factors* series, works were created in which the numbers of objects depicted were based on the first few prime numbers. Rather than a single object representing a specific number (as in the new series), sets of related objects formed cardinal representations of specific numbers.

The pair of works, *2000.15a* and *2000.15b* (figure 8.8), show two opposite views of the same three-dimensional (3D) structure. The bulbous arms extending from each of the

Figure 8.6 *99.13.*

eight sides of the images represent {1, 2, 3, 5, 7, 11, 13, 17}, the identity and the first seven prime numbers.

Each layer of objects in *2000.24* (figure 8.9) is differentiated by scale and color. Each also contains a specific number of objects—from background to foreground: two, three, five, and seven—representing the first four prime numbers.

Most recently, the quantity of objects in a given work has increased at least an order of magnitude over that in previous works. In the case of *2002.12a* (figure 8.10) more than 2300 objects form nested patterns similar to those found in fingerprints. Here the pattern formed by the group of objects is more important than the specific number of objects or even the individual forms of the objects, as is also the case with *2002.1* in figures 8.3 and 8.4.

Figure 8.7 Detail of *99.13*.

Why Prime Numbers?

In previous work, controlled random values have been used to create variation. For example, objects would be individually and randomly scaled to make each structure unique. The random values involved were always within a specified range and frequently weighted to a particular portion of the range. In *99.16* (figure 8.11, created in 1999), each object is made of up two smaller objects, a rounded-edge disc and a sphere. The sphere and the discs were randomly scaled for each pairing, creating hundreds of unique groups.

This technique was excellent for producing variation, and artistic control was maintained by managing the range of random values along with the forms involved. More structure and control was desired, however. Rather than having pattern and structure

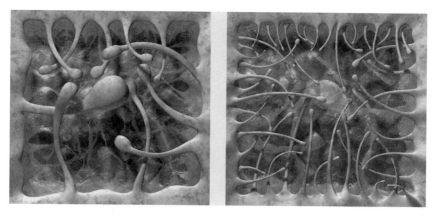

Figure 8.8 *2000.15a* (left) and *2000.15b*.

only in the placement of the objects, as in *2002.12a* (figure 8.10), we felt a need to create pattern, structure, and meaning in the individual objects themselves.

A first thought was to use the sequence of digits from *pi* (3.141592653589...), selecting sequential groups of digits (for example, "314," "159," etc.) to determine the structure of objects. We quickly realized that unless the objects were visually connected to show the original sequence, the result would be the random numbers used before. The sequence of digits in a particular work also would always have to start at the beginning (3.14...) for the encoded values to be placed in a meaningful context.

The idea of using prime numbers—a known, identifiable sequence of numbers with a rich intellectual history—seemed appropriate. The sequence of prime numbers has random characteristics and contains interesting patterns. As an infinite sequence of numbers, it would ensure no limit of possible variations. Once decoded, the content or meaning of an object would be readily understand—a number.

Unlike the digits of *pi*, with which each object encodes a random sequence of digits, encoding prime numbers results in unique objects, each with a specific and unique identification. At this point, the "prime number encoding" pieces were completed, including *2000.15a*, *2000.15b*, and *2000.24* (figures 8.8 and 8.9). In these works, a number of methods were used to create variation, including changing scale and surface details of individual objects, but a specific numerical content also was included in the number of objects portrayed.

Many sketches show sequences of numbers in which the objects representing prime numbers were differentiated from those representing composite numbers, revealing the

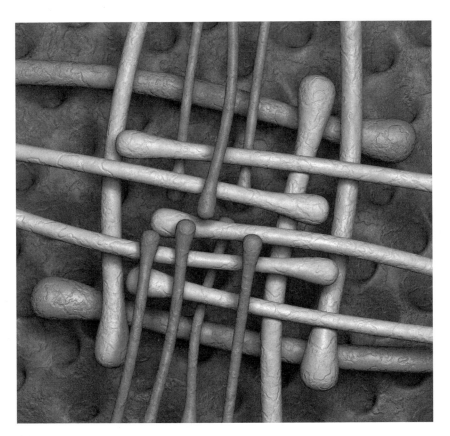

Figure 8.9 *2000.24.*

patterns of the placement of primes in the positive integer sequence. Though the idea of representing sequences of numbers was intriguing, we wished not to be bound to using sequences. The differentiation of prime numbers had meaning only in the context of the other numbers in the sequence, and the number of objects in a group, not the structure of the individual objects themselves, was encoding additional information. Over time, these ideas and sketches evolved into the current series.

An Artist's Lexicon

These works are not meant to be purely representational, in the sense of conveying a precise interpretation of a particular physical object. At the same time, they also are not purely abstract, as they contain objects with a physical level of detail and realism and are

Figure 8.10 *2002.12a.*

Figure 8.11 *99.16.*

initially often mistaken for photographs. This is part of the work's very purposeful ambiguity. The idea that these things look as if they could exist, that they simultaneously resemble any number of forms, objects, or materials in a physically realistic manner, makes more powerful the realization that they are entirely imagined artifices.

Early on, we decided not to give the work verbal titles, instead using numbers based on the year a piece was created. While verbal labels or interpretations of individual works is undesirable, maintaining a consistent vocabulary when discussing its themes is very useful. Some of the terms are generalizations or partial definitions from mathematics; others are words and phrases that have come to be used to describe specific ideas, objects, and patterns.

A *prime number* is a positive integer greater than 1 that is wholly divisible (no remainder) only by itself and 1. Positive integers other than 1 that are not prime are called *composite numbers*. The *factors* of a positive integer are the integers that wholly divide it. The fundamental theorem of arithmetic (Hardy and Wright) states that every positive integer greater than 1 can be expressed uniquely as a product of prime numbers, apart from the rearrangement of factors. This unique group is known as the set of *prime factors* of the particular number. Forty-two is a composite number. Its factors are $\{1, 2, 3, 7, 21, 42\}$ and its prime factors are $\{2, 3, 7\}$. Forty-three, a prime number, has factors of $\{1, 43\}$.

Source integers are the positive integers—those integers greater than or equal to 1. This is the numerical domain of this body of work.

An *encoded object* is the embodiment or manifestation of a single source integer and is constructed of one or more *elements*—individual visual indications (form, material, color, etc.) representing some part of the encoding of a particular source integer, similar to the way the dots and dashes visually represent the letters and numbers of Morse Code. The combination of virtual forms and materials and the rules that govern their application in a specific way to visually encode the prime factorization of particular source integers is an *encoding scheme*.

The term *identity* refers to the multiplicative identity of one in the series of positive integers and also to a single, specific element in each encoded object. The identity in mathematics is the number 1 and is so called because multiplying any number by 1 results in the original number. (This is a simplified version of the mathematical concepts of identity and multiplicative identity.) In that sense and in this work, the number 1 also is a factor of any number. Great advantage is taken of this fact by including a specific element in each encoded object, which not only encodes the multiplicative identity of 1 but also provides a visual starting point from which the object can be read or decoded. The *identity element* in a sense marks the beginning of the sentence that is an encoded number.

By using an identity element and always using it as the starting point for interpretation, we may orient the encoded object in 3D space without constraint. Encoded objects may be constructed from left to right, right to left, clockwise, counterclockwise, up, down, or sideways—in whatever direction best suits the theme and composition of the encoding scheme and the final work. (Figure 8.16 shows an example of the ambiguity that arises when an identity element is not used.)

The *reading spine* of an encoded object starts at the identity element and continues through the encoded elements in the order in which they are encoded and interpreted. In some encoding schemes, the reading spine is visible; in others it is implied.

Each positive integer greater than 1 can be factored into a unique sequence of prime factors. Each of the prime factors of a given integer is a *used factor*. Those prime numbers that are not factors of a given integer and fall between 1 and the largest prime factor for the given integer are considered *skipped primes*. The idea of a skipped prime is distinct from the mathematical concept of a *prime gap*, defined as the number of positive integers between two consecutive prime numbers (for example, the prime gap between 23 and 29 would be 5). Prime numbers larger than the largest factor of a given integer are ignored. Because of this, an encoded object will always end with a used factor element.

Referring back to the prime factorization of 42, the prime number 5 is not a factor of 42 and is therefore a skipped prime. Two, 3, and 7 are all used factors, while prime numbers greater than 7 would be ignored in the encoding of 42. Forty-three is the fourteenth prime number, and encoding it involves skipping the first thirteen primes (2, 3, 5, 7, 11, 13, 17, 19, 23, 29, 31, 37, and 41).

Indicator elements are those that encode the fact that either a single factor in the sequence of prime numbers is used (to the first power) or a single prime is skipped in the encoding of a specific source integer.

The purpose of a *bracket element* varies with whether the bracket is showing a used factor (with an exponent greater than 1) or a series of skipped primes in the sequence of prime numbers. Bracket elements for used factors enclose the exponent of the factor. The exponent is recursively encoded following the same rules as the overall encoding. Brackets for skipped primes enclose the encoding of the number of primes in the sequence of prime numbers to be passed over in the interpretation of the visual encoding. (Figure 8.26 will illustrate that the nesting of brackets can cause ambiguity if the opening and closing brackets are not visually differentiated.)

Additional Considerations

In the context of this work, it is important to remember that the prime factors of a given source integer are always arranged in ascending order. It is the entire sequence of elements

Identity	i
Used indicator	|
Skipped indicator	-
Used opening bracket	[
Used closing bracket	]
Skipped opening bracket	{
Skipped closing bracket	}

Figure 8.12 The symbols of a text encoding scheme.

and the order in which they appear that are critical to the encoding of a source integer. If the prime factors were not listed sequentially, there would be no point of reference from which to interpret the individual elements, let alone the entire encoded object. The sequence of all prime numbers also is always considered in ascending order, starting with the prime integer 2.

Development of the Concept and Some Examples

Encoding Using Text Symbols

It is necessary to differentiate seven unique visual elements: the identity, a used indicator, a used opening bracket, a used closing bracket, a skipped indicator, a skipped opening bracket, and a skipped closing bracket. During the development of this series of works, a text encoding scheme was created (figure 8.12) that is used as a shorthand and fed into the custom software tools to communicate the structures of encoded objects. The text encodings for the numbers 1 through 20 are shown in figure 8.13.

An illustrative encoding scheme was used for the objects in the figure, which shows the source integers, the encoded objects, and the text encoding. Some encoded objects merit special comment, rendering the remainder self-explanatory. For reference, the prime numbers in this sequence, indicated in the figure, are 2, 3, 5, 7, 11, 13, 17, and 19.

One, the identity element, is encoded using a medium gray form and subsequently appears at the beginning of each encoded object. In this scheme, the reading spine starts at the identity element and extends to the right, as illustrated in figure 8.15.

Two, the first prime number, is encoded with the identity element followed by a dark element serving as the used factor indicator.

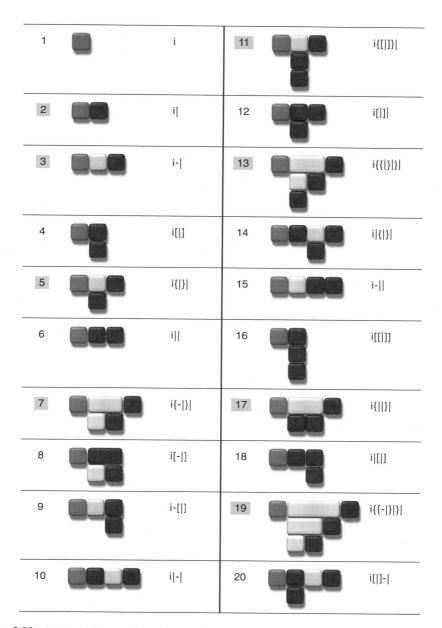

Figure 8.13 An illustrative encoding scheme applied to the numbers "1" through "20."

Three, the second prime number, is encoded with the used factor indicator at the right end of the encoded object while a skipped prime indicator (the light gray element) appears in the middle position representing the skipping of the prime integer 2.

Four, the first composite number, has a prime factorization of 2 to the second power (2^2). The exponent of the prime factor 2 is indicated by placing the encoded representation of 2 (less the identity element) adjacent to the factor element. While not readily apparent in this encoded object, the used factor element immediately to the right of the identity element is actually a used bracket element. This bracketing becomes more apparent with the skipped prime brackets of the encodings of the numbers 7, 13, 17, and 19 and the used factor bracket of the encoding of the number 8, as each includes elongated elements spanning multiple adjacent elements.

Five, the third prime number, is encoded by skipping the first two prime integers (2 and 3) and using the third prime integer (5). Similar to the indication of the exponent of 2 in the encoding of the number 4, two primes are being skipped; the encoding of the number 2 is therefore placed below the skip element (just to the right of the identity element). Here, also, the skip element (light gray) is actually a bracket element, but in the case of skip brackets, it is used to show the number of primes passed over rather than the exponent of a used factor.

The prime factorization of 6 is 2 times 3. Each of the first two prime integers is used, and therefore two used indicator elements follow the identity element.

Seven is the fourth prime number. The nature of a bracketing element becomes more apparent here as a skip bracket element extends to run alongside the encoding for the number 3 (the number of primes skipped).

The encoded object for the number 8 includes the first (and in the range of numbers represented in the figure, only) instance of a extended used bracket element, in this case encoding 2 to the third power (2^3).

For the number 13, notice the hierarchy of nested elements (here encoding a skip of five primes) does not include the identity element. As described earlier, the main purpose of the identity element is to establish the start and the reading direction of the encoding. The initial identity element serves this purpose, and any additional identity elements would be extraneous.

Thirteen, 17, and 19, the remaining prime source integers in this sequence, also show a developing pattern for encoded source integers that are prime—the identity, followed by a skipped element of varying complexity, followed by a single used indicator element. This pattern is most apparent when the elements running directly along the reading spine of an encoded object are considered in isolation.

Figure 8.14   The number 712,080 encoded.

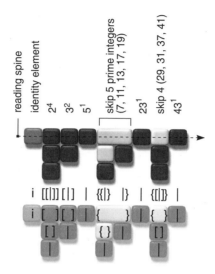

Figure 8.15   The encoding of 712,080 with labeled elements.

As a more complex example of this encoding scheme, 712,080 is encoded in figure 8.14. The text encoding of 712,080 is "i[[l]]{[l]{{l}l}l{[l]}l"; its factors are $2^4 \cdot 3^2 \cdot 5 \cdot 23 \cdot 43$. There are five skipped prime integers between 5 and 23 and four skipped prime integers between 23 and 43. The various elements of the encoding are labeled in figure 8.15, along with relationships between the encoded elements and the elements of the text encoding.

The Necessity of the Identity Element

Mathematically, the identity (and therefore the identity element in this work) does not affect the numerical outcome, but *identity elements* do affect the reading order and therefore the interpretation of encoded objects.

As an example, the encoded object in figure 8.16 is interpreted as "[l-l]l" or $2^{10} \cdot 3^1 = 3,072$, if read from left to right, but as "l[l-l]", or $2^1 \cdot 3^{10} = 118,098$ if read

Figure 8.16 An ambiguous encoded object.

from right to left. The addition of the identity element eliminates ambiguity based on the reading direction.

In addition to eliminating the possibility of multiple interpretations of the same encoded object, the use of an identity element allows complete freedom of orientation for encoded objects in 3D space. This freedom of orientation is used in all of the *Encoding with Prime Factors Series* works that follow (see figures 8.17, 8.19, 8.28, and 8.31).

An Example from the Series

EPF:2003:IV:A:99,961 (figure 8.17) is an example of an implemented encoding scheme. The source integers for the work are 99,961–99,971. Two prime numbers start, finish, and are the only prime numbers in the sequence. Works in the series often represent continuous sequences of source integers. The quantity of numbers in the sequence is often a prime number, and the sequences often start and end with prime integers. The eleven discrete encoded objects are arranged in a clockwise sequential order starting with 99,961 at the three o'clock position.

For each encoded object, each limb signifies either a bracket or an indicator. The main reading spine starts at the large black sphere in the center and ends in a tapered point. All other branches end in small spheres, the color of which is significant. Black spheres are used elements and white spheres are skipped elements. If a limb has no other limbs attached, it is an indicator. Limbs with other limbs branching from them are brackets. Once a limb has branched off the reading spine, the length of the limb is significant, with longer limbs representing brackets. An attached limb is not longer than its parent limb unless it is attached to the reading spine or the length would not cause an encoding ambiguity.

The two prime numbers encoded can be distinguished by the particular sequence and number of limbs. Each has two limbs, a skipped bracket followed by a used indicator. The encoded object for 99,971 (at approximately the two o'clock position in figure 8.15, and the other prime number in the sequence) maintains the pattern of a skipped bracket followed by a single used indicator.

The text encoding of 99,961 is "i{[|]|{[|]}|{{-|}|}|}|". Figure 8.18 highlights some specific manifestations of the elements and bracketed element groups; 99,961 is the 9589th

Figure 8.17 *EPF:2003:IV:A:99,961.*

99,961 : i { [|] | { [|] } | { { - | } | } | } |

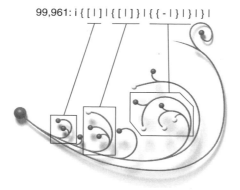

Figure 8.18 The object from *EPF:2003:IV:A:99,961*, which encodes 99,961.

Visually Encoding Numbers Utilizing Prime Factors

155

prime number. The most complicated branch encodes the skipping of the first 9588 prime integers.

During the creation of this work, the first to use this encoding scheme, we realized the arbitrary nature with which the forms were constructed inhibits establishing larger patterns in the sequence of objects. The image has unique, obviously related structures, but the deeper patterns of the encoding scheme are hidden by the wide range of variations in limb structure and placement. While there is some sense of order, the rules of construction should be stricter to highlight larger patterns. The viewer can potentially decode the objects into the appropriate source integer, but grander patterns, such as the occurrence of prime numbers within a longer sequence of numbers, are indistinguishable.

It was decided that the source of variation in the objects should be based primarily and most significantly on the encoded source integer rather than arbitrary or random changes in structure. Figures 8.19, 8.20, and 8.21 show a work in which the encoding scheme defines the structural changes in a more constrained fashion.

Encoded in *EPF:2003:VI:A:673* (figure 8.19) are the forty-seven source integers from 673 to 719, inclusive. The seven prime numbers in that range of integers are 673, 677, 683, 691, 701, and 709, differentiated by the darker material. The encoded objects are arranged on a rough 5 by 5 grid of two layers. Objects are placed on the grid, left to right, from top to bottom, starting in the upper left corner. Odd numbers appear on the bottom layer, even numbers on the top layer. This stacking is shown in the detail of the work in figure 8.20.

Introduced is the idea of *secondary encoded objects*, which encode specific integers but are not necessarily decipherable because of their placement in the composition. In this work, the large-scale backdrop objects encode 380 through 417, leftover integers from the number ranges used as primary encoding sources in the *VI:A* series.

The encoding scheme consists of straight limbs optionally terminated by a square block for used indicators and used brackets. A limb with additional limbs attached to it is a bracket element. The identity element is the square block with a hole in the center, and the reading spine is the limb extending out from the identity element.

Children limbs alternate orientation along their parent limb. For odd numbers, the first child limb branches in a counterclockwise direction from the parent, and in a clockwise direction for even numbers. This rule applies recursively to all child branches.

The objects built using this encoding scheme are primarily planar. Normally, each alternating child branch is separated from its siblings and from the base of its parent branch by a fixed distance. In cases where elements would collide, additional space was inserted on an interactive, somewhat arbitrary basis. In figure 8.21, the encoded object for 684 has had two units of additional space added at the base of the third branch, which encodes the skipping of five prime integers.

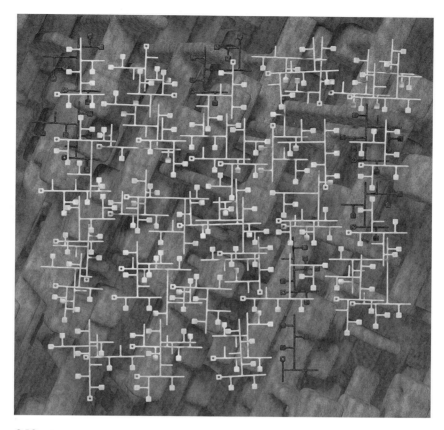

Figure 8.19 *EPF:2003:VI:A:673.*

Two Types of Encoding Schemes

All the encoding schemes created fall into two major categories: hierarchical and sequential. The examples given so far have all been *hierarchical* schemes. The encoded object has a central axis (the "reading spine," not necessarily a straight line) connected to which are similar groups of encoded elements representing used factor exponents greater than one or sequences of one or more skipped prime factors. Elements could also be stacked (imagine the encoded objects in figure 8.13 as lateral cross-sections of larger forms). *Sequential* encoding schemes, the other category, consist of elements in a series, one element after another.

The nesting of used and skipped bracket elements makes all encoding schemes hierarchies, but here these terms are used in connection with the construction and arrangement

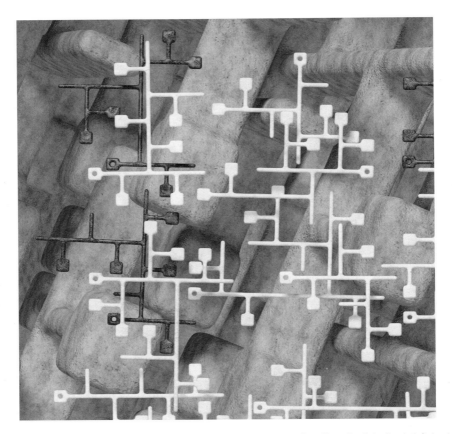

Figure 8.20 Detail of *EPF:2003:VI:A:673* showing the objects encoding (from back to front, left to right) 673 (prime), 674, 675, and 676 in the top row; 683 (prime), 684, 685, and 686 in the bottom row.

of the visual encoding elements. When the elements are stacked or branching, I refer to them as "hierarchical," while encoding elements arranged in a line are "sequential." Sequential encoding schemes always use distinct elements for opening and closing brackets, whereas hierarchical schemes usually only use one element to encode both the opening and closing brackets.

The scalariform markings of the plant leaf shown in figure 8.22 are an example of a natural pattern that served as the inspiration for a number of sequential encoding schemes.

The shorthand text encoding scheme described earlier (in figures 8.12 and 8.13) is an example of a sequential encoding scheme. In that scheme, each of the seven necessary encoding elements is represented by a distinct symbol. Another example of a sequential encoding scheme is shown in figure 8.23.

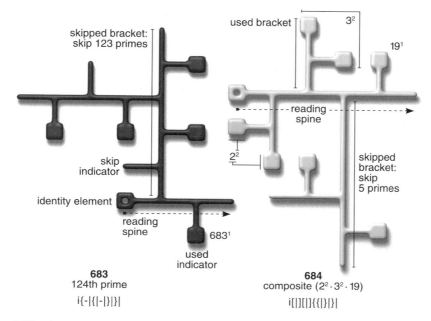

skipped bracket:
skip 123 primes

used bracket

3^2

19^1

skip
indicator

reading
spine

identity element

reading
spine

2^2

skipped
bracket:
skip
5 primes

683^1

used
indicator

683
124th prime
i{-|{|-|}|}|

684
composite ($2^2 \cdot 3^2 \cdot 19$)
i[]][[]]{{|}|}|

Figure 8.21 The encoded objects for 683 and 684, isolated, unstacked, and labeled.

Figure 8.22 A close-up photograph of a plant leaf.

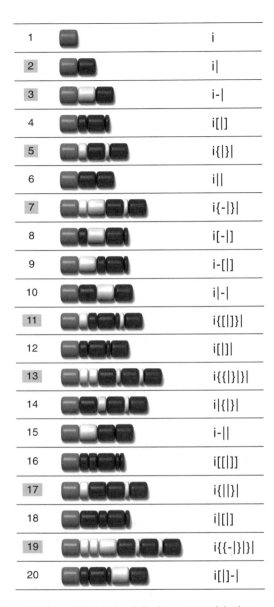

1		i
2		i|
3		i-|
4		i[|]
5		i{|}|
6		i||
7		i{-|}|
8		i[-|]
9		i-[|]
10		i|-|
11		i{[|]}|
12		i[|]|
13		i{{|}|}|
14		i|{|}|
15		i-||
16		i[[|]]
17		i{||}|
18		i|[|]
19		i{{-|}|}|
20		i[|]-|

Figure 8.23 The numbers "1" through "20," encoded using a sequential scheme.

Identity	i	●
Used indicator	|	●
Skipped indicator	-	●
Used opening bracket	[	●
Used closing bracket	]	●
Skipped opening bracket	{	●
Skipped closing bracket	}	●

Figure 8.24 The seven distinct encoding elements of the sequential encoding scheme.

i [[|]][|] | {{ | } | } | { [|]} |

Figure 8.25 A sequential encoding of 712,080.

In this illustrative scheme, the color coding from the hierarchical encoding scheme of figure 8.13 is maintained. Rather than creating elements that visually span other elements to indicate bracketing, two elements, one narrower than the other, are placed on either side of the enclosed elements. The widest elements are the identity, along with the used factor and skipped factor indicators (figure 8.24).

Encoding 712,080 with this sequential encoding scheme results in the encoded object shown in figure 8.25 (compare this with the hierarchically encoded version in figure 8.14). Once again, the text encoding is "i[[|]][|]|{{|}|}|{[|]}|" and is shown above the corresponding elements.

A Sequential Ambiguity

During the development of a number of sequential encoding schemes, an ambiguity became apparent that emphasized the need to differentiate opening and closing brackets.

Assuming that the light gray element is the identity and the narrow and wide dark elements represent used brackets and used indicators, respectively (for the moment, opening and closing brackets are not differentiated), the encoded object shown in figure 8.26 can be interpreted in two ways. Converted to the text encoding, the two possible

Figure 8.26 A sequentially encoded object with bracket ambiguity.

i [| [|] |]   i [|] | [|]

2^{90}  300

Figure 8.27 A sequentially encoded object without bracket ambiguity.

valid interpretations are "i[|[|]|]" and "i[|]|[|]". The first interpretation encodes 2^{90} (1,237,940,039,285,380,274,899,124,224), the second encodes 300 ($2^2 \cdot 3 \cdot 5^2$).

By creating some discernible difference between opening and closing brackets, we eliminate the ambiguity (figure 8.27). In this case, opening brackets are encoded with medium-width elements, and closing brackets with the narrowest elements. The number encoded on the left of the figure is 2^{90}, and 300 is encoded on the right.

An Example of a Sequential Encoding Scheme

EPF:2003:V:A:997,141 (figure 8.28) encodes the sequence of twenty-three numbers (itself a prime number) 997,141–997,163. The sequence starts and ends with prime numbers. It contains three additional prime numbers (997,147; 997,151; and 997,153), for a total of five prime numbers (itself a prime number). Each of the twenty-three spiral forms encodes a single source integer. A light gray identity indicator is at the center of the spiral, and the reading spine extends from the center outward. Used elements are encoded with a white material and skipped elements are in a black material. The widest elements are indicators, the medium-width are opening brackets, and the narrowest are closing brackets. The objects encoding prime numbers are differentiated by scale and by the reading spine spiraling in the opposite direction (counterclockwise, compared to clockwise for the encoded composite source integers). The solid dark spiral forms in the background refer to the fact the twenty-three numbers encoded are part of an infinite series of numbers.

The encoded objects are arranged on a 5-by-5 cell grid, read from left to right, top to bottom. The diagonal grouping of the objects encoding prime numbers seen in the top three rows is an artifact of the number of columns of the grid and the fact that all prime numbers are odd numbers (with the exception of the number 2). If the grid-cell dimensions had been different, other diagonal or vertical groupings might have appeared. Figure 8.29 shows the positions of odd numbers on a grid with an odd number of columns compared to a grid with an even number of columns.

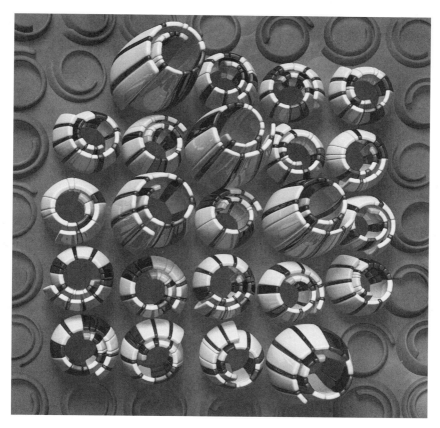

Figure 8.28 *EPF:2003:V:A:997,141,* an example of a sequential encoding scheme.

1	2	3	4	5
6	7	8	9	10
11	12	13	14	15
16	17	18	19	20
21	22	23	24	25

1	2	3	4	5	6
7	8	9	10	11	12
13	14	15	16	17	18
19	20	21	22	23	24
25	26	27	28	29	30

Figure 8.29 Comparison of placement of odd numbers on grids with odd and even number of columns.

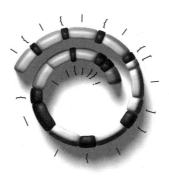

Figure 8.30 From *EPF:2003:V:A:997,141*, a cross-section of the object encoding 997,151.

The isolated encoded object in figure 8.30 represents the third prime number in the sequence, 997,151, and is a cross-section of the top of the original object shown in figure 8.28 (second column, third row). The text encoding for the integer is "i{{{|}||{-|{|{{|}|}|}|}|}|" and the figure shows these text elements in relation to their corresponding 3D representations; 997,151 is the 78,296th prime number. The majority of the elements, with the exception of the first and last, encode the skipping of 78,295 prime integers.

Expanding on the encoding scheme for *EPF:2003:V:A:997,141*, figure 8.31 shows a similar scheme implemented in a work consisting of twenty-five 1-foot-square panels. The objects in each panel encode nonoverlapping sequences of seven numbers starting and ending on a prime. Starting from one, the first such sequence is 5 through 11 and is encoded in the panel in the upper left corner of the work. That panel is one of nine panels in which encoded sequences contain three prime integers, while the remaining panels each encode sequences with two prime integers. The last panel in the lower right corner, encodes 383 through 389. The panels are arranged from left to right, top to bottom. The darker objects around the perimeter of each panel do not encode numbers.

This encoding scheme uses a narrow dark plate at the center of the spiral as the identity element. Transparent plates are skip elements and the opaque are used elements. The widest plates are indicators, with the medium-width and narrowest plates encoding opening and closing brackets, respectively. The object in figure 8.32 encodes 273, the prime factorization of which is $3^1 \cdot 7^1 \cdot 13^1$. The text encoding would be "i-|-|-|". The prime integers 2, 5, and 11 are skipped in the encoding and are represented by the transparent plates. Figure 8.33 shows this encoded object in the context of its panel, *EPF:2003:V:B:271.*

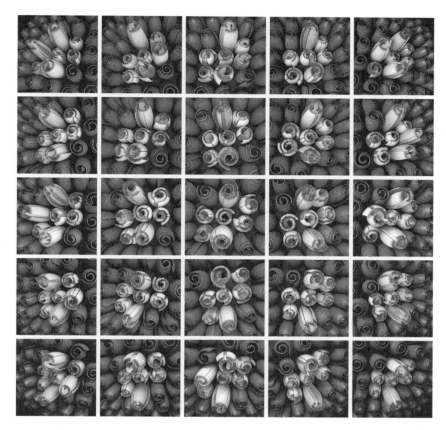

Figure 8.31 *EPF:2003:V:B:5::383(25).*

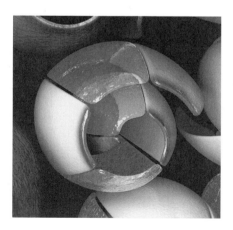

Figure 8.32 *EPF:2003:V:B:271,* the twentieth panel of *EPF:2003:V:B:5::383(25).*

Visually Encoding Numbers Utilizing Prime Factors

Figure 8.33 A detail of *EPF:2003:V:B:271* showing the object encoding 273.

Conclusion

This chapter has presented a method to create the infinite multitudes of similar yet uniquely varied objects integral to one artist's body of work. This process is not meant as a practical alternative representation of numerical information. For that purpose, one of many difficulties would be the requirement of prior knowledge not only of the sequence of prime numbers but also the order in which they occur. Those practicalities aside, the process does give a guaranteed and discernible set of unique variations while maintaining the possibility of an additional layer of meaning. As the purposeful ambiguities in the entire body of work allow for and embrace multiple interpretations, aesthetic computing allows for the individualization of a computing experience, recognizing the lifetime of experience that make each of us unique.

Acknowledgments

The author would like to thank Sean Rush, without whose support, encouragement, and feedback, his work and life would not be as rich. Gratitude is also expressed to Dr. Paul Fishwick whose interest, enthusiasm, and invitation to participate in this book are all greatly appreciated. Many of the works shown were completed using software made available through grants by Alias Systems. All of the *Encoding with Prime Factors* series works were rendered with software provided under a grant from mental images.

Note

Full-color images and illustrations for this chapter can be found at http://www.kennethahuff.com/epf/ac/. The continuing *Encoding with Prime Factors* series is fully documented at http://www.kennethahuff.com/epf/.

References

Hardy, G. H., and Wright, E. M. 1979. "Statement of the Fundamental Theorem of Arithmetic". In *An Introduction to the Theory of Numbers*, 5th ed. New York: Oxford University Press, p. 3.

Huff, Kenneth A. 1999. "The Application of a Non-periodic Tiling Pattern in the Creation of Artistic Images." In *SIGGRAPH 99 Conference Abstracts and Applications*; ACM SIGGRAPH, p. 209. Also available (expanded and illustrated) on the artist's website at http://www.kennethahuff.com/Presentations/SIGGRAPH99Sketch/.

9

From the Poesy of Programming to Research as Art Form

Laurent Mignonneau and Christa Sommerer

Since the early 1990s we have been developing and programming interactive computer systems that take the users' interaction input as important components for self-generating software structures that are not predefined by us as artists but constantly change, grow, develop, evolve, and adapt to the environment.

One of our main goals in creating these systems is to show how interaction is a key component in the creation of complexity, diversity, and emergence, not only in real life, but in artificial systems as well. We have applied principles of complex adaptive systems and artificial life to the creation of interactive software structures that constantly change when users interact with them. We created dynamic interactive artworks that are not static, but instead process-based, open-ended, adaptable, and environment centered. We call this "Art as a Living System" (Sommerer and Mignonneau 1998, 148–61), in reference to natural systems that are always dynamic, flexible, and input dependent. Before describing some of the research principles we apply to creating these artworks, let us consider a few basic questions on the role of programming, the function of the artist/programmer, and the importance of research and development in our artworks.

Research as Art Form

For each of our interactive artworks we have designed and developed custom-made software programs as well as special hardware interfaces (Mignonneau and Sommerer 2000). We concentrate a significant amount of energy on finding novel interfaces as well as novel programming algorithms for novel artistic concepts. Our artistic activity has become a research activity and the artworks we create have become research projects that expand and explore the status quo of what is known and commercially available.

A main motivation for writing our own software programs and developing our own hardware interfaces, rather than using off-the-shelf software packages or commercially available interface technology, is our wish to develop systems that investigate new questions and explore novel technical, conceptual, and artistic approaches. As media artists, we have chosen to become artists/researchers or researchers/artists who define and shape new questions of creation, and set out to explore the forefront of creativity and digital technology, investigating the very question of creation, invention, and discovery.

Beyond End-User Art and the Art of Discovery

Having worked for around 10 years at advanced research centers in Germany (Fraunhofer Gesellschaft), the United States (Beckmann Institute), and Japan (ATR Advanced Telecommunications Research Center), we witnessed the usual time lag of a few years before a novel research prototype becomes part of the software or hardware market. This means that available software and hardware products usually lag a few years behind the already scientifically and technically explored.

Working as an artist in research and development thus not only provides insight into today's visions and inventions that might shape the future, it also enables one to define new artistic research topics that might as well shape the future of art, design, product, and society at large. While it is of course perfectly legitimate to be an "end-user artist," developing her artwork through the currently available software or hardware packages, works produced with these packages always have a certain kind of creative limitation and aesthetic resemblance. The liberty of designing one's own software and creating one's own hardware could be compared to mixing one's own colors from pigments instead of using a paint set with premixed colors. It is experimenting with the details as well as the sometimes accidental discovery of novel features that make programming itself a highly creative experience. During the programming process, essential new discoveries can be made by chance or even by misconception. The programming language itself is designed to be used in a certain way (the grammar and the words, the syntax), but what this language describes has not been fixed, leaving the programmer great freedom to use this language. Programming is a process of constant discovery, and asking others to create a program on one's behalf excludes many creative details essential to the work's final look and even its final content.

The Poesy of Programming

Programming can be compared to writing a novel: even though the language of the novel is defined (say, French, German, or English), its content is subject to the author's imagination and creative expression. The same holds true for the art of programming: each programmer has his or her own code writing style, and the results usually depend on the programmer's skill and experiences. Especially in the area of interface programming, which can be quite complex in its need to consider user input, there are large differences between programming styles and the personal creativity of the programmer.

Returning to the novel metaphor, one could imagine asking two writers to produce a novel on the same topic, using the same language. The resulting two novels will certainly differ greatly, even though both authors may even have used the same words. One of the novels might be more interesting than the other, depending on how this author managed to convey his or her imagination and ideas. Full control over language combined with complete openness toward discoveries and experiments help an author produce an outcome (be it a computer program or a novel) that expresses and transcends his or her creative vision.

The Role of the Code in Our Artworks

Let us now look at the function of code in our own artworks. One of our main goals in creating interactive systems is to show how dynamic and complex life is. Or, as Dennett puts it, "William Paley was right about one thing: our need to explain how it can be that the universe contains many wonderfully designed things" (Dennett 1995).

Deeply fascinated by the workings of nature, we created several artificial systems reflecting on real-life systems by recreating and interpreting some of its beauty and complexity of design. From analyzing principles of nature, such as the emergence of life, the emergence of order and complexity, and the dynamics of interactions, we were inspired to create artificial systems that model some of these processes.

To do this, it became necessary to create software structures that themselves are dynamic and open-ended. Over the years, we have been instrumental in developing and establishing a research field called Artificial Life Art, Generative Art, and art that creates complex adaptive systems through interactivity (Sommerer 2001). Let us briefly summarize some of the underlying research areas.

Complex Systems

Complex system sciences study how parts of a system give rise to the collective behaviors of the system and how the system interacts with its environment. Social systems forming, in part, out of people, the brain forming out of neurons, molecules forming out of atoms, and the weather forming out of air currents are all examples of complex systems.

Complex system science, as a field of research, has emerged in the past decade. It approaches the question of how life on earth could have appeared by searching for inherent structures in living systems and trying to define common patterns within these structures.

A whole branch of research—not only within biology but also crossing into physics and computer science—deals with complex dynamic systems and can be seen as the attempt to find basic organizing principles.

Complex systems science focuses on certain questions about parts, wholes, and relationships. Efforts to describe and define the notions of complexity have been made by many scholars including Ashby (1962), Baas (1994), Bennett (1988), Cariani (1992), Casti (1994), Chaitin (1992), Jantsch (1980), Kauffman (1993), Landauer (1988), Langton (1989), Pagels (1988), Wicken (1987), Wolfram (1984) and Yates (1987), among others.

Although there is no exact definition of a complex system, we now understand that when a set of evolving autonomous particles or agents interact, the resulting global system displays emergent collective properties, evolution, and critical behavior that exhibits universal characteristics. Such a system is fundamentally novel and not divisible into its mere parts. These agents or particles may be complex molecules, cells, living organisms, animal groups, human societies, industrial firms, or competing technologies. All of these elements are aggregates of matter, energy, and information that display the following characteristics:

- couple to each other;
- learn, adapt, and organize;
- mutate and evolve;
- expand their diversity;
- react to their neighbors and to external control;
- explore their options;
- replicate;
- organize a hierarchy of higher-order structures.

Emergence

In the study of complex systems, the idea of emergence indicates the rising patterns, structures, or properties that do not seem adequately explained by the system's preexisting components and their interaction alone. Emergence becomes increasingly important as an explanatory construct when the system is characterized by the following features:

- when the organization of the system, that is, its global order, appears to be more salient and of a different kind than the components alone;
- when the components can be replaced without an accompanying decommissioning of the whole system; and

- when the new global patterns or properties are radically novel with respect to the preexisting components and the emergent patterns are unpredictable, nondeducible, and irreducible.

Interactivity

Interactivity plays a central role in the creation of complexity and emergence. By coupling to each other and exchanging salient information that, in return, triggers the creation of new information, interactivity can be described as a key principle in the organization and transformation of components within a complex dynamical system.

Emergent Design through Dynamic Programming Structures and User Interaction

Intrigued by the idea that order, structure, and design can emerge through the interaction of particles or agents in a system, we explored (since 1992) complex dynamical systems that are open-ended, process-based, adaptable, and environment centered.

From an artistic point of view, we aim to create artworks that are like dynamical living systems (Sommerer and Mignonneau 1998a, 148–61), as they constantly change, adapt, and diversify according to their environmental input parameters. The idea of creating a dynamic and emergent software structure also requires a new programming approach: instead of asking the computer to execute only a given set of instructions, the code should reorganize itself "on-the-fly," while the dynamic input parameters are processed.

Just as in natural complex dynamical systems, components of the software code and the users' input parameters from the interaction are coupled to each other; this leads to an adaptive system that can reorganize itself, mutates and evolves, expands its diversity, reacts to its neighbors and external control, explores its options, and replicates and finally organizes a hierarchy of higher-order structures.

Emergent Aesthetics

It is of artistic interest in this process is to see how creation (whether natural or artistic) is an emergent property that can produce unexpected and novel results. Through the dynamic software structure and a linked user interaction, novel content and new forms of expression can emerge. The final outcome is not so much a predetermined "result" as a dynamic process of constant reconfiguration and adaptation. The aesthetic quality of the outcome becomes secondary as the focus shifts to the process creating this constantly changing and evolving output.

Figures 9.1 and 9.2 show our work "Life Spacies," created in 1997. We use language as a genetic code to create artificial online creatures that live, mate, evolve, feed on text, and

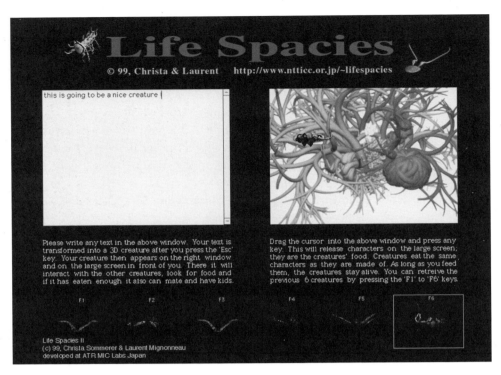

Figure 9.1 "Life Spacies II"—graphical user interface. Written text is used as the genetic code and food for artificial life creatures. "Life Spacies II" ©1997–99, Christa Sommerer & Laurent Mignonneau, collection of the NTT-ICC Museum Japan.

die. Users can create these creatures by simply writing text and feeding the creatures with text characters. In this work, the code of language is used literally, as the genetic code for artificial life forms. An in-depth description of this system is provided by Sommerer, Mignonneau, and Lopez-Gulliver (1999). Some of the earlier generative artworks we created since 1992, using dynamic and generative image processes, are described in the literature (Sommerer and Mignonneau 1997; 1998b; 2000).

Generating and Interacting with Complexity on the Internet

The Internet is an ever-expanding database of images, text, and sound files that currently contains several billion documents. These data and their internal organization are constantly changing, as new documents are being uploaded, new websites created, and old links deleted. New connections between various sites are also constantly built, and the

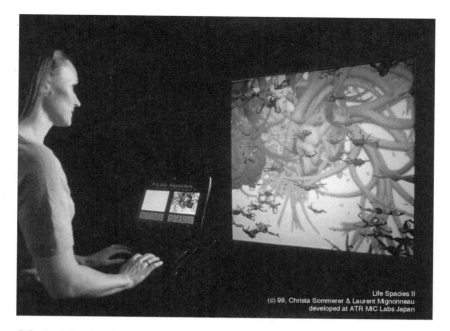

Life Spacies II
(c) 99, Christa Sommerer & Laurent Mignonneau
developed at ATR MIC Labs Japan

Figure 9.2 "Life Spacies II"—user as she creates and feeds various artificial creatures that mate, eat, die, interact, and evolve, creating an open-ended, complex dynamical system. "Life Spacies II" ©1997–99, Christa Sommerer & Laurent Mignonneau, collection of the NTT-ICC Museum Japan.

Internet itself has basically become an evolving, reconnecting, and reconfiguring network of user-driven data input and output. Since 1999, we have created various interactive systems that directly tap into this complexity, linking it to multimodal interaction experiences.

The first system we created, in 1999, is called "Riding the Net" (Mignonneau, Sommerer, Lopez-Gulliver, Jones 2001). Users can use speech communication to retrieve images from the Internet, watch these images as they stream by, and interact by touching them. Two users can interact in this system simultaneously, and as they communicate, their conversation will be supported and visualized in real time through images as well as sounds streamed from the Internet. Figure 9.3 provides an example of this interaction, at Siggraph 2001.

In 2001, we adapted the "Riding the Net" image retrieval software for an interactive information environment called "The Living Room" (figure 9.4). The system was developed for the "Bo01-Living in the Future" architecture exhibition held in Malmoe, Sweden, in May 2001. Users in this system enter a 6 × 6-meters large space that consists of

(a)

Figure 9.3 (a) "Riding the Net"—multimodal interaction with complex data on the Internet. (b) Screen shot from the "Riding the Net" installation, with keywords "veil" and "beauty" downloading images from the Internet. (c) Screen shot from the "Riding the Net" installation with keywords "world" and "baby" downloading images from the Internet. "Riding the Net," ©2000, Christa Sommerer, Laurent Mignonneau, and Roberto Lopez-Gulliver, ATR Media Integration and Communications Research Lab Kyoto.

four 4 × 3-meter screens; as they talk, microphones placed on the ceiling of the space detect their conversations. Detected keywords are then used to generate word icons, which appear and float on the four screens. When users touch any of these word icons, their touch triggers the downloading of corresponding images from the Internet. Up to thirty users in the system can touch the various word icons, generating constantly changing image and sound downloads. As a result of these multiuser interactions, a dynamic, self-organizing, and constantly changing information space emerges. It represents the users' individual conversations, their individual interests in certain topics, and their collective interaction with the shared information.

(b)

(c)

Figure 9.3 (continued)

(a)

Figure 9.4 (a) ''The Living Room''—A user as he interacts with the interactive Internet environment. (b) ''The Living Room''—Two users interacting with the interactive touchscreens to download images and sounds from the Internet. ''The Living Room'' ©2001, Christa Sommerer, Laurent Mignonneau, and Roberto Lopez-Gulliver, developed for ''Bo01—Living in The Future Exhibition,'' Malmö Sweden 2001, ATR Media Integration and Communications Research Lab Kyoto.

In May 2002, we adapted "The Living Room" software to the 3D immersive environment of the CAVE™ system (figure 9.5). In this system, called "The Living Web," users can actually "enter the Internet" and interact with the available image and sound information in three dimensions. When users talk into their headset microphones, images relating to their conversations are streamed from the Internet, surrounding them in 3D displays. By grabbing one of the floating images, the user can retrieve more information about this specific image (for example, its URL), place the icon in a 3D space for bookmarking, and sort the various selected icons as 3D bookmarks to create further links, weights of interests, and connections between the various selected topics.

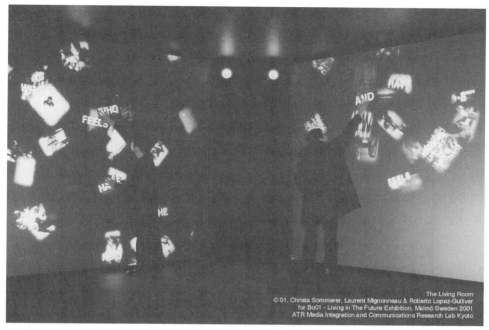

The Living Room
© 01, Christa Sommerer, Laurent Mignonneau & Roberto Lopez-Gulliver
for Bo01 - Living in The Future Exhibition, Malmö Sweden 2001
ATR Media Integration and Communications Research Lab Kyoto

(b)

Figure 9.4 (continued)

As in the "Riding the Net" and "The Living Room" systems, the imprecision of the speech recognition system and the randomized choice of images from the various search results are used intentionally to create a dynamic system that is unpredictable, full of surprise, and compliant with some of the definitions of a complex system. Users have some control over the kind of image and sound downloads triggered, but the sheer quantity of available information makes straightforward selection impossible. For each keyword, typically several hundred or at times several thousand image and sound documents are available and users can perceive only a fraction of the available data. To manage this complex and constantly changing database of images and sounds and allow intuitive as well as creative data browsing, these systems were designed to deal with randomness and order, allowing partly directed and partly undirected searches (Lopez-Gulliver, Sommerer, and Mignonneau 2002). Again, as in the principles of complex systems, it is exactly this notion of order and randomness, predictability, and surprise that make dynamic complex systems interesting, emergent, and full of discoveries.

Figure 9.5 User interacting with the Internet-based image data inside "The Living Web" CAVE™ environment. "The Living Web," ©2002, Christa Sommerer, Laurent Mignonneau, and Roberto Lopez-Gulliver, developed at ATR Media Information Science Research Lab Kyoto, FhG-IMK Frauenhofer Institute for Mediacommunication Bonn, and IAMAS Institute of Advanced Media Arts and Sciences, Gifu, Japan; supported by the BEC Bonner Entwicklungswerkstatt für Computermedien.

Transcending the Code

Writing computer programs is a complicated task, involving extended knowledge of the ever-changing programming languages, their capacity, and their inner structures. In addition, knowledge of the computer's internal hardware architecture as well as its resources and infrastructure can be of great advantage in extending the already known and explored. It is important to know both hardware and software structures when one wants to explore new forms of expressions and become less dependent on today's predesigns and the limitations of computer hardware and software. Such in-depth knowledge provides extra freedom, as one can change, modify, and extend any part and use both hardware and software as flexible materials to express and shape one's imagination and artistic vision.

Only when all the components of the materials are known can one begin to transcend the actual technology and create outputs beyond the purely technical and materialistic. As in biological systems, in which the phenotype differs greatly from the genotype, programming as art form is not a question of the code purely for its own sake, but rather how this code is expressed, how it is linked to other environmental influences, and what it actually means. Instead of focusing only on technical details and rational questions of the code, artists have to transcend the software code and hardware constraints to create artworks with this technology. They have to present us with intellectually as well as emotionally challenging ideas and questions by tapping into the emotional, metaphorical, irrational, and sensual layers of human knowledge.

Summary

The most difficult part in creating artworks with computers is thus not so much acquiring technical skills or learning the software languages, but evaluating and estimating their technical possibilities, as well as exploring new technical and intellectual ideas by balancing their conceptual and technical capacity and value. As any creative field of expression requires mastery (think of the dancer's mastery over the body as essential to the dance performance), computer-dependent art requires mastery over the material to express itself in a higher and more transcendant form.

The quality of a media artist lies in her sensitivity to new visions and ability to explore new tools and structures to support these visions and create content and experiences that transcend time and material, touching deeper emotions not readily explained through code, numbers, or aesthetic experiences alone.

References

Ashby, W. Ross. 1962. "Principles of the Self-Organizing System." In *Principles of Self-Organization.* Heinz Von Foerster and George W. Zopf, eds. Oxford: Pergamon Press.

ATR Advanced Telecommunications Research Center, Kyoto, Japan. Available at http://www.atr.co.jp.

Baas, N. A. 1994. "Emergence, Hierarchies, and Hyperstructures." In *Alife III, Santa Fe Studies in the Sciences of Complexity.* C. G. Langton, ed. Proceedings Volume XVII. Redwood City, CA: Addison-Wesley, pp. 515–37.

Beckmann Institute. NSCA National Center for Super Computing Applications. Champain/Urbana, IL. Available at http://www.beckman.uiuc.edu.

Bennett, C. H. 1988. "Logical Depth and Physical Complexity." In *The Universal Turing Machine*. Rolf Herken, ed. Oxford: Oxford University Press, pp. 227–57.

Cariani, P. 1992. "Emergence and Artificial Life." In *Artificial Life II*. Christopher G. Langton, Charles Taylor, J. Doyne Farmer and Steen Rasmussen, eds. Santa Fe Institute Studies in the Sciences of Complexity. Proceedings Vol. X. Redwood City, CA: Addison-Wesley, pp. 775–97.

Casti, J. L. 1994. *Complexification*. London: Abacus.

Chaitin, G. J. 1992. *Information Theoretic Incompleteness*. Singapore: World Scientific.

Dennett, D. 1995. *Darwin's Dangerous Idea: Evolution and the Meanings of Life*. New York: Simon and Schuster.

Fraunhofer Gesellschaft, Bonn, Germany. Available at http://www.fraunhofer.de.

Jantsch, E. 1980. *The Self-Organizing Universe*. Oxford and New York: Pergamon.

Kauffman, St. 1993. *The Origins of Order. Self-organization and Selection in Evolution*. Oxford: Oxford University Press.

Landauer, R. 1988. "A Simple Measure of Complexity." *Nature* 336: 306–07.

Langton, C. 1989. "Artificial Life." In *Artificial Life*. C. Langton, ed. Redwood City, CA: Addison-Wesley, pp. 1–47.

Lopez-Gulliver, R., Sommerer, C., and Mignonneau, L. 2002. "Interfacing the Web: Multi-modal and Immersive Interaction with the Internet." In *VSMM 2002 Proceedings of the Eight International Conference on Virtual Systems and MultiMedia*, Gyeongju, Korea, pp. 753–64.

Mignonneau, L., and Sommerer, C. 2000. "Designing Interfaces for Interactive Artworks." In *KES 2000 Knowledge Based Engineering Systems Conference Proceedings*. University of Brighton, Brighton, UK, pp. 80–84.

Mignonneau, L., Sommerer, C., Lopez-Gulliver, R., and Jones, S. 2001. "Riding the Net: a Novel, Intuitive and Entertaining Tool to Browse the Internet." In *SCI 2001—5th World Multiconference on Systemics, Cybernetics and Informatics Conference Proceedings*. Orland, Florida: International Institute of Informatics and Systemics, pp. 57–63.

Pagels, H. 1988. *The Dreams of Reason*. New York: Simon & Shuster.

Sommerer, C. 2001. "ALife in Art, Design, Edutainment, Game and Research." *LEONARDO Journal* 2001; 34(4): 297–98.

Sommerer, C., and Mignonneau, L. 1997. "Interacting with Artificial Life: A-Volve." *Complexity Journal* 2; 6: 13–21.

Sommerer, C., and Mignonneau, L. 1998a. "Art as a Living System." In *Art @ Science*. C. Sommerer and L. Mignonneau, eds. Vienna/New York: Springer-Verlag.

Sommerer, C., and Mignonneau, L. 1998b. "The Application of Artificial Life to Interactive Computer Installations." *Artificial Life and Robotics Journal* 2; 4: 151–56.

Sommerer, C., and Mignonneau, L. 2000. "Modeling Emergence of Complexity: The Application of Complex System and Origin of Life Theory to Interactive Art on the Internet." In *Artificial Life VII*. M. A. Bedau, J. S. McCaskill, N. H. Packard, and St. Rasmussen, eds. Boston: MIT Press, pp. 547–54.

Sommerer, C., Mignonneau, L., and Lopez-Gulliver, R. 1999. "LIFE SPACIES II: From Text to Form on the Internet Using Language as Genetic Code." In *Proceedings ICAT'99 9th International Conference on Artificial Reality and Tele-Existence*. Tokyo: Virtual Reality Society, pp. 215–20.

Wicken, J. S. 1987. *Evolution, Thermodynamics, and Information*. Oxford: Oxford University Press.

Wolfram, S. 1984. "Cellular Automata as Models of Complexity." *Nature* 311: 419–24.

Yates, F. E., ed. 1987. "Self-Organizing Systems." In *The Emergence of Order*. New York: Plenum Press.

10

Transdisciplinary Collaboration in "Cell"

Jane Prophet and Mark d'Inverno

The ideas we describe in this chapter on transdisciplinary collaboration, and our belief that such collaboration can have a positive impact on the practice of computing, are based on the experience of working on an interdisciplinary project (Cell) looking into innovative theories of stem cell behavior. The collaboration involved an artist (Jane Prophet), a mathematician (Mark d'Inverno), a liver pathologist (Neil Theise), an artificial life (Alife) programmer (Rob Saunders), and a curator/producer (Peter Ride). We report on the project, our backgrounds, and the nature of process-based interdisciplinary research. We discuss our experience of negotiating discipline-specific positions on a number of aesthetic qualities that have in turn led to a change in our understanding of the aesthetics of computing. In the right circumstances, we propose, interdisciplinary research transcends the individual disciplines and can potentially be what we call *transdisciplinary*—that is, the impact of disciplines on each other is strong enough to fundamentally affect the disciplines themselves, including computer science.

The Cell Project

Cell is a collaboration between the individuals mentioned above. It is an interdisciplinary project to look at the modeling, visualization, and understanding of new theoretical and experimental developments in adult stem cell research. These new theories challenge existing paradigms of stem cell behavior particularly in terms of what is known as *plasticity*. In the old paradigm, stem cells have specific properties including the ability to generate new daughter cells along a particular differentiation lineage, eventually (and deterministically) producing cells of a specific type (such as red blood cells). The new theories of Theise and associates and others challenge this view. New paradigms propose that cell lineages are reversible, and plastic (cells from one line can produce daughter cells of a different line).

Our collaboration had a number of outcomes:

- Papers in peer reviewed medical journals, mathematical modeling journals, simulation journals, art journals
- A mathematical model of the new paradigm
- A dynamical simulation of the mathematical model
- Art installations exploring the nature of scientific representation
- 3D illustrations of cells and their behavior, generated using Alife techniques
- Detailed documentation of all the processes involved in this project

All team members have an impact, either explicitly or implicitly, on the form and content of these artifacts.

The Cell Team

To understand some of the insights we have gained through working together on this project, it is worth presenting a very brief background of each collaborator. Prophet is an established artist and professor of visual art and new media at University of Westminster. Her work includes Alife artworks such as TechnoSphere (Prophet 2001) and a series of artworks that challenge ideas about landscape and nature (Prophet 2001). D'Inverno is a professor of computer science at University of Westminster whose research focuses on building mathematical models of new technologies in computer science and is best known for his work in multiagent systems (d'Inverno and Luck 2003). Theise is a liver pathologist based at Beth Israel Medical Center. He was among the first to show that adult bone marrow stem cells have surprising plasticity and transform themselves into the mature cells of other organs (Theise et al. 2001). Saunders is a pioneer in developing computational models of curiosity using specialized neural networks, he also models creativity, focusing on the roles of novelty and emergence in creative processes (Rob Saunders homepages). Ride commissions and produces artworks that address artists' use of digital technology, developing new forms and systems that enable them to create innovative work. He is the Artistic Director of DA2, Digital Arts Development Agency (Digital Arts Development Agency homepages), and codirects the Centre for Arts Research, Technology and Education (CARTE), University of Westminster (CARTE's homepages) with Prophet.

The Working Process

Our collaboration began following a successful application to the Wellcome Trust's sciart (science and art) fund for research and development (Sciart homepages). This supported a series of studio and laboratory visits between Prophet, Ride, and Theise. The Cell team uses e-mail, telephone, and fax as well as face-to-face meetings to develop ideas and produce the outputs listed previously. We keep records of all correspondence and meetings (which are audio and video recorded). The collaboration has been conducted in a triangle of different experimental research environments: Theise's medical laboratory; d'Inverno's and Saunders's respective mathematical and computer science labs; and Prophet's art studio. Each discipline and environment provides a different context for the work, and each has associated methodologies and aesthetics.

Photographs: Medical Science versus Contemporary Art

Theise and Prophet became immersed in each other's working cultures and identified significant differences. For example, in cell biology the "photographs" of tissue slides have a truth status, and are accepted as "proof" of experiments and hypotheses within papers. Surprisingly, the beauty of representations produced as part of laboratory research (figure 10.1) appears to be important to biomedical scientists such as Theise in general. In addition, there is an apparent correlation between aesthetic quality (specifically how beautiful a representation is considered to be) and the publication rate of associated papers.

Figure 10.1 is one example of Theise's "beautiful" images, representing skin tissue from a female mouse that received a bone marrow transplant from a male mouse. Blue nuclei of hair follicle lining cells surround the orange, autofluorscent hair shaft (large arrow). Two of these nuclei contain fluorescently labeled Y chromosomes (small arrows), indicating that they derive from the donated male bone marrow, not from the female's own original cells. Thus, bone marrow stem cells have given rise to skin-type lining cells.

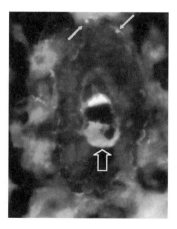

Figure 10.1   Hair follicle with lining cells derived from bone marrow.

Figure 10.2 Petworth House, 2003, by Jane Prophet. Duratran from digital file, 190cm × 87cm. Fractal tree by Gordon Selley.

By contrast, in contemporary art practice, photographic representations have no automatic truth status (quite the contrary) but are assumed to be subjective. Many such images artists make deliberately draw attention to their construction and artifice (figure 10.2). In this image, the photographic representation is of the parkland at Petworth House in Sussex, England. The landscape is well known, and views of it were painted by Turner. But the landscape formation is not "natural." It was constructed by the eighteenth-century landscape designer Lancelot "Capability" Brown, drawing on compositional techniques from contemporaneous landscape painting. Figure 10.2 is based on a photograph of the park as it is now, with a superimposed tree generated using fractal mathematics.

The Role of Formal Modeling

In terms of mathematical modeling, we can think of a number of aesthetic principles. First, any mathematical model needs to have an internal integrity. Second, the model has to be as *simple* as possible; mathematicians often create structures for their own sake without understanding the need to use the mathematics to provide a "portability of ideas." Without simplicity, the model cannot provide the necessary fabric to create a *common conceptual framework* in which scientists (and in the case of our project, also artists) have the same base from which to discuss and develop new ideas whether formally or otherwise. Language was a real problem between Prophet, Theise, and d'Inverno and our developing model catalyzed a precise and clear meaning for words, structures, and processes. Without

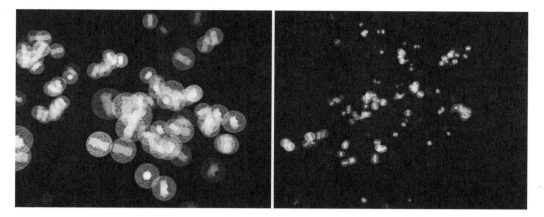

Figure 10.3 Two 3D Alife representations from Cell.

this common language, initial meetings were often spent "disambiguating" terms and concepts.

We found that in building a formal model describing in plain English the rules that together defined stem cell behavior, we were able to identify gaps in each of our understandings. These gaps in understanding were not only in relation to Theise's theory, but in both Prophet's and d'Inverno's understanding of the developing model. We were all struck by the way the process of developing the formal model not only highlighted differences in our understanding but also illuminated the different ways in which we each conceptualized the same properties of cells.

Last but not least, the formal model helped by providing a bridge between the real system of the human body and the simulated system we see on the computer screen (see figures 10.3 and 10.4). Using logical proof rules, we can ensure that the simulation encapsulates the formal model. Of course, we can never be sure the model incorporates the theory exactly, only that by recursively developing and revising the model, it is as close as we can possibly make it.

Using Alife Techniques

Theise's research examines the plasticity of adult stem cells and their function. To do this he uses methods based on hypothesis and hypothesis testing, specifically repeatable laboratory experiments and the analysis of cell tissue specimens. The tissue is dead at the time it is analyzed, and the tissue slides (for example, figure 10.1) therefore represent a frozen moment in time seen from one perspective, from which researchers hope to understand another aspect of stem cell behavior, and extrapolate further hypotheses to test. Prophet's experience as an artist working with time-based media and Alife suggests a different approach to assessing stem cell behavior. We therefore decided to develop an Alife engine to enable the scientist to look at *simulated stem cell behavior as it happens*, within the complex system of a wider community of cell types and enzymes.

Our simulation treats each cell as a reactive autonomous agent responding to local environmental factors. One goal is to produce a set of local environmental rules for each agent such that the resulting system exhibits a number of global properties, for example, maintaining a balance of different cells under varying conditions. It then becomes possible to alter conditions to replicate disease and life-threatening events and environments. We can experiment to find out how the system might recover by changing environmental factors or properties of stem cell behavior.

In general, agents are reactive autonomous entities reacting to local environmental conditions with no control over their behavior from human intervention. The overall behavior of a large system of such agents can never be predicted but emerges as a result of the combination of the multitude of individual behaviors. This is very different to commonly held definitions of works of art that are usually of a fixed appearance, and if time-based then changing in accordance with the predetermined direction of the artist whose hand in determining sequence, pace, and other qualities is clear. In such works of art (and their associated aesthetics), little is nondeterministic or unexpected. By contrast Alife artworks, that have a graphical and sound output generated from an Alife engine, challenge traditional notions of authorship and artistic control and intent. These artworks (see Alife used by contemporary artists) are autonomous, not controlled or made by the artist or illustrator in the usual top-down sense (for example, in the way figure 10.2 was "made").

In addition, it is significant to how we make meaning from them, or interpret them, that these artworks are time-based, not still (in contrast to the slide image of figure 10.1 or the still art image of figure 10.2). They are not constant or predictable (like prerecorded narrative film or video art), as the visual or aural outputs are produced in real time to represent the software running beneath them, which is itself constantly changing as a complex system of interactions between entities (agents) take place. They are not the result of top-down behavior or decision-making by the artist or scientist, but the result of bottom-up and potentially emergent behavior. Unexpected behavior represented as images or sounds emerges from many interactions between a large number of entities whose individual behavior is based on simple rules. The closest genre from the arts is improvisation, in which the live performers respond to each other, feedback loops of music, and the environment that they themselves have in part created.

Discussion: The Experience of Interdisciplinary Collaboration

While this may strike the reader as obvious, it was not clear to us at first that we each had different aims for the project. The project progressed by continually assessing our working process and redefining individual and joint goals. Once we had set initial short-term goals and found a common language, it was then possible to conduct research across disciplines and converge or focus on agreed longer-term goals and deliverables.

Our understanding of ourselves has deepened as we each have had to articulate to Cell colleagues from different disciplines our positions within the context of our discipline. As we became aware of each other's disciplines, and more familiar with their key characteristics, it became easier to converge on, and agree on, goals and outcomes. However, we note here that once we have a broad understanding of each discipline, a lack of more detailed understanding can be beneficial. For example, as an artist and a mathematician we were not shackled by a training in medical science, and, as a result were able to think "out of the box" to suggest radical new mechanisms or processes that might explain some observed scientific data. Of course, the downside of this lack of knowledge is that we were not able to eliminate ridiculous theories quickly and had to rely on Theise to filter all our ideas.

We quickly decided that it was important to produce a range of outputs from the Cell project, rather than focusing on only one joint art exhibition or one scientific visualization. This enabled us to identify a wide range of separate but connected elements in the research and made it possible to define a program for discussing and investigating almost all of them. Divergence at the point of outputs has been noted by Glaser (2003) as a useful model in art/science collaborations. At regular intervals, we discussed how our work together might contribute to each individual's research. This included individual and joint authoring (e.g., Theise and d'Inverno 2004), as agreed to on a case by case basis. We decided that our approach to the dissemination of each output would be by submitting it to the most appropriate forum for peer review. We choose to submit outputs to the scrutiny of peer review not simply because we are academics, but because it drives us to maintain standards within each discipline as well as across disciplines. By submitting different outputs to different kinds of peer-review process, and aiming to submit at least one output to each of our disciplines, we hope to avoid privileging one discipline over another, and to contribute quantifiably to each discipline.

Scale

Aesthetic debates concerning scale are central to the Cell project. Prophet has been interested in the "sublime" in contemporary culture for a number of years, particularly fractal mathematics and an apparent cultural shift to a sublime in the very small and detailed. This develops ideas of the natural or religious sublime (Burke and Phillips 1998), based on our experience of the human body in landscapes so large and overwhelming that they prompt a sense of awe and momentary terror. Prophet suggests, in an update to Kant's thesis on the sublime and small scale (Kant 1952), that there is now a sublime of the micro, nano, and virtual, a similar awe and terror as we try to grasp an inner landscape of a scale too small in relation to the human body for most of us to comprehend.

Theise's theory challenges the paradigm of the progressively differentiating adult stem cell and of cells being one of the body's smallest building blocks. He draws attention to the role of technology (the microscope) in assigning high status to the unit of the cell— bounded by the cell wall and made visible for the first time by microscopes. Determining the bounded cell as a key unit is central to our thinking of scale and reinforces a reductive model of the human body in medicine. Theise notes that if a different imaging technology had been invented (instead of the microscope), for example, one that showed patterns of energy or fluid movement through the body, we would be less inclined to reductionism (unpublished conversation between Prophet, Ride, and Theise). Any subsequent development of the microscope would have qualified the fluid model to note that fluids sometimes moved across boundaries (i.e., across cell walls).

Saunders and d'Inverno have a different interest in scale as it is also the case that emergence arises in multiagent/complex systems only when the number of interacting autonomous agents is sufficiently large. Moreover, we envisage in any adequate model of stem cells the individual agents will not be stem cells themselves, but entities that might potentially exhibit some properties of stem cell behavior if the local environment is suitably orientated. Our intuition tells us it makes no sense for stem cells to be individually defined or modeled in isolation. "Stem cell-ness" is meaningful only as a set of potential functional or behavioral properties of some subset of entities in a massive, complex system.

In choosing to manifest the mathematical model by developing software using open software standards, Saunders has kept the project sensitive to scale at the level of the computer code itself. During the various stages of development, a number of open standards and languages have been used, including Java, C++, and OpenGL, providing the project with a range of tools that can be used on different types of computer and computers of differing speeds (figure 10.4). Consequently, the software that has been developed can run on machines ranging from laptops and desktop computers to distributed computing platforms typically used to perform complex scientific calculations. Scalability has become

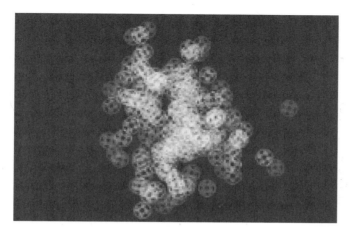

Figure 10.4 A 2D Java Alife representation from Cell.

central to the ethos used to design the Cell software. Discipline-specific theories of scale converge in the proposed project to become a key theme in the project.

Aesthetics and Problems with Visualization

Contemporary scientific visions and hypotheses about biotechnologies of the near future are frequently disseminated using visualizations that present digital images as reality. The observer therefore misinterprets what amounts to nothing more than artistic illustrations as a physical or biological reality or truth. This is exacerbated by the photorealistic quality of the digital images presented (this use of digital images or simulations is rife in contemporary publications and presentations about nano science).

Photorealism in computer graphics is informed by the medium, material, and aesthetics of photography. The computer game industry is dominated by the aesthetic of photorealism and real-time 3D rendering. These pervasive aesthetics from flight and gaming simulations have "contaminated" the 3D version of Cell; the characteristic focus on surface rendering, depth, and transparency particularly reflects the genres' relentless drive toward photorealism (see figure 10.3).

In developing the look and feel of the scientific visualization, Prophet has emphasized that as a contemporary artist she was educated to resist *beautifying* the graphics. As far as possible, the graphic look and feel that Prophet favors is one that reflects most closely the underlying software, drawing attention to the essence of the idea or concept with as little decoration as possible. From Prophet's standpoint, the Java version (see figure 10.4) is a more satisfying outcome than the 3D version. The 3D version, favored by Theise, has been influenced by the aesthetics of medical illustration and its goal of explaining via precise observation of *the appearance of things*: this is at odds with our emphasis on *the behavior of things* (in this case stem cells) and their material qualities. Its appeal lies in its familiarity (the graphic representations of cells look more like the cells seen through a microscope). What is key for us both is to transmit a sense of "stem cell-ness." What is captivating about our contemporary understanding of these cells seems to be the way they behave rather than the way they look, but employing computer graphic devices such as 3D modeling, transparency, collision detection, and an increasing the sense of depth of field by including flotsam in the environment may be useful by allowing medical researchers to suspend their disbelief and focus on the cells' behavior. Not using these computer graphic devices may contribute to observers from a medical background focusing on the unfamiliar representations of cells as simple graphics (as seen in the 2D Java representation of the simulation) rather than assessing the behavior of the cells, and our use of abstraction can become counterproductive.

The relationship between the aesthetics of art and the aesthetics of computing is not simply a one-way transfer from art to computing. At the very least, it is a dialogic process in which computing affects the aesthetics of the art. For example, the infinite reproducibility of the digital image without loss of quality has taken to new heights art historical arguments about the reproduction of art and the subsequent loss of aura. In fact, we believe art and computer science affect each other in a hermeneutic circle.

Conclusion

Some interdisciplinary projects draw on the practice of each discipline without challenging or altering those disciplines as a result. In our experience with this project, however, each discipline has been challenged and altered as a result of the continuing debates and negotiation between us and the dissemination of our outputs. Such *transdisciplinary* collaborations, we believe, are fundamentally different from interdisciplinary projects (see Marcos Novak's homepages). Such projects can fundamentally affect the disciplines themselves, and have a significant impact on the way artistic and scientific investigations should proceed. Transdisciplinary collaborations will enable disciplines to recursively affect the very nature of each other.

Acknowledgments

This chapter is based on discussions with Peter Ride, Rob Saunders, and Neil Theise. Cell research has been conducted with awards from The Wellcome Trust sciart; Shinkansen Future Physical "BioTech," and The Quintin Hogg Trust.

References

Alife used by contemporary artists. See, for example, the work of Christa Sommerer and Laurent Mignonneau (http://www.iamas.ac.jp/~christa/); Kenneth Rinaldo (http://www.cgrg.ohio-state .edu/~rinaldo/); The VIDA Art & Artificial Life International Competition (http://www.fundacion .telefonica.com/at/vida/english/index.html).

Burke, Edmund, and Phillips, Adam, eds. 1998. *Philosophical Enquiry into the Origin of Our Ideas of the Sublime and Beautiful*. Oxford: Oxford University Press.

CARTE's homepages, http://www.carte.org.uk.

Digital Arts Development Agency homepages, http://www.da2.org.uk.

d'Inverno, Mark, and Luck, Michael. 2003. *Understanding Agent System*. 2nd ed. New York: Springer.

Glaser, Daniel. 2003. University College London Academic and Institute of Contemporary Art, London, Scientist in Residence, speaking at a conference in Colchester, UK. Documentation of this event at http://www.futurephysical.org/pages/content/biotechnology/cal_interchangetimeline .html.

Kant, Immanuel. 1952. *Critique of Judgement. Book I, Analytic of the Beautiful; Book II, Analytic of the Sublime.* James Creed Meredith, trans. Oxford: Clarendon Press. Immanuel Kant acknowledged that "nothing can be given in nature, no matter how great we may judge it to be, which, regarded in some other relation, may not be degraded to the level of the infinitely little, and nothing so small which in comparison with some still smaller standard may not for our imagination be enlarged to the greatness of the world."

Krause, Diane S., Theise, Neil D., Collector, Michael I., et al. 2001. "Multi-Organ, Multi-Lineage Engraftment by a Single Bone Marrow-Derived Stem Cell." *Cell* 105: 369–77.

Marcos Novak homepage. AlienSpace. Information on Novak's work. Available at http://www.mat .ucsb.edu/~marcos/Centrifuge_Site/MainFrameSet.html.

Prophet, Jane. 2001a. "TechnoSphere: Real Time Artificial Life." *Leonardo: The Journal of the International Society for The Arts, Sciences and Technology* 34(4): 309–12.

Prophet, Jane. 2001b. *Decoy*. London: Film & Video Umbrella & Norwich School of Arts.

Rob Saunders homepages, http://www.robsaunders.net.

Sciart award scheme website. Sciart "provides a unique opportunity for scientists and artists to re-search in collaboration, and develop and produce projects likely to result in innovative public engagement. These partnerships may involve scientists interested in creating new forms of expression, artists nspired by scientific research or a combination of both." Information on the sciart award scheme at http://www.sciart.org.

Theise, Neil D., and d'Inverno, Mark. 2004. "Understanding Cell Lineages as Complex Adaptive Systems." *Blood, Cells, Molecules, and Diseases (BCMD)* 41: 17–20.

11

Processing Code: Programming within the Context of Visual Art and Design

Casey Reas and Ben Fry

Graphical user interfaces (GUIs) became mainstream nearly 20 years ago, but programming fundamentals are still primarily taught through the command line interface. Classes proceed from outputting text to the screen, to GUI, to computer graphics (if at all). It is possible to teach programming in a way that moves graphics and concepts of interaction closer to the surface. The "Hello World" program can be replaced by drawing a line, thus shifting the focus of computing from ASCII to images and engaging people with visual and spatial inclinations.

This chapter presents alternative programming environments, visualizations, and curricula to introduce new audiences to computer programming and encourage hybrid artist/designer/programmers.

The Aesthetics and Computation Group

The Aesthetics and Computation (ACG) group was active at the MIT Media Laboratory from 1996 to 2003. Led by Professor John Maeda, the group worked toward designing advanced system architectures and thought processes to enable the creation of (as yet) unimaginable forms and spaces. During its 7-year tenure, diverse experimentation was executed in input devices, visualization, kinetic sculpture, typography, audiovisual performance, wearables, and design pedagogy. The belief that computers are a unique medium with extraordinary and untapped potential was at the core of this work. One strategy for realizing this potential was to develop programming libraries and environments that would enable current and future generations of artists and designers to expand their thinking beyond commercially available software tools.

Figure 11.1 dbn_maeda.tif. John Maeda. Design By Numbers programming environment.

Design By Numbers

Design By Numbers (DBN) is a programming language and environment created for visual designers and artists (figure 11.1). Released in 1999, it was designed to teach the "idea" of computation in the belief that the quality of design and media art can be improved only by establishing appropriate educational infrastructure in arts and technology schools. DBN has the goal of fostering the cross-disciplinary individuals that will create future innovations. The environment provides a unified space for writing and running programs, and the language introduces basic ideas of computer programming within a context of drawing and interaction. Visual elements such as dot, line, and field are combined with the computational ideas of variables, conditional statements, and functions.

Professor John Maeda initiated DBN after years of teaching programming workshops and courses within the design context. Maeda has said that

Distilling a basic vocabulary of computational visual art requires years of experience in practice and instruction of basic principles.... I hesitated before undertaking the definition of a basic programming language for art and design education. However, having seen Java and C++ (languages that would easily discourage the most ardent young futurists) take hold as the de facto method for stu-

Casey Reas and Ben Fry

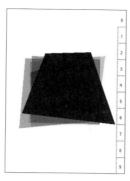

Figure 11.2 square_maeda.tif. John Maeda. Reactive Square (1995).

dents to acquire computational skills, I chose to prescribe a minimal degree of knowledge in the ongoing Design By Numbers project. (Maeda 2000, p. 444)

His experiments from the mid-1990s, such as the Reactive Square (figure 11.2), were some of the first sophisticated syntheses of visual design and interactive graphics and they allowed the design community to see the relation between their work and computation. Preceding the Macromedia Flash environment, these experiments had a large influence on that community.

The primary quality of DBN is its minimal syntax and restrictions. For example, programs can only be 100 by 100 pixels in dimension and use grayscale values. These self-imposed restrictions are in the tradition of established, rigorous design foundation studies and make the entire language and environment clearly comprehensible to novices. People can begin writing programs within minutes and gradually build complexity as they learn. Even in this reduced framework, students are motivated by the emphasis on creating responsive drawings with code, and it is possible to teach core concepts of computation. A program for drawing a line on the screen is only two lines of code (figure 11.3):

```
paper 0
line 20 20 80 80
```

This program is easily modified to be responsive through receiving input from the mouse (figure 11.4):

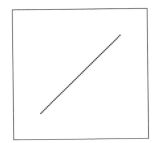

Figure 11.3   line_dbn.tif.

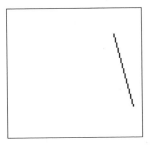

Figure 11.4   mouseline_dbn.tif.

```
forever
{
    paper 0
    line <mouse 1> <mouse 2> 80 80
}
```

A more complex example reveals the structures for setting individual pixels, variables, and logical statements (figure 11.5):

```
forever
{
    set msec <time 4>
    set sec <time 3>
    set [msec 50] 20
    set [sec 50] 50
```

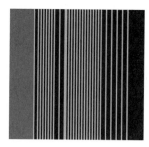

Figure 11.5 time_dbn.tif.

```
repeat x 0 100
{
    notsame? [x 50] 0
    {
        pen ([x 50] - 1)
        line (x-1) 0 (x-1) 100
    }
    pen 100
    line 100 0 100 100
}
}
```

DBN was designed for a visually sophisticated, but computationally inexperienced audience. The infrastructure is tailored to creating visual interactive work, and many of the tedious programming tasks such as double-buffering and threading for animation are implicit to the environment. This allows people using the software to focus on interaction and communication, rather than technical code. The reference material for the language, published as a well-conceived book, appeals to a visually sophisticated audience. For an audience of designers and artists, the visual design of the environment and reference materials are critical to the project's success.

Studying DBN is the first step toward computational literacy and was not designed as a general and comprehensive language. The same elements that make DBN appropriate for beginners make it frustrating for experienced programmers. Its reduced syntax excludes floating point numbers, arrays, and other common language primitives, and this forces programmers to develop elaborate hacks for implementing basic code elements they may want to use. In addition, there is no clear transition for beginners to make after learning basic computational concepts through DBN.

Courses in Computational Media Design

A series of undergraduate and graduate courses developed through the Aesthetics and Computation Group suggest a core curriculum for integrating computation with the visual arts.

The MIT undergraduate course Fundamentals of Computational Media design has been a laboratory for experimenting with different programming environments and teaching methods. Taught by Professor Maeda and his graduate students since the spring of 1999, it uses Java, DBN, Processing, and other software tools for teaching a hybrid curriculum merging ideas from the traditional arts and computation. In the class, students work with software, photography, typography, 3D graphics, electronics, paper, clay, and other materials. Instruction ranges from explaining the Bresenham line drawing algorithm to discussing the nuances of ikebana, the Japanese art of flower arranging. In this eclectic mix, students are free to explore the natural intersections of diverse media and technologies. Students who think of themselves as "technical" rather than "artistic" find there is no contradiction in these terms.

In addition to the undergraduate curriculum, Professor Maeda has also explored a series of more advanced graduate courses. Beginning in 1997, they have focused on topics including visual interface design, digital typography, numeric photography, and organic form. Unlike the undergraduate classes, which emphasize a visual and interaction foundation for more technical pupils, the graduate courses include students with degrees in architecture, design, studio art, mathematics, and engineering. By completing problem sets and participating in critiques, each student learns more rapidly from their colleagues than if they were in a class of students exclusively from their own discipline. This diverse mix is extremely beneficial for learning if the professor (or professors) is able to communicate across the diverse disciplines and also critique the work on its conceptual, technical, and aesthetic merits. It is necessary for each student to have the aptitude for learning technical skills and have had some experience with programming before entering the course.

In the Principles of Visual Interface Design course, students created basic exercises in interactive parameterized form and recursion (figure 11.6) and space/time connections before moving on to more challenging exercises in constructing software for balancing randomness with order (figure 11.7). Courses such as Numeric Photography focus deeply on a narrow domain. Students spent the semester taking photographs and developing software for processing the images according to their weekly exercise. Various personal innovations in interactive image interpretation (figures 11.8 and 11.9) emerged as the students moved

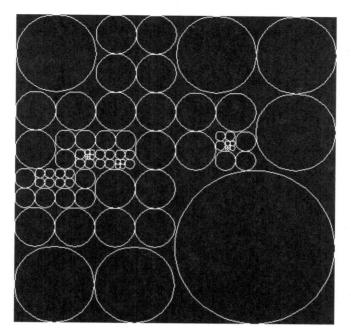

Figure 11.6 recursion_tiongson.tif. Phillip Tiongson. Software for building recursive parameterized form.

Figure 11.7 random_white.tif. Tom White. Reducing randomness through interpolating two disparate colors.

Figure 11.8 hand_levin.tif. Golan Levin. Depositing graphic form to reveal a photographic image.

beyond the constraints of existing imaging software. These courses have defined a potential curriculum for a degree in computational design.

Processing

Like its direct predecessor DBN, Processing integrates a programming language, development environment, and teaching methodology into a unified structure for learning. Unlike DBN, Processing allows people to make a smooth transition from beginner to advanced programmer, and the intended audience of Processing is much wider. Processing makes it possible to introduce programming in the context of art and design and also to open electronic art concepts to a programming audience. Processing is an open project initiated by Ben Fry of the MIT Media Lab and Casey Reas of UCLA and the Interaction Design Institute Ivrea. Development began in 2001, with the first public software release in August 2002.

Concept

The concept of Processing is to create a text programming language specifically for making responsive images, rather than creating a visual programming language. The language

Figure 11.9 erode_co.tif. Elise Co. Deconstructing a photographic image.

Figure 11.10   processing_thumbs.tif. Examples of software written with Processing.

enables sophisticated visual and responsive structures and balances features and ease of use. Many computer graphics and interaction techniques can be discussed including vector/ raster drawing, image processing, color models, events, network communication, and information visualization (figure 11.10). It includes a custom 2D/3D engine that draws its feature set from PostScript and OpenGL and the language is easily extended by writing additional code or integrating existing Java libraries. Processing allows similar functionality of Java and C++ but with a simplified syntax, and it is more general than other design environments such as Macromedia's Flash and Director.

Processing is designed to be a prototyping and learning environment. In the same way that architects use cardboard to build models and musicians use a keyboard to develop arrangements, Processing can be used as a tool for writing software sketches. Ideas can quickly be realized in code, with programs often half as long as their Java or C++ equivalents. The generality and origins of the Processing syntax make it a base for future learning. Skills learned through Processing enable people to learn languages and APIs suitable for different contexts including web authoring (ActionScript), networking and communications (Java), microcontrollers (C), and computer graphics (OpenGL).

Programming Language/Environment

Processing provides three modes of programming—each more structurally complex than the previous. In the most basic mode, similar to the structure of DBN, programs are single-line commands for drawing primitive shapes to the screen (figure 11.11):

Figure 11.11   line_processing.tif.

Figure 11.12   mouseline_processing.tif.

```
background(255);
line(20, 20, 80, 80);
```

The intermediate mode allows for the creation of dynamic software in a hybrid procedural/object-oriented structure (figure 11.12). A simple example follows:

```
void draw() {
  background(255);
  line(mouseX, mouseY, 80, 80);
}
```

As people gain skills, programs can be enhanced with additional layers of complexity. This program loads a static image and represents the color data as a stream of kinetic lines (figure 11.13):

```
BImage a;
int direction = 1;
float signal;
void setup()
{
  size(200, 200);
  stroke(255);
  a = loadImage("florence03.jpg");
}
void draw()
{
```

Figure 11.13 image_processing.tif.

```
signal += (0.1*direction);
if (signal > width-1 || signal < 0) {
  direction *= -1;
}
for (int i=0; i<width*height; i++) {
  pixels[i] =
a.pixels[int((width*int(signal))+(i%width))];
}
}
```

In the most complex Processing mode, Java code may be written within the environment. This allows people to write fully developed Java applications within the environment, thus making the complete transition from the simplified context-specific Processing syntax to the general-purpose Java language.

Even for people who have moderate experience using tools like Flash and Director, a significant gap remains between the fundamentals learned in their respective scripting languages and more advanced programming languages such as Java or C++. Developers interested in making the jump to the latter are likely to find the switch frustrating, since they must first learn the idiosyncrasies of developing a graphical application for their com-

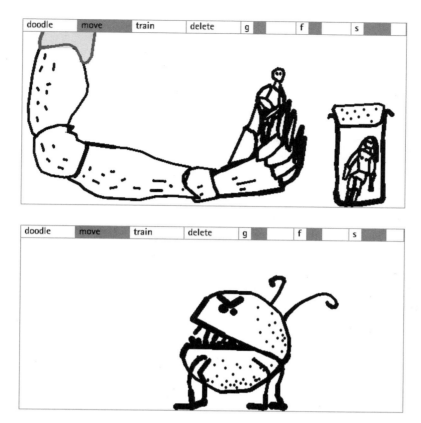

Figure 11.14 moovl_burton.tif. Ed Burton. Moovl, a behavioral drawing tool.

puting environment, a task that often involves pages of code before even the simplest objects can be drawn on the screen.

Experienced programmers find Processing useful as a prototyping tool. They are able to quickly encode their ideas in the syntax and see the results. For example, Ed Burton from Soda has been developing the ideas for his newest software project called Moovl (figure 11.14) within the Processing environment because it lets him focus on the design tasks, rather than on cumbersome syntax and infrastructure.

Processing strives to achieve a balance between features and clarity, which encourages experimentation and reduces the learning curve. Because the project is built around Java, the programming skills learned using Processing are directly transferable to these more advanced environments once the time is appropriate. It supports many of the existing Java structures, but with a simplified syntax, and operates by translating programs written

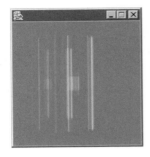

```
int size = 200;
int[] gre = new int[size*size];
int[] blu = new int[size*size];
int mx, pmx, my = 0;
int dif = 0;

void setup()
{
  size(200, 200);
  noBackground();

  for (int i=0; i<width*height; i++) {
    gre[i] = 0;
    blu[i] = 204;
  }
```

Figure 11.15   gui_processing.tif. The Processing programming environment.

in its own syntax into Java code and using an existing Java compiler to create executable programs.

The development environment (figure 11.15) includes a minimal toolbar for running, stopping, opening, saving, exporting, and creating a new project. More advanced features are embedded in the menus, but it is possible to learn all of the environment basics in a few minutes.

Networked Environment

The Internet's potential and culture have been designed into the Processing initiative, allowing the project to grow in unexpected ways. Thousands of students, educators, and practitioners across five continents are involved in using the software. The website for the project, http://www.processing.org, serves as the communication hub for the project, but development takes place remotely in cities such as Bogota, Istanbul, Manila, Boston, New York, and Los Angeles. The Processing website hosts a set of extended examples and a complete reference for the language. Standardized Web structures such as bulletin boards host discussions about features, bugs, and related events.

Processing programs can be simply exported in the Web-ready format of Java applets, and this supports the creation of a global educational community and provides motivation

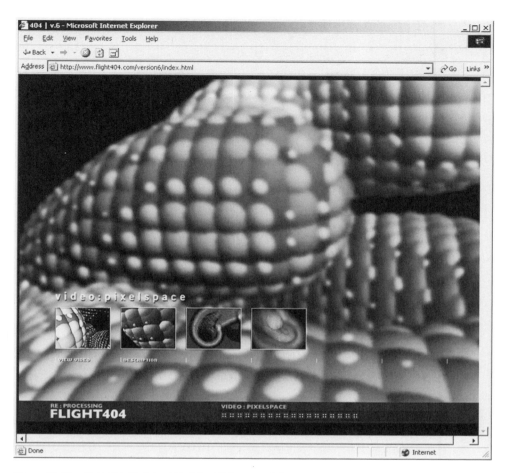

Figure 11.16 flight404.tif. Robert Hodgin. Flight404 website.

for learning. Designers thrive on sharing their work, and talented practitioners such as Robert Hodgin of the exploratory design site Flight404 (figure 11.16) and students such as Mikkel Koser of the Royal College of Art (figure 11.17) have been rapidly learning and inspiring others. People are encouraged to expose their source code. Just as the "view source" function in Web browsers encouraged the rapid expansion of the Web, access to Processing source code enables members of the community to learn from each other and raises the skills of community as a unit. For example, Karsten Schmidt's execution of the Perlin noise algorithm (figure 11.18) inspired others to expand their own knowledge and push the original author's aesthetics. Many algorithms that have remained exclusive to

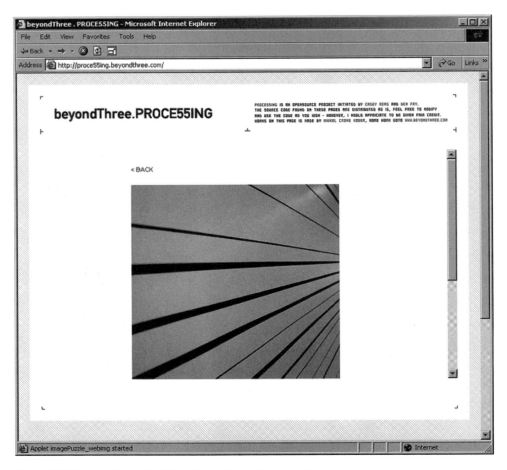

Figure 11.17   beyondthree.tif. Mikkel Moser. BeyondThree website.

computer science and computer graphics are now being distributed to the mass community of artists and designers.

Curriculum

There are many established introductory curricula for computer science (and thousands of variants), but by comparison very few classes have been striving to integrate traditional visual arts knowledge with core concepts of computation. Using the classes initiated by John Maeda as a model, diverse courses are begin created around Processing by using ideas from the computer science community to support assignments in visual and interaction

Figure 11.18 noise_toxi.tif. Perlin noise generated landscape by Karsten Schmidt.

design. These workshops and courses have been used at diverse universities and institutions in the United States (MIT, Yale, New York University, Columbia, UCLA, University of Florida, etc.), Europe (Royal College of Art, Central Saint Martins, University of the Arts Berlin, Interaction Design Institute Ivrea, etc.), and Asia (Hongik Univeristy, Ateneo de Manila University, etc.).

Processing has proved to be a useful environment for short workshops ranging from one day to a few weeks. Because the environment is so minimal, students are able to begin programming after a few minutes of instruction. The Processing syntax, similar to those of Java and Actionscript, is already familiar to many people and this allows experienced

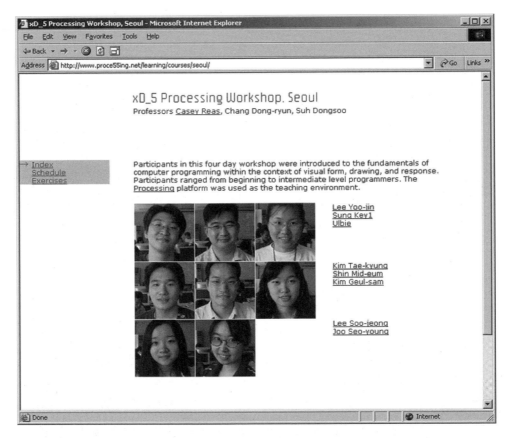

Figure 11.19   workshop_seoul.tif. Website for Processing workshop at Hongik University in Seoul.

programmers to begin writing advanced syntax almost immediately. In the one-week workshop at Hongik University in Seoul (figure 11.19), the students were a mix of computer science and design majors and both groups worked toward synthesis. Some work was more visually sophisticated and some more technically sophisticated, but it was all evaluated within the same set of criteria.

In a university situation, Processing has been used for teaching introductory classes and advanced topical graduate-level courses. The Design for Interactive Media course at UCLA looks at familiar visual elements (form, image, typography, animation, and interface) by writing short programs. Because the language is easily extended with external classes, educators can tailor the content to their specific needs. For his Model Based design class at the

Figure 11.20 mkim.tif. Malaika Kim. Image rendered from DXF file exported from Processing.

Yale School of Architecture, Simon Greenwold extended Processing to export DXF files, a common 3D file format, thus allowing his students to export computationally generated models and render them in specialized rendering environments (figure 11.20). For his classes at New York University, Amit Pitaru wrote a library to merging JSyn, a popular Java audio library, with Processing to give him and his students more refined control over audio data than the base library provides. Using this extension, Amit wrote the Sonic Wire Sculpture application (figure 11.21), which generates sound from 3D lines as they move through space.

Future Directions

There is an enormous area for innovation beyond the creation of text-based programming environments such as Processing and Design By Numbers. We don't see the creation of these languages as a revolutionary advance, but as an important step in the evolution of programming languages and environments for visual art and design. Other explorations within the Aesthetics and Computation Group reveal innovative ideas about the future of computation. These experiments remove programming from its one-dimensional text representation by introducing space, color, and motion. The Visual Machines of Jared

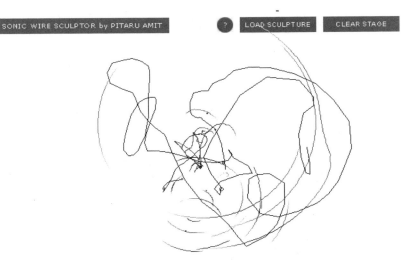

Figure 11.21   wiresculpture_pitaru.tif. Amit Pitaru. Sonic Wire Sculpture, the JSyn audio library generates tones by reading a 3D linear form.

Schiffman and the Visually Deconstructing Code series by Ben Fry create a base for future exploration in software tools and pedagogy. Each of the studies presented in the following pages is a working software prototype.

Visual Machines

Jared Schiffman has developed a Visual Machine Model and a series of Visual Machine Languages (Schiffman 2001). His goal is to make computation visible and therefore more accessible by improving the process of programming with new kinds of visual programming languages and environments. Each of these explorations allows the programmer to observe the computation continuously and directly interact with it by adjusting values and logical structures while the program is running.

Turing

Turing is a reinterpretation and visualization of Alan Turing's theoretical computing machine and its one-dimensional tape. It enables the user to draw a program as a series of nodes and connections and then watch the program execute. Each node is a state in the constructed finite state diagram, and each connection defines a transition with an input symbol, output symbol, and direction in which the tape should move. The program rep-

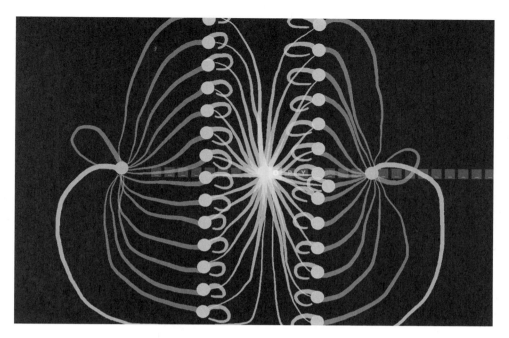

Figure 11.22 turing_schiffman.tif. Jared Schiffman. Turing.

resented in figure 11.22 copies any piece of text from one point in the tape to another. This model of programming is more similar to drawing than to writing.

Plate

Plate is derived from text-based programming languages, but the form of the language is defined by embedded structural layers. There are ten separate types of layers for the different elements of the language and they are instantiated by selecting from contextual menus. Plate is a syntax-directed editing environment, assisting the programmer to construct valid syntax. Programs can be executed normally or step-by-step and on execution, the layers fold backward and forward to place emphasis on the code that is currently executing (figure 11.23). This allows the programmer to clearly see the correlation between the running code and the result.

Pablo

Pablo is based in the functional data flow paradigm. It borrows visual elements from precedents such as Prograph, but extends the concept by visually animating the data

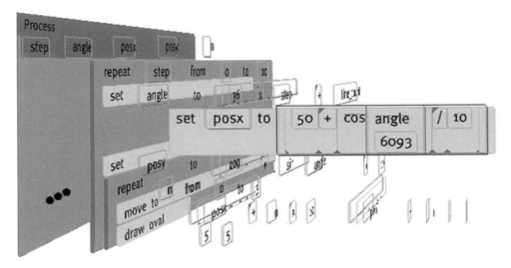

Figure 11.23 plate_schiffman.tif. Jared Schiffman. Plate.

moving through the structure. This reinforces the conceptual model and allows contextual access to the changing data as it flows through the program (figure 11.24). Pablo programs execute in a continuous visual space, with elements such as functions expanding and collapsing during runtime to reveal their infrastructure as the data flows through.

Nerpa

Visual elements in Nerpa replace the structural elements of text-based programming languages. It is a purely functional language, meaning each expression within the program evaluates to a value. Each expression is represented by a shape with two sides—one showing the expression and the opposite side showing the resulting value. Each function is enclosed inside a circular disc, with the center area returning the final value. As functions execute, they operate from the outside to the center, smoothly pulling in the attached elements as the calculation takes place (figure 11.25). After the program runs, the user may reexpand the structure and observe each of the values.

Visually Deconstructing Code

Visually Deconstructing Code by Ben Fry is a series of experiments looking at the form of code. This collection searches for alternative perspectives to text, machine language, and binary software codes and visualizes the abstract structures and processes buried within.

Casey Reas and Ben Fry

Figure 11.24 pablo_schiffman.tif. Jared Schiffman. Pablo.

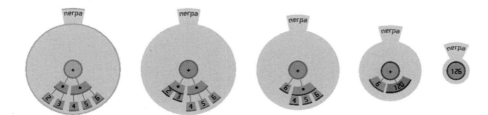

Figure 11.25 nerpa_schiffman.tif. Jared Schiffman. Nerpa.

The Evolution of Software Projects

While it's obvious that the code in a software project changes over time, less obvious is the nature of how individual changes have taken place in a broader context. Projects are typically structured as a collection of files that are added, removed, and reorganized throughout the course of development. The contents of the individual files are modified, line by line or in large pieces for every fix and feature.

The first experiment in this set is an interactive application that shows the evolution of the structure and content of the Processing project over time from its initial inception through forty releases. The experiment consists of large-format printed pieces depicting broader changes over time. Figure 11.26 shows an overall picture of the changes, with each column representing one version of the software. Lines are drawn between the columns to connect lines that have changed. Notable changes can be seen for the removal of one large file (bottom, middle), and the later addition of a new file (top, right), or a spike in activity (about two-thirds to the right) coinciding with a push for the initial alpha

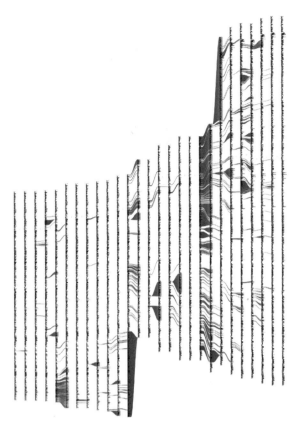

Figure 11.26 evolution1_fry.tif. Ben Fry. Visualizing the evolution of the Processing code.

release of the project. Figure 11.27 shows a detail of the image enlarged thirteen times to make the text of one portion of a column legible.

While the method of depicting changes between versions of a file is not new, representing many versions in a single instance is less conventional. The result is a depiction of the organic process in which even the smallest pieces of software code mature through the course of its development, as it is passed between developers, revisited for later refinement, merged, removed, and simplified.

Packaging of Data Within Code

Any piece of executable code is also commingled with data, ranging from simple sentences of text for error messages to entire sets of graphics for the application. In older cartridge-

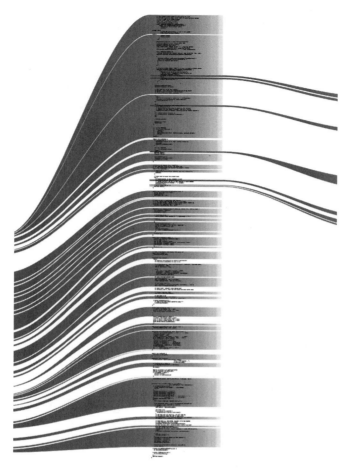

Figure 11.27 evolution2_fry.tif. Ben Fry. Visualizing the evolution of the Processing code (detail).

based console games, the images for each of the small on-screen images (the "sprites") were often stored as raw data embedded after the program's instructions. This piece examines the unpacking of a Nintendo game cartridge, decoding the program as a four-color image, to reveal a beautiful soup of the thousands of individual visual elements making up the game screen.

The images are a long series of 8 × 8 pixel "tiles." Looking at the cartridge memory directly (with a black pixel for an "on" bit, and a white pixel for an "off") reveals the sequence of black and white (one bit) 8 × 8 images. Each pair of images is mixed together to produce a two-bit (four-color) image. The blue represents the first sequence of image

Figure 11.28 packagingdata_fry.tif. Ben Fry. Revealing images stored as raw data on a Nintendo cartridge.

data, the red acetate sheet is the second set of data that is read, and together they produce the proper mixed-color image depicting the actual image data (figure 11.28).

Seeing Time in the Operation of Code

Programs on modern computers are eventually compiled into machine language, a series of basic and direct instructions understood by the microprocessor. Programs are flattened from their hierarchical state into a long series of simple mathematical instructions (e.g., "multiply" or "add with carry") and interspersed with commands for jumping to another location in the program. Figure 11.29 shows the program for the "Excite Bike" game for the original Nintendo (this console was chosen for its simplicity). The blocks of gray text are "data" sections used to store images or game scenarios. The curved lines connect locations in the program where "jumps" occur, which can be a function or a conditional choice made by the software. Figure 11.30 depicts the original "Super Mario Brothers" game. The images were created in appreciation of the elegant structure of such software, rather than as a diagnostic tool for understanding their operation. (The binary of the cartridge program is disassembled from the text list seen here with a program called *NESrev* written by Kent Hansen.)

Visual Mathematics in Code Algorithms

A class of software algorithms including cryptography, error checking, and serial number testing works like the mathematical equivalent of the ridges found on an intricate key. Their operation is a series of gymnastics performed with a group of numbers comprising the key.

This piece examines such an algorithm that simulates the process of how the serial numbers for software products by the manufacturer Adobe are generated and tested (figure 11.31). It begins with a simple seed number, and then walks through several mathematical steps, mostly simple addition or multiplication, to generate a multidigit key for the

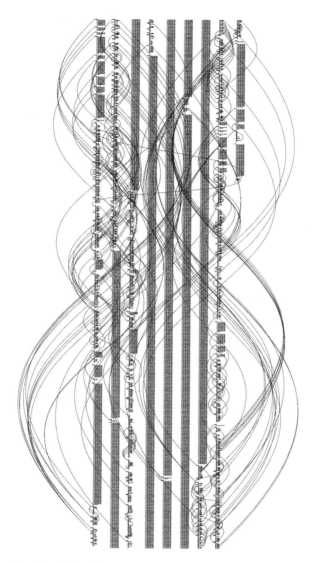

Figure 11.29   operation1_fry.tif. Ben Fry. Excite Bike code visualization.

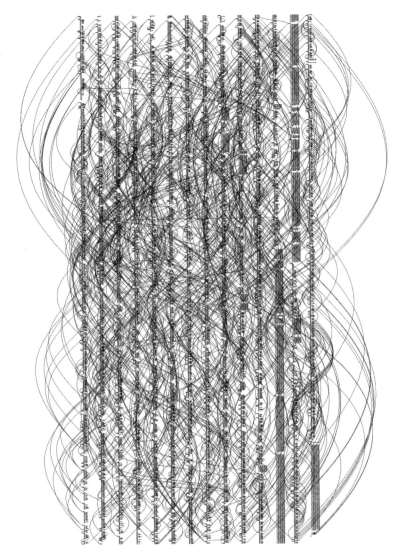

Figure 11.30 operation2_fry.tif. Ben Fry. Super Mario Brothers code visualization.

Figure 11.31 serial_fry.tif. Ben Fry. Examining the algorithmic structure of serial numbers.

product. An application such as Photoshop or Illustrator will use such an algorithm to test whether the key entered by the user is proper; while the same algorithm can also be used to generate a myriad of fake but working keys for anyone who wants his or her own. The nature of this experiment is to illustrate the elegance and simplicity of a process kept intentionally as opaque as possible to the end-user.

Each of these experiments begins with the question, "How can this aspect of code be understood visually?" As individual projects, they are simple ideas, but as a collection, they provide a visual perspective on how code works and behaves, introducing a mental model for code that is more organic than common tools of depiction like text, tables, and graphs.

Conclusion

The development of alternative programming environments and languages is not a unique pursuit, and we have been highly influenced by pioneering work such as Seymour Papert's LOGO, Miller Puckette's MAX, and Jitter by Cycling '74. These languages were each developed for a specific context, and Processing and its related curriculum have been developed for their own context within the art and visual design communities.

In the same way the graphical user interface (GUI) innovation made it possible for more people to use computers, we hope a future innovation will enable more people to begin programming computational machines for their own desires and needs. The Apple Macintosh was definitely not the first computer with a GUI, but it started the revolution. Our goal is to contribute to the foundation of the next revolution in which the ideas behind computer programming, not simply the use of computers, can become as ubiquitous as basic skills in writing and mathematics.

References

Aesthetics and Computation Group, at http://acg.media.mit.edu.

Beyond Three, at http://proce55ing.beyondthree.com/Flight404; http://www.flight404.com/.

Fry, Ben. 2003. "Visually Desconstructing Code." In Ars Electronica 2003: CODE—The Language of Our Times, Hatje Cantz.

Maeda, John. 1999. *Design By Numbers*. Cambridge, MA: MIT Press.

Maeda, John. 2000. Maeda@Media. London: Thames & Hudson.

Moovl, at http://www.soda.co.uk/moovl.

Processing, at http://processing.org.

Schiffman, Jared. 2001. "Aesthetics of Computation—Unveiling the Visual Machine." MIT Media Laboratory MS thesis. Available at http://acg.media.mit.edu/people/jarfish/VisualMachineThesis.pdf.

Sonia, at http://pitaru.com/.

Mathematics and Computing

Aesthetics and the Visualization and Quality of Software

Stephan Diehl and Carsten Görg

Software has many facets. Users and developers perceive different facets, or at least perceive them in different ways. Users typically run software and interact with it through a graphical user interface, while developers spend much time with visual representations to design, implement, and analyze software. The majority of these representations are text and graph based. In the following we discuss the relation of the visual beauty of software to its quality—in particular, whether nice implies good. To this end we look at the field of software visualization first, that is, the use of computer graphical representation to show the development process, structure, and behavior of software (Stasko et al. 1998; Diehl 2001).

Beauty—Scientifically

Humans assign beauty to objects that please the senses, or the intellect. Beauty is a very subjective property and differs from culture to culture. Nevertheless, many scientists attempt to define and even measure it. The first step toward this goal is to identify elementary properties that as a whole make up or at least contribute to beauty. If we can count or in some way quantify all these properties, then we can quantify beauty by the sum of the elementary measures. In essence, therefore, beauty is reduced to a number and once we measure the beauty of two objects, we can say one is nicer than the other if its measure is greater. Since introduced by Euclid in about 300 B.C., the golden ratio has a long history as a measure of beauty in art (for a critical account see Livio 2003). All mathematical approaches to measuring beauty have to ignore some contributing aspects to cope with the complexity of a real world, but isn't that true for all science?

Software Quality

Aspects of software quality include ease of use, speed, correctness, reliability, security, extensibility, and maintainability. The quality of a particular piece of software is dominated by some of these aspects, depending on its purpose. Software engineers have come up with an abundance of software metrics to quantify different facets of software and relate them to aspects of software quality. As an example of how quality is measured, we look at coupling. Coupling is the degree to which components in software systems depend on one another. Larger software systems consist of different libraries, modules, classes, and functions —in decreasing order of granularity. If we look, for example, at the function level we find that functions call other functions. Functions called by another function are coupled. So, as a simple metric for coupling we can define the coupling of a particular function as the number of functions it calls and the number of functions it is called by. Such a coupling metric quantifies the complexity of the dependencies in a software system. Typically, the more dependencies there are, the more difficult it is to understand or replace a function.

Similarly, we can define measures for coupling on other levels of granularity. As a rule of thumb, software developers strive for low coupling, in particular at the higher levels of granularity such as classes or modules.

Aesthetics and Software Visualization

To develop new or understand existing software, we often need to represent it in a human readable form, for example, the program text. Note that the program text is not the software, but just a representation of it. The program text is written in an artificial language with a strict syntax and typically well-defined semantics. Often program text is "pretty printed" to make it more appealing and understandable to the human eye. Pretty printing produces a formatted, textual representation of the source code. Originally, pretty printing was restricted to the use of indentation, spaces, and line breaks to make the structure of a program more explicit. Later, tabbing was added for vertical alignment of declarations, and different widths of spaces between operators and operands made operator precedence more explicit. With technological advances fonts, font faces, and colors are now also used, for example, boldface for keywords and italics for comments, as shown in the left part of figure 12.1. Different font sizes can indicate nesting levels (lexical scope).

The more the scale and functionality of modern software systems expand, the more the program text used to represent the software increases. Trying to understand a real software system by reading its millions of lines of program text is a pointless task, even if it is pretty printed. As a consequence, many tools have been developed to support software understanding. Often such tools rely on analysis and visualization techniques. The SeeSoft system (Eick et al. 1992; Ball and Eick 1996) represents each line of code as a line of pixels

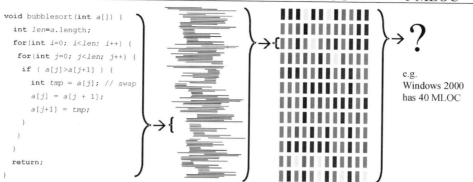

| 10 LOC | 100 LOC | 1KLOC | 1 MLOC |

```
void bubblesort(int a[]) {
  int len=a.length;
  for(int i=0; i<len; i++) {
    for(int j=0; j<len; j++) {
      if ( a[j]>a[j+1] ) {
        int tmp = a[j]; // swap
        a[j] = a[j + 1];
        a[j+1] = tmp;
      }
    }
  }
  return;
}
```

e.g.
Windows 2000
has 40 MLOC

Figure 12.1 Pretty printed program code and color-coded pixel representations of program code (LOC = lines of code).

or even a single pixel (see figure 12.1). Metrics computed by different kinds of analysis are color-coded, that is, the color of each pixel indicates the value of the metric for a particular line of code. For example, red (in SeeSoft, hot) is used for lines that have been changed recently, whereas blue (in SeeSoft, cold) indicates lines that have not been changed for a long time. With this color-code, the user can easily see what parts of a program are under current development.

In figure 12.2 a graphical representation of a program, its call graph, is shown. In addition, the graph contains some information computed by a program analysis. With the help of this visualization developers can detect certain kinds of errors, so-called stack overflows, in their programs (AbsInt 2004). A stack overflow is an error condition that is the result of trying to put additional items onto a stack (area of memory) when there is no room for them. In the call graph shown, the number of edge crossings and bends has been reduced and directed edges are mostly drawn downwards. The nodes of a call graph represent elements of a software system that access other elements, where the edge set represents such access. A visual representation of such a call graph, consisting of rendered nodes and edges, is referred to as a graph drawing. Quigley discusses some graph drawing aesthetics in more detail in another chapter. These aesthetics are quantitative, for each layout of a graph, each aesthetic measure yields a number, thus producing a nice graph layout is reduced to the problem of minimizing or maximizing the value of each measure. Unfortunately, when trying to minimize the number of edge crossings, the number of bends usually increases. So, often the optimization goals are conflicting and a nice graph drawing is a compromise, trading one aesthetic measure for another.

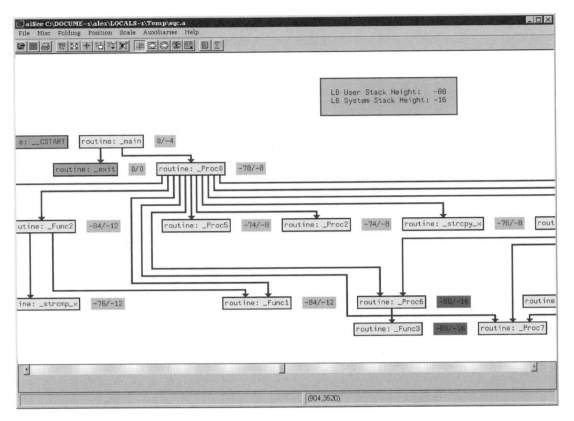

Figure 12.2   Call graph of program with stack usage information computed by static program analysis.

Software is often designed using diagrams. In recent years, a collection of diagram types called the Unified Modeling Language (UML) has been standardized and is widely used in industry (Fowler 2003). Despite its widespread use, the visual efficiency of these diagrams is very low (Purchase et al. 2003). In recent studies, geons have been used to draw diagrams of software architectures (Irani and Ware 2000). Geons are a collection of twenty-four primitive, viewpoint-invariant 3D objects, which means they are easy to recognize even when projected into 2D.

Several experiments with computer science students showed they could visually analyze geon diagrams much faster and with more accuracy, and they could recall them better than with equivalent UML diagrams. Figure 12.3 shows a UML diagram and a geon diagram of a car. It inherits from conveyance and consists of a motor and several wheels. Note

Stephan Diehl and Carsten Görg

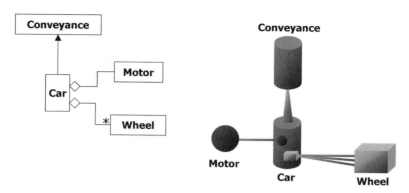

Figure 12.3 UML diagram and an equivalent geon diagram.

that, unlike in typical UML diagrams, the geons of the aggregated classes in the geon diagram are also drawn in reduced size within the geon representing the aggregating class.

Aesthetics and Software Quality

In this section we discuss the question of correspondence between the aesthetics of software visualization and the software quality. Or more precisely, is the software quality high if the visualization is beautiful and vice versa?

As an example, we consider the visualization of the control-flow graph of a program that is a directed graph whose nodes are the program's instructions. Two nodes, i and j, are connected by an edge if an execution of the program exists in which instruction j is executed directly after instruction i. Furthermore, a control-flow graph has two special nodes: the entry and exit points of the program.

A program is called structured if its control-flow graph is a series-parallel graph. Series-parallel graphs are recursively defined (Kannan and Proebsting 1995):

1. A graph consisting of two nodes with an edge between them is a series-parallel graph.
2. A series connection of two series-parallel graphs is a series-parallel graph.
3. A parallel connection of two series-parallel graphs is a series-parallel graph.

The series-parallel graphs can be drawn nicely, because these graphs are planar (i.e., they have no edge crossings) and well structured and it is easy to follow the flow. Because common constructs in modern programming languages like loops and conditional statements lead to series-parallel control-flow graphs, it is appropriate to claim there is a correspondence between aesthetics and software quality: structured programs that usually have better quality than unstructured programs (because they are easier to extend and maintain and are not as error-prone) lead to series-parallel control-flow graphs, which are more beautiful than those of unstructured programs. These graphs are usually not series-parallel and in some cases not even planar because of the excessive use of goto statements. The same holds in the inverse direction as well: a series-parallel control-flow graph leads to a structured program with good quality, whereas an unaesthetic control-flow graph that is not planar leads to some "spaghetti-code" program of low quality. Note that we have only identified a relation between a single measure of beauty and a single measure of software quality, here structuredness. Nice drawings result as a compromise of different aesthetic criteria. When we actually draw a certain control-flow graph, other measures might be important as well, for example, one might trade crossing edges for length of edges. Furthermore, program code can be structured at one level of abstraction while very unstructured at another one.

As a second example of the visual aesthetics–software quality relationship, we return to coupling as a measure of software quality. In his book *Machine Beauty*, David Gelernter presents many examples of computer systems that draw their beauty from being powerful, yet simple (Gelernter 1998). We think that this is true for some software visualization techniques, too. Although technically they are very simple, they provide new insights about software and its development process.

As an example, consider the pixel map shown in figure 12.4. In this map, the color of the pixel at position (x, y) represents the number of times file f_x and f_y have been changed together relative to the total number of times file f_x has been changed. This figure shows the developer how strongly different files are coupled. We call this evolutionary coupling (Zimmermann et al. 2003), because it is based on the change history of files, to distinguish it from the logical coupling usually used in software engineering. As the files are sorted by the containing directory, the pixels form blocks. These blocks indicate that files within a directory are coupled, that is, often changed together. Software developers are mainly interested in the outliers—those pixels representing couplings between files in different directories, such as those labeled "Patches" in figure 12.4. Outliers can be a sign of a bad system architecture. In other words, if we do not find rectangular areas nicely aligned along the diagonal in the pixel map, the system should be restructured.

Software Beauty

The previous sections discussed the relation of the visual beauty of representations of software. Two additional aspects of software haven't yet been covered: the visual beauty of the graphical user interface and the beauty of software as a theory, for example, whether it is elegant, ingenious, tricky, or just a hack. Several chapters of this book address the first

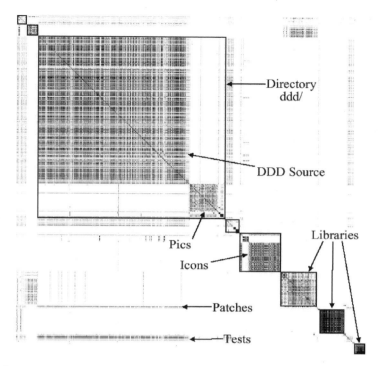

Figure 12.4   Pixel map showing the evolutionary coupling of the GNU Data Display Debugger (DDD).

aspect, so we discuss only the second aspect here using as an example the computation of prime numbers. An integer greater than 1 is prime if it is divisible only by itself and 1. The straightforward algorithm to compute all prime numbers from 1 to N is performing a simple primality test for each number n, that is, test whether n is divisible by a smaller number greater than 1. In about 240 B.C. the Greek mathematician Eratosthenes devised an algorithm, considered beautiful by many computer scientists, to solve this problem more efficiently. This algorithm, also known as "the sieve of Eratosthenes," uses the previously computed smaller prime numbers in its primality test, which divides the number n by all the primes less than the square root of n. The algorithm draws its beauty from its efficiency and concise formulation, both resulting from mathematical insights and the reuse of previously computed results.

Summary

We looked at the interrelations of aesthetics, software visualization, and software quality. First, we discussed the aesthetics of several software visualizations, then gave examples in which nice visualizations implied good software quality. If carefully chosen, a visualization can be an indicator of the quality of a software system. For the series-parallel control-flow graphs, we found that the inverse implication also holds. In our examples, it was important that we reduced beauty to some simple properties that could be objectively measured. We did not address the relationship between subjective, visual beauty and software quality.

References

AbsInt GmbH. 2004. aiCall StackAnalyzer. Available at http://www.aicall.de.

Ball, Thomas, and Eick, Stephen G. 1996. "Software Visualization in the Large." *IEEE Computer Society Press* 29(4): 33–43.

Diehl, Stephan, ed. 2001. *Software Visualization.* New York: Springer Verlag, LNCS 2269.

Eick, Stephen G., Steffen, Joseph L., and Sumner, Eric E. 1992. "SeeSoft—A Tool for Visualizing Line Oriented Software Statistics." *IEEE Transactions on Software Engineering* 18(11): 957–68.

Fishwick, Paul, Diehl, Stephan, Prophet, Jane, and Lowgren, Jonas. 2004. "Perspectives on Aesthetic Computing." *Leonardo.* Cambridge, MA: MIT Press. 38(2): 133–41.

Fowler, Martin. 2003. *UML Distilled.* New York: Addison Wesley.

Gelernter, David. 1998. *Machine Beauty: Elegance and the Heart of Technology.* Basic Books.

Irani, P. Pourang, and Ware, Colin. 2000. "3D Diagrams Based on Theories of Structural Perception." In *ACM Advanced Visual Interfaces, Palermo, Italy.* New York: ACM Press, pp. 61–67.

Kannan, Sampath, and Proebsting, Todd. 1995. "Register Allocation in Structured Programs." In *Proceedings of the Sixth Annual ACM-SIAM Symposium on Discrete Algorithm.* Philadelphia, PA: Society for Industrial and Applied Mathematics, pp. 360–68.

Livio, Mario. 2003. *The Golden Ratio: The Story of Phi, the World's Most Astonishing Number.* New York: Broadway Books.

Purchase, Helen C., Colpoys, Linda, Carrington, David, and McGill, Matthew. 2003. "Comprehension of UML Class Diagrams." In *Software Visualization—From Theory to Practice.* Zhang, Kang, ed. New York: Kluwer Academic Publishers, pp. 149–78.

Stasko, John, Domingue, John, Brown, Marc, and Price, Blaine, eds. 1998. *Software Visualization: Programming as a Multimedia Experience.* Cambridge, MA: MIT Press.

Zimmermann, Thomas, Diehl, Stephan, and Zeller, Andreas. 2003. "How History Justifies System Architecture." In *Proceedings of International Workshop on Principles of Software Evolution IWPSE'2003, Helsinki, Finland.* IEEE Computer Society Press.

13

Aesthetics and Mathematics: Connections Throughout History

Michele Emmer

Many mathematicians feel their activity is highly creative and possesses a special beauty. They go so far as to say that aesthetic criteria determine many of the decisions taken in writing proofs and the interest of certain theories. One source of this viewpoint is Plato. In his dialogue *Timaeus*, Plato describes the five regular solids of three-dimensional (3D) space as the most beautiful shapes the human mind is capable of imagining. These are not physical objects, which one can make a model of, but ideas—Platonic ideas, one might say, or "the essence of the spirit," as Robert Musil puts it in his book *A Man Without Qualities* (Musil 1929), whose main character is a mathematician. Interestingly, many mathematicians who have written about aesthetics cited the five Platonic solids among the most fascinating of mathematical entities.

No doubt the intrinsic beauty and harmony of these solids, as well as the theory of proportions contained in Euclid's *Elements*, provoked interest in geometry and mathematics among the great artists of the Italian Renaissance. And it was a mathematician, Luca Pacioli (a close friend of Piero della Francesca, portrayed in *La Madonna dell'ovo*), who possibly coined the term "divine proportion," in his well-known book, *De Divina Proportione*, a work published in 1509 that also included Leonardo da Vinci's famous illustrations of the spatial solids.

Returning to the present day, Morris Kline wrote in his book *The Mathematics of Western Culture* (Kline 1953) that "The determination of the precise assertions contained in the theorems, and the proofs which establish those theorems, are acts of creation. As in the arts, each detail of the final work is not discovered but composed. Of course the creative process must produce a work that has design, harmony and beauty. These qualities too, are present in mathematical creations." In my comments on Kline's words, I wrote in "Mathematics and Art" that

while it may not be profitable to discuss mathematicians' ideas about art, it is still worth pointing out that an artistic ambition is widespread in the mathematical community. Complementary to this ambition, there is the need for the artistic creativity of mathematicians to be recognized by outsiders—recognition that is not usually forthcoming, especially from those who deal with art. Also because this would mean attempting to understand something about contemporary mathematics.

Kline is fully aware of this problem when he says that "the ultimate test of a work of art is its contribution to aesthetic pleasure or beauty," even though this may not be so clear for contemporary art. But that is beyond the scope of this discussion. "Fortunately or unfortunately, this is a subjective test and depends on the cultivation of a special taste. Hence the question of whether mathematics possesses beauty can be answered only by those who have studied the subject. Unfortunately it requires years of study to master mathematical ideas and there is no royal road that effectively shortens the process."

When speaking of beauty, mathematicians also hope to communicate to those who are not mathematicians, philosophers, or art historians. They must therefore rely on well-known and simple examples to be understood. Few mathematicians not working directly in the field can grasp the beauty and elegance of the theorem and the proof of singularities for minimal surfaces in dimensions greater than 7. Examples must, first, be useful to clarify ideas.

It is always difficult to examine intellectual processes. And the difficulties encountered are even greater when dealing with mathematics, a discipline that is hard to explain to those who don't have sufficient experience in this field. On the other hand, this is true for almost any field of human knowledge. When the answers are difficult, or rather when the questions are difficult, mathematicians usually look for examples or try to modify the question to simplify its answer. And this is what we must do—not attempt to find conclusive answers to these questions (which would not be possible), but determine how to formulate the problems and the questions to try to understand them.

A new phenomenon has occurred in mathematics research in the last 25 years: the use of computers in proving theorems (e.g., the famous proof of the Four Color Theorem) and computer graphics for better understanding problems, visualizing and proving nontrivial results. One of the most interesting uses of computer graphics is in the proof by David Hoffman, William Meeks, and J. T. Hoffman of the Costa surface in solving an old conjecture on infinite minimal surfaces not self-intersecting, with topological genus greater than zero, let us say with "holes." Another example is the visualization of the behavior of the unknown solution to nonlinear PDE or ODE to understand their behavior, as in the case of the Lorenz attractor. Fractal geometry and all possible applications is another interesting example.

All of these new areas of mathematics have stimulated many questions in the mathematical community regarding the meaning of proving a result, as well as questions related to aesthetics and mathematics in connection with computing. Many mathematicians working in these new areas of "visual mathematics" are naturally attracted to consider the "beauty," that is, the aesthetics of the new forms discovered in their work. B. Mandelbrot, D. Hoofman, M. Field, and H. O. Peitgen, among others have written books and articles on the possible connections of their work with art and on the aesthetics of their virtual images. Others have organized traveling exhibitions on the "beauty" of mathematics. Their work has focused, in part, on the aesthetic impact of the images, analyzing the best way to present their work visually to a wide public. For example, in the introduction to their book *The Beauty of Fractals* (Peitgen and Richter 1986) Peitgen and Richter wrote: "Science and art: two complementary ways of setting up a relation with the real world, analytical the first, intuitive the second. The thinking man, in his efforts to resolve all the complexity of phenomena in a few basic law, is himself a visionary, no less than the person, a lover of beauty, who immerses themselves in the richness of shapes, feeling themselves to be part of the eternity to come."

Consideration of the aesthetic aspects of mathematics started well before the use of computers. As the well-known example of the Platonic solids as well as similar "classical" examples of symmetry, proportions, and the Golden ratio, the mathematicians' appreciation of the "beauty" of mathematics is very old. Understanding the reasons and motivations of the mathematicians who have written on mathematics and aesthetics can help clarify the attitude toward an aesthetic of the new computing medium. This chapter focuses on some of these attitudes.

Diehl and Görg, in another chapter, define beauty as follows:

Humans assign beauty to objects that please the senses, or the intellect. Beauty is a very subjective property and differs from culture to culture. Nevertheless, many scientists tried to define and even more measure it. The first step toward this goal is to identify elementary properties which as a whole make up or at least contribute to beauty. If we can count or in some way quantify all these properties, then we can quantify beauty by the sum of the elementary measures. In essence, therefore, beauty is reduced to a number and once we measure beauty of two objects, we can say one is nicer than the other if its measure is greater.

Is it possible to have aesthetics criteria than can be measurable and objective? What follows is a short history of a selection of papers and books on the beauty of mathematics. First, let us consider Francis Hutcheson's words on beauty written three centuries ago. Many of the questions he raised were revisited in subsequent centuries.

Francis Hutcheson: The Beauty of Theorems

The first edition of *Inquiry into the Origin of Our Ideas of Beauty and Virtue* was published in London in 1729 (Hutcheson 1729). In the eighteenth century, aesthetics became an autonomous philosophical discipline. The term "aesthetics" was not in current use when Hutcheson published this first organic treatment of the subject whose aim was to investigate the nature of aesthetics, taking beauty as its most basic aspect.

As Ermanno Migliorini wrote in the preface to the Italian edition in 1988 (Migliorini 1988), Hutcheson's work is

a systematic investigation into the origin of the idea of beauty, order, harmony and design. It probably marks the first appearance of ideas such as the universality of the sense of beauty and the links between original and comparative beauty, the regularity of nature, uniformity in variety, as well as the beauty of theorems. Of course, it also deals with the field of arts, and is full of subtle observations on painting, sculpture, architecture, landscape gardening, music and poetry.

These subjects would be taken up again by Kant in his *Critique of the Faculty of Judgment*, in which he writes (Kant 1790) "Beauty is what is represented, without pre-conceptions, as an object of universal pleasure" and again, "an object of pleasure with no purpose beyond its own existence." This is a subject dear to mathematicians championing the beauty of their discipline.

Kant also wrote that: "Anything that conforms too rigidly to rules (similar to mathematical rules) has within itself something that is contrary to pleasure; in other words, it does not keep our attention long enough to remember it, and it leads to boredom since it does not aim expressly at knowledge or a specific practical purpose." Many years later, Ernst Gombrich dedicated a chapter of his book *The Sense of Order* (Gombrich 1979) to precise rules. This is my starting point in examining the question of the relationship between mathematics and aesthetics. Hutcheson says in his preface (Hutcheson 1729, preface, pp. XII, XIII):

There is scarcely any object which our minds are employed about, which is not thus constituted the necessary occasion of some pleasure or pain. Thus we find ourselves pleased with a regular form, a piece of architecture or painting, a composition of notes, a theorem, an action, an affection, a character. And we are conscious that this pleasure necessarily arises from the contemplation of the idea, which is then present to our minds, with all its circumstances, although some of these ideas have nothing of what we commonly call sensible perception in them, [as in the case of mathematical theorems whose peculiarity is their abstraction.]

One needs to have a particular type of sensibility, an "internal sense" (Hutcheson 1729, p. 9) Hutcheson continues,

There will appear another reason perhaps hereafter, for calling this power of perceiving the ideas of beauty, an internal sense; from this, as in some other affairs where our external senses are not much concerned, we discern a sort of beauty, very like, in many respects, to that observed in sensible objects, and accompanied with like pleasure: such is that beauty perceived in theorems, or universal truths, in general causes, and in some extensive principles of action.

As with any theory, Hutcheson has to provide examples of this original or absolute beauty (Hutcheson 1729, p. 14):

What we call beautiful in objects, to speak in the mathematical style, seems to be in a compound ratio of uniformity and variety, so that where the uniformity of bodies is equal, the beauty is as the variety; and where the variety is equal, the beauty is as the uniformity. This will be plain from examples. First, the variety increases the beauty in equal uniformity. The beauty of an equilateral triangle is less than that of the square; which is less than that of a pentagon; and this again is surpassed by the hexagon. When indeed the number of sides is much increased the proportion of them to the radius or diameter of the figure, or of the circle to which regular polygons have an obvious relation, is so much lost to our observation that the beauty does not always increase with the number of sides; and the want of parallelism in the sides of heptagons, and other figures of odd numbers, may also diminish their beauty. So in solids, the icosahedron surpasses the dodecahedron, and this the octahedron, which is still more beautiful than the cube; and this again passes the regular pyramid: the obvious ground of this is greater variety with equal uniformity.

Clearly, Hutcheson deals with Platonic solids, which one might say is where everything starts. It is always difficult to provide significant examples that are also comprehensible to nonmathematicians. The regular solids have both qualities. It is interesting to note that the mathematician George David Birkhoff formulated a full theory of mathematics and aesthetics in the 1930s. To provide examples, he analyzed the aesthetics of the geometrical figures, concluding (as opposed to Plato) that the construction of 3D spatial figures was based on the "most beautiful of the triangles, the one that, when doubled, generates a third triangle which is equilateral." This is the right-angled scalene triangle in which the cathetus is equal to half the hypotenuse. Birkhoff developed a formula to calculate a measure of aesthetic value. By applying it to the right-angled triangle, he obtained a minimum of beauty. He felt that numerical determination of aesthetic spatial perception would be a great help since, if the *aesthetic mechanism* were subject to a mathematical law, at least in theory it would be possible to express the laws governing shapes with the help of a mathematical formula. Birkhoff's formula for the feeling of aesthetic pleasure is introduced in his long essay, "A Mathematical Approach to Aesthetics" (Birkhoff 1931).

The legitimacy of mathematical aesthetics was based on the fact that all psychological and social phenomena seemed to have logical structures in the eyes of *homo mathematicus* who, as Birkhoff notes (Birkhoff 1934), is led to believe that further progress along this difficult path would be possible only once more adequate mathematical concepts and methods had been developed. Moreover, for Birkhoff, the vast field of pure mathematical thought testifies unequivocally that the objective and subjective world is of a mathematical nature.

This led Birkhoff to the idea that, in the field of aesthetics, one can recognize and quantify mathematical order determined by factors such as symmetry, rotation, equilibrium, and simplicity. To express the aesthetic measurement of an object, all that is needed (in the simplest terms) is to work out the function M (representing the feeling of aesthetic pleasure) as a ratio $M = O/C$, where O is the order of the object, and C its complexity. Birkhoff's theory leaves the main question open—what we see and feel when we experience a visual composition or a piece of music and whether this seeing and feeling lends itself to mathematical analysis. Of course, finding an answer is extremely difficult.

Returning to the beauty of mathematics, Hutcheson's theory would be less interesting if it were limited to geometric shapes generally considered "beautiful" from Plato's time through the Renaissance. The chapter of Hutcheson's book that interests me most (Hutcheson 1729, p. 30) discusses the beauty of theorems:

The beauty of theorems, or universal truth demonstrated, deserves a distinct consideration, being of a nature pretty different from the former kinds of beauty; and yet there is none in which we shall see such an amazing variety with uniformity; and hence arise a very great pleasure distinct from prospects of any farther advantage. For in one theorem we may find included, with the most exact agreement, an infinite multitude of particular truths; nay, often an infinity of infinities; so that although the necessity of forming abstract ideas and universal theorems, arises perhaps from the limitation of our minds, which cannot admit an infinite multitude of singular ideas or judgments at once, yet this power gives us an evidence of the largeness of the human capacity above our imagination.

Hutcheson provides examples, such as proposition 47 in Euclid's first book dealing with the "infinite possible sizes of right-angled triangles" of a fixed area;

in algebraic and fluxional calculations, we shall still find a greater variety of particular truths included in general theorems; not only in general equations applicable to all kinds of quantity, but in more particular investigations of areas and tangents: in which one manner of operation shall discover theorems applicable to infinite orders or species of curves, to the infinite sizes of each species, and to the infinite points of the infinite individuals of each size.

Another type of beauty in theorems is when a theorem contains a vast number of corollaries that are easily deductible (Hutcheson 1729, p. 35):

It is easy to see how men are charmed with the beauty of such knowledge, besides its usefulness; and how this sets them upon deducing the properties of each figure from one genesis. This pleasure we enjoy even when we have no prospect of obtaining any other advantage from such manner of deduction, than the immediate pleasure of contemplating the beauty.

The important part of this statement is the charm of the beauty of such knowledge, regardless of its usefulness.

Hutcheson goes on to say (Hutcheson 1729, pp. 35–36) that

It is no less easy to see into what absurd attempts men have been led by this sense of beauty, and an affectation of obtaining it in the other sciences as well as the mathematics. Men perceive the beauty of uniformity in the sciences even from the contortions of common sense they are led into by pursuing it. This delight which accompanies sciences, or universal theorems, may really be called a kind of sensation; since it necessarily accompanies the discovery of any proposition, and is distinct from bare knowledge itself, being most violent at first, whereas the knowledge is uniformly the same.

Nearly three hundred years ago, Hutcheson gave a general outline for a theory of aesthetics, in particular for mathematics, pointing out several peculiarities: that the beauty of theorems lies in the many consequences deriving from them, the strong feelings they engender, their practical lack of utility, and the existence of a special "sixth sense" that enables only a few people to experience this feeling. In the following centuries mathematicians would deal with these themes, at least by those interested in mathematical aesthetics (though I have never seen Hutcheson cited).

Aesthetical Criteria in Mathematical Research

Many mathematicians have expressed their ideas regarding the relationship between mathematics and aesthetics. And it is clearly a field in which unanimity is unlikely. The great mathematician John von Neumann describes a mathematician's work as follows (von Neumann 1956):

A discussion on the nature of intellectual work is a difficult question in any field, even in fields that are not far removed from the central area of our common human intellectual effort as mathematics still is.... Any discussion of the nature of intellectual effort in any field is difficult, unless it presupposes an easy, routine familiarity with that field. In mathematics this limitation becomes very severe, if the discussion is to be kept on a non-mathematical plane. The discussion will then necessarily show some very weak features; points which are made can never be properly documented; and a certain overall superficiality of the discussion becomes unavoidable.... Mathematics falls into a great number of subdivisions, differing from one another widely in character, style, aims and influence. I doubt that any mathematician now living has much of a relationship to more than a quarter.

The problem is that mathematics is almost incomprehensible to many people, even to mathematicians themselves working in different fields. But what does a mathematician's work consist of? Why are they so fascinated by their subject?

John von Neumann goes on to say

The mathematician has a wide variety of fields to which he may turn, and he enjoys a very considerable freedom in what he does with them. To come to the decisive point: I think that it is correct to say that his criteria of selection, and also those of success, are mainly aesthetical. I realize that this assertion is controversial and that it is impossible to "prove" it, or indeed to go very far in substantiating it. One expects a mathematical theorem or a mathematical theory not only to describe and to classify in a simple and elegant way numerous and a priori disparate special cases. One also expects "elegance" in its "architectural" and structural makeup. These criteria are clearly those of any creative art, and the existence of some underlying empirical, worldly motive in the background is assumed—often in the very remote background, overgrown by "aesthetic" developments and followed into a multitude of labyrinthine variants—all this is much more akin to the atmosphere of art pure and simple than to that of empirical sciences.

In addition, the mathematician must have that "sixth sense" that Hutcheson refers to. It is this freedom that brings mathematicians closer to artists. So there is much space for intuition, imagination, emotion. Here is an example. After years of lonely research, Andrew Wiles was able to announce on October 25, 1994, that he had delivered the manuscripts for two articles in which he had proved *Fermat's Last Theorem*. Simon Singh, with a PhD in physics from Cambridge University, was commissioned to interview Wiles for a documentary that the BBC wanted to make on the event. Wiles recounted his feelings about what he had achieved, how he had pursued his childhood dream for 30 years, how without his realizing it all the mathematics he had studied had become a set of tools for working on Fermat's problem, how nothing would be the same again, his feeling of loss that the problem would no longer dog him every day, and the strong sense of relief he now feels. For Wiles, it was the end of a chapter in his life. The BBC documentary, "Fermat's Last Theorem" (Singh 1996), includes several really moving moments. For example, Wiles describes how he finally reached the definitive proof of the theorem. Though several months have gone by, he's unable to hide his emotion:

One Monday morning, September 19 to be exact, I was sitting at my desk. Suddenly, and quite unexpectedly, I had this incredible revelation. It was a solution so indescribably beautiful, it was so simple and so elegant. I couldn't understand why I hadn't noticed it before, I stared at it in disbelief for twenty minutes. Then, during the day, I wandered round the department and kept on going back to my desk to see if the solution was still there. It was still there. I couldn't contain myself, I was so excited. It was the most important moment of my working life. Nothing I ever do in the future will mean so much.

Strong emotions, the intuition of beauty in the solution, can be understood by very few people, and few mathematicians are able to interpret and understand the proof of the theorem. The beauty of mathematics is only for the few. Or rather, the beauty of complex results that solve great problems. It's not easy to understand what is meant by "the beauty of mathematics" because mathematicians themselves have different ideas on the subject, and the word beauty can take on a variety of very different meanings.

Beauty Is Absolute?

On May 7, 1981, the mathematician A. Borel gave a lecture at the *Carl Friedrich von Siemes Stiftung* in Munich (Borel 1983), on the subject of mathematics: art and science (*Mathematik: Kunst und Wissenschaft*). Borel deals with another question Hutcheson had examined: Is beauty absolute, or can a scale of values be established? And if so, what are the possible methods?

The question immediately arises as to how one can make value judgments. Surely not all concepts and theorems are equal. Are there then internal criteria which can lead to a more or less objective hierarchy? You will notice that the same basic question can be asked about painting, music, or art in general. It thus becomes a question of aesthetics. Indeed, a usual answer is that mathematics is to a great extent an art, an art whose development has been derived from, guided by, and judged according to aesthetic criteria. For the non-specialist it is often surprising to learn that one can speak of aesthetic criteria in such a discipline as mathematics. But this feeling is very strong for the mathematician, even though it is difficult to explain. What are the rules of this aesthetics? Wherein lies the beauty of a theorem, of a theory? Of course there is no one answer that will satisfy all mathematicians, but there is a surprising level of agreement, to a far greater extent than exists in music or painting.

Quoting from von Neumann's article "The Mathematician," Borel recalls that "Still others have taken a more intermediate stance—they fully recognize the importance of the aesthetic side of mathematics but feel that it is dangerous to push mathematics too far for its own sake." Poincaré, for example, had written earlier (Poincaré 1905):

Mathematics has a triple aim. It can provide an instrument for studying nature. But that's not all: it has a philosophical aim and dares to have an aesthetic aim. It helps philosophy to take a closer look at notions of number, space and time. And above all, its practitioners experience a sense of joy akin to that provided by painting and music. They admire the delicate harmony of numbers and shapes; they marvel when a new discovery reveals unexpected perspectives; and doesn't the joy they experience have its aesthetic side, even though they don't take part directly? It's true that not many fortunate people are invited to enjoy it fully, but isn't that what happens to the most noble arts?

Poincaré adds an observation on mathematics and art that Borel does not share: "If you will allow me to pursue my comparison with the fine arts, a mathematician, while being oblivious to the external world, is similar to a painter who knows how to combine colors and shapes harmoniously, but lacks models. His creative power would soon be exhausted."

Borel lived in Munich, a center of twentieth-century abstract art. He could not help replying to Poincaré's statement by commenting on "the possibility of abstract painting." This strikes me as especially noteworthy in Munich, where, not much later, the artist Wassily Kandinsky would concern himself quite deeply with this question.

One day in the early 1900s, Kandinsky was looking at one of his own paintings when he suddenly realized that the subject is sometimes detrimental to a painting in that it may obstruct direct access to shapes and colors—that is, to the actual artistic qualities of the work itself. But, as he later wrote, "a frightening gap" and a host of questions confronted him, the most important of which was "What should replace the missing subject?" Kandinsky was fully aware of the danger of ornamentation, of purely decorative art, and wanted to avoid it at all costs. Contrary to Poincaré, however, he did not conclude that painting without a real subject had to be fruitless. In fact, he even came up with a theory of "inner necessity" and "intellectual content" of painting. From about 1910 he and many other painters devoted themselves to what is called abstract or pure painting, which has little or nothing to do with nature and reality (Bill 1949). Borel adds that mathematics is like abstract art: "It is an art because it is primarily a creation of the mind and progress is achieved by intellectual means, many of which issue from the depth of the human mind, and for which aesthetic criteria are the final arbiters." However, he goes on to say: "But this intellectual freedom to move in a world of pure thought must be governed to some extent by possible applications in the natural sciences."

Creativity and Mathematics: The Mathematical Unconscious

Poincaré believes that the "sixth sense" for mathematics is innate. In an article entitled "The Mathematical Unconscious" (Papert 1988), Seymour A. Papert investigates the Frenchman's approach to mathematical creativity: "For Poincaré the distinguishing feature of the mathematical mind is not logical but aesthetic. He also believes that this aesthetic sense is innate; some people happen to be born with the faculty of developing an appreciation for mathematical beauty, and those are the ones who can become creative mathematicians. The others not...."

Papert shows how Poincaré establishes a scale in the application of aesthetics to mathematics: "The first is a stage of deliberate conscious analysis. If the problem is difficult, the first stage will never yield the solution. Its role is to create the elements out of which the solution will be constructed. A stage of unconscious work, according to Poincaré, which might appear to the mathematician as temporarily abandoning the task, or leaving the problem to incubate, has to intervene." The problem is how the unconscious mind knows what to pass back to the conscious mind. "This is where Poincaré sees the role of aesthetics. He believes that ideas passed back are not necessarily correct solutions to the original problem. But the ideas passed up do always have the stamp of mathematical beauty. The function of the third stage of the work is to consciously and rigorously examine the results obtained from the unconscious." A sort of Freudian censor, said Papert: "Its job is to scan the changing kaleidoscope of unconscious patterns allowing only those which satisfy its aesthetic criteria to pass through the portal between the minds."

In an interview I conducted a few years ago with leading Italian mathematicians, Alessandro Figà Talamanca, referring to Ennio De Giorgi, said that there are those who work by intuition, without much effort; they are highly creative and mathematics is part of their makeup, while for others becoming creative is extremely hard work (Emmer 1996). The opinions mentioned earlier follow the lines set out by Hutcheson, trying to establish a method and a scale of values to explain the famous "sixth sense."

Theorems Are Not All Equally Beautiful

In his paper "The Phenomenology of Mathematical Beauty" (Rota 1997) Gian Carlo Rota poses the question right from the outset: "What kind of mathematics can be beautiful?" And he distinguishes between theorems and proofs:

Theorems, proofs, entire mathematical theories and definitions, a short step in the proof of some theorem, are at various times thought to be beautiful or ugly by mathematicians. Most frequently the word "beautiful" is applied to theorems. In the second place we find proofs: a proof that is deemed beautiful tends to be short. Beautiful theories are also thought of as short, self-contained chapters fitting within broader theories.

Moreover, mathematicians and nonmathematicians may hold very different ideas: "Theories that mathematicians consider to be beautiful seldom agree with the mathematics thought to be beautiful by the educated people. For example, classic Euclidean geometry is often proposed by non-mathematicians as a paradigm of a beautiful theory, but I have not heard it classified as such by professional mathematicians."

In particular, Rota notes that "a peculiarity of twentieth century mathematics is the appearance of theories where the definitions far exceed the theorems in beauty." Among the examples Rota provides is naturally the five Platonic solids. "The theorem stating that in three dimensions there are only five regular solids (the Platonic solids) is generally considered to be beautiful; none of the proofs of this theorem, however, at least none of those I know of, can be said to be beautiful."

Other examples include Picard's theorem for the functions of a complex variable, Church's axiomatic system, E. H. Moore's theory of finite fields, and Galois's theory of equations.

Rota also observes that, as in any cultural field,

the rise and fall of synthetic geometry shows that the beauty of a piece of mathematics is dependent upon schools and periods. The beauty of a piece of mathematics does not consist merely of the subjective feelings experienced by an observer. The beauty of a theorem is an objective property on a par with its truth. The truth of a theorem does not differ from its beauty by a greater degree of objectivity.

Rota goes on to clarify what he means by the concept of mathematical beauty:

Mathematicians are concerned with the truth. In mathematics however there is an ambiguity in the use of the word "truth." This ambiguity can be observed whenever mathematicians claim that beauty is the *raison d'être* of mathematics, or that mathematical beauty is that feature that gives mathematics a unique standing among science. These claims are as old as mathematics, and lead us to suspect that mathematical truth and beauty may be related. They share one important property. Neither of them admits degrees. Mathematicians are annoyed by the "graded" truths which they observe in other science.

Rota's Definition of Mathematical Beauty

Rota defines mathematical beauty as

the expression mathematicians have invented in order to obliquely admit the phenomenon of enlightenment while avoiding acknowledgment of the fuzziness of this phenomenon. They say that a theorem is beautiful when they mean to say that the theorem is enlightening. We acknowledge a theorem's beauty when we see how the theorem "fits" in its place, how it sheds light around itself, like "*Lichtung*," a clearing in the woods. We say that a proof is beautiful when it gives away the secret of the theorem, when it leads us to perceive the inevitability of the statement being proved. The term "mathematical beauty" is a trick mathematicians have devised to avoid facing up to the messy phenomenon of enlightenment.

It is important to remember that, when speaking of mathematics and aesthetics, one cannot expect full and unequivocal answers. Clearly, when mathematicians say that certain theorems or theories are "beautiful" they probably have in mind something they know well and are working on. There are dozens of sectors in modern mathematics, and even a good mathematician is probably capable of working on only four or five, not more. Absolute beauty, beauty without degrees, importance in mathematical research, unconscious activity, enlightment, that is, mathematical beauty is a phenomenon mathematicians agree on but still find difficult to explain. This is what interests not only mathematicians but also philosophers of science who observe things "from outside," at least in part. James W. McAllister has devoted a book to the subject of "beauty and revolution in science."

Proofs and Theorems: Where Is Beauty?

In his paper "Mathematical Beauty and the Evolution of the Standards of Mathematical Proof" (McAllister 2004), McAllister stresses how the idea of a proof and mathematical rigor have changed and how, as a result, the idea of beauty in mathematics changes. First, referring to Hutcheson's ideas he asks

How should we interpret an observer's claim that a certain entity is beautiful? The most natural interpretation is that the entity has a property named "beauty" which the observer has perceived. I do not regard this interpretation as satisfactory, however. I regard beauty as a value that is projected into or attributed to objects by observers, and not a property that intrinsically resides in objects. Whether a certain observer projects beauty into a certain object is determined by two factors: the aesthetic criteria held by the observer, and the object's true intrinsic properties.

It is worth noting that most mathematicians are not very interested in the "essence" of mathematical subjects. As Courant and Robbins said in their famous definition, what interests mathematicians most is relationships (Courant and Robbins 1941; Giusti 1999).

It is clear that two observers can have different aesthetic criteria. Therefore, "a mathematical entity has certain aesthetic properties, such as simplicity and symmetry. On the strength of perceiving these properties in a mathematical entity, and by virtue of holding to aesthetic criteria that attach value to these properties, an observer is moved to project beauty into the entity. A different observer, holding different aesthetic criteria, could decline to attribute beauty to this entity." Another important aspect to note is that today's mathematicians tend to attribute "beauty" to theories and theorems developed in recent years (difficult to understand for most) while nonmathematicians tend to refer to classical mathematics (even that of ancient Greece). Naturally one of the properties most mentioned is "symmetry," though it has so many meanings it doesn't really signify much.

McAllister makes an interesting point concerning

a tentative distinction between two classes of mathematical entities to which beauty may be attributed: processes and products. Processes include problem-solving techniques, calculation methods, computer programs, proofs, and other operations, algorithms, procedures, and approaches used in mathematics. Products, which are outcomes of processes, include numbers, equations, problems, theories, theorems, conjectures, propositions of other sorts, curves, patterns, geometrical figures and constructions, and all other mathematical structures.

Examples are numbers such as "e," class of numbers, polygons and tiling, Platonic solids (not only mathematicians seem to agree!), the golden section, and fractals. McCallister put forward an explanation with a model he calls "aesthetic induction."

Aesthetic induction is the procedure by which scientists attribute weightings to aesthetic properties of theories. Scientists at a given time attach aesthetic value to an aesthetic property roughly in proportion to the degree of empirical success scored up to that time by a set of all past theories that exhibit the property. Thus, if a property is exhibited by a set of empirically very successful theories, scientists attach a great aesthetic value to it, and thereby see theories that exhibit that property as beautiful.

In particular, he goes on to say,

On the basis of the reception of computer-assisted proofs, I conjecture that the evolution of aesthetic criteria applied to mathematical proofs is also governed by aesthetic induction. This suggests that mathematicians' aesthetic preferences evolve in response to the perceived practical utility of mathematical constructs—a conclusion that contradicts both the view that mathematicians' aesthetic preferences are innate and the view that they are disinterested with respect to practical utility.

The problem clearly emerges that it is very difficult to build a "scientific" theory of mathematical aesthetics. On the other hand, if the ability to grasp the beauty of mathematics, the ability to be a mathematician, hinges on a special "sixth sense," an innate ability that may even be partly subconscious, formulating a convincing theory becomes extremely difficult.

Aesthetics Theories Are Impossible in Mathematics?

Jerry P. King has a long chapter on "aesthetics" in his book *The Art of Mathematics* (King 1992), in which he states that it is impossible to find a theory of this kind, or rather that it is a good thing no theory of "the mathematics of mathematical aesthetics" exists. In the preface, King says that "To write about mathematics you must deal with each of these: beauty, truth, and reality." At the beginning of the chapter on aesthetics, he states that "Mathematicians do mathematics for aesthetic reasons." He then states that "what we need are aesthetic theories which will address the specific questions: what is mathematical beauty? Alas, specific theories do not exist."

King also considers the possibility that the absence of a precise aesthetic theory may simply be in the nature of things because "A true aesthetic theory which includes mathematics cannot exist. In a certain real sense, all true theories are mathematical theories." So the question is: "Whether or not a mathematical aesthetic theory can exist which includes mathematics. The answer seems clearly negative" even if "before us remains the inescapable fact that mathematicians do mathematics for aesthetic reasons."

New Criteria for Aesthetics in Mathematics

But in all this, mathematicians do not lose heart. In 2001, in their article dedicated to Gian Carlo Rota, Domenico Napoletani and Daniele Struppa put forward some new criteria for the "aesthetics of mathematics" (Napoletani and Struppa 2001), returning to the question posed by Borel: "We put forward a method to describe the various levels at which the beauty of a mathematical subject can be explored."

First of all, they define what a mathematical subject is: a definition, a theorem, an article, a series of articles, a theory, the work of a mathematical school. Another important word to define is the "context." "We suggest that mathematical beauty can be found in the relationship between an object and its context," where context is "the corpus of mathematical knowledge together with its bibliographic references." To describe the different levels of beauty in mathematics, they use a metaphor taken from the theory of singularities: "We might say that beauty appears when there is a singularity between past and future. The creation of this singularity, in which the tension of the past merges in the present with the potential of the future, gives us the opportunity to experience beauty."

The second level occurs when the singularity is resolved, creating a context within which the problem can be understood. The subsequent level is that of analyzing the new variety that arises from the resolution of the singularity. The topology of the new variety measures its beauty. So, while the parts of the new context are organized at the second level, the subsequent level is that of its lemmas. "It can be seen that the previous levels represent an approximation of the original singularity. The beauty consists in its applicability. Here, beauty, power, truth and utility coincide. The previous levels of beauty were external, this is internal." The final level is that of the text, the theorem, the article, and the theory. The authors claim that these pointers open the way to further research "if it is felt that a full statement of this aesthetic theory is necessary."

Final Remarks

We have tried to give an overview of mathematicians' opinions in the last 300 years regarding the possible links between mathematics and aesthetics. As was clear from the outset, one cannot imagine or even assume that there is a single opinion or a "mathematical theory" of aesthetics, as King says. And it is natural that things should be so. Rather than mathematical aesthetics, mathematicians have an urge to discuss the problem of aesthetics in mathematics, because (as Roger Penrose pointed out) the major theorems are "works of God" (Penrose 1989).

If opinions differ, and some mathematicians give priority to certain results, theorems, and theories over others, perhaps we can pinpoint some common features that are changing as a result of the wide-scale recognition that applied mathematics is acquiring in scientific circles:

- The difficulty of being understood by nonmathematicians; the "sixth sense"
- The simplicity and clarity of definitions and statements making them "beautiful"
- Words that seem obvious but in fact conceal a profound truth—mathematicians know when statements, theorems, and proofs have "aesthetic" properties, even though opinions on the subject may differ and be difficult to compare.

It is certainly true that one factor in mathematicians' motivation to find beauty in their work is the unique, elitist nature of their activity, which produces results that are appreciated by only a few people. At root, the theory of beauty in mathematics is a sort of self-justification for the lonely work that mathematicians undertake. They are proud of their work, but at the same time would like more people to appreciate what they do and the results they achieve. Mathematicians know their discipline produces results that are valid for all times. This leads to a certain sense of superiority and to claims that mathematics is the true art (Hardy 1940).

An important part of mathematics is building links and bridges between different sectors. In Singh's film on "Fermat's Last Theorem," it is no accident that there are several shots of San Francisco's Golden Gate bridge. This is one of the most important aspects of a mathematician's work. Linked problems and theories, bridges, lead to progress in sectors that seemed very far apart. This is the same enthusiasm and satisfaction a child feels when he or she understands the proof of a basic mathematical problem, a personal challenge without the interference of "external reality," or the risk of disappointment and failure, as recounted by Apostolos Doxiadis in "Uncle Petros and the Goldbach's conjecture" (Doxiadis 2000).

I have deliberately avoided the question of images and visual objects, partly because I dealt with them in other books, and partly because they present different problems (Emmer 1993). The fairly simple ideas outlined in this article go much deeper than may at first be apparent, and lead to a rare occurrence in the scientific field—the desire of many mathematicians to discuss their work in aesthetic terms. As I pointed out at the beginning of this chapter, these motivations were at the origin of the interest, let us say of the "natural" interest, in the aesthetic aspects of the new results mathematicians have obtained in the last 25 years in "visual mathematics" using computers. The aim was to bring them to mind and pose questions on mathematics and aesthetics. The answers are another story.

References

Bill, Max. 1949. *"Die mathematische denkweise in der kunstunserer zeit,"* *Werk*, 3; reprinted in English with corrections by the author. In *The Visual Mind*. M. Emmer, ed. Cambridge, MA: MIT Press, 1993.

Birkhoff, George D. 1931. "A Mathematical Approach to Aesthetics." *Scientia*.

————. 1934. "Mathematics: Quantity and Order." *Science Today*; see also G. D. Birkhoff. 1993. *Aesthetic Measure*. Cambridge, MA: Harvard University Press.

Borel, A. 1983. "Mathematics: Art and Science." *The Mathematical Intelligencer* 5(4): 9–17. Translated from German.

Courant, Richard, and Robbins, Herbert. 1941. *What Is Mathematics: An Elementary Approach to Ideas and Methods*. New York: Oxford University Press.

Doxiadis, Apostols. 2000. *Uncle Petros and the Goldbach Conjecture*. London: Faber & Faber.

Emmer, Michele, ed. 1993. *The Visual Mind*. Boston: MIT Press; see also Emmer, Michele, ed. 2004. *The Visual Mind 2*, Boston: MIT Press; Emmer, Michele. 1991. *La perfezione visibile*. Rome: Theoria.

————. 1996. *Mathematicians* (video). Naples: Città della Scienza.

Giusti, Enrico. 1999. *Ipotesi sulla natura degli oggetti matematici*. Turin: Bollati Boringhieri.

Gombrich, Ernst. 1979. *The Sense of Order: A Study in the Psychology of Decorative Art*. Oxford: Phaidon Press.

Hardy, G. H. 1940. *A Mathematician's Apology*. New York: Cambridge University Press.

Hutcheson, Francis. 1729. *Inquiry into the Origin of Our ideas of Beauty and Virtue, in two Treatises*. Third ed. London. Reprinted as the original by Kessinger Publishing, nd.

Kant, Immanuel. 1790. *Critik der Urtheilskraft*. Berlin; Italian ed., E. Garroni and H. Hohenegger, eds., Turin: Einaudi, 1999.

King, Jerry. 1992. *The Art of Mathematics*. New York: Plenum Press, p. 123.

Kline, Morris. 1953. *Mathematics in Western Culture*. Oxford: Oxford University Press; reprinted New York: Penguin Books, 1977, p. 523.

McAllister, James. 2004. "Mathematical Beauty and the Evolution of the Standards of Mathematical Proof." In *The Visual Mind 2*. M. Emmer, ed. Cambridge, MA: MIT Press.

Migliorini, Ermanno. 1988. Preface. In Francis Hutcheson. *L'origine della bellezza*. E. Migliorini, ed. Palermo: Aesthetica edizioni.

Musil, Robert. 1929. *Der Mann ohne Eigenschaften*. Wien: Rowolhlt.

Napoletani, Domenico, and Struppa, Daniele. 2001. "*L'estetica in matematica*." *Lettera Matematica* 39–40 (March–June): 44–51.

Papert, Seymour A. 1988. "The Mathematical Unconscious." In *On Aesthetics in Science*. J. Wechsler. Boston: Birkhauser, pp. 105–19.

Peitgen, H.-O., and Richter, P. H. 1986. *The Beauty of Fractals*. Berlin: Springer.

Penrose, Roger. 1989. *The Emperor's New Mind*. Oxford: Oxford University Press, pp. 74–78.

Poincaré, Henri. 1905. *La valeur de la science*. Paris: E. Flammarion; reprinted in 1970, p. 139.

Rota, Gian Carlo. 1997. "The Phenomenology of Mathematical Beauty." *Synthese* 111: 172–82.

Singh, Simon. 1996. *Fermat's Last Theorem* (video). London: BBC Horizon, J. Lynch producer.

Von Neumann, John. 1956. "The Mathematician." In *The World of Mathematics*. J. R. Newman, ed. New York: Simon & Schuster, pp. 2053–63.

14

Aesthetic Computing and Shape

Frederic Fol Leymarie

In this chapter, we address the problem of three-dimensional (3D) shape representation:[1] aesthetic principles of shape, as proposed by the Gestalt theory of perception (Wertheimer 1923; Koffka 1935), lead to symmetry-based representations for which we present a hierarchical model taking the form of a 3D graph—that is, a *virtual scaffolding in space* made of special nodes linked by special curves. Together, these nodes and linking curves make explicit certain symmetries of the original object, as well as important shape features, such as surface ridges (e.g., of a face's nose), corners, main axial curves (e.g., of fingers), bumps, and indentations. The same representation can be applied to the surrounding space, thus also permitting to characterize the "shape" of the voids between objects (e.g., the distance and interaction between dancers or molecules).

From a mathematical perspective, this representation for shape brings together the geometry of "contact spheres" with the singularities of differential (Lie) groups used to model geometric wave propagation in space, making explicit natural phenomena such as Archimedes' light caustics and their variations (Arnold 1991). From an aesthetic perspective, the obtained scaffoldings capture perceptually significant symmetries as well as the relative density of shape features, in a fashion similar to what a painter or sculptor might use. From a computational perspective, the representation is well-grounded in geometric principles that permit one to accurately, uniquely, and efficiently obtain such 3D graphs for the gamut of possible shapes of interest encountered in applications, ranging from astronomy to chemistry, via archaeology, sculpting, medicine, and so on.

The 3D graph for shape we propose as a useful framework for aesthetic computing is derived from a combined analysis of the topology and geometry of maximal contact spheres, that is, spheres that kiss the boundary of an object at two or more contact points,

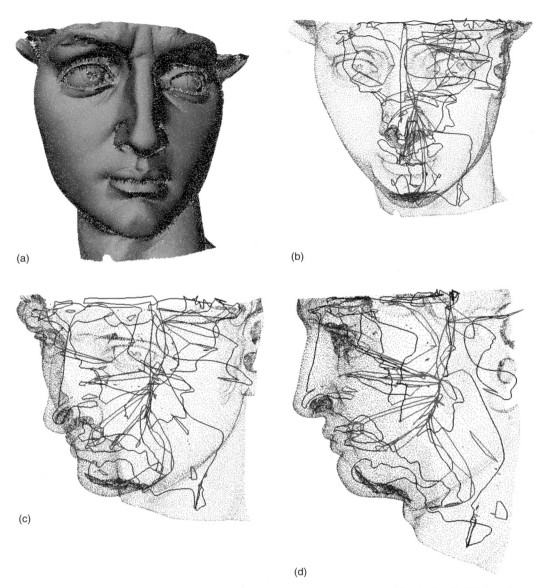

(a)

(b)

(c)

(d)

Figure 14.1 (a) The face of Michelangelo's David (31,000 points, laser scanned by the Stanford University Graphics group (Levoy 2000)) as a triangulated surface. Three views (b–d) of the *shock scaffold*, a shape-specific 3D graph structure, where red curves indicate axial symmetries, while blue curves are in relation to surface ridges (notice the long curve of symmetry for the nose, and the looping structures for the chin and mouth). (e) A long flexible cylinder that was tied as a complicated knot (reconstructed from 10,000 points,

Frederic Fol Leymarie

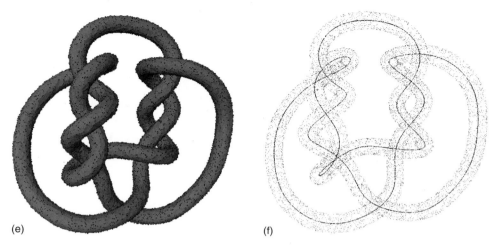

(e)　　　　　　　　　　　　　　　　(f)

Figure 14.1 (continued)

randomly spread on its surface; Leymarie 2003). (f) View of the computed shock scaffold, which is reduced to axial (red) curves only representing a *generalized axis* structure (Binford 1987), along which a circular cross-section may be swept to recreate the original shape (see also chapter 15, and the discussion on shape generation by "transfer").

in a way that no other sphere can be contained in their interior while osculating the same boundary points. By tracing their centers and studying the variation of their associated radius, we are able to locate a set of special nodes at singular values of this variation and link these into a graph structure we call the *shock scaffold*.[2] This graph for shape is directly computable from the raw data such as provided by modern laser scanners in the form of clouds of points sampling the surfaces of an object (figure 14.1).

The "Beauty of Shape"

Consider the human face: what constitutes a pleasing figure? Look closely at one eye: the round pattern of the iris with its varying, yet repetitive, set of colored patches can be called "beautiful." The nose of a Nefertiti or a David, with its elongated symmetry of the slope is pleasing. But what about the face as a whole? A pair of otherwise "beautiful" eyes will look awkward if their interdistance is "too large" or "too small" with respect to the remaining overall figure, particularly to their position in relation to the nose. We could repeat this experiment with the lips, ears, and so on. In a picture, be it a photograph, a snapshot of what your brain registers, or a painting, it is the juxtaposition of the elements and their mutual relationships, which accounts for successfully passing the "test of beauty" in our eyes.[3]

Psychologists and art historians have attempted to characterize the beauty of shape, trying to measure what is pleasing to the eye, and thereby provide "physical" theories for analyzing human perception and works of arts. The first such important theory, which emerged as a cohesive set of principles before World War II, came under the works of the "Gestalt school" (Koehler 1947) and their pupils who promoted, and applied their discoveries, particularly in Arnheim's (Arnheim 1971; 1974) analysis of films and paintings. The Gestalt[4] theory of human perception, in a nutshell, proposes generic principles that permit to description of the regional characteristics of shape elements, such as a set of lines or points sampling the outline of a figure.[5]

Gestalt Principles

The original Gestalt principles can be listed as (1) figure and ground, (2) similarity, (3) proximity or contiguity, (4) continuity, (5) closure, (6) area, and (7) symmetry. Some of these seven principles may imply visual cues other than shape, such as color, shading, and contrast; nevertheless they are all applicable to the problem of shape representation. These principles all have a common thread, when applied to shape: *they require at least binary relationships* to be established between visual elements, such as points, edges, curve segments, and surface patches. That is, the analysis moves away from the "calculus" approach of looking at a point, or at a single atom, to determine its nature, and the focus is rather on notions of relationships between elements (or points or atoms). In particular, Gestalt psychologists had noticed from the late 1800s on that the human eye is sensitive to illusory patterns, "creating" paths of relationships where there is no signal, as illustrated, for example, by the famous images of Kanizsa and others (Kanizsa 1979).

Arnheim's Application of the Gestalt Principles to the Arts

Rudolph Arnheim, a student of the German Gestalt school of the early 1900s, applied the Gestalt principles to the arts, including cinema, sculpting, painting, and drawing. Arnheim considered the influence of boundaries in a finite space where the art piece is set to be observed. In accordance with the physical paradigm favored by the Gestalt school, Arnheim thinks of the visual experience as a field of forces, with its balance, dynamics, and lines of main attraction and repulsion. Noticeably, he describes a concept that will emerge as a computing framework in pattern theory a few years later: the idea of a *structural skeleton*, the locus in the visual field where force lines tend to converge (Arnheim 1974, ch. I).[6]

For example, the influence of the frame or limited canvas extent, and its (often) rectangular shape has a direct impact on the way the artist lays down the paint, even before a first line or brush trace has been applied. Painting is analyzed as a sequential process in which constant visual feedback is provided by the visual force field dynamics, "any line drawn on a sheet of paper ... is like a rock thrown into a pond. It upsets the repose, it mobilizes space" (Arnheim 1974, p. 16).

While the Gestalt school works provided insights and guidelines into understanding how shape is perceived, it lacked a clear mathematical framework permitting the realization of a *computational model of the aesthetics of shape*, its implementation, and its use. A first step toward this goal was achieved in the works of Harry Blum in the 1960s and 1970s (Blum 1973). From the 1980s on, Michael Leyton has proposed a comprehensive and unifying framework (Leyton 1987, 1988, 2001; see also ch. 15 in this book). In the following section, after summarizing the model of Blum based on symmetry and some of Leyton's advances, we describe the *shock scaffold*, a representation that supports aesthetic computing for 3D shape; that is, it captures the original Gestalt principles and gives one possible computational framework to implement (at least part of) the more general theory of Leyton based on transfer and recoverability.

A Computational Model for Shape

The Medial Axis of Blum

A few years after Arnheim published his seminal work in 1954 (Arnheim 1974), Harry Blum, a radio engineer, proposed in the early 1960s a mathematical framework based on the notion of wave propagation and the locus where waves coalesce (Blum 1961; 1962; 1964). If one restricts waves initiated at the elements of interest, for example, the edges of a contour, to propagate through space and label it uniquely except at the locus where waves meet, one obtains a description of shapes that in 2D takes the structure of a stick figure making explicit certain symmetries of a shape (figure 14.2a). Early on, Blum and his contemporaries noticed that a strictly equivalent definition was to consider the centers of empty discs osculating the contour fragments at two or more loci (figure 14.2b). Blum took a further step by associating to this diagram a vector field by following the gradient of the distance from the boundary along the diagram, resulting in directed paths (figure 14.2c). Together, the diagram and associated field of distance is named *medial axis* and denoted *MA*.[7]

It is important to note here how Blum's model provides a *toolbox to capture aesthetic principles of shape* such as those proposed by the Gestalt school. The *MA* captures the topology of a shape and of its surrounding space (if one applies wave propagation to both the "inside" and the "outside" of an outline) and preserves the figure-ground dichotomy. Similarities between equivalent *MA* diagrams can be measured via attributes provided by the distance field. Distance attributes of the diagram computed for the space between shapes permits to evaluate proximity. Continuity is reflected in the smoothness (or lack thereof)

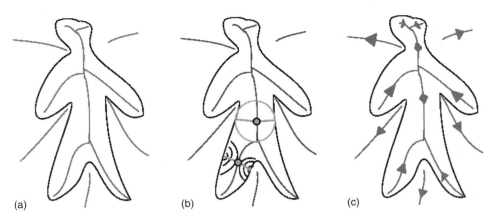

Figure 14.2 (a) A stick figure representation is obtained from an anthropomorphic outline. (b) The computation of the stick figure can be equivalently obtained from *(i)* the locus of meeting wavefronts initiated from the boundary and navigating at constant unit speed; *(ii)* the centers of empty discs kissing the boundary in two or more loci. (c) By associating the distance from the boundary of meeting wavefronts (or the radii of empty osculating discs) to this stick figure, one gets a vector field along the diagram (adapted from Blum 1973, where arrows indicate direction of increasing distance).

of diagram segments. Closure, area, and symmetry as defined in Gestalt theory are all derivable from the *MA*. Essentially, the *MA* combines topology with geometry (Sherbrooke et al. 1996). For example, curvature extrema are mapped to endpoints of the diagram (Leyton 1987), while genus is preserved by its overall connectivity and loop structure. Object "symmetry," which involves overlapping in Gestalt theory, is also computable (Blum 1973; Tek et al. 1997; Tek 1999).

By combining the *MA* and its computation via wave propagation, one fills all of the visual space, thereby obtaining a possible implementation of Arnheim's visual field.[8] The *structural skeleton* is then nothing more than the part of the *MA* representing the "outside" of space with respect to the shapes of interest.

From the Medial Axis to Shock Graphs and Scaffolds

At first glance Blum's model seems to provide most if not all the ingredients to make it a pleasing embodiment of the Gestalt principles of shape via a computational model based on two complementary views: wave propagation and their quenching loci, and a geometry of empty spheres osculating outlines.

Yet, 40 years have passed since the early proposals and studies of Blum and his collaborators and numerous followers, and no single computational model has been recognized as satisfying by the computing community. There are three main reasons for this: (1) the computations in the discrete world have proven difficult, (2) the *MA* is rather sensitive to perturbations of its boundary, and (3) although the *MA* makes explicit information not directly available in the original outline (e.g., curvature extrema and the topology of the entire shape or surrounding space), it can itself result in complicated shapes (as a diagram) that are not easy to retrieve nor obvious to exploit, particularly when considering 3D shapes.[9]

Most approaches to the computation of the *MA* have relied on a discrete grid tesselating space and shape outlines, thus introducing a number of difficulties, such as the need to mimic Euclidean wave propagation to achieve greater accuracy. The lack of an understanding until recently of the dynamic behavior of the resulting diagrams under deformation and perturbations has also resulted in a strong critique of the approach from a theoretical point of view. Finally, mapping an outline to another set of outlines does not readily summarize data, nor does it permit one to address the aesthetic principle of *structural ordering* by simplification or tension reduction in Arnheim's fields (Arnheim 1971); this may also be understood as a form of "maximization of transfer and recoverability" in Leyton's theory (Leyton 2001).

Starting in the mid-1980s, two steps were taken that would eventually lead to addressing these potential foes of the *MA*. Leyton, after studying the local nature of the *MA* and showing how curvature extrema were related to the end of *MA* branches (Leyton 1987), initiated groundwork on the dynamics of the *MA* representation and proposed a grammar for 2D shape understanding, where changes in the topology of the diagram, under deformation of the original shape, are bound to happen in a very restrictive set of possibilities and sequences (Leyton 1987; 1988).[10] The key insight here was that the *MA* diagram should be understood not merely as a static representation of an outline, but also be studied under deformations. On the one hand, this offers the advantages of, first, providing a natural way to deal with the sensitivity of the diagrams under perturbations by offering a way to smooth out their effect (e.g., how much deformation is required to change the topology of the *MA* can be used to determine a saliency measure) and, second, allowing them to relate similar shapes. On the other hand, it leads Leyton to propose a general theory of shape dynamics in which a history explaining the structure of a shape can be formally associated to it (Leyton 2001).

The second step in generalizing the scope of the *MA* has been explored since the early 1990s chiefly by Kimia, Siddiqi, and their collaborators and followers (Siddiqi and Kimia 1996; Siddiqi et al. 1999; Tek 1999), who proposed a simplified model for the *MA* aiming at addressing the computing problems of accuracy, efficiency, and simplicity. It was realized that only a "small" subset of the *MA* was important, namely, those in which the distance flow had its sources, relays, and sinks (essentially, where the vector field along the

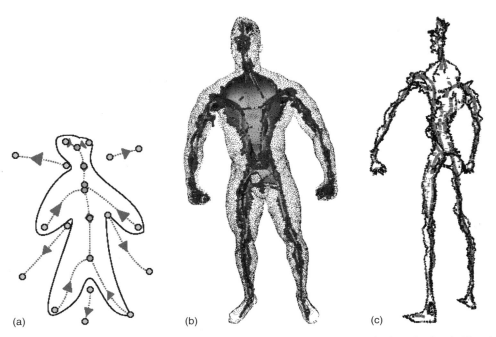

(a)   (b)   (c)

Figure 14.3 (a) The mapping in 2D of the *MA* to the shock graph made of special points, the singularities of the distance flow along the *MA* and their connectivity. (b) An example of the 3D *MA* representation of a human body sampled by a laser scanner. (c) An example of the shock scaffold (*SC*) version of (b), which retains only special nodes and their connectivity. NB: In 3D the interior of medial surfaces are only made implicit as loops of the *SC*.

MA is singular). This has the advantage of defining a set of nodes, or points in space, which can then be linked by selected paths along the remaining structure of the *MA*, transforming the representation into one of a directed graph. In 2D, this model was called the *shock graph* (figure 14.3a). In 3D, the equivalent notion was explored in my doctoral thesis (Leymarie 2003) and named the *shock scaffold*, denoted *SC* (figure 14.3c). A summary of this computational representation for shape follows.

The Shock Scaffold

The symmetry set (*SS*) is the closure of the locus of centers of spheres tangent to smooth surface patches in two or more loci; such bitangent spheres are called "contact spheres." The medial axis (*MA*) is the subset of the *SS* for which all such spheres are maximal, that is, such that no other contact spheres are contained in them.[11] To obtain a uniquely defined 3D graph structure from the *MA*, two ingredients are useful: a classification of *MA*

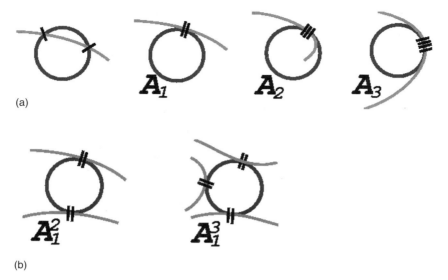

Figure 14.4 Illustration of the notation A_k^n based on contact of a curve with a circle (from Giblin and Kimia 2004). $k + 1$ counts order or degree of contact (indicated by straight short dark segments): (a) A_1 is regular tangent contact, A_2 is regular "curvature" contact, A_3 is a curvature maximum contact. (b) The superscript n counts the number of contact points, so that A_1^2 means two A_1 contacts. A similar definition holds for the contact of surfaces with spheres.

points in terms of types of contacts combined with a notion of singularity of flow along the *MA*.

A classification of *MA* points was introduced by Giblin and Kimia (Giblin and Kimia 1998; 1999; 2000; 2004), which we now summarize. Let A_k^n denote a circle (in 2D) or a sphere (in 3D) osculating a boundary element at n distinct points, each with $k + 1$ degree of contact, figure 14.4: $k = 1$ denotes regular tangency; $k = 2$ denotes a sphere of curvature for a surface patch; $k = 3$ denotes a sphere of curvature at a ridge point; $k = 4$ denotes a sphere of curvature at a turning point of a ridge (Halliman et al. 1999, ch. 6). Only odd orders of contact (i.e., $k = 1, 3$) can contribute to an *MA* type of shock, that is, as being the center of a maximal sphere. Then, a classification based on the number and order of contact (Giblin and Kimia 2004) leads to five principal types of shock points: A_1^2, A_1^3, A_3, A_1^4, and $A_1 A_3$ (figure 14.4).[12]

1. A_1^2 contact: this is a sphere with two ordinary A_1 contacts. The local form of the A_1^2 is such that the centers of the contact spheres trace a surface, called sheet, which is locally smooth.

2. A_3 contact: this is the limiting case of two A_1^2 points that come together; it corresponds in 2D to the center of curvature at a curvature extrema and in 3D to rib curves associated to ridges on the boundary.

3. A_1^3 contact: the contact sphere has three ordinary A_1 contacts. The local form is one in which three sheets come together at a curve, that is, choosing any two of these three tangency points and moving the sphere so that it remains bitangent to the bounding surface at points close to these two, results in a smooth sheet of the SS or MA for each pair.

4. $A_1 A_3$ contact: it contains the centers of spheres that have contact with the surface in two places, one near the original A_1 point (i.e., ordinary tangency) and one near the A_3 rib point. Furthermore, at an $A_1 A_3$ point, an A_1^3 curve also "terminates" together with the A_3 curve.

5. A_1^4 contact: the contact sphere has four ordinary contacts, which is generic, that is, four points in space determine a unique sphere (such that they are not colinear nor cocircular). At the center of the sphere passes six smooth A_1^2 sheets of the MA (i.e., six distinct pairs from four contact points). An alternative view of this event is as the combination/intersection of four A_1^3 curves (i.e., four distinct triplets from four contact points).

Two observations are significant here (Giblin and Kimia 2004). First, the topology of each of these types is as follows: A_1^2 points are interior points of a medial surface, called "sheet"; A_3 points organize into curves representing ridges on surfaces and are the "exterior" boundary of MA sheets, called "ribs" or "skeletal edges"; A_1^3 points organize into curves that are the intersection of three A_1^2 sheets—these curves often correspond to "generalized axes" (Binford 1987) as well as to "interior" boundaries of MA sheets, and are sometimes called "seams" or "axial curves"; A_1^4 and $A_1 A_3$ are isolated points where four A_1^3 or a pair of A_1^3 and A_3 curves intersect, respectively.

The shock structure arises from a "dynamic" interpretation of the MA, as the locus of singularities—or shocks—formed in the course of wave propagation from boundaries with associated direction and speed of flow, as in Blum's grassfire (Blum 1973). The flow for each MA point is defined in the direction of increasing radius, R, of associated maximal contact spheres in a neighborhood of that point. Flow is thus a vector field, taken as the projection of the gradient of R on the MA. This flow itself can have singularities, and shocks thereby can "flow" along sheets (A_1^2) or curves (A_3 and A_1^3) in various ways (Giblin and Kimia 2004), as summarized in the following:

Regular shock (or 1st order)   A shock point at which flow goes through smoothly *(i)* along a sheet: A_1^2-1; *(ii)* along a curve: A_1^3-1, A_3-1.

Table 14.1 Final classification of 18 possible shock points based on contact with spheres, A_k^n, and flow type

Shocks	Regular	Source	Relay	Sink
Sheet	A_1^2-1	A_1^2-2	A_1^2-3*	A_1^2-4
Rib	A_3-1	A_3-2	A_3-3*	A_3-4
Axis	A_1^3-1	A_1^3-2	A_1^3-3*	A_1^3-4
Rib end	—	A_1A_3-2	A_1A_3-3	A_1A_3-4
Axis end	—	—	A_1^4-2, A_1^4-3	A_1^4-4

There are 3 regular shock types and 15 singular ones: the sources, relays, and sinks for the flow.
* Degeneracies are possible and considered special cases of relays where shocks flow simultaneously in and out.

Shock source (2nd order) A shock that initiates flow *(i)* along a sheet: A_1^2-2; *(ii)* along a curve: A_1^3-2, A_3-2; *(iii)* at a vertex: A_1A_3-2.
Shock relay (3rd order) A shock that is both a source and sink for the flow *(i)* for a sheet: A_1^2-3; *(ii)* for a curve: A_1^3-3, A_3-2; *(iii)* for a vertex: A_1^4-2, A_1^4-3, A_1A_3-3.
Shock sink (4th order) A shock at which flow type terminates *(i)* for a sheet: A_1^2-4; *(ii)* for a curve: A_1^3-4, A_3-4; *(iii)* for a vertex: A_1^4-4, A_1A_3-4.

This classification of the MA into eighteen types of shock points (table 14.1) leads to a powerful graph structure for its representation, where *regular shock points need not be traced explicitly*. Based on this classification the MA representation is transformed into an explicit 3D graph whose nodes are taken from the set of fifteen types of shock singularities, that is, sources, relays, and sinks and whose links connect the selected nodes. Note that MA sheets can still be represented as hyperlinks if the precise geometry of an object is to be preserved. However, note that a hierarchical representation for shape that gradually makes implicit the geometry of an object while preserving the topological information is now possible. This hierarchy comprises five levels (Leymarie 2003).

We start with a general hypergraph that includes all special points as nodes, special curves as links, and sheets as hyperlinks. We then present coarser versions in which hyperlinks have been removed, therefore leaving a graph that is the shock scaffold proper, that is, made of shock point singularities as nodes, and linked by curve segments forming in space a structure resembling the scaffoldings used to erect buildings. We follow standard definitions of hypergraphs and graphs from the literature, which are constructed from the pair "nodes and (hyper)links." First, we define the elements we will use to construct the various representations in the hierarchy, that is, nodes, links, and hyperlinks:

Shock nodes, P   The set of shock nodes, denoted P, is composed of shock sources, relays, and sinks for shock curves and vertices.

Shock (curve) links, L   A shock link, L, for each curve segment between two shock nodes is an ordered (by the radius function) pair of these two shock nodes, and it has attributes describing its geometry and dynamics.

Shock (sheet) hyperlinks, H   A shock hyperlink, H, for each sheet is the ordered, cyclic set of shock nodes of its associated bounding curves and vertices. A hyperlink is attributed with geometry and dynamics of the sheet.

Note that a hyperlink therefore gives an orientation to the shock sheet.

We can now define the first level in our hierarchy, which augments the *MA* with a directed graph structure.

Augmented shock scaffold, SC+   The augmented shock scaffold, is the *MA* augmented with the set of shock nodes, P, connected by links L and hyperlinks H.

The advantage of the augmented graph structure over the ("classical") trace of the *MA* is that it organizes the *MA* information into groups and specifies their connectivity. It is precisely the connectivity among these groups that contains the qualitative information, while the remaining information allows for an exact reconstruction or an approximation of the shape from the shock hypergraph (Giblin and Kimia 1999).

If we drop from this *SC+* the hyperlinks, H, which contain the explicit representation of the sheets and their interior, we are left with an "ordinary" graph structure that defines the connectivity among the retained shock nodes via explicit links only. This graph summarizes the *MA* (figure 14.5).

Shock scaffold, SC   The shock scaffold is a directed graph, with nodes P and links L.

The *SC* is not a tree in general, that is, it contains circuits (chains of links forming closed loops) that are the boundaries of shock sheets. Despite the lack of an explicit representation of the interior of sheets, from the *SC* alone, we are still able to get a fairly good idea of the shape of the object due to the remaining connectivity. If we also make the representation of shock curves implicit, we obtain a simpler graph.

Reduced shock scaffold, SC−   The reduced shock scaffold is the *SC* in which link attributes (i.e., geometry and dynamics) have been discarded.

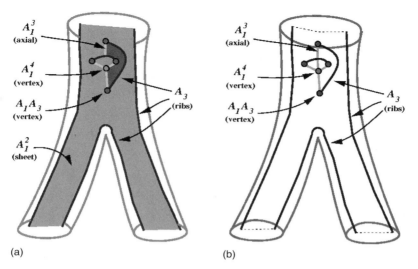

Figure 14.5 The 3D augmented shock scaffold, $SC+$, is illustrated in (a) for a branching structure that, at the top, is a cylinder whose base grows from a triangle to an ellipse, and that splits into two cylindrical structures with elliptic bases (only the hyperlink interior to the shape is shown); the corresponding scaffold, SC, is shown in (b).

This three-tier hierarchical representation for the MA is illustrated in figure 14.6. We also note that at the very coarsest level, only connectivity among nodes need be retained. That is, we could do away with the precise loci of nodes and define a graph devoid of geometry, where a node is simply a representative of a sheet, curve, or vertex. We call this representation the *topological scaffold*, and denote it TS (figure 14.7b). Finally, at the other end of the spectrum, we can further characterize the interior of shock sheets by building a network connecting their nodes (i.e., sources, relays, and sinks) together with the nodes at the boundaries of sheets, that is, with nodes of bounding curves and vertices, thereby defining a "full" shock hypergraph, denoted as SH (figure 14.7a).[13] The full scaffold hierarchy is summarized in table 14.2; this hierarchy permits to make explicit groupings of similar shapes, ranging from geometric exactness at one end (with the SH) to loose geometrical similitude, yet with similar topological attributes, at the other end (with the TS).[14]

Note that by going from the "classical" MA trace, which is a continuum of surfaces and curves of symmetry, to a discrete graph in the form of the shock scaffold, SC, we have considerably reduced the burden of computation. Recently, we introduced a near-linear scheme for computing the SC from unorganized point clouds sampling an object such as a sculpture or a human being (Leymarie 2003; Leymarie and Kimia 2003). This method

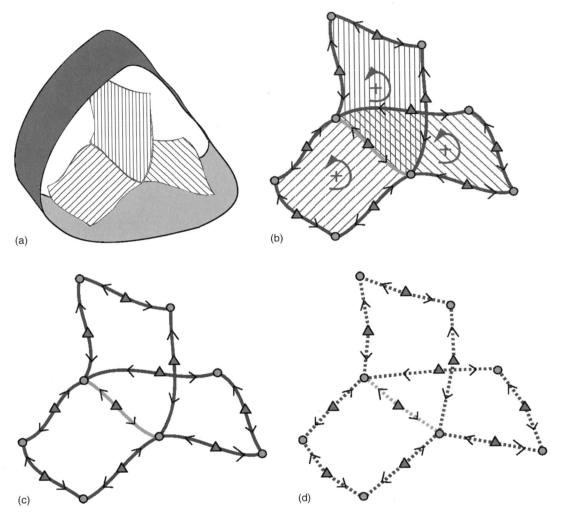

Figure 14.6 From the "classical" *MA* static representation to the shock scaffold hierarchy. (a) Typical situation in 3D, where three medial sheets intersect into a medial curve. (b) Equivalent representation by the augmented shock scaffold, *SC+*, where shock nodes along curves are connected by directed links; hyperlinks cyclic order is indicated by a counterclockwise arrow. (c) Representation by the *SC*, where the interior of sheets is implicit. (d) Representation by the reduced shock scaffold, *SC−*, where the trace of shock sheets and curves is implicit. Red points correspond to shock (or *MA*) vertices, that is, A_1^4 or A_1A_3. Green triangles correspond to shock nodes along curves, for example, A_1^3 − 2 source points.

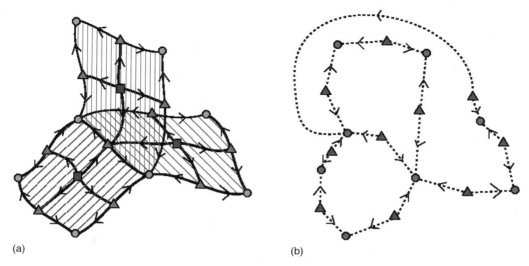

(a)

(b)

Figure 14.7 Possible additional levels in the shock scaffold hierarchy. (a) The shock hypergraph, *SH*, adds to *SC+* sources, relays, and sinks of shock sheets (indicated as blue squares) and links among these as well as with respect to the sheet boundaries. (b) The topological scaffold, *TS*, is obtained from the *SC* when only the topology of the graph structure is preserved.

Table 14.2 The complete scaffold hierarchy is composed of five levels

Level	Symbol	Features
I	$\mathscr{S}\mathscr{H}$	All shock flow singularities, connected via links and hyperlinks
II	$\mathscr{S}\mathscr{C}^+$	Set of nodes P, links L, and hyperlinks H
III	$\mathscr{S}\mathscr{C}$	Directed graph $\{P, L\}$
IV	$\mathscr{S}\mathscr{C}^-$	Set of nodes P, and links stripped of geometry
V	$\mathscr{T}\mathscr{S}$	Set of nodes and links stripped of geometry

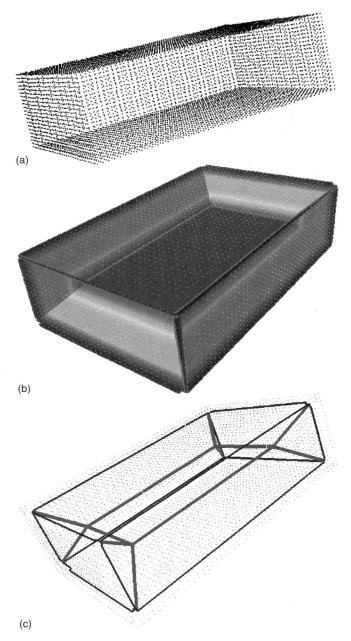

(a)

(b)

(c)

Figure 14.8 The augmented shock scaffold, $SC+$, of a rectangular box sampled by 7326 points (a) is depicted in (b). The flow along sheets is shown using the color spectrum, where blue means close to the boundary, and red means as far away as possible. In (c) the geometry for the interior of the shock sheets is left implicit, and

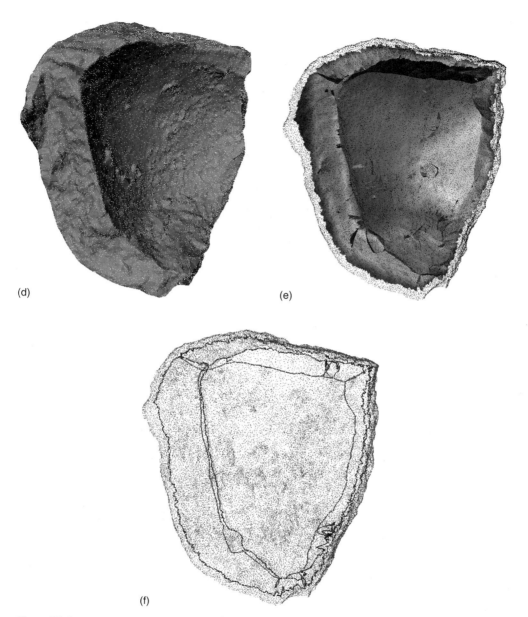

(d)

(e)

(f)

Figure 14.8 (continued)

(A_1^3) axial curves at the intercepts of shock sheets are shown in pink, while (A_3) ribs at the boundaries of shock sheets are shown in blue. (d) A pot shard is shown (approximatively 40,000 point samples here, obtained by laser scanning). $SC+$ of this shard is shown in (e) with the flow along sheets color-coded similarly to (b); the ("outer") symmetries, away from the concave part of the pot shard, are not shown here; white dots indicate input data. (f) The corresponding SC (input point samples in black) after transitions (see Leymarie 2004 for details). Observe how the SC in (f) can be seen as a deformed version of the SC in (c).

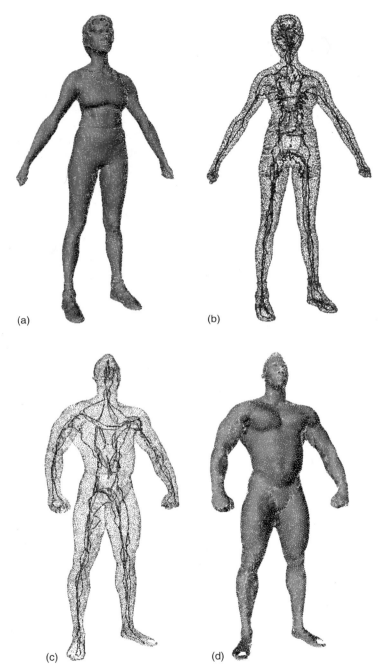

Figure 14.9 Real-life human female (a and b) and male (c and d) bodies, laser-scanned (by Cyberware, Inc.), composed of 30,430 and 21,500 points, respectively. In (b) and (c) are shown the computed SC for each body. Notice how similar the general topological features are (i.e., the loop structures in the graph).

fully exploits the compactness of the representation by focusing the computations on the shock singularities.

We conclude this section by comparing the representations computed for a synthetic dataset (a rectangular box) and an archaeological fragment of a pot (figure 14.8), as well as for a pair of human bodies (figure 14.9). The synthetic example in figure 14.8 serves as a *prototype* of many real shapes, such as the pot shard that can be thought of as a *deformed* rectangular box with additional surface *perturbations*.

From the Shock Scaffold to Shape Dynamics

With the shock graph in 2D and the shock scaffold (*SC*) in 3D, we now have a good mathematical and computational toolbox to address the Gestalt principles of shape. The simplified representation not only permits the more efficient computation and storage of the *MA* model, but it also allows one to put the focus of the analysis on the graph structure, to study its dynamics under perturbations and deformation. This represents a first step toward making this technology more fully compatible with Leyton's theory of aesthetics (ch. 15).

As we noted earlier, the *MA* is inherently unstable, and in 3D as the surface outline is deformed, the graph structure of the *SC* can change abruptly. This is also the case for sudden transitions in 2D shock graphs (Siddiqi et al. 1999; Sebastian et al. 2004). A solution for the practical use of 2D shock graphs in applications was to classify the set of such instabilities, or transitions, and employ these as an explicit representation when relating two shapes in 2D (Giblin and Kimia 1999; Tek and Kimia 2001; Sebastian et al. 2004). Likewise, when representing 3D shapes, the transitions arising from small deformations must be classified and represented. Giblin and Kimia have formally classified the set of generic transitions of the *MA* (Giblin and Kimia 2002), which is a specialized subset of the full gamut of transitions for the *SS* (Bogaevsky 2002). Figure 14.10 shows two of the seven possible transitions relevant to the *MA* (and thus the *SC*). The first one, the A_1A_3-I transition, corresponds to a surface being pulled out slightly, resulting in a new medial sheet being generated in the direction of the pull. The second one, the A_1^5 transition, shows how compressing a shape can abruptly change its *SC*. Finally, figure 14.11 shows an application of using transitions to undo deformations, thus permitting the recovery of a "regularized" shape representation (Leymarie et al. 2004).

Conclusion

We presented a powerful computational model for dealing with the representation of 3D shape, the shock scaffold: a directed graph model capturing many of the the aesthetic principles of shape as advocated by the Gestalt school. Together with a study of transitions

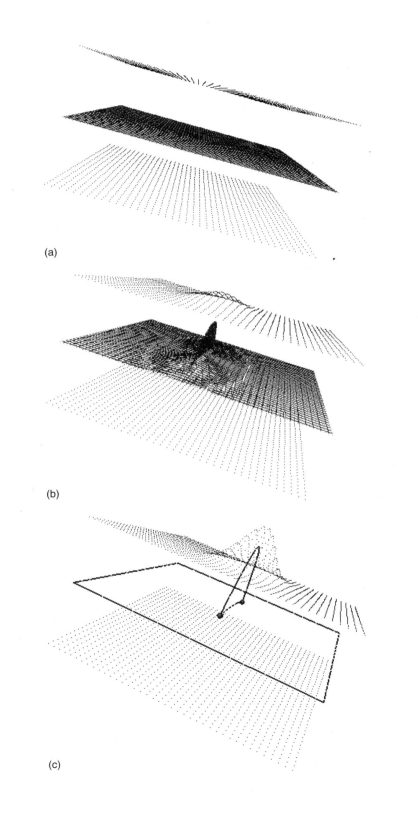

(a)

(b)

(c)

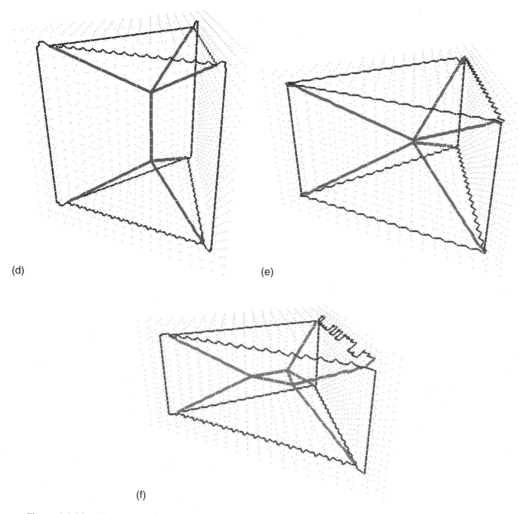

(d)

(e)

(f)

Figure 14.10   Illustration of two of the seven 3D transitions (after Giblin and Kimia 2002), where the shape deforms from left to right, passing through an A_1A_3-I transition in (a), (b), and (c), and through an A_1^5 transition in (d), (e), and (f). The former represents the effect of pulling a *protrusion* out of an otherwise smooth pair of surfaces (a), generating a new loop structure in the SC made of an A_3 rib of a ridge (in blue), an A_1^3 axial curve (in red) joined at a pair of A_1A_3 vertices (c). The latter represents a *squashing* effect of a cakelike object (or prism), which brings an A_1^3 axial link in the SC (d), to a point at the transition (e), to a loop structure made of three A_1^3 axial curves (f) bounding a new A_1^2 sheet of the corresponding MA.

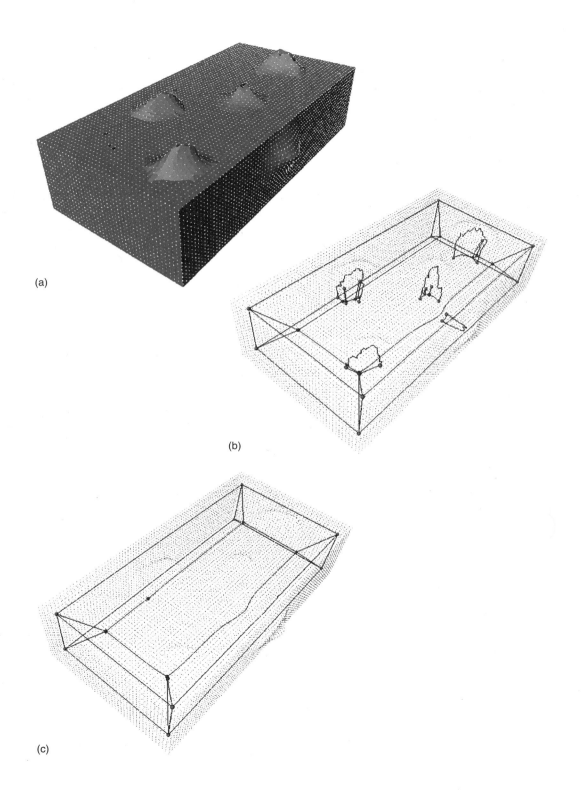

(a)

(b)

(c)

(d)

(e)

(f)

Figure 14.11   An example of how transitions can regularize the shock scaffold (after Leymarie 2004). (a) The box of figure 14.8 was deformed by five protrusions: four on the top and one on the side. (b) The initial SC where smaller loop structures are due to the protrusions. (c) The SC after transition removal. (d) The pot shard of figure 14.8 and (e) its initial SC. (f) The resulting SC after transition removal.

under perturbations and deformations, which is presently under development (Giblin and Kimia 2002; Leymarie et al. 2004; Chang et al. 2004), this model should permit one to study shape dynamics and relate it more formally to Leyton's theory of aesthetics (ch. 15). Furthermore, its relative simplicity allows the development of efficient computational schemes for its retrieval, as was recently demonstrated (Leymarie 2003; Leymarie et al. 2004; Chang et al. 2004).

Acknowledgments

This work would not have been possible without a grant from the National Science Foundation of the USA (ITR-0205477).

Glossary

Object A region of a given space, such as the Euclidean 3D space, E^3, having some homogeneous characteristic. For example, define an object as a region, $\mathbf{x}$ of E^3 whose density, r, is above some fiducial value, $K : r(\mathbf{x}) > K$. For more details on this topic, refer to the concept of solid shape and tolerances for shape by Koenderink (Koenderink 1990, ch. 2).

Outline Lines (curves) that mark the outer limits of an object. Also, a sketch in which object contours (not necessarily boundaries) are marked without shading (e.g., a line-drawing of a figure).

Shape Quantitative description of the boundary or of the outline of an object. Such a "description" might simply consist of a quantitative study of the outline itself; for example, an ordered enumeration of the contour points. Alternatively, a "description" of some of the distinctive features extracted from the outline can define "shape," for example, the three corners of a triangle. Thus, this description will depend on the method used to probe the object's outline. As such, one may say that "shape is operationally defined" (Koenderink 1990, p. 15).

Form Qualitative representation of the boundary of an object. For example, one may talk of the "round form" of the sphere or of an ellipsoid. Thus, the notion of "object" corresponds to the physical body present in the scene. The notion of "shape" corresponds to the description of the "available" outline of this object. Usually it is derived from some projection of the body in the scene onto the image (or retinal) plane. Finally the notion of "form" is a more abstract (qualitative) concept. Many shapes may have the same form. Shape is the "content" of form; that is, it gives a more precise meaning or identity to a form. Form is like a "metashape," a concept useful for object classification and recognition.

Notes

1. A short glossary at the end of the chapter gives a few definitions for "object," "outline," "shape," and "form."

2. The *shock scaffold* is a generic representation for 3D shape that was recently defined based on the collaborative works of B. B. Kimia (at Brown University), P. J. Giblin (at Liverpool University), and myself, F. F. Leymarie (at Brown).

3. Why we are sensitive to such beauty is another (anthropological and psychological) matter: consider that certain studies show that very symmetric features, for example, of a face or body, are synonymous with youth or a robust immune system. We will not go further into this topic, but it could be interesting to attempt to relate beauty to biophysical properties, or even to energy optimization (e.g., in the symmetric arrangements of galaxies; Icke 1991).

4. Gestalt, derived from the German word *gestellt*, meaning to "put together," assemble in a "cohesive whole." The essential meaning of Gestalt is that "the whole is more [important] than simply the sum of the parts" in cognitive percepts.

5. There is much more in the Gestalt literature, including the works of Arnheim and his contemporaries (e.g., see Gapenne and Rovira 1999). Our focus here is on the ideas relevant to establishing a simple computational model for shape representation from aesthetic principles.

6. The concept of a structural skeleton where visual force lines generated by outlines tend to converge is likely to be an ancient one; for example, it has recently been proposed to explain the layouts of certain sixteenth-century Japanese gardens (van Tonder et al. 2002).

7. Other names can be found in the literature, such as "medial loci," "Voronoi skeleton," "symmetry axis," and "cut locus," to describe an equivalent notion (Pizer et al. 2003; Wolter et al. 2004). The computational process used to obtain the diagram is sometime called a "transform," mapping the boundary outline into a skeletal or symmetry outline; in topology this notion is called a "deformation retract" (Sherbrooke et al. 1996).

8. Technically speaking, this also shows a close relationship between Blum's model and an older mathematical construct—the Voronoi diagram (Okabe et al. 2000; Leymarie 2003).

9. Blum's model, as well the Gestalt principles of shape, are applicable to higher (and lower) dimensional shapes. In this chapter we focus on 3D worlds.

10. Leyton introduces a variant of the 2D *MA*, denoted *PISA*—Process Inferring Symmetry Axis—where the skeletal diagram is obtained by tracing mid-arc points of maximal circles of contact, rather than their centers, as for Blum's "classical" *MA*. This permits one to explicitly represent each curvature extrema of an outline.

11. Contact with isolated input points is taken as the limit of a contact with tiny spheres with radii shrinking to zero. The maximality criterion is equivalent to "emptiness," that is, a maximal contact sphere is such that it contains no other input points.

12. This notation corresponds to the one used to describe singularity varieties of minima functions of three variables in the singularity theory of dynamical systems; see, for example, the works of Arnold (1991). The "A" comes from the relation to the simple Lie groups of type A.

13. An early attempt at representing 3D MA sheets in a similar way was advocated by Nackman and Pizer (1985), by creating a "critical point configuration graph" linking sources to relays and sinks of an MA sheet seen as a topographic map (with an associated height field). This was motivated by the classical "hills and dales" representation of Cayley (1859) and Maxwell (1870).

14. The lower levels in the hierarchy—$SC-$ and TS—give possible embodiments of the notion of "form," while the top levels, SH and $SC+$, give precise descriptions of the "shape" of an "object" under scrutiny (see Glossary).

References

Arnheim, Rudolf. 1971. *Entropy and Art: an Essay on Disorder and Order.* Berkeley: University of California Press.

———. 1974. *Art and Visual Perception: A Psychology of the Creative Eye.* Berkeley: University of California Press. Expanded and revised edition of the 1954 original.

Arnold, Vladimir I. 1991. *Theory of Singularities and Its Applications.* Lezione Fermiane. Cambridge: Cambridge University Press.

Binford, Thomas. 1987. "Generalized Cylinders Representation." In *Encyclopedia of Artificial Intelligence.* S. C. Shapiro, ed. Pp. 321–23, New York: John Wiley & Sons.

Blum, Harry. 1961. "An Associative Machine for Dealing with the Visual Field and Some of Its Biological Implications." In *Biological Prototypes and Synthetic Systems.* Bernard, E. and Kare, M., eds. 1: 244–60. New York: Plenum Press, 1962. Proceedings of the 2nd Annual Bionics Symposium, held at Cornell University, 1961.

———. 1962. "A Machine for Performing Visual Recognition by Use of Antenna-Propagation Concepts." In *Proceedings of the Institute of Radio Engineers, Wescon Convention Record*, 6;4, session 6.4, August 1962.

————. 1964. "A Transformation for Extracting New Descriptors of Shape." In *Models for the Perception of Speech and Visual Form.* Wathen-Dunn, W., ed. Pp. 362–80. Cambridge, MA: MIT Press, 1967. Proceedings of a symposium held in Boston, November 1964.

————. 1973. "Biological Shape and Visual Science." *Journal of Theoretical Biology* 38: 205–87.

Bogaevsky, Ilya. 2002. *Perestroikas of Shocks and Singularities of Minimum Functions.* Available at http://arXiv.org/abs/math.AP/0204237.

Cayley, Arthur. 1859. "On Contour and Slope Lines." *The London Edinburgh, and Dublin Philosophical Magazine and Journal of Science* XVIII: 264–68.

Chang, Ming-Ching, Leymarie, Frederic F., and Kimia, Benjamin. 2004. "3D Shape Registration Using Regularized Medial Scaffolds." *IEEE Proc. of the 2nd International Symposium on 3D Data Processing, Visualization, and Transmission (3DPVT)*, Greece, pp. 987–94.

Gapenne, Olivier, and Rovira, Katia. 1999. "Gestalt Psychologie et cognition sans langage—Actualite' d'une figure historique." *Intellectica* 28: 229–50.

Giblin, Peter, and Kimia, Benjamin. 1998. "On the Intrinsic Reconstruction of Shape from Its Symmetries." *Proc. of the Conference on Computer Vision and Pattern Recognition (CVPR'98)*, pp. 79–84; extended version published in the *IEEE Trans. of PAMI* 2003; 25(7): 895–911.

————. 1999. "On the Local Form and Transitions of Symmetry Sets, and Medial Axes, and Shocks in 2D." *Proc. of the 7th International Conference on Computer Vision* 1: 385–91. Greece: IEEE Computer Society; extended version published in *International Journal of Computer Vision* 2003; 54(1–3): 143–57.

————. 2000. "On the Local Form of Symmetry Sets, and Medial Axes, and Shocks in 3D." *Proc. of the Conference on Computer Vision and Pattern Recognition (CVPR'00)*, pp. 566–73. South Carolina: IEEE Computer Society.

————. 2002. "Transitions of the 3D Medial Axis under a One-Parameter Family of Deformations." In *Computer Vision—ECCV*, LNCS 2351, Part II in Lecture Notes in Computer Science. Berlin: Springer-Verlag. Pp. 719–34.

————. 2004. "A Formal Classification of 3D Medial Axis Points and Their Local Geometry." *IEEE Trans. of Pattern Analysis and Machine Intelligence* (PAMI) 26(2): 238–51.

Halliman, P., Gordon, G., Yuille, A., Giblin, P., and Mumford, D. 1999. *Two- and Three-Dimensional Patterns of the Face*. Natick, MA: A. K. Peters.

Icke, V., and van de Weygaert, R. 1991. "The Galaxy Distribution as a Voronoi Foam." *Quaterly Journal of the Royal Astronomical Society* 32(2): 85–112.

Kanizsa, Gaetano, ed. 1979. *Organization in Vision*. New York: Praeger.

Koenderink, Jan. 1990. *Solid Shape*. A.I. Series. Cambridge, MA: MIT Press.

Koehler, Wolfgang, 1947. *Gestalt Psychology, an Introduction to New Concepts in Modern Psychology*. New York: Liveright Pub. Corp.

Koffka, Kurt. 1935. *Principles of Gestalt Psychology*. New York: Harcourt, Brace.

Leymarie, Frederic Fol. 2003. *Three-Dimensional Shape Representation via Shock Flows*. PhD thesis. Brown University, Division of Engineering, Providence, RI. Available at http://www.lems.brown .edu/~leymarie/phd/.

Leymarie, Frederic F., and Kimia, Benjamin. 2003. "Computation of the Shock Scaffold for Unorganized Point Clouds in 3D." *IEEE Proc. of the Conference on Computer Vision and Pattern Recognition (CVPR'03)* 1: 821–27.

Leymarie, Frederic F., Kimia, Benjamin, and Giblin, Peter. 2004. "Towards Surface Regularization via Medial Axis Transitions." *Proc. of the 17th International Conference on Pattern Recognition (ICPR'04)* 3: 123–26.

Levoy, Mark, et al. 2000. "The Digital Michelangelo Project: 3D Scanning of Large Statues." *ACM Proc. of SIGGRAPH'00*, pp. 131–44.

Leyton, Michael. 1987. "Symmetry-Curvature Duality." *Computer Vision, Graphics and Image Processing* 38: 327–41.

———. 1988. "A Process Grammar for Shape." *Journal of Artificial Intelligence* 34(2): 213–47.

———. 2001. *A Generative Theory of Shape*. LNCS 2145 in Lecture Notes in Computer Science. Berlin: Springer-Verlag.

Maxwell, James Clerk. 1870. "On Hills and Dales." *London Edinburgh, and Dublin Philosophical Magazine and Journal of Science* 40: 421–25.

Nackman, Lee, and Pizer, Stephen. 1985. "Three-Dimensional Shape Description Using The Symmetric Axis Transform I: Theory." *IEEE Trans. on Pattern Analysis and Machine Intelligence* (PAMI) 7: 187–202.

Okabe, Atsuyuki, Boots, Barry, Sugihara, Kokichi, and Chiu, Sung~Nok. 2000. *Spatial Tessellations: Concepts and Applications of Voronoi Diagrams. Probability and Statistics.* 2nd ed. New York: John Wiley & Sons.

Pizer, Stephen, Siddiqi, Kaleem, Szekely, Damon, James, and Zucker, Steven. 2003. "Multiscal Medial Loci and Their Properties." *International Journal of Computer Vision* 55(2–3): 155–79.

Sebastian, Thomas, Klein, Philip, and Kimia, Benjamin. 2004. "Recognition of Shapes by Editing Their Shock Graphs." *IEEE Trans. on Pattern Analysis and Machine Intelligence* (PAMI) 26(5): 550–71.

Sherbrooke, Evan, Patrikalakis, Nicholas, and Wolter, Franz-Erich. 1996. "Differential and Topological Properties of Medial Axis Transforms." *Graphical Models and Image Processing* 58(6): 574–92.

Siddiqi, Kaleem, and Kimia, Benjamin. 1996. "A Shock Grammar for Recognition." *IEEE Proc. of the Conference on Computer Vision and Pattern Recognition (CVPR'96)*, pp. 507–13.

Siddiqi, Kaleem, Shokoufandeh, Ali, Dickinson, Sven, and Zucker, Steven. 1999. "Shock Graph and Shape Matching." *International Journal of Computer Vision* 35(1): 13–32.

Tek, Huseyin. 1999. *The Role of Symmetry Maps.* PhD thesis. Brown University, Division of Engineering, Providence, RI.

Tek, Huseyin, and Kimia, Benjamin. 2001. "Boundary Smoothing via Symmetry Transforms." *Journal of Mathematical Imaging and Vision* 14(3): 211–23.

Tek, Huseyin, Leymarie, Frederic F., and Kimia, Benjamin. 1997. "Interpenetrating Waves and Multiple Generation Shocks via the CEDT." *Advances in Visual Form Analysis*, pp. 582–93. World Scientific.

van Tonder, Gert, Lyons, M., and Ejima, Y. 2002. "Visual Structure of a Japanese Garden." *Nature* 419: 359–60; extended version in *Journal of the IEICE—Special Issue* 2003; 86(10): 742–46.

Wertheimer, M. 1923. "Laws of Organization in Perceptual Forms." In *A Source Book of Gestalt Psychology*. W. D. Ellis, ed. Pp. 71–88. New York: Harcourt, Brace, 1938.

Wolter, Franz-Erich, Peinecke, Niklas, and Reuter, Martin. 2004. "Geometric Modeling of Technical Objects." In *Encyclopedia of Computational Mechanics*, Vol. 1, ch. 16. Stein, E. et al. eds. New York: John Wiley & Sons.

15

The Foundations of Aesthetics

Michael Leyton

This chapter summarizes the theory of aesthetics that comes from the new foundations for geometry developed in my books. The new geometric foundations are based on two principles of aesthetics: (1) maximizing transfer of structure and (2) maximizing recoverability of the generative operations.

These principles are fundamental to aesthetic judgment in (1) the arts, in which we examine painting, music, and poetry; (2) the sciences, in which we examine general relativity and quantum mechanics; and (3) computer programming, in which we examine object-oriented programming. We show that all these areas are driven by the same two underlying principles: maximization of transfer and recoverability. Transfer is formalized in terms of particular products of groups. It is shown to be the basis of Gestalt. Recoverability is shown to depend on a new theory of symmetry breaking, provided in the geometric theory. Together, transfer and recoverability are shown to be the basis of memory storage; and our rigorous theory of aesthetics says that *the rules of aesthetics are the rules of memory storage*. In particular, both the arts and the sciences are driven by the single goal of maximizing memory storage. Finally, these principles are applied to explain core phenomena in object-oriented programming. For a full analysis of each of these areas, the reader should consult my books *Symmetry, Causality, Mind, A Generative Theory of Shape, Shape as Memory,* and *The Structure of Paintings*.

Transfer in Art and Science

As stated previously, the new foundations for geometry I developed are based on two principles of aesthetic judgment in the arts, sciences, and computation—maximization

Figure 15.1 Line drawing of Holbein's Ann of Cleves.

of transfer and maximization of recoverability. The next few sections examine the first principle (maximization of transfer), and then we move on to the second principle.

In examining some of the evidence that transfer has a fundamental role in aesthetics, let us begin by looking at Holbein's painting of Ann of Cleves, shown in figure 15.1. I analyze this in considerable detail in my book *The Structure of Paintings*, which is summarized here.

The generative history of this painting begins with a circle, appropriately, in the region of the face—in both the top line of the head and the neck. The circle is then deformed vertically into an ellipse; for example, we see this in the successive downward necklaces. The downward end of the ellipse is a curvature maximum (extreme of bend). It is made successively more extreme in the successive downward necklaces.

In the next stage, this downward curvature maximum branches into two copies of itself, left and right, creating a *bay* in the dress band, as shown in figure 15.2. The two copies are shown at the ends of the two arrows.

In the next stage of the generative history, the center of the bay, which is a curvature minimum (extreme of flatness), itself splits into two copies of itself that move to the sides.

Figure 15.2 The bay in the dress band.

The resulting shape is a *deepened bay*, which is shown as the arm line in figure 15.3. That is, the flattened center of original bay (above the arms), has now become the two flattened parts of the lower bay, indicated by the two forearms.

Now notice the following crucial point: Holbein *transfers* any downward action just described onto a corresponding upward action. For example, the downward creation of the bay, in figure 15.2, now appears as the upward creation of the bay in the veil, as shown in figure 15.4. Furthermore, the deepened bay, in figure 15.3, now appears as the top line of the head. My books analyze painting at length, showing that transfer is its fundamental structuring principle.

Transfer is also the fundamental principle of music. A movement of a Beethoven symphony has remarkably few basic elements. The entire movement is generated by the transfer of these elements into different pitches, major and minor forms, overlapping positions in counterpoint, and so on. For example, figure 15.5 shows the famous motif in Beethoven's 5th Symphony being transferred to different levels of pitch, in eight successive bars from the symphony. Almost the entire score looks like this.

Figure 15.3   Deepened bay.

Furthermore, transfer is the basis of not only the pitch structure of music, but also the meter structure. Meter is composed of an accent hierarchy with the following successive levels:

1.   Primary accent grouping (division into bars).
2.   Secondary accent grouping (first subdivision of the bar).
3.   Division into beats.
4.   Division of beats.
5.   Subdivision of beats.

Each level *transfers* the level below it. For example, figure 15.6 illustrates the meter structure of a single bar in 9/8 time. This will be transferred onto the next bar. Furthermore, within this hierarchy, each node transfers the nodes that it dominates, as indicated by the arrow below it. See Leyton (2001, 2003) for an extensive discussion.

I have also demonstrated that poetry is structured by transfer. For example, consider figure 15.7, which is from a sonnet by Shakespeare. This is propelled forward by an exqui-

Figure 15.4   The bay in the veil.

Figure 15.5   Transfer in a Beethoven symphony.

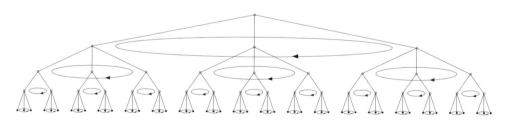

Figure 15.6   The accent hierarchy of a bar.

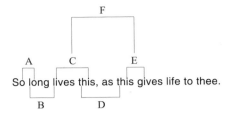

Figure 15.7 Transfer in a Shakespeare sonnet.

site sequence of transfers: First, the *o* sound is transferred, as indicated by bracket A. Then the *l* sound is transferred, as indicated by bracket B. Then the *i* sound is transferred, as indicated by bracket C. Then the *th* sound is transferred, as indicated by bracket D. Then the *i* sound is transferred, as indicated by bracket E.

Observe that bracket F marks a powerful phenomenon. It captures the fact that bracket E is a transfer of bracket C, because both brackets are the transfer of the *i* sound. That is, bracket F transfers bracket C onto bracket E. However, bracket F also indicates another transfer. The phrase "lives this" undergoes a mirror transformation, becoming the phrase "this gives." Finally, at the end of the line, the pair of sounds "l- th-", in the phrase, "life to thee" is a transfer of the earlier "l- th-" in the phrase "lives this."

Note also that the meter structure of poetry conforms to the transfer theory of musical meter. Having seen that art aesthetics are based on transfer, we can now turn to science to find that scientific aesthetics are also based on transfer.

A comprehensive survey of the use of the term *aesthetics* in science reveals that this term is consistently used about the fundamental phenomenon of *symmetries of laws*. These symmetries have led to the major discoveries of physics—the conservation laws, the existence of particles, the existence of dynamical equations, the unification of forces, and the very concept of a force. To understand what is meant by *symmetries of laws*, we see that this is a powerful example of *transfer* that reinforces my claim that transfer is a crucial element of aesthetics.

All branches of physics are founded on a law that determines how their systems, evolve over time. This is the *dynamical law*, or dynamical equation. For example, in Newtonian mechanics, the dynamical equation is Newton's second law, $F = ma$, which determines the trajectory of a system in classical mechanics. In quantum mechanics, the dynamical law is Schrodinger's equation, which determines how a quantum-mechanical state will evolve over time. In Hamiltonian mechanics, Hamilton's equations determine how a point moves in phase space.

Let us now consider what is meant by *symmetries* of the dynamical law.[1] Consider figure 15.8. The bottom trajectory in the figure shows an experiment being run in a laboratory in

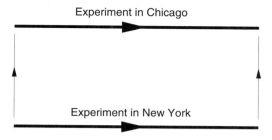

Figure 15.8 The transfer of a scientific experiment.

New York, and the upper trajectory shows the same experiment being run in a laboratory in Chicago. Let us suppose that we discover a fundamental law that prescribes both trajectories. Any such law, being a dynamical law, prescribes a *flow*. The two trajectories shown would be part of the flow prescribed by the law.

The most important question one can ask in physics is this: Is there a transformation that takes the flow-line in New York onto the flow-line in Chicago? Let us suppose there is, and the transformation is translation. This translation is shown by the vertical arrows in figure 15.8. One says, in this case, that the equation (the flow) has *translational symmetry*; that is, translation will send flow-lines of the equation onto each other.

Our illustration used translation as the transformation that sent flow-lines onto flow-lines. But the transformation could have been rotation, in which case the dynamical law would have rotational symmetry.

Hunting for symmetries of a dynamical law is important because the fundamental discoveries come from this. For example, for every symmetry transformation discovered, there is a conservation law. If the discovered symmetry transformation is temporal translation, for example, then one has the conservation of energy; if the discovered symmetry transformation is spatial translation, then one has the conservation of linear momentum; if the discovered symmetry transformation is spatial rotation, then one has the conservation of angular momentum.

Clearly the phenomenon we have been describing is one of *transfer*. That is, a dynamical equation has a symmetry if the flow-lines can be *transferred* onto each other. Succinctly, we use the term *aesthetics* in science regarding symmetries of a law; however, symmetries of a law mean *transfer* of the law's flow-lines onto each other.

This section has examined some of the evidence that transfer is basic to aesthetics in both art and science. For much more extensive evidence, the reader should consult my books (Leyton 1992; 2001; 2005a; 2005b).

Groups

In the next section, we examine the structure of transfer in greater depth, but this requires understanding the concept of *group*, which is explained in this section. Intuitively, one can say that *a group is a complete system of transformations*. Following are examples of groups:

1. *Rotations*   The complete system of rotations around a circle.
2. *Translations*   The complete system of translations along a line.
3. *Deformations*   The complete system of deformations of an object.

To explain the word "complete," let us suppose we can list the collection of transformations T_i in a group, G, thus:

$$G = \{T_0, T_1, T_2, \ldots\}.$$

For example, the transformations T_i might be rotations. The condition that this collection is *complete*, means satisfying the following three properties:

1. *Closure*   For any two transformations in the group, their combination is also in the group. For example, if the transformation *rotation by* $30°$ is in the group, and the transformation *rotation by* $60°$ is in the group, then the combination, *rotation by* $90°$, is also in the group.
2. *Identity element*   The collection of transformations must contain the "null" transformation, that is, the transformation that has no effect. Thus, if the transformations are rotations, then the null transformation is *rotation by zero degrees*. Generally, one labels the null transformation e, and calls it the *identity element*. In the preceding list, we can consider T_0 to be the identity element.
3. *Inverses*   For any transformation in the group, its inverse transformation is also in the group. Thus, if the transformation *clockwise rotation by* $30°$ is in the group, then its inverse, *anticlockwise rotation by* $30°$, is also in the group.

A fourth condition on groups, called associativity, is so simple that we need not consider it here.

Generating a Shape by Transfer

Recall that, according to my new foundations for geometry, aesthetics is based on two principles: maximization of transfer and maximization of recoverability. The second prin-

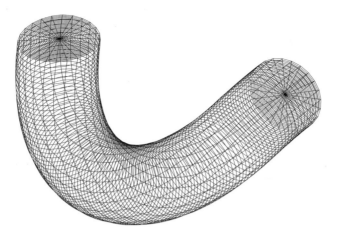

Figure 15.9 A deformed cylinder.

ciple will be introduced in the section on Recoverability. But first we will examine the first principle in greater depth.

The new foundations for geometry is a *generative theory of shape*. Such a theory characterizes the structure of a shape by a sequence of actions needed to generate it. According to the new foundations, these actions must maximize transfer:

Maximization of Transfer   Make one part of the generative history a transfer of another part of the generative history, whenever possible.

We now illustrate the means of generating a shape by transfer. Figure 15.9 shows a deformed cylinder. To generate it entirely by transfer, we proceed as follows:

Stage 1   Create a single point in space.
Stage 2   Transfer the point around space by rotating it, thus producing a circle, as illustrated in figure 15.10.
Stage 3   Transfer the circle through space by translating it, producing a straight cylinder, as illustrated in figure 15.11.
Stage 4   Transfer the straight cylinder onto the deformed cylinder by deforming it.

Now observe that these four successive stages created a succession of four structures:

Point → Circle → Straight cylinder → Deformed cylinder.

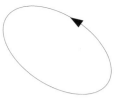

Figure 15.10   A point is transferred by rotations, producing a circle.

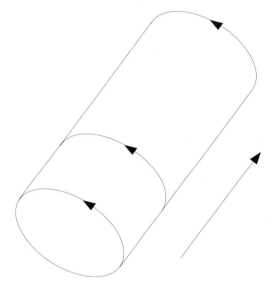

Figure 15.11   The circle is then transferred by translations, producing a straight cylinder.

Most important, observe that each stage created its structure by *transferring* the structure created at the previous stage; that is, there is transfer of transfer of transfer. The final object is therefore created by a *hierarchy of transfers*. Furthermore, the transfer at each stage was carried out by applying a set of actions to the previous stage; thus, stage 2 applied the group Rotations to stage 1; stage 3 applied the group Translations to stage 2; stage 4 applied the group Deformations to stage 3. This hierarchy of transfer can be written as follows:

Point ⓣ Rotations ⓣ Translations ⓣ Deformations

The symbol ⓣ means "transfer." Each group, along this expression, transfers its left-subsequence, that is, the entire sequence to its left, going successively, left-to-right along the following sequence: (1) the group Rotations transfers its left-subsequence Point to create a circle, (2) the group Translations transfers its left-subsequence Point ⓉRotations (the circle) to create a straight cylinder, and finally, (3) Deformations transfers its left-subsequence Point ⓉRotations ⓉTranslations (the straight cylinder) to create the deformed cylinder.

Fiber and Control

The transfer operation Ⓣ always relates two groups, thus

$$G_1 \, Ⓣ \, G_2$$

The lower group, that to the left of Ⓣ, is *transferred* by the upper group, that to the right of Ⓣ. The lower group is called the *fiber group*, and the upper group is the *control group*. Thus, we have

Fiber Group Ⓣ Control Group

The reason for this terminology is illustrated with the straight cylinder. Here, the lower group was Rotations, which generated the cross-section, and the upper group was Translations, which transferred the cross-section along the cylinder:

Rotations Ⓣ Translations

   The thing to observe is that this transfer structure causes the cylinder to decompose into *fibers*, the cross-sections, as shown in figure 15.12. Each fiber, a cross-section, is individually generated by the lower group, Rotations. It is for this reason that I call the lower group, the *fiber group*. Notice, also from figure 15.12, that the other group, Translations, *controls* the position of the fiber along the cylinder. This is why I call the upper group, the *control group*.
   Generally, a transfer structure causes a *fibering* of some space. As a further illustration, consider what happened when we created the deformed cylinder by adding Deformations, above the straight cylinder:

Rotations Ⓣ Translations Ⓣ Deformations

Here Deformations acts as a control group, and the group to its left, Rotations Ⓣ Translations, acts as its fiber group. In this case, the fibers are now the various deformed versions

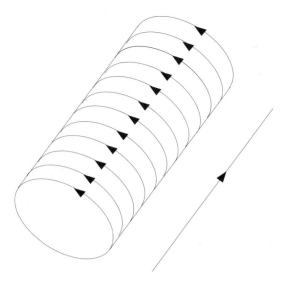

Figure 15.12   Under transfer, a cylinder decomposes into fibers.

of the cylinder. For example, the straight cylinder is the initial fiber, and any of its deformed versions (created by the control group), are also fibers.

My book *A Generative Theory of Shape* presents a comprehensive mathematical theory of transfer. The operation ⓉT is formalized in terms of a group-theoretic construct called a *wreath product*. To make this discussion available to a larger readership, we omit the mathematical technicalities here.

Theory of Gestalt

Since the beginning of perceptual psychology, over a hundred years ago, a major unsolved problem has been how the mind forms cohesive wholes, that is, Gestalts. Using the preceding concepts, we can now solve this problem, defining Gestalt theory as follows: The human perceptual system forms cohesive wholes, that is, Gestalts, by *transferring* stimuli onto each other. Stimuli are thus bound together by *transfer*. Consequently, a Gestalt is an *n*-fold transfer hierarchy, $G_1 \, ⓉT \, G_2 \, ⓉT \, \cdots \, ⓉT \, G_n$.

Recoverability

Recall that *aesthetics* is based on the two principles of maximization of transfer and maximization of recoverability. It is now necessary to bring in the concept of recoverability. Given a dataset, we recover or infer a sequence of operations that generate the set.

N. Riche

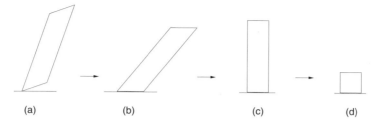

Figure 15.13 Psychological results found in Leyton (1986b, 1986c).

(a)   (b)   (c)   (d)

In *Symmetry, Causality, Mind* (Leyton 1992), I analyzed this problem, concluding, among other things, with the asymmetry principle.

Asymmetry Principle   The only recoverable operations are symmetry-breaking; that is, a generative history is recoverable only if it is symmetry-breaking on each of the successively generated states.

It is worth considering a psychological example of this principle at work. In a series of experiments (Leyton 1986b, 1986c), I found that subjects presented with a parallelogram oriented in the picture plane, as shown in figure 15.13a, see it as a rotated version of the parallelogram (figure 15.13b), then as a sheared version of the rectangle in figure 15.13c, and finally as a stretched version of the square in figure 15.13d. The remarkable thing is that the first figure, the rotated parallelogram, is the only object subjects are given. Their minds recovered the generative history shown in the figure.

The most important thing is that, to carry out this recovery of successively previous states, their minds successively removed asymmetries and recovered symmetries. Thus, subjects conjectured that the generative history was *symmetry-breaking in the forward-time direction*, from square to rotated parallelogram.

New Theory of Symmetry-Breaking

The asymmetry principle states that recoverability of history is possible only if each asymmetry in the present goes back to a past symmetry. This means that the history must have been symmetry-breaking.

Currently, in mathematics and physics, symmetry-breaking is described by reduction of a group. This is true because a symmetrical object is described by a group of transformations that correspond to its symmetries; when some symmetries are destroyed, the corresponding transformations are lost, therefore reducing the group.

In our system, however, symmetry-breaking is associated with the expansion of the group. For instance, recall the case of the straight cylinder, given by the group

Point ⊕ Rotations ⊕ Translations

Taking this group as fiber, and extending it by the Deformations group, using the transfer operation ⊕,

Point ⊕ Rotations ⊕ Translations ⊕ Deformations

results in the deformed cylinder. The added group, Deformations, breaks the symmetry of the straight cylinder. However, the straight cylinder group is not lost in this expression. It is retained as fiber. In fact, it is *transferred* onto the deformed cylinder, allowing us to see the latter cylinder as a *deformed version* of the straight cylinder. Thus, we have a new view of symmetry-breaking:

Symmetry-Breaking　When breaking the symmetry of an object that has symmetry group, G_1, take this group as fiber, and extend it by the group G_2, using the transfer operation ⊕. Thus,

$G_1 ⊕ G_2$

where G_2 is the group of the asymmetrizing action.

Maximizing Memory Storage

The new foundations to geometry directly oppose the foundations that have existed from Euclid to modern physics, including Einsteinian theory. In the standard foundations, a geometric object consists of those properties of a figure that do not change under a set of actions. These properties are called the *invariants* of the actions. Geometry began with the study of invariance, with Euclid's concept of *congruence*, which is really a concern with invariance (properties that do not change). Modern physics is also based on invariance. For example, Einstein's principle of relativity states that physics is the study of those properties that are invariant (unchanged) under transformations between observers.

The problem with invariants, however, is that they are *memoryless*. If a property is invariant (unchanged) under an action, then one cannot infer from the property that the action has taken place. In other words, *invariants cannot act as memory stores*. Thus, I conclude that geometry, from Euclid to Einstein, has been concerned with *memorylessness*. In fact, since standard geometry, including Einstein's relativity theory, tries to maximize the discovery of invariants, it is essentially trying to maximize memorylessness. These foundations to geometry are inappropriate to the computational age. People buy computers that have greater memory storage, not less. The medical profession fights diseases such as Altzheimer's because these diseases attack memory, and memory not only allows intelligence, but is equated with the person's identity.

As a consequence, I embarked on a 30-year project to build up an entirely new system for geometry—a system I recently completed and published in *A Generative Theory of Shape* (Leyton 2001). Rather than basing geometry on the *maximization of memorylessness* (the aim from Euclid to Einstein), I base geometry on the *maximization of memory storage*. The result is a profoundly different system, on both a conceptual level and a detailed mathematical level. The basic principle of the new foundations is

Shape ≡ Memory storage

In particular, the claim is that all memory storage takes place via shape.

The theory, then, shows that the maximization of memory storage in shape is achieved by the two principles of maximization of recoverability and maximization of transfer. These two principles are fundamental to memory because recoverability means the reconstruction of the past from what is available in the present, and transfer means seeing the present in terms of the past, that is, as a transfer of the past. The crucial concept is therefore that shape maximizes memory storage, if it is given a generative (historical) description that maximizes transfer and recoverability.

To illustrate, let us go back to the example of the deformed cylinder. We showed how this cylinder can be generated, all the way up from a point, by layers of transfer: one starts with a point, then transfers the point by rotations to create a circle, then transfers the circle by translations to create a straight cylinder, and finally transfers the straight cylinder by deformations to produce the deformed cylinder. This means that, forward in time, one goes through a sequence of four stages that create a succession of four structures:

Point → Circle → Straight cylinder → Deformed cylinder

Each stage creates its structure by transferring the structure created in the previous stage.

The arrows in the above sequence of four structures represent the forward direction of time. Now let us consider how one *recovers* that history. This means that one must reverse the arrows, going backward in time:

Deformed cylinder $\longrightarrow$ Straight cylinder $\longrightarrow$ Circle $\longrightarrow$ Point.

Thus, starting with the deformed cylinder *in the present*, one must *recover* the backward history through these stages. How is this recovery of the past possible? The answer comes from our asymmetry principle: to ensure recoverability of the past, any asymmetry in the present must go back to a symmetry in the past.

In mathematics and physics, "asymmetry" really means *distinguishability*, and "symmetry" really means *indistinguisability*. Thus, the asymmetry principle really says that, to ensure recoverability, any distinguishability in the present must go back to an indistinguishability in the past. In fact, the backward-time sequence is recovered exactly as follows:

1. *Deformed cylinder $\longrightarrow$ Straight cylinder*   The deformed cylinder has distinguishable (different) curvatures at different points on its surface. By removing these distinguishabilities (differences) in curvature, one obtains the straight cylinder, which has the same curvature at each point on its surface; that is, indistinguishable curvature across its surface.
2. *Straight cylinder $\longrightarrow$ Circle*   The straight cylinder has a set of cross-sections that are distinguishable by position along the cylinder. By removing this distinguishability in position for the cross-sections, one obtains only one position for a cross-section, the starting position; that is, one obtains the first circle on the cylinder.
3. *Circle $\longrightarrow$ Point*   The first circle consists of a set of points that are distinguishable by position around the circle. By removing this distinguishability in position for the points, one obtains only one position for a point, the starting position; that is, one obtains the first point on the circle.

We therefore see that each stage, in the backward-time direction, is recovered by converting a distinguishability into an indistinguishability. This means that each stage, in the forward-time direction, creates a distinguishability from an indistinguishability in the previous stage. Let us check this with the example of the deformed cylinder. The sequence of actions used to generate the deformed cylinder from a point are

Point $\textcircled{T}$ Rotations $\textcircled{T}$ Translations $\textcircled{T}$ Deformations

Each level creates a distinguishability from an indistinguishability in the previous level. That is, Rotations produces a cross-section by creating distinguishability in position for the single point on the previous level. Then Translations produces a straight cylinder by creating distinguishability in position for the single cross-section on the previous level.

Finally, Deformations produces a deformed cylinder by creating distinguishability in curvature on the surface of the straight cylinder of the previous level.

The fact that each level creates a distinguishability (asymmetry) from an indistinguishability (symmetry) in the previous level, means that each level is *symmetry-breaking* on the previous level. However, we have also seen that each level *transfers* the previous level. This is a fundamental point: *Each level must act by both symmetry-breaking and transferring its previous level.* To fully understand the importance of this point, let us state it within the main argument of this section.

Maximization of memory storage   Requires (1) maximizing the recoverability of generative operations and (2) maximizing the transfer of generative operations. This means that each stage of the history must fulfill two conditions: (1) it must be symmetry-breaking on the previous stage; (2) it must act by transferring the previous stage. That is, each stage must be a *symmetry-breaking transfer* of the previous stage.

The concept of symmetry-breaking transfer is fundamental to the new foundations for geometry. It means that each successive control group must be symmetry-breaking on its fiber.

Rigorous Definition of Aesthetics

We are now ready to rigorously define aesthetics. The new foundations to geometry proposes that aesthetics is based on two principles: (1) maximization of transfer and (2) maximization of recoverability. We have put forward examples of the first principle from the arts including painting, music, and poetry, and examples from science including the symmetries of laws. In all cases, we saw that maximization of transfer was basic to aesthetic judgment. Now let us turn to the second principle, maximization of recoverability.

First consider art. We saw that the composition of Holbein's Ann of Cleves is based on the following generative sequence. The circle in the neck extends downwards to become an ellipse in a necklace, which has a curvature maximum (bottom of the necklace) that did not exist in the circle. This maximum branches then sideways into two copies of itself, to produce a bay. Next, the central curvature minimum (flatness) of the bay branches sideways into two copies of itself, to produce a deepened bay. The history is therefore

circle $\rightarrow$ ellipse $\rightarrow$ bay $\rightarrow$ deepened bay

where, at each stage, the number of curvature extremes (maxima or minima) increases.

Now it is important to understand that a curvature extreme creates greater *distinguishability* in curvature around the curve, because an extreme involves a fluctuation in curvature. This means that, at each stage in the preceding history, the introduction of a new curvature extreme has a symmetry-breaking effect on the previous stage (i.e., creates greater curvature distinguishability). Therefore, the generative history accords with our asymmetry principle, which states that a generative history is recoverable only if it is symmetry-breaking at each of the successively generated states.

The fact that the generative history is recoverable from the structure of the painting means that the painting acts as a *memory store* for the generative actions:

Artworks Are Maximal Memory Stores

This is the crucial function of artworks, the reason they are so valued. Furthermore, I have argued that computer scientists can significantly increase the power of memory stores in computers by learning the rules by which artworks are constructed, given by the new foundations to geometry (Leyton 1992; 2001; 2005a; 2005b).

Although I have presented several hundred rules for the construction of shapes as memory stores, I will illustrate the method with just two of these rules. They concern the extraction of history from curvature extrema, that is, the conversion of curvature extrema into memory stores:

Symmetry-Curvature Duality Theorem (Leyton 1987b)   To each curvature extremum, there is a unique symmetry axis leading to and terminating at the extremum.
Interaction Principle (Leyton 1984)   A symmetry axis is the most likely direction along which a process moved.

Figure 15.14 shows the application of these rules to a painting by Picasso. The arrows lie along the symmetry axes leading to extrema, and represent the inferred processes of deformation that went along those axes. Thus, the figure shows the painting as a *memory store*.

Now let us turn to science. Current models explaining the physical constitution of the universe argue for a succession of symmetry-breakings from the underlying starting state (first to hypercharge, isospin, and color, and then to the electromagnetic gauge group). There is considerable puzzlement in physics as to why such backward symmetrization occurs, as Wigner expressed in his famous phrase, the "unreasonable power of mathematics" in physics, by which he really meant the unreasonable power of symmetry.

Figure 15.14 The force structure of Picasso's still life.

However, according to our theory, backward symmetrization is entirely explicable. It comes from the asymmetry principle, that a generative history is *recoverable* only if present asymmetries go back to past symmetries in the generative history.

With this in mind, let us return to the issue of *aesthetics* in science. Aesthetics in physics is often linked to the use of symmetries to represent past generative states. Therefore, putting this notion together with the considerations of section on transfer in art and science, there appear to be two uses in physics for the term aesthetics: (1) the characterization of transfer and (2) the characterization of recovered states.

The question therefore is to what extent are these two situations of aesthetic judgment separate from each other? Our theory says they are not separate. We showed in earlier sections that each level of the transfer hierarchy necessarily simultaneously takes on the role of transfer and recoverability. To use physics as an example, *the symmetry group acts as both the past state and the operational structure that transfers flow-lines of the dynamical law onto each other.*

We illustrate this with both general relativity and quantum mechanics. First, in general relativity, the gravitational force breaks the symmetry of flat space-time, making it curved. Corresponding to this, it breaks the conservation laws, which act globally in flat space-time and only infinitessimally in curved space-time. This means that, in flat space-time, one can *transfer* flow-lines onto flow-lines, in the dynamical laws; but in curved space-time this transfer is lost. Thus, as previously stated, the symmetry group acts as both the past state and the operational structure that transfers flow-lines of the dynamical law onto each other. In other words, the two forms of aesthetic judgment in physics—symmetries of the dynamical laws (transfer) and the description of past states (recoverability)—are made coincident.

Notice the relationship of this to memory storage: curved space-time has an asymmetry (curvature) that stores the effect of the action of the gravitational force.

Exactly the same kind of situation exists in quantum mechanics. As an example, consider the modeling of the hydrogen atom. The atom involves a number of complex factors, such as the interaction between the electron's spin and orbital angular momentum, and the interaction between the proton and electron spins. One starts with empty space (the "free particle" situation). This has the most symmetrical energy function (Hamiltonian potential) possible—simply a flat constant surface, that is, a translationally and rotationally symmetric surface. Then one introduces the simplest form of the hydrogen atom, called the Coulomb electrostatic model. This breaks some of the symmetries of the flat energy surface of empty space, but retains some of its other symmetries. Then, one adds the interaction between the electron's spin and orbital angular momentum. This breaks still more of the symmetry. This is the fine-structure splitting of the Coulomb model. One then adds the interaction between the proton and electron spins, breaking still more of the symmetry. This is called hyperfine splitting.

In these successive symmetry-breakings, one looses the transfer of flow-lines onto flow-lines of the dynamic law (Schroedinger's equation). Thus, as stated earlier, the symmetry group acts as both the past state and the operational structure that transfers flow-lines of the dynamical law onto each other. Again, the two forms of aesthetic judgment in physics—symmetries of the dynamical law (transfer) and description of past states (recoverability)—are coincident.

Notice the relation of this to memory storage. The successively added asymmetries, in building the model of the hydrogen atom, are memory stores for the successively added interactions.

Now let us take stock. I have argued that the term "aesthetic" is used in science when maximization of transfer and recoverability exist. This leads to the rigorous theory of aesthetics:

Aesthetics is the maximization of transfer and recoverability.

We have also seen that maximization of transfer and recoverability serves the goal of *maximization of memory storage*, leading to the related claim:

The rules of aesthetics are the rules of memory storage.

Let us look at this issue more deeply with respect to science. We know that the main concern of science is explaining how things are caused. In *Symmetry, Causality, Mind* (Leyton 1992) I show that "explaining how things are caused" is the same as "converting them into memory stores." That is, extracting the causal history from an object is the same as viewing it as a memory store of that history. The latter formulation is more powerful, however, since it is tied to the very concept of computation. Thus whereas, conventionally, the causal and the computational (calculation) aspects of physics are separate, my new foundations for geometry unifies these two by showing the causal aspects are actually a means of setting up computational components, that is, memory stores. In fact, I argue that

In science, the concept of causality should be replaced by the concept of memory storage. In other words, causal constructs in science should be replaced by computational ones.

In this view, science is the extension of a computational system to encompass the environment as extra memory stores. For example, the purpose of general relativity and quantum mechanics is to add curved space-time and the hydrogen atom as extra memory stores. Physics, in other words, is just a hard drive.

The argument leads to the fundamental conclusion that, since science always tries to maximize the causal explanation in a situation, my conversion of causal constructs into memory constructs shows that *science is the conversion of the environment into maximal memory stores*. For a full elaboration of this theory, the reader should see my books (Leyton 1992; 2001; 2005a; 2005b).

Earlier, I stated that *artworks* are maximal memory stores. This means that both the sciences and the arts are driven by the same goal: producing maximal memory stores. Furthermore, this is what aesthetics is.

The issue that then arises is if sciences and the arts are driven by the same goal, what is the difference between them? I argue that computation involves two basic operations: (1) reading a memory store and (2) writing a memory store. *Science* is therefore the process of *reading* a memory store; and *art* is the process of *writing* a memory store.

To explain this further, according to the above theory, both scientist and artist are interested in *maximization* of memory information extractable from an object. The scientist focuses on maximizing the memory information obtained by *reading*. This means that the scientist *converts* the existing environmental objects into memory stores (e.g., curved space-time, the hydrogen atom). In contrast, the artist focuses on maximizing memory information by actually *creating* new objects in the environment that will act as memory stores. To state the situation succinctly:

The goal of both science and art is the production of maximal memory stores. Science achieves this by converting existing objects into maximal memory stores. Art achieves this by creating new objects as maximal memory stores.

The Aesthetics of Computing

Aesthetics is a major driving force in the organization of computer programs. The reason is that programs are often such large, complex structures their construction must accord with principles of good organization so that they can be read, understood, and modified by programmers who need to use them.

The new foundations to geometry give considerable insight into the methods of organizing and using computer programs. My extensive discussion in *Generative Theory of Shape* is briefly summarized in present section.

First, it is generally understood that *reusability* is a major factor driving program organization. For example, modern computing is largely based on objects (e.g., rectangles, cubes), not only because human beings find that manipulating objects is conceptually easy, but because objects are reusable items. Not only are programs decomposed into objects, but they are decomposed into larger reusable units, which help the programmers and clients use and adapt them with ease.

In the new foundations to geometry, reusability is formalized as *transfer*, that is, to reuse an item is to transfer it. Since maximization of transfer is one of the two basic principles of our geometric theory, we can see that this corresponds to the computer scientist's goal of maximizing reusability. Notice the relation between this and aesthetics in the arts—for example, the movement of a Beethoven symphony is propelled forward by the continual *reuse* of the motival material.

Most crucially, since the new geometry gives an extensive mathematical theory of transfer, in terms of wreath products, the geometry thereby gives an extensive mathematical theory of reusability in software (as it does in the arts).

For example, the very notion of an object (class) is modeled by transfer, in the following way: each geometric class (e.g., a rectangle) consists of an internal symmetry group, which is usually specified in the invariants clauses of the software text for the class, and an external group consisting of command operations, such as deformations, specified in the feature clauses of the class text. A principle claim of the theory is that the relation between the internal symmetry group and command structure, in the software text, is given by the following structure:

$$G_{sym} \textcircled{T} G(C)$$

where G_{sym} is the internal symmetry group and $G(C)$ is the group of command operations. In other words, because the object is itself a group, G_{sym}, the true action of the command operations can be viewed as *transferring* that group. This transfer follows the theory of symmetry-breaking; that is, the command operations act by breaking the symmetry of the internal group—for example, deforming the object or moving it from its default position (which breaks the symmetry by misalignment). Therefore, the object-structure accords with the theory of recoverability discussed earlier. The very concept of object is organized by our principles of aesthetics.

Also, transfer is the basis of *Gestalt*, that is, *cohesion* is formed by transfer. This is illustrated in the present example. Our transfer-based theory of object-orientedness is explaining cohesion in programming.

As another example, the theory provides a deep understanding of *inheritance*, which is a basic tool in object-oriented programming. Inheritance refers to the passing of properties from a parent to a child (Meyer 1997). The child incorporates these parent properties, but also adds its own. This kind of structure covers two types of situation. The first is class inheritance, which is a static software concept, and the second is a type of dynamic linking created at run-time. The geometric theory gives an algebraic theory of both types of inheritance, but we deal here with only the latter. This type is fundamental to all computer-aided design, assembly, robotics, animation, and so on. A typical example is a child object inheriting the transform of a parent object, and adding its own.

As we have seen, the very structure of an object is organized by transfer. We now see that the inheritance relationship between two objects is also organized by transfer.

Algebraic Theory of Inheritance   Inheritance arises from a transfer hierarchy:

$$G_{child} \textcircled{T} G_{parent}$$

where G_{child} is the command group of the child object, and G_{parent} is the command group of the parent object.

To illustrate, in many situations, such as robotics and animation, objects can be strung together in an n-fold inheritance hierarchy. For example, limbs are put together in a serial-link manipulator; or the sun, earth, and moon are combined in an animation of the solar system. Our geometric theory says the following about this.

Group of Entire Transform Structure   Consider a set of $n + 1$ objects: object 1 to n, and the world. Suppose that they are linked so that object i is the child of object $i + 1$, and object n is the child of the world. Then the group of the entire transform structure is the transfer hierarchy:

$$_{F1}G_1^{F2} \, \textcircled{T} \, _{F2}G_2^{F3} \, \textcircled{T} \, \cdots \, \textcircled{T} \, _{Fn}G_n^{W}$$

where (1) object i has personal transform group G_i and frame F_i; (2) personal transform group G_i relates frame F_{i+1} of the parent, upper index, to the personal frame F_i, lower index. (The world frame is written as W.)

Notice that, initially, all frames F_i are coincident, and the action of the transforms is to move the frames out of alignment; that is, breaking their symmetries. This means that the transfer hierarchy is a symmetry-breaking one, in accord with the theory of recoverability.

Conclusion

This chapter has summarized the theory of aesthetics based on my new foundations for geometry. Their two principles—maximization of transfer and maximization of recoverability—are also the basic principles of aesthetics. I have shown that they are fundamental to aesthetic judgment in (1) the arts (painting, music, and poetry); (2) the sciences (general relativity and quantum mechanics); and (3) computer programming (object-oriented programming). All of these areas are driven by the same underlying principles.

Note

1. A dynamical law is always in the form of a differential equation. In the present section, for ease of illustration, we will assume that the equation is first-order. Higher-order equations follow the same basic principles, but at higher levels.

References

Leyton, Michael. 1974. *Mathematical-Logical Postulates at the Foundations of Art.* Tech Report. University of Warwick, Mathematics Department.

————. 1984. "Perceptual Organization as Nested Control." *Biological Cybernetics* 51: 141–53.

————. 1986a. "Principles of Information Structure Common to Six Levels of the Human Cognitive System." *Information Sciences* 38: 1–120.

————. 1986b. "A Theory of Information Structure I: General Principles." *Journal of Mathematical Psychology* 30: 103–60.

————. 1986c. "A Theory of Information Structure II: A Theory of Perceptual Organization." *Journal of Mathematical Psychology* 30: 257–305.

————. 1987a. "Nested Structures of Control: An Intuitive View." *Computer Vision, Graphics, and Image Processing* 37: 20–53.

————. 1987b. "Symmetry-Curvature Duality." *Computer Vision, Graphics, and Image Processing* 38: 327–41.

————. 1992. *Symmetry, Causality, Mind*. Cambridge, MA: MIT Press.

————. 1999. "New Foundations for Perception." In *Invitation to Cognitive Science*. Pp. 121–71. Oxford: Blackwell.

————. 2001. *A Generative Theory of Shape*. Berlin: Springer-Verlag.

————. 2003. "Musical Works Are Maximal Memory Stores." In *Perspectives in Mathematical and Computer-Aided Music Theory*. Osnabruck: Osnabruck Music Publishing.

————. 2005a. *Shape as Memory: A Geometric Theory of Architecture*. Basel: Birkhauser.

————. 2005b. *The Structure of Paintings*. (submitted).

Meyer, Bertrand. 1997. *Object-Oriented Software Construction*. Upper Saddle River, NJ: Prentice Hall.

16

Aesthetics of Large-Scale Relational Information Visualization in Practice

Aaron Quigley

. . . all life is only a set of pictures in the brain, among which there is no difference betwixt those born of real things and those born of inward dreamings, and there is no cause to value one above the other.

——H. P. LOVECRAFT

Speaking to the Eye

This chapter reviews aesthetic computing as it pertains to information visualization, graph drawing, and graph drawing aesthetics embodied in the FADE paradigm for large-scale graph drawing.

Societies' continued reliance on information and communications technologies has resulted in organizations generating, gathering, and storing "raw data" at a rate that is growing every year. Research has shown that shipped hard drive capacity is doubling every year (Lyman and Varian 2000). The ability of a mid-sized organization to store tens to hundreds of terabytes of data is within easy reach. The availability of massive storage technology is rapidly outstripping our ability to effectively analyse, explore, and understand such voluminous data. Clearly these raw data are of little value unless useful information and hence knowledge can be derived from it. One approach to understanding such a large amount of data is to use visual analytics based on *information visualization* (Ware 1999), in which visualization can be thought of as the process of "speaking to the eye" (Kinloch 1992). Our research in this area addresses a number of issues associated with the scale of the data in question (Quigley 2002; 2001; Quigley and Eades 2000).

Aesthetic computing as applied to information visualization draws on techniques from art to aid the expression, abstraction, representation, form, presentation, and visual appeal of such pictorial forms of data. Typically the data in question are collected automatically or are based on derived data from simple aggregation or filtering of the raw data. Such data are often without geometric form, that is, they are abstract data. Examples include software analysis (Ball and Eick 1996), financial trading data, stock market prices and movements, biological analysis, reverse engineering (Quigley 2002), traffic and airline data, and weather pattern data. Take, for example, the price movement and trades of gold on any given day. On a global scale these data are voluminous and "raw" in the sense that no higher order knowledge has been inferred (either through visual analytics or automatic analysis). However, a gold trader can use analysis tools to "infer," based on historical knowledge and local patterns, that gold prices will continue to move upwards for the next 3 days. This higher-order data or knowledge is typically concise compared to the voluminous raw data and requires the application of a combination of techniques ranging from data mining through visualization to experienced trader analysis.

One approach to the human analysis task is to *automatically* convert the data into *pictures* and *models* that can be graphically displayed, typically referred to as an information visualization process. Behind the development of the field of visual analytics is the intuition that human beings are inherently skilled at understanding data in visual forms. However, unlike artistic forms of expression produced by humans, the picture or visual form is typically produced automatically or semiautomatically. The goal in information visualization is often to codify measurable aesthetic principles and practice in their production.

The information visualization in figure 16.1 represents the results (abstract data) obtained for the modeling of a number of input parameters to a semiautomatic antenna design system, using sampling and visualization for use in a visual analysis process. Here each element represents thousands of permutations of a particular antenna's output characteristics based on a discovered configuration (Quigley 2002). The element's position and color represent various attributes of each antenna design. For example, here the color of the element is a measure of the vertical standing wave ratio (VSWR) of that antenna design, and the interelement distance is a measure of similarity. An antenna designer can view and hence analyze such data in this visual form to find patterns to help identify problems or opportunities for a particular design.

It is becoming increasingly apparent that more powerful graphical information exploration tools are required as the amount and complexity of data these tools are expected to handle steadily increases.

Background

Large-scale information visualization is the process of graphically representing large amounts of abstract information on screen, which a user can interpret in ways not possible

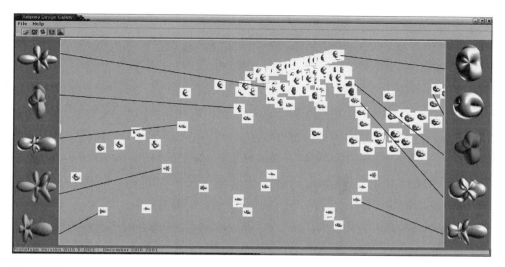

Figure 16.1 Human Guided Antenna Design Gallery system from MERL.

from the raw data alone. In some application domains, the information space can be modeled in terms of its atomic entities and their interrelationships, that is, as *relational information*. Techniques that produce graphical representations or abstract views of such relational information now form a substantive component of many graphical software systems (Jerding, Stasko and Ball 1997). Other chapters in this book present various forms of aesthetic computing visualization, where notions of form and factor are closely followed in the human production of the visualization. Here, we limit our discussion to previously studied *relational information aesthetics* and their application to the automatic production of pictures, that is, automatic visualization creation.

Relational information is typically modeled in terms of a graph; the atomic entities of the domain form the set of nodes and the interrelationships form the set of edges. Figure 16.2 shows an example of visualization of relational information, in which the edges represent links between web pages. The problem of creating a high-quality picture of a graph is in assigning a location for each node and a route for each edge so that the picture is easy to follow; this is the classical problem in *graph drawing* (Di Battista et al. 1999).

Graph drawing is a widely researched field that is computationally hard. The problem is to draw huge complex graphs with many nodes and many edges in such a way that only unavoidable edge crossings are permitted and, hopefully, symmetry and other groupings of nodes are used in an attempt to achieve pleasing results. The readability of such

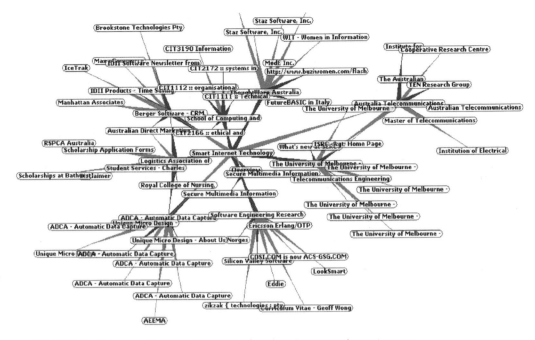

Figure 16.2 Web page visualization of depth 2 from http://www.smartinternet.com.au.

drawings relates to aesthetic computing in which aesthetics is understood to pertain to human perception.

A good visual representation of a graph can effectively convey information to the user, but a poor representation can confuse or, worse, mislead. Graph drawing aims to develop algorithms and methods of producing high-quality pictures that are easy to follow. Generally, our research into the development of the FADE (Force Algorithms by Decomposed Estimation) paradigm has identified four related problems when dealing with the visualization of large graphs:

1. *Graph drawing aesthetics* The field of graph drawing has codified a number of "graph drawing aesthetics," which are typically measurable attributes of the visualization. These aesthetics include line crossings, node overlaps, drawing area, and drawing aspect ratio. Although codified as such, many aesthetics are contradictory and cannot all be achieved in one drawing (except for the smallest examples). In practice, a graph drawing algorithm achieves good results for one or two such aesthetics, such as the individual layers shown in figure 16.3.

Aaron Quigley

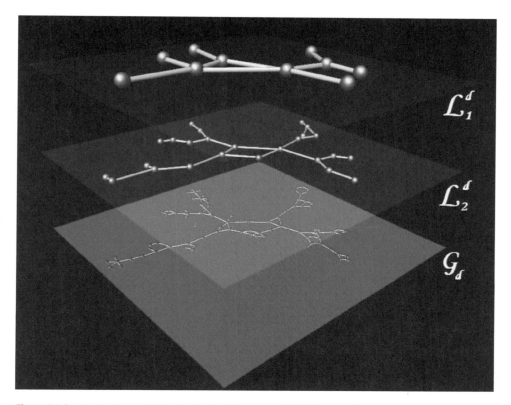

Figure 16.3 Underlying and abstract visual précis drawn with FADE algorithms.

2. *Computation* Until quite recently graph drawing algorithms and approaches tended to deal only with relatively small graphs. This has resulted in the development of techniques that are unable to scale when drawing larger graphs. The primary bottleneck is the large amount of computational effort these methods require to layout even medium-sized graphs. Our underlying FADE methods used to produce the layout in figure 16.3 takes N log N time, based on tree-codes (Barnes and Hut 1986), as opposed to the classical quadratic time algorithm.

3. *Screen space aesthetics* The challenging problem of making fast algorithms is further compounded by the need to make effective and aesthetic use of the screen space. Showing part of the entire layout in detail or zooming out to fit the entire drawing are common techniques. A variety of other visualization techniques attempt to fit large amounts of relational information onto a computer screen. Sophisticated interactive systems employ

the recursive use of glyphs to elide parts of the drawing or warp the visual space. One approach, shown in FADE, makes effective use of the screen by eliding the underlying graph and allowing the visualization of abstract representations.

4. *Cognitive load*   Related to the problem of the effective use of screen space is the issue of load related to cognition. Even if the problems of computational cost and screen space can be solved, there is clearly a need to reduce the cognitive load drawing too much extraneous information places on the user. When dealing with large amounts of information, the overriding desire is to simplify the drawing to highlight the global structures while deemphasizing the irrelevant detail. Figure 16.3 shows an example drawing from one of our approaches. This example allows us to highlight the global structure while deemphasizing the underlying graph.

> ... if a visualization isn't worth a thousand words, the hell with it.
> —TUFTE 1997

Visualization

Visualization is classically defined as the process of forming a mental image of some scene as described. Since the advent of graphic workstations, however, it has become synonymous with the computational process of making data visible. With graphic workstations now ubiquitous in day-to-day life, it is prosaic to motivate interest in visualization by stating that images are a powerful way to show data. We know visualization is important; more important is addressing the question of "readability." Bad information visualizations are, unfortunately, all too common. The central question of visualization is not "Do we use graphics to represent information?" but rather "How do we create graphical presentations that are easy to understand and effectively and efficiently convey information?"

With information visualization there is typically no a priori geometric model but rather abstract data in the form of a symbolic model of information (Ware 1999). A symbolic model consists of a set of symbols that represent actual elements of information. To allow the symbolic model to be visualized, it can be assigned a geometry. This geometry allows abstract concepts or measures to be visualized. An important issue in visualization is readability, that is, the degree to which something is intelligible and can easily be understood. Classically, readability has not been an aesthetic measure of artistic worth or visual appeal. Instead, the question of readability has been confined to the field of typography, in which issues of design, arrangement, style, and appearance of type are among the factors affecting the readability of text. Several readability measures for textual documents are available. Quantifying the structure of language use and its relative level of complexity, these measures include the Flesch reading ease measure and the Flesch-Kincaid grade-level measure.

The goal for relational information visualization is to pursue a visual aesthetic that is both measurable and has been empirically shown to be visually pleasing and aid understanding. Regardless of the visual form, our aim is to convey the relational information as clearly as possible with less "visual ink" (Tufte 1997).

Relational Information Visualization

Relational information consists of elements of information and their interrelationships. Typically this is modeled on a graph of nodes and edges. For complex relational information, other graph models such as an "attributed graph" can be used. An attributed graph models information that contains more than one attribute per data element. Relational information visualization is hence a simplified drawing that conveys the relations, elements, and attributes of the underlying abstract symbolic model of the information (Herman et al. 2000).

Visual Abstraction

In data modeling, abstraction is the process of deriving the essential features of the data. Abstraction comes from the Latin *abstrahere*, meaning "to withdraw," indicates that an abstraction process should remove unnecessary detail to create the abstract form of the data, which typically highlights its essential features. Figure 16.3 shows two levels of visual abstraction, L1 and L2, based on underlying data. Visual abstraction is the process of creating an image, which departs to some extent from representational accuracy (Strothotte 1998). Abstract artists, such as Picasso, often used abstraction to select and then exaggerate or simplify the forms suggested by the world around them. The simplified drawings in medical illustrations, architectural sketches, and subway maps all employ some degree of visual abstraction to create the simplification. In general, drawings of a model or information differ from photorealistic visualizations in terms of context sensitivity, information filtering, information hiding, visual distortion, elision, aesthetic appeal, and user control as described in the following sections.

Context Sensitivity

Medical illustrations of sections of the human brain typically show an overview with fine levels of detail where they are needed. This *detail-in-context* view allows certain parts of the visualization to be selectively emphasized (while other parts are deemphasized). Often the "context" of the drawing can be on a different scale, allowing more space for the detailed parts of the illustration.

Filtering

Depending on the domain, filtering is often used before any visualization takes place. Elements of the model can be assigned an a priori importance or classification type, then only elements above a certain threshold or in a particular category are considered. Filtering is typically a preprocessing step that results in certain parts of the model being effectively ignored.

Distortion

Distortion techniques include intelligent zoom, presentation emphasis, fisheye views, and hyperbolic views as shown in figure 16.4 (Lamping and Rao 1996). As the models become large, however, the cognitive load on the user or computational effort required to render such large amounts of graphical information becomes prohibitive. Hybrid hyperbolic

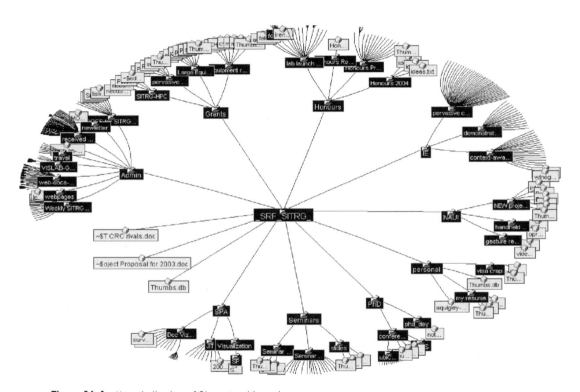

Figure 16.4 Hyperbolic view of file system hierarchy.

viewers for tree exploration, based on filtering coupled with "elision" techniques, have been developed.

Hiding and Elision

Often in information visualization the amount of data in the model to be visualized is large. Information hiding is the computational process of selectively ignoring or not yet presenting parts of the information. Information hiding can be based on the notion of visual elision. Unlike filtering or simple hiding, elision methods attempt to "hint" at information that is not fully displayed. To convey information about the hidden part of the model, numerous methods employ "glyphs," visual symbols, such as a stylized figure that imparts information nonverbally. Glyphs can be stylized (coded) according to attributes such as color, size, orientation, shape, or texture. Some applications use the natural clustering or hierarchical structure of the data to decide what parts are to be hidden. For example, a model of a car can be described in hierarchical terms with a part-of relationship. Then, instead of drawing the wheels at the greatest level of detail (tread, color, letters, nuts, and bolts), a simple cylinder glyph can be used to suggest the wheel while the rest is hidden by elision.

Graph Drawing

Graph drawing is the process of making a picture from relational information. Research in graph drawing has developed considerably since graphics workstations were introduced in the 1980s (Di Battista et al. 1999). The problem is to develop a graph drawing algorithm, which assigns a location for every node and a route for every edge, as shown in figure 16.5. Once the graph drawing algorithm has assigned a geometry, one can then render a picture, that is, a visualization of the graph.

Drawing Conventions

The combinatorial properties of a graph can be determined before any graph drawing. Graph theoretic properties such as whether the graph is directed or undirected, or the graph is planar or not, determine the class of the graph. Often this class indicates which

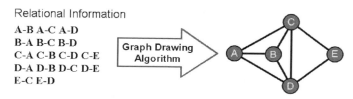

Figure 16.5 Graph drawing algorithm.

particular graph drawing convention should be used. Common drawing conventions include:

- Planar drawing, in which no two edges cross; straight-line drawing, in which edges are drawn as straight lines.
- Polyline drawing, in which edges are drawn as a sequence of connected lines.
- Orthogonal drawing, in which edges are drawn as polylines, consisting of horizontal and vertical segments. Nodes are drawn at integer x, y coordinates of a rectangular grid.
- Downward drawing, in which the edges of an acyclic digraph are drawn as monotonically decreasing arcs in the vertical direction.

The most appropriate drawing conventions for a graph are typically application domain specific and dependent on the graph's combinatorial properties. If these conflict, then it becomes a matter of determining an appropriate tradeoff or changing the combinatorial properties of the graph to suit the convention required.

Drawing Aesthetics

As previously noted, the question of readability does not just pertain to text; it also clearly applies to *drawings*. For drawings, the question is "For a given drawing how easy is it to understand and how effectively and efficiently does that drawing convey information?" Graph drawing algorithms attempt to find a geometrical configuration of nodes and edges that has a high level of readability, according to some set of criteria. Regardless of the nature of the graph, or the method used to draw that graph, the primary requirement is that the resultant drawing should be *readable*. Research has shown that maximizing the readability of a drawing is crucial to conveying the information contained in the underlying graph (Purchase 1997). Unfortunately, readability is often a highly subjective matter and measuring the readability of a specific drawing is open to even more aspects of personal taste and preference.

Without objective measures, it is impossible to compare and contrast two drawings or even two layout methods in a scientific manner. The identification of important *features of drawings* has been researched since graph drawing algorithms were first developed. The features identified, typically called *aesthetic criteria*, are used to form measures of readability and have been codified as a set of formal aesthetics. Broadly speaking, measuring a graph drawing by these aesthetic criteria shows whether or not the drawing has "great beauty." Although the features of the drawing that impact the formal aesthetic are not independent, a broadly accepted set of base goals (aesthetic criteria) has been identified. Some of the more significant aesthetic measures are informally described in the following sections.

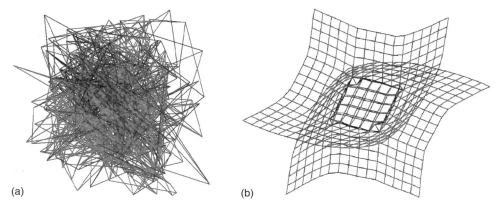

Figure 16.6 (a) Random 2D positioning of nodes from graph dw512b of the Matrix Market; (b) FADE 2D positioning of nodes from graph dw512b of the Matrix Market.

Minimizing the number of edge crossings has been shown to be among the most important goals for the creation of an aesthetically pleasing graph drawing. Drawings with a large number of crossings, especially those caused by long edges, are difficult to follow. The drawings in figure 16.6a and b show the difference between a drawing with many edge crossings (a) due to a random positioning of the nodes and those (b) due to a graph drawing algorithm.

Maximizing edge length uniformity is often used in applications where all edges are of equal significance. One way of representing this is by ensuring that the lengths of all edges in the drawing are uniform; figure 16.6b shows uniformity in edge length and uses color to encode relative edge strength. These aesthetic criteria can be extended to edge set length uniformity, where edges are assigned to categories, each of which has a desired edge length. Often we wish to maximize the uniformity of the lengths of all edges or sets of edges.

Maximizing the distance between nonadjacent nodes ensures that no false relationships, based on proximity, are inferred. If related nodes are drawn close together, then nodes with no direct relationship should not be drawn close. Cognitively, the worst case occurs when geometrically close yet nonadjacent nodes appear to the user as being logically connected. Most of the nonadjacent nodes are drawn far apart in the two-dimensional (2D) image shown in figure 16.6b. If this aesthetic is important for a given application domain, however, the topology of this example graph means the use of a three-dimensional (3D) layout will result in a much better nonadjacency measure (in three dimensions). Two views of a 3D drawing of the same graph are shown in figure 16.7a and b.

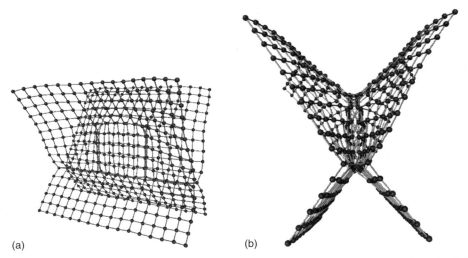

(a)   (b)

Figure 16.7   (a) 3D FADE positioning of nodes from graph dw512b of the Matrix Market (viewpoint a). (b) 3D FADE positioning of nodes from graph dw512b of the Matrix Market (viewpoint b).

Maximizing the symmetries in the drawing aims to display whether the underlying graph has duplicate, or near-duplicate, parts in its structure. The symmetrical graph drawing should reflect a balance in displaying those symmetries. Typically, symmetries provide a formal balance to the layout that can make the process of understanding the graph easier. If repeated or near-repeated sections of the graph are drawn with rotational or reflexive symmetry, then the understanding of one section often results in faster comprehension of the other symmetric sections. Graph theoretic measures for symmetry exist, but developing formal measures for symmetry or near symmetry in drawings is difficult. Informally, we can say the drawings shown in figure 16.7a and b have much visual symmetry.

Maximizing the angular resolution of the drawing aims to ensure the individual edges drawn are clear and distinct. The angular resolution of a drawing is the minimum angle formed between a pair of edges that are either crossing or incident on the same node. A drawing that exhibits a low angular resolution typically suffers a visual effect called blobbing, which makes identifying individual edges difficult and hence makes the drawing hard to follow and understand.

Area is a measure of how efficiently a drawing uses available screen space. The area occupied by a drawing is typically measured by the maximum x and y-extent of the node positions, and the z-extent in the case of measuring volume for 3D drawings. The goal of this aesthetic is to ensure that area efficient drawings are produced, since screen real estate is a valuable commodity not to be wasted.

Aspect ratio is a measure of the ratio of the longest side length to the shortest side length of a rectangle that encloses all the nodes of the drawing. A drawing with a high aspect ratio may be difficult to visualize effectively, as it will not fit conveniently on a computer monitor.

Abstract Representation Aesthetics

As noted earlier, when dealing with large amounts of relational information, it is useful to consider visual abstraction techniques. As such, we introduce several other important criteria that any reasonable multilevel layout technique should meet. Three such criteria are informally described in the following paragraphs.

Minimize the introduction of edge crossings by abstraction to ensure that higher-level views or visual précis are not less aesthetically pleasant than the drawing of the underlying graph. Any abstraction represents a simplified form of the underlying graph. Depending on the size and combinatorial properties of the graph, this simplification departs from representational accuracy, to a variable range of possible degrees. Using an automatic simplification method, it is entirely possible to generate a simplified drawing with edge crossings, where the underlying graph drawing has none. Any simplification method should aim to minimize the introduction of such artifacts of the simplification process.

Glyphs representing groups of nodes should not overlap, as this would severely affect the readability of the drawing. An abstraction process groups nodes, which are then drawn using a glyph. As with the underlying drawing, nodes drawn close together or overlapping imply relationships where none exist. At higher levels of abstraction, the false positives may result in a more distorted view of the underlying elements and their interrelationships.

Minimize the variance in abstraction aspect ratios to ensure a smooth visual mapping between abstraction levels. The FADE drawing paradigm is based on providing high-level simplified views of the underlying graph structure. Users can move between levels or can selectively show various parts at different levels of abstraction. Maintaining a similar aspect ratio between each visual précis of the graph provides a visual landmark to aid the user in moving between levels of detail. Typically, altering the layout of a graph to improve one aesthetic criterion can have a negative impact of another, that is, the criteria are not independent and some tradeoff between the criteria must be determined. This determination is often based on the nature of the application, the type of the graph and the purpose to which the drawings are put. This determination gives rise to a subset of aesthetic criteria that are important for a given application domain. This determination is crucial, as attempting to satisfy a large number of criteria simultaneously is at best computationally expensive and at worse futile and infeasible.

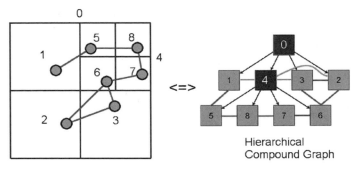

Figure 16.8 Space decomposition used to form an inclusion tree for a hierarchical compound graph.

FADE: Graph Drawing Paradigm

The FADE paradigm includes clustering (to create abstractions of the large graph) and visualization (to create pictures of different levels of abstraction) (Quigley 2001). The method uses a combination of geometric and combinatorial techniques. We map the graph nodes to geometric points, cluster these points using geometric methods, then use the result to produce our "hierarchical compound graph," as shown in figure 16.8.

This figure shows both a geometric and a graph theoretic view of the underlying graph and its associated hierarchical compound graph. The image on the left shows a graph drawing (nodes and edges) overlaid with a recursive space decomposition (a quad tree). On the right, we see the inclusion tree based on this geometric decomposition of space, where the root node 0 includes all the graph nodes, and edges and internal node 4 include nodes 5, 6, 7, 8, and three edges. The edges (1-4, 4-3, 4-2) represent "implied" or inter-cluster edges.

As noted in other domains, to realize this model we must address two problems: graph nodes have no intrinsic geometric information; we must synthesize the geometry. Geometric clustering is suitable for a graph *only* if the geometric distance between node images reflects the underlying graph theoretic relationships. The FADE drawing paradigm described here addresses both of these problems. In fact, all graph algorithms address the first problem, that is, their goal is to synthesize geometry for the graph so that it can be visualized. The second problem is specifically addressed by force-directed graph drawing methods (Eades 1984), such as those in FADE. Force-directed methods attempt to produce a drawing so that related nodes are drawn close together. The FADE paradigm operates on both geometric and combinatorial models for clustering and visual abstraction (Quigley 2001).

FADE: Fast Force-Directed Layout

Force-directed algorithms tend to emphasize the aesthetics of symmetry, maximize edge length uniformity, maximize the distance between nonadjacent nodes, have good angular resolution, and as a byproduct, tend to minimize the number of edge crossings. Force-directed algorithms view the graph as a virtual physical system, in which the graph's nodes are bodies of the system. These bodies have forces acting on or between them. Often the forces are physics based, and therefore have a natural analogy, such as magnetic repulsion or gravitational attraction. Classical force-directed methods are based on the direct computation of all node-to-node forces, which dramatically limits the number of nodes that these quadratic time algorithms can handle.

In FADE, the node-to-node force calculations are approximated based on the notion of well-separated clusters within the hierarchical compound graph, as in other N-body–based methods from physics (Barnes and Hut 1986). The notion of well-separated clusters is based on the distance between the center of mass of a cluster and an individual node. This measure is used to determine the closeness between a cluster (cell) and a node. If the center of a cluster is far enough away, according to a "cell-opening criterion," then the node-to-pseudonode nonedge force is computed (Quigley and Eades 2000). If the cluster is too close, its daughter cells are resolved and the process continues. This approach means that the contribution of close nodes is computed directly, as per the classical method, whereas the contribution of distant nodes is taken into account only by including node-to-pseudonode forces, representing many node pairs.

FADE: Visual Précis

To address the effective use of screen real estate and the computational effort involved in rendering large graphs. We use the hierarchical compound graph model to support our notion of a "visual précis," which is simply an abstract visual representation of the underlying graph. Our visual précis is related to mesh generation in the field of surface modeling. This relationship comes about because the space decomposition methods, such as quad trees, are used in both the formation of hierarchical compound graphs and approximate mesh generation. In surface modeling, however, a mesh point is an approximation of some point in space.

In a visual précis, a region of space defines a cluster, which is an abstract representation of a set of relational data elements and their interrelationships. Formally, a visual précis is a 2D or 3D projection of a précis extracted from a hierarchical compound graph. Recall that a précis consists of a set of clusters, implied edges, real nodes, and real edges. A précis may contain any combination of these, as long as it represents an abstract view of the entire underlying graph.

Précis containing primarily clusters and implied edges are called high-level précis. In a précis, the only graph edges are between nodes that are both included in the précis. All other edges are included as implied edges or are abstracted into clusters. The definition of a précis can apply to any type of inclusion tree, regardless of its arity. As a result, regardless of the shape of space decomposition used to form the hierarchical compound graph (HCG), these visual précis drawing techniques can be applied.

Figure 16.9 shows four views from a hierarchical compound graph, the top left is a visual précis without any clusters or implied edges, that is, the underlying graph drawing; the top right is a view with a particular level in the inclusion tree superimposed on the

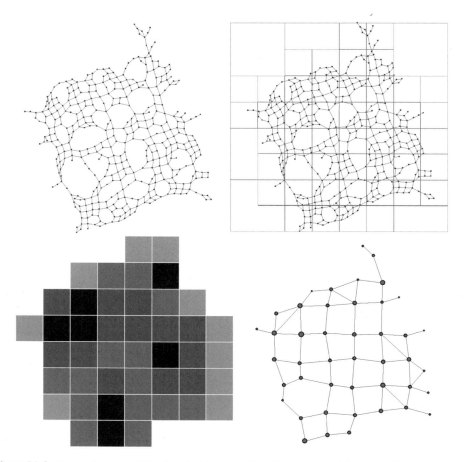

Figure 16.9 Graph drawing with horizon (précis) overlaid and two drawings (visual précis).

Aaron Quigley

underlying drawing. The bottom right is a horizon visual précis consisting of clusters and implied edges from the HCG. The bottom left is a tree map visualization showing node density for the same horizon view.

Reflections

The application of visual aesthetics to the field of relational information visualization has codified many desirable visual properties of such drawings. Our work in this area and the development of our graph model and its uses allow us to make more effective use of screen space. Extracted from our model are précis, which we render as visual précis in two and three dimensions. High-level précis form very approximate views of the underlying graph but generally have a "visual weight" that is a small fraction of the underlying graph drawing. This approach allows for the drawing of abstract representations with good resolution.

For high-level views, the nodes and edges of the visual précis can be clearly identified in the drawing. By reducing the size of the graph and drawing more abstract views on screen, we have reduced the direct cognitive load on the user. If the précis accurately reflects the structures and connectivity in the underlying graph, the cost of comprehending this abstract representation is minimized. The smaller visual précis, which can represent many thousands of nodes and edges, are also computationally inexpensive to render in two and three dimensions. Overall, our hierarchical compound graph with the drawing, representation, and rendering methods introduced address the four problems of computation, screen space, cognitive load, and rendering.

References

Ball, T., and Eick, S. G. 1996. "Software Visualization in the Large." *Computer* 29(4): 33–43.

Barnes, J., and Hut, P. 1986. "A Hierarchical O(n log n) Force-Calculation Algorithm." *Nature* 324(4): 446–49.

Coleman, M. K., and Parker, D. S. 1986. "Aesthetics-Based Graph Layout for Human Consumption." *Software Practice and Experience* 26(12): 1415–38.

Di Battista, G., Eades, P., Tamassia, R., and Tollis, I. G. 1999. *Graph Drawing: Algorithms for the Visualization of Graphs.* Upper Saddle River, NJ: Prentice-Hall.

Eades, P. 1984. "A Heuristic for Graph Drawing." *Congresses Numerantium* 42: 149–60.

Herman, Melancon G., and Marshall, M. S. 2000. "Graph Visualization and Navigation in Information Visualization: A Survey." *IEEE Transactions on Visualization and Computer Graphics*. H. Hagen, ed. Vol. 6(1). Washington, DC: IEEE Computer Society, pp. 24–43.

Herman, I. 1999. "Skeletal Images as Visual Cues in Graph Visualization." *Proceedings of the Joint Eurographics—IEEE TCCG Symposium on Visualization.* H. L. E. Groller and W. Ribarsky, eds. Vienna, Austria: Springer, pp. 13–22.

Jerding, D. F., Stasko, J. T., and Ball, T. 1997. "Visualizing Interactions in Program Executions." *Proceedings of the 19th International Conference on Software Engineering (ICSE '97).* New York, ACM, pp. 360–71.

Kinloch, D. P. 1992. The Thought and Art of Joseph Joubert. New York: Oxford University Press.

Lamping, J., and Rao, R. 1996. "Visualizing Large Trees Using the Hyperbolic Browser." *Proceedings of ACM CHI 96 Conference on Human Factors in Computing Systems. VIDEOS: Visualization*, Vol. 2. pp. 388–89.

Lyman, Peter, and Varian, Hal R. 2000. *How Much Information*. Available at http://www.sims .berkeley.edu/how-much-info. Accessed on July 31st 2003.

Purchase, H. 1997. "Which Aesthetic Has the Greatest Effect on Human Understanding?" *Proc. 5th International Symposium Graph Drawing, GD.* G. Di Battista, ed. Lecture Notes in Computer Science, LNCS. Vol. 1353. Heidelberg: New York: Springer-Verlag, pp. 248–61.

Quigley, A. J. 2002. "Experience with FADE for the Visualization and Abstraction of Software Views." Proceeding of the 10th International Workshop on Program Comprehension (IWPC'02). June 26–29, 2002. Paris, France, pp. 11–21.

Quigley, A. J. 2001. "Large Scale Relational Information Visualization, Clustering, and Abstraction." PhD thesis. University of Newcastle, Australia.

Quigley, A., and Eades, P. 2000. "FADE: Graph Drawing, Clustering, and Visual Abstraction." *Proc. 8th International Symposium Graph Drawing, GD.* J. Marks, ed. Vol. 1984, Lecture Notes in Computer Science, LNCS. Heidelberg: New York: Springer-Verlag, pp. 197–210.

Quigley, A., Leigh, D. L., Lesh, N. B., et al. 2002a. "Semi-Automatic Antenna Design via Sampling and Visualization." *IEEE Antennas and Propagation Society International Symposium* 2: 342–45.

Strothotte, T. 1998. *Computational Visualization. Graphics, Abstraction, and Interactivity*. Heidelberg: Springer-Verlag.

Tufte, E. R. 1997. *Visual Explanations: Images and Quantities, Evidence and Narrative*. Cheshire, CT: Graphics Press.

Ware, C. 1999. *Information Visualization: Perception for Design*. San Francisco, CA: The Morgan Kaufmann Series in Interactive Technologies.

17

The Well-Tempered Compiler? The Aesthetics of Program Auralization

Paul Vickers and James L. Alty

Like angels stopped upon the wing by sound
Of harmony from Heaven's remotest spheres.
—WORDSWORTH: "THE PRELUDE"

In this chapter we are concerned with external auditory representations of programs, also known as program auralization. As program auralization systems tend to use musical representations, they are necessarily affected by artistic and aesthetic considerations. Therefore, it is instructive to explore program auralization in the light of aesthetic computing principles. In *The Music of the Spheres*, James (1993) writes of music and science that "at the beginning of Western civilisation ... the two were identified so profoundly that anyone who suggested that there was any essential difference between them would have been considered an ignoramus." This is in stark contrast to today, when anyone suggesting they have anything in common "runs the risk of being labelled a philistine by one group and a dilettante by the other and, most damning of all, a popularizer by both."

The Great Theme of early philosopher scientists of a universe of perfect order in which everything has a purpose and a place, a universe whose very fabric sounded to continual heavenly music (which music obeyed the beautiful rules of the mathematics of Pythagoras and Plato), was discarded over the years of the Renaissance and into the Age of Reason. Though many present-day scientists have a great appreciation of the arts, those involved in the humanities often eschew the cold empiricism of science. This is the age of C.P. Snow's Two Cultures,[1] which James describes as a "psychotic bifurcation." James elaborates:

In the modern age it is a basic assumption that music appeals directly to the soul and bypasses the brain altogether, while science operates in just the reverse fashion, confining itself to the realm of pure ratiocination and having no contact at all with the soul. Another way of stating this duality is to marshal on the side of music Oscar Wilde's dictum that "All art is quite useless," while postulating that science is the apotheosis of earthly usefulness, having no connection with anything that is not tangibly of this world.

Despite centuries of divergence, there are indications that some are starting to build bridges between the cultures again. In Douglas Adams's comedy novel *Dirk Gently's Holistic Detective Agency* (1988), the lead character, Richard MacDuff, attempts to produce music from mathematical representations of the dynamics of swallows in flight. In a marvellous reiteration of the Great Theme, Adams writes of MacDuff's belief that "if . . . the rhythms and harmonies of music which he found most satisfying could be found in, or at least derived from, the rhythms and harmonies of naturally occurring phenomena, then satisfying forms of modality and intonation should emerge naturally as well."

Although a single work of comic fiction is not scientific evidence of a swing away from the Two Cultures, Adams's thinking is indicative of a growing trend in the computer science research community. It is doubtful that MacDuff's beliefs were an intentional move by Adams toward reestablishing the philosophy of the early scientists among modern researchers; however, the fact remains that computer scientists (unwittingly or not) are making increasing use of artistic forms (be they aural or visual) in their work.

Auditory Display

Since the introduction of the visual display unit, much research effort has gone into finding new and better ways to maximize the use of the video channel. Developers have been quick to maximize the use of graphical display capabilities from the use of menus on character-based displays to the visually impressive graphical user interfaces of today.

Along with the development of visual presentation, psychologists spent much time analyzing and studying the effects on computer users of different methods of information display. This has produced a well-established body of research into the exploitation of the visual medium as a means of interfacing the increasingly powerful and sophisticated computer technology with a more discerning and expectant user community.

Although simple audio signals were experimented with in the early days of computing, the research community was slow to recognize audio as a useful carrier of information in the world of software development. This can be attributed in part to the relatively late arrival of widely available and cheap sound-generating devices for computers. By the time affordable sound-generating equipment became available to the average computer user, the study of the visual medium was well advanced. For largely technological reasons, the human–computer interface has been almost entirely visual in its construction from the start. With advances in display technology came an inertia that led to an increasing bias toward visual interfaces. This is reflected in the natural language of cultures that rely on the written word for communication (particularly English), which by using words like "imagery" to describe mental processes, shows an inclination toward explaining ideas with visual metaphors. Contrast this with cultures with oral traditions, whose communication is much more multisensory:

Speakers in non-literate cultures, including children in all cultures who have not yet learned to read, tend to use many inflections and gestures. But as people become educated in literate cultures they are often taught to "modulate" their vocal inflections, stand still as they talk, and not use gestures. Thus speech becomes reduced to the single element which can be coded by writing or printing: the meaning of the words themselves. (Somers 1998)

In *Dirk Gently's Holistic Detective Agency*, MacDuff made himself wealthy by devising a spreadsheet program that allowed company accounts to be represented musically. MacDuff states sarcastically that the "yearly accounts of most British companies emerged sounding like the Dead March from Saul" (Adams 1988). Although Adams's idea of the musical spreadsheet may have seemed absurd in 1988, science fiction often precedes science fact, and researchers such as Kramer (1994a) have since reported the successful use of auditory displays of stock market data to identify market trends.

The idea of auditory imagery has relatively recently begun to attract attention in the cognitive fields (e.g., see Reisberg 1992). Where graphical visualization is informed by complementary research in cognitive science, auditory display draws on corresponding auditory image research in addition to the audio engineering/sound production fields to allow the communication of information and data through nonspeech sound (figure 17.1). Auditory imagery is, of course, vital for blind users. Up until the 1970s, blind people were quite involved in computing. The selective development of visual interfaces was a severe blow to them.

Although not always explicit in the literature, auditory display work is also informed to a greater or lesser extent by aesthetic considerations.

The Programming Problem

Computer programming poses an interesting problem for information display. Program events are in the time domain while visual mappings provide predominantly spatial representations. Visual techniques give us good descriptions of spatial relations and structural details (as Fourier analysis does for soundwaves), but do not naturally represent temporal details. Sound presents us with a complementary modality that increases the diagnostic

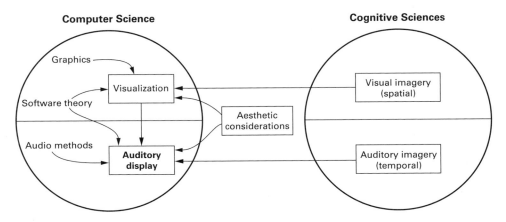

Figure 17.1 The emerging discipline of auditory display.

tools available by giving a temporal view of software (as the waveform plot does for a soundwave). In fact, audio was used quite a lot in the early days of computing. Machines such as the ICL 1900 series had sound output on their operator consoles and it was often used by operators and engineers who, by listening to the patterns of sounds from the loudspeaker, learned to monitor CPU behavior and identify errant program behavior. However, most sound output was primitive and required much effort to produce.

Jackson and Francioni (1992) argued that some types of programming error (such as those that can be spotted through pattern recognition) are more intuitively obvious to our ears than our eyes. Also, they pointed out that, unlike images, sound can be processed by the brain passively, that is, we can be aware of sounds without actively listening to them. The representation of program information in sound is known as program auralization (Kramer 1994b). One of the first auralization systems was described by Sonnenwald and associates (1990), followed by DiGiano (1992), DiGiano and Baecker (1992), Brown and Hershberger (1992), Jameson (1994a; 1994b), Bock (1994; 1995a; 1995b) Mathur and associates (1994), and Boardman and associates (1995). These early systems all used complex tones in their auditory mappings but, like much other auditory display work, this was done without regard to the *musicality* of the representations. That is, simple mappings were often employed, such as quantizing the value of a data item to a chromatic pitch in the 128-tone range offered by MIDI-compatible tone generators. Furthermore, the pitches were typically atonal and combined with sound effects (e.g., a machine sound to represent a function processing some data). Effort was largely invested in demonstrating that data could be mapped to sound with much less attention given to the aesthetic qualities of the auditory displays.

Alty (1995) was one of the first to explicitly use musical principles in his auralization of the bubble-sort algorithm. Leyton (see chapter 15 of this volume) argues that strong aesthetics maximize the transfer of structure. Indeed, where aesthetic considerations are taken into account, auditory displays become much easier to listen to and comprehend (as evidenced by Alty 1995) as the transfer of information from the computer domain to the auditory domain is facilitated. Mayer-Kress and colleagues (1994) mapped chaotic attractor functions to musical structures in which the functions' similar but never-the-same regions could be clearly heard. The use of a musical aesthetic meant that the resultant music could be appreciated in its own right without needing to know its generative history (how it was produced).

Music in Auralizations

In his *Seismic Sonata* Quinn (2000) used the aesthetics of tonal musical form to sonify data from the 1994 Northridge, California, earthquake. Using data to assist with composition is not new. Cohen (1994) suggested it was John Cage who first put forth the principles of auditory display in the 1950s, citing Cage's works *Music of Changes* (1952) and *Reunion* (1968) as early examples of data sonification. In *Music of Changes*, the score was written by mapping the results of coin tosses to pitch, duration, amplitude, and timbre. Even changes in tempo and the number of measures in a given section were controlled by coin tosses. Reunion developed the idea by using photoelectric switches on a chessboard to trigger the playing of different pieces of music. Whether Cage intended to communicate information regarding data sets by music or merely used data as a mechanism for the creation of new music (i.e., was the music a byproduct or the intentional product) is moot; what is interesting is that Cage believed the relationship between music and data could be exploited. Indeed, King and Angus (1996) believed that musical aesthetics would provide a sufficiently well-understood framework on which to build a useful auditory display of the DNA gene sequence of the brain's serotonin receptors that the resultant sonification also appeared as the CD album track *S2 Translation* (The Shamen 1995).

Arguing that music offers a powerful medium for communication, Vickers and Alty (2002b) looked for ways to use its structures and organizational principles to better communicate program information. Francioni and coworkers (1991) suggested that musical representation can highlight situations that could easily be missed in a visual representation (and no doubt the opposite is true in some cases). To give a simple example, shifting a single note by one semitone can change the whole sense of a chord, producing an immediate and compelling effect. This happens when a major triad has its mediant (the third degree of the scale) flattened to produce a minor chord (e.g., see figure 17.2): a similar movement in the value of one data variable in a graph might not be noticed. Of course,

(a) C-Major chord   (b) C-Minor chord

Figure 17.2 A semitone shift produces a very noticeable effect: (a) a C-major chord in first inversion (the mediant at the bottom) and (b) a C-minor chord in first inversion.

not all semitone shifts would be as dramatic, but may merely serve to color a chord rather than change its type. However, the fact remains that, within a tonal music framework, very small changes in pitch are readily discernable when they change the balance of the melody (or the melodic contour) and may even sound out of place if they fall outside the organizing rules of the particular musical style. Thus, as perturbations in the data being explored can be mapped to easily perceived musical events, the aesthetics of tonal music increase the transferability of this information to the listener.

Figure 17.2a shows a C-major triad in first inversion form, in which the bottom note is the mediant E. In part b of the figure, the E is flattened, changing the chord into a C-minor triad (also in first inversion form). Although the change is small (a frequency shift of approximately 6 percent from 329.6 Hz to 311.1 Hz), the effect is very noticeable. In program debugging, the richness of a musical representation may offer fairly precise bug location possibilities (whether used in isolation or in conjunction with the visual media).

The key issue is how to map domain entities to musical structures. Alty (1995) showed that algorithms (such as the bubble sort and minimum-path) can have information about their run-time behavior communicated successfully through musical mappings. The results suggest that, music can transfer information successfully if precise numerical relationships are not being communicated. In their development of a musical diagram reader for the visually impaired, Alty and Rigas (1998) concluded that musical messages should be designed within a consistent framework (much as elements of successful graphical user interfaces follow common design principles). With the CAITLIN musical program auralization system, Vickers and Alty (2002a; 2002b; 2002c; 2003) demonstrated that a musical auralization framework for communicating run-time behavior of Pascal programs was successful in assisting with bug location tasks.

In the CAITLIN system, motifs (signature tunes) were composed for the program language features to be displayed (in this case, the language constructs WHILE, REPEAT, FOR . . . TO, FOR . . . DOWNTO, IF, IF . . . ELSE, CASE, and CASE . . . ELSE). The motifs were organized around a unified and structured tonal framework (see Vickers and

Alty 2002a), and their design was strongly influenced by current thinking in music theory and music cognition. The aim was to create a musical environment that would be easily and quickly learned, that did not depend on prior musical training or expertise, and that could thus communicate information about the run-time behavior of a program. Diatonic (seven-note scale) forms were used, as these underlie much Western popular and orchestral music and so already have wide exposure in the general population from which the experimental subjects were drawn. Figure 17.3 shows Pascal code for a loop and a selection construct and the resultant auralizations.

Until programs become self-aware and can identify their own bugs, the programmer must diagnose the symptoms of a malfunctioning program and deduce where its defects lie. Thus, the auralizations themselves do not have musical features that represent bugs: a bug causes a perturbation in program flow, and it is these perturbations that are looked for. For example, the auralization in figure 17.3d, generated from the code in figure 17.3c, shows that the variable "a" did not have any of the values 1, 2, or 3. If, at this point in the program, "a" was supposed to have a value in the range 1 . . . 3, then either the statement that assigns a value to "a" or the earlier statement that gives "b" a value (not shown) is in error: either way, the fact that "a" does not have an expected value is manifested in the auralization, which tells the listener that the CASE statement's ELSE path was followed. If "a" did have a value in the range 1 . . . 3, then the auralization would sound different as we would hear a major motif signifying a match, as in figure 17.3e.[2]

An Aesthetic Perspective on Auralization

With the CAITLIN system, we showed that simple diatonic auralizations were useful (Vickers and Alty 2002c; 2003). One could argue that, given sufficient training, any auralization framework can be learnable and usable. However, that goes against the more recent efforts to improve design aesthetics, as espoused, for example, by Norman (2004). The underlying principle of aesthetic computing is that art theory and practice should influence the design of computer systems and artifacts (Fishwick 2002). As art theory and practice embody customization, personalization, preference, culture, and emotion (Fishwick 2003; and chapter 1 of this volume), there is much for the auralization designer to consider.

Customization and Personalization

Many of the early program auralization systems let the user define the mappings of data to sound. While this allows almost unlimited customization, personalization, and preference, it requires some sound-design skills on the part of the user. It's like giving someone the

(a)

```
FOR counter := 1 TO 6 DO
    counter := counter + 1 ;
```

The Pascal code (a) results in the auralization (b). Bar 1 has a percussive motif played on an open triangle that pre xes all iterations Bar 2 and beat1 of bar 3 show the tune denoting entry to the loop. The notes in the remainder of bar 3 and in bar 4 represent six iterations of the loop, the nal iteration being supplemented by a sleighbell sound. Bars 5 and 6 denote exit from the loop (the closed triangle motif in bar 6 terminates all iterations).

(b)

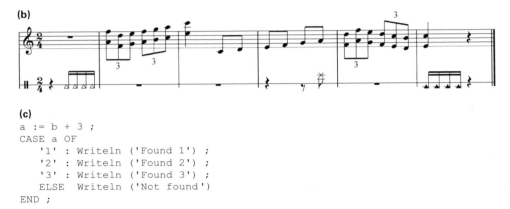

(c)

```
a := b + 3 ;
CASE a OF
    '1' : Writeln ('Found 1') ;
    '2' : Writeln ('Found 2') ;
    '3' : Writeln ('Found 3') ;
    ELSE  Writeln ('Not found')
END ;
```

The Pascal code (c) results in the auralization (d) when the assignment to variable 'a' gives a value greater than 3 and in the auralization (e) when the assignment gives 'a' the value 3. Bar 1 contains a percussive motif that is pre xed to all selections. Bar 2 and beat 1 of bar 3 show the tune denoting entry to the CASE construct.

Figure 17.3 CAITLIN motifs for a FOR...TO loop (b) and a CASE...ELSE statement. Two auralizations for the CASE...ELSE are given: one with a match (d) and one with no match (e).

twelve notes of the chromatic scale and asking them to compose a sonata—without knowledge of, and training in, composition techniques, this would be nearly impossible. Customization and personalization must be balanced by the knowledge and skills required to make use of them. In the CAITLIN system we took the opposite approach and decided to use fixed auralizations, such as those shown in figure 17.3. The hierarchically designed motifs were preassigned to the various language constructs so that all selections were variations on a common theme and all iterations were variations on a different common theme. The system allows the timbre for each construct to be altered, and in some cases the musical scale (e.g., major, minor, ten-note blues, etc.) can also be selected (notably for the FOR loops). However, in the experimental setting (Vickers and Alty 2002a; 2002c), only the overall tempo was user adjustable, so as not to confound the results.

(d)
A cowbell sound is played as each case instance is tested (bottom staff, bars 3 and 4). The tune in bars 5 and 6 signi es exit from the construct. In this example, no match was found for the case selector (meaning the variable 'a' did not have a value in the range 1...3), so a minor chord (beat 1, bar 5) is played to signal following of the ELSE patch and then the construct nishes with the exit motif in a minor key. In the CAITLIN system the major mode was used to denote Boolean true and minor for Boolean false.

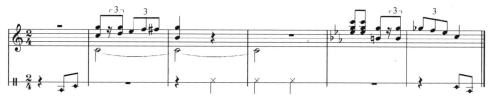

(e)
In the auralization below we can see a major chord on beat 2 of bar 4 played above the cowbell sound that denotes testing the third CASE instance. This means that the value of 'a' matched that of the third CASE instance (i.e., it had the value 3). The construct now exits in a major key (bars 5 and 6) because of a successful match.

Figure 17.3 (continued)

Preference

User preference is certainly an important factor. A study of surgeons who listened to music while operating showed that their speed and task accuracy were greater when they listened to self-selected music than to music chosen by the experimenters (Allen and Blascovich 1994). In our experiments, we noticed a definite preference among subjects for motifs with a strong melody. This was especially apparent in the early pilot studies in which the motif design was less refined. In the early versions of the system, some constructs had motifs that were much less musical than others. For example, the first version of the system used a metaphoric mapping for the IF and IF...ELSE statements: a pitch bend was applied to mimic the rising and falling inflection of the human voice when posing and answering questions. In fact, as several of the subjects in the experiment observed, this ended up sounding like a comical ship's fog horn (Vickers 1999).

In the most recent version, users expressed a preference for the FOR motifs, which were also the most melodic; that is, the melodic contour was more elaborate than the simpler up-and-down scale-based motifs of the selection constructs and the harmonically richer motifs of the WHILE and REPEAT loops. Contour was judged by subjects in our studies as being a useful aide-mémoire for recalling the motifs. Edworthy (1985) and Dowling (1982) observed that contour becomes even more important when the tonal context is weak or confusing; contour is less important in familiar melodies and melodies retained over a period of time.

Emotion

Music clearly has an emotional dimension. We talk of mood music and can be strongly moved by certain pieces. One emotion auralization systems are susceptible to inducing is annoyance. Gaver and Smith (1990) noted that sounds in the interface can be annoying and what "seems cute and clever at first may grow tiresome after a few exposures." In our experience, tiresome sounds are usually those that have not been designed with listening aesthetics in mind—that is, the mental and cognitive processing loads the sounds themselves require reduce the amount of attention the listener can give to the information transfer function. Designers go to great lengths to ensure that auditory signals and alarms in safety critical environments (such as aircraft cockpits and nuclear power plants) sit well within their auditory ecology, but these rigors are not so well followed in other auditory displays. It is easy to make a display that clashes with, or masks, other events, or that is simply tiring (both emotionally and cognitively) to use. Approximately half of the subjects in an experiment using the CAITLIN system found the auralizations to be moderately annoying, the other half suffering almost no annoyance (Vickers 1999). The ambiguity of this result gives hope that we can produce auralizations that do not trigger a negative emotional response but cautions us that we must pay very careful attention to this aspect.

Cultural Aspects

Early auralization systems used musical pitches and MIDI data, but they were simply mapping program data to common frequencies to effect the auralizations without regard for the output's musicality. Weinberg (1998) described programming as a "communication between two alien species," and Conner and Malmin (1983) said we must recognize there may be a gap in understanding between the communicator and the receiver. Successful communication requires a common medium between the two so that the gap can be bridged. Meyer (1956) observed that meaning and communication "cannot be separated from the cultural context in which they arise. Apart from the social situation there can be neither meaning nor communication."

Music aesthetics are thus culturally dependent, and so the aesthetics of an auditory display have a pivotal role in determining how successful the display is. Watkins and Dyson

(1985) found that music performed in a style familiar to the listener is easier to recognize and understand. In the CAITLIN system, it was vital that the auralizations were not so far from the programmer's frame of reference as to be rendered useless. If music is to be used, it must not rely on forms and intervals that are too unfamiliar or indistinguishable to the average person. That is, the aesthetics must be complementary with, or accessible to, those of the listener. Composers organize music according to defined structures, schemas, or sets of rules. Structuring auralizations according to simple syntactical rules offers the hope of music forming the basis for a bridge of the semantic gap between an incorrectly functioning program and the programmer.

Alty (2002) observed that just as designers would never create a chair 12 meters high because it would not be generally useable, composers must not produce works that are beyond the cognitive processing capabilities of the listener. For example, some composers have chosen to use transformations that are simply not cognitively identifiable. In the same vein, auralizations must be mappable to different musical idioms so that the user can select a familiar representation. Just as software interfaces undergo internationalization to take account of cultural differences and social constructs, so auralizations need to be designed with the listener in mind. What is particularly interesting about music is that recall of melody appears to be an innate skill. That is, people do not need to be trained to recognize melodies (the ability to sing, whistle, or hum a tune after only a few hearings is evidence of this). Thus, auralizations that use melodies as carriers of information stand a good chance of being understood and retained in the listener's mind.

The diatonic scale is so common in Western music that one can be fooled into thinking it is somehow a form of nature. But, as Parncutt (1989, p. 5) observed, it is not "an inevitable consequence of the psychophysics of tone perception." In the nineteenth century, Helmholtz believed that the development of musical styles was heavily influenced by culture and aesthetics. This is evident in the divergence of Eastern and Western musical traditions. The Western classical tradition (especially in the eighteenth century) was driven by a desire to explore harmony. Eastern music, on the other hand, focused less on harmony and much more on rhythmic structures (see Parncutt 1989, p. 6). The ancient Greeks strongly debated the relative spiritual merits and vices of the different modal schemes (scales) that were common right up until the Middle Ages.

The argument that diatonic systems are in some way more natural than atonal systems is belied by the fact that concert repertoires continue to include new music styles. However, as Parncutt (1989) observes, most of the atonal systems have not been incorporated into mainstream (or popular) music, as they require more information processing by the listener; studies have shown that the organizing principles of twelve-tone music, with no tonal center to the music and equal weight to each degree of the scale (e.g., the music of

Schoenberg and Stockhausen), are often imperceptible even to trained listeners. Alty (2002) explains this in terms of the limits of working memory which, according to Miller (1956), can handle around seven concurrent bits (or chunks) of information. In experiments on melody recall, Sloboda and Parker (1985) found that the most fundamental feature preserved in a recalled melody was its metrical structure. Musicians and nonmusicians differed significantly on only one measure, that of the ability to retain the harmonic structure of the original melody. Therefore, it is wise not to rely on ability to discriminate between harmonic structures in the auralization motifs, and so we do not commend atonal music systems as good vehicles for auralization.

Of course, cultural as well as perceptual factors are at work here as the seven-note diatonic tonal scheme is a Western, not a world, music form. That said, evidence suggests the scheme shares characteristics with other world music forms. For instance, melodies from around the world tend to center on a particular pitch, a key feature of tonality (Parncutt 1989, p. 70). Furthermore, the twelve-note chromatic scale (of which the diatonic scale is a subset) developed independently in different musical cultures (ancient China, India, Persia, and then the West) and the use of the octave, fourth, and fifth intervals (important in tonal forms) is widespread in music throughout the world. The international success of Western rock and pop bands is further evidence that even Western musical structures are widely (if not universally) accepted, especially in the computer-using world (Vickers and Alty 2002b).

As designers of auditory displays we must nevertheless be aware that even an idiom (such as Western pop music) that is widely *accepted* is not necessarily *interpreted* the same way around the world, for the boundary between sensory and cultural influences is not clear. For example, consonance and dissonance are important concepts, but ones that appear to be specific to Western music (Parncutt 1989). This means that comprehension (or rather, specific interpretations) of particular musical structures cannot be taken for granted. An auralization system that uses dissonance to draw attention to exceptional events, for example, may fail for listeners who are more influenced by musical forms that do not emphasize consonance and dissonance. So, we can see that the aesthetic issues of program auralization systems are complex and strongly culturally dependent.

Conclusion and Future Work

In an attempt to avoid the pitfalls of requiring programmers to be able to specify good auditory mappings, the CAITLIN musical program auralization system was built with fixed motifs designed within a coherent and self-consistent tonal framework (see Vickers and Alty 2002a). This helped ensure that the aural ecology of the system was healthy and no individual parts of the auralizations dominated the mix or conflicted with others. The benefits of this approach are that the listener receives output consistent with a unifying aesthetic framework. A disadvantage is that the system is much less configurable to suit different preferences and emotional or cultural needs. In a sense, an aural equivalent of XML is needed to allow the content (information or data) to be separated from its presentation (in this case, the auditory metaphor). Designers could then produce sets of auditory mappings in much the same way that visual interfaces (or skins) are produced for popular programs today. For example, there could be a jazz schema, a Bach chorale schema, a Javanese Gamelan music set, or even a Chinese classical opera style. In addition, we envisage providing multiple motifs within each set so that program objects and events can be tagged by the user with the motif of preference, in the knowledge that each motif conforms to the aesthetic qualities of the others. Such a development could be considered to be extending the principles of literate programming (Knuth 1984; Pardoe and Wade 1988). Where literate programming tools of the past concentrated on typography and external visual representations to enhance presentation and comprehension of programs (e.g., Vickers, Pardoe, Wade 1991a; 1991b), the tools of the future can make use of auditory and musical aesthetics to extend the programmer's toolbox and visualization set.

Of course, more experimentation is needed to explore just how sensitive auralizations are to the cultural and aesthetic background of the listener. So far, the CAITLIN system has been tested within a Western tonal system only with Western subjects. Actually, we would be surprised if the simple musical forms of the CAITLIN system were not comprehensible to people from other cultures given the tendency of other world music systems to have tonal characteristics. Indeed, we have found in many other tests with subjects from many countries that the cultural differences are minor if simple forms and structures are used.

In the pursuit of aesthetic excellence, we must be careful not to tip the balance too far in favor of artistic form. Much current art music would, perhaps, not be appropriate for a generally usable auralization system. The vernacular is popular music, the aesthetics of which are often far removed from the ideals of the music theorists and experimentalists. Lucas (1994) showed that the recognition accuracy of an auditory display was increased when users were made aware of the display's musical design principles. Watkins and Dyson (1985) demonstrated that melodies that follow the rules of Western tonal music are easier to learn, organize (cognitively), and discriminate between than control tone sequences of similar complexity. So, it would seem that the cognitive organizational overhead associated with the aesthetics of atonal systems makes them less well suited as carriers of program information.

The sonifications of Quinn (2000) and King and Angus (1996) and the generative music of Mayer-Kress and associates (1994) had a dual function of standing on their own as music while shedding light on the underlying data. In a sense, a program auralization system is a generative music system in that the musical output depends on the input data; changing the data changes the behavior of the program, and thus the music. However, the purpose of auralization systems is not to entertain or to convey mood and emotion, but to assist programmers with understanding software and its behavior. The intentional product of an auralization system is the communication of information or knowledge with the music as the carrier. The music itself, inasmuch as it exists as an entity in its own right, is not the intentional product but a byproduct of the auralization process. Therefore, whatever music systems and aesthetics are employed they must not detract from the prime purpose, which is to communicate information. Of course, if the mappings can be organized such that the music byproduct can exist and be appreciated independent of its context (as is the case with the generative chaotic attractor music of Mayer-Kress et al., for example), then so much the better.

Very few formal studies of program auralization have been published. The experiments described by Vickers and Alty (2002a; 2002c) indicate that music can be used to communicate information about program flow and assist with bug location. The results highlighted two areas in which the music seemed particularly efficacious: where the program output contained no clue as to the bugs' location and where programs contained complex Boolean expressions. When the output gives clues (e.g., a loop displays only six output records instead of an expected ten), a bug's location is relatively easy to guess because the auralization very quickly showed the loop to be at fault. When no such clue exists, however, the job is harder to do. In the case of multiple complex Boolean expressions, auralization made it very easy to hear which expressions were at fault; without the auralization subjects had to evaluate the expressions by hand (or use a visualization).

Auralization support for object-oriented and multithreaded programming environments is necessary. The potential for musical sound in program comprehension in such a domain needs to be explored. For example, the orchestral model of families of timbres (e.g., woodwind, brass, strings, percussion, and keyboards) could be applied to help programmers to distinguish between the activities of different threads. Furthermore, rather than replacing visual displays (though this would be useful for the visually impaired), we anticipate that combination audiovisual displays will be the most powerful. We expect that the temporal-spatial communication space provided by a combination auralization-visualization system will offer the programmer a powerful set of tools for writing, comprehending, and debugging code. For example, we envisage a scenario in which a graphical visualization displays the state of a data structure while an auralization renders the program's control flow (or, perhaps, the passing of messages between object methods and program threads). Auralization tools must be integrated into software development environments to allow common debugging techniques (such as breakpoints and step-and-trace facilities) to be extended into the auditory domain.

The use of a bimodal system offers exciting opportunities for program comprehension and debugging tasks. The ease with which music and nonspeech audio can now be incorporated into programming environments (especially the Java platform) means that such a system is a realizable goal in the short to medium term. As long as the auditory aesthetics are well-designed, and thus support the transfer of information from the symbolic programming domain to the temporal auditory domain, we believe such a tool will be a valuable addition to the software development community.

Notes

1. The Two Cultures refers to the existence of two separate cultures, with little contact between them; one culture is based on the humanities and the other on the sciences. The phrase gained popularity after C.P. (Lord) Snow's Rede Lecture, later published as *The Two Cultures and the Scientific Revolution* (1959); c.f., Matthew Arnold, *Culture and Anarchy* (1869), and his Rede Lecture *Literature and Science* (1882) (Brewer 1989).

2. Space does not permit a score for an auralization of a complete program here, but a short annotated example can be found in Vickers and Alty (2003). An audio file of that auralization, together with other examples, can be heard at www.auralisation.org (spelt with an "s" and not a "z").

References

Adams, D. 1988. *Dirk Gently's Holistic Detective Agency.* New York: Pocket.

Allen, K., and Blascovich, J. 1994. "Effects of Music on Cardiovascular Reactivity among Surgeons." *Journal of the American Medical Association* 272(11): 882–84.

Alty, J. L. 1995. "Can We Use Music in Computer-Human Communication?" In *People and Computers X: Proceedings of HCI '95.* M. A. R. Kirby, A. J. Dix, and J. E. Finlay eds. Pp. 409–23. Cambridge: Cambridge University Press.

Alty, J. L. 2002. "Engineering for the Mind: Cognitive Science and Musical Composition." *Journal of New Music Research* 31(3): 249–55.

Alty, J. L., and Rigas, D. I. 1998. "Communicating Graphical Information to Blind Users Using Music: The Role of Context in Design." Paper presented at the CHI98 Conference on Human Factors in Computing Systems, Los Angeles, CA, April 18–23, 1998.

Boardman, D. B., Greene, G., Khandelwal, V., and Mathur, A. P. 1995. "LISTEN: A Tool to Investigate the Use of Sound for the Analysis of Program Behaviour." Paper presented at the 19th International Computer Software and Applications Conference, Dallas, TX, August 9–11, 1995.

Bock, D. S. 1994. "ADSL: An Auditory Domain Specification Language for Program Auralization." Paper presented at the ICAD '94 Second International Conference on Auditory Display, Santa Fe, NM, November 7–9, 1994.

Bock, D. S. 1995a. "Auditory Software Fault Diagnosis Using a Sound Domain Specification Language." Unpublished PhD thesis. Syracuse University, Syracuse, NY.

Bock, D. S. 1995b. "Sound Enhanced Visualization: A Design Approach Based on Natural Paradigms." Unpublished MSc dissertation. Syracuse University, Syracuse, NY.

Brewer, E. C. 1989. *Brewer's Dictionary of Phrase and Fable* 14 ed. London: Cassell Publishers Ltd.

Brown, M. H., and Hershberger, J. 1992. "Color and Sound in Algorithm Animation." *Computer* 25(12): 52–63.

Cohen, J. 1994. "Monitoring Background Activities." In G. Kramer, ed. *Auditory Display*. Pp. 499–532. Reading, MA: Addison-Wesley.

Conner, K. J., and Malmin, K. 1983. *Interpreting the Scriptures: A Textbook on How to Interpret the Bible.* Portland, OR: Bible Temple Publications.

DiGiano, C. J. 1992. "Visualizing Program Behaviour Using Non-speech Audio." Unpublished MSc dissertation. University of Toronto, Toronto.

DiGiano, C. J., and Baecker, R. M. 1992. "Program Auralization: Sound Enhancements to the Programming Environment." Paper presented at the Graphics Interface '92.

Dowling, W. J. 1982. "Melodic Information Processing and Its Development." In *The Psychology of Music*. D. Deutsch ed. Pp. 413–29. New York: Academic Press.

Edworthy, J. 1985. Melodic Contour and Musical Structure. In *Musical Structure and Cognition*. P. Howell, I. Cross and R. West eds. Pp. 169–88. New York: Academic Press.

Fishwick, P. 2002. "Aesthetic Programming: Crafting Personalized Software." *Leonardo* 35(4): 383–90.

Fishwick, P. 2003. Personal communication.

Francioni, J. M., Albright, L., and Jackson, J. A. 1991. "Debugging Parallel Programs Using Sound." *SIGPLAN Notices* 26(12): 68–75.

Gaver, W. W., and Smith, R. B. 1990. "Auditory Icons in Large-Scale Collaborative Environments." Paper presented at the Human-Computer Interaction: Interact '90. Cambridge, UK.

Jackson, J. A., and Francioni, J. M. 1992. "Aural Signatures of Parallel Programs." Paper presented at the Twenty-Fifth Hawaii International Conference on System Sciences.

James, J. 1993. *The Music of the Spheres*. New York: Springer-Verlag.

Jameson, D. H. 1994a. "The Run-Time Components of Sonnet." Paper presented at the ICAD '94 Second International Conference on Auditory Display, Santa Fe, NM, November 7–9, 1994.

Jameson, D. H. 1994b. "Sonnet: Audio-Enhanced Monitoring and Debugging." In *Auditory Display*. G. Kramer ed. Pp. 253–65. Reading, MA: Addison-Wesley.

King, R. D., and Angus, C. 1996. "PM—Protein Music. *CABIOS*." 12(3): 251–52.

Knuth, D. E. 1984. "Literate Programming." *Computer Journal* (May).

Kramer, G. 1994a. "Some Organizing Principles for Representing Data with Sound." In *Auditory Display*. G. Kramer, ed. Pp. 185–222. Reading, MA: Addison-Wesley.

Kramer, G., ed. 1994b. *Auditory Display*. Reading, MA: Addison-Wesley.

Lucas, P. A. 1994. "An Evaluation of the Communicative Ability of Auditory Icons and Earcons." Paper presented at the ICAD '94 Second International Conference on Auditory Display, Santa Fe, NM, November 7–9, 1994.

Mathur, A. P., Boardman, D. B., and Khandelwal, V. 1994. *LSL: A Specification Language for Program Auralization.* Paper presented at the ICAD '94 Second International Conference on Auditory Display, Santa Fe, NM, November 7–9, 1994.

Mayer-Kress, G., Bargar, R., and Choi, I. 1994. "Musical Structures in Data from Chaotic Attractors." In *Auditory Display*. G. Kramer, ed. Pp. 341–68. Reading, MA: Addison-Wesley.

Meyer, L. B. 1956. *Emotion and Meaning in Music*. Chicago: Chicago University Press.

Miller, G. A. 1956. "The Magical Number Seven, Plus or Minus Two: Some Limits on our Capacity for Processing Information." *Psychological Review* 63: 81–96.

Norman, D. A. 2004. *Emotional Design: Why We Love (or Hate) Everyday Things*. New York: Basic Books.

Pardoe, J. P., and Wade, S. J. 1988. "Knuth With Knobs On—Literate Program Development." In *Automating Systems Development*. D. Benyon and S. Skidmore, eds. New York: Plenum.

Parncutt, R. 1989. *Harmony: A Psychoacoustical Approach*. Berlin: Springer-Verlag.

Quinn, M. 2000. *Seismic Sonata: A Musical Replay of the 1994 Northridge, California Earthquake*. Lee, NH: Marty Quinn.

Reisberg, D., ed. 1992. *Auditory Imagery*. Hillsdale, NJ: Lawrence Erlbaum Associates, Inc.

Sloboda, J. A., and Parker, D. H. H. 1985. "Immediate Recall of Melodies." In *Musical Structure and Cognition*. P. Howell, I. Cross and R. West, eds. Pp. 143–67. New York: Academic Press.

Somers, E. 1998. "A Pedagogy of Creative Thinking Based on Sonification of Visual Structures and Visualization of Aural Structures." Paper presented at the ICAD '98 Fifth International Conference on Auditory Display, Glasgow, November 1–4, 1998.

Sonnenwald, D. H., Gopinath, B., Haberman, G. O., et al. 1990. "InfoSound: An Audio Aid to Program Comprehension." Paper presented at the Twenty-Third Hawaii International Conference on System Sciences.

The Shamen (artist). 1995. *S2 Translation*, on Axis Mutatis [CD], One Little Indian Records Ltd., Warner Chappell Music TPLP52CDL.

Vickers, P. 1999. "CAITLIN: Implementation of a Musical Program Auralisation System to Study the Effects on Debugging Tasks as Performed by Novice Pascal Programmers." Unpublished PhD thesis. Loughborough University, Loughborough.

Vickers, P., and Alty, J. L. 2002a. "Musical Program Auralisation: A Structured Approach to Motif Design." *Interacting with Computers* 14(5): 457–85.

———. 2002b. "Using Music to Communicate Computing Information." *Interacting with Computers* 14(5): 435–56.

———. 2002c. "When Bugs Sing." *Interacting with Computers* 14(6): 793–819.

———. 2003. "Siren Songs and Swan Songs: Debugging with Music." *Communications of the ACM* 46(7): 86–92.

Vickers, P., Pardoe, J. P., and Wade, S. J. 1991a. "Software Assisted Program Design." Paper presented at the Computer Assisted Learning of Computing, Manchester Polytechnic, September 17, 1991.

———. 1991b. "The Use of Literate Program Development Tools." Paper presented at the Software Supported Programming Instruction Workshop, University of Ulster, June 14, 1991.

Watkins, A. J., and Dyson, M. C. 1985. "On the Perceptual Organisation of Tone Sequences and Melodies." In *Musical Structure and Cognition*. P. Howell, I. Cross and R. West, eds. Pp. 71–119. New York: Academic Press.

Weinberg, G. 1998. *The Psychology of Computer Programming: Silver Anniversary Edition*. New York: Dorset House Publishing Co. Inc.

IV

Interface and Interaction

18

Tertiary Artifacts at the Interface

Olav W. Bertelsen

At a lecture on computer systems development many years ago, I absentmindedly observed the forest of TV antennas on the rooftops through the windows. In my imagination, the TV antennas became a jazz orchestra, and suddenly I understood that systems development was like the improvisation of a jazz band.

This everyday aesthetics in modernity is not easily found in the user interface. The problem is that there is no functional point in seeing the TV antennas, and because the designer (in principle) can exclude anything from the interface that does not contribute to "getting the job done" in a transparent manner, the TV antennas of the computer system, do not become visible.

In this chapter, I discuss how an aesthetic approach to computing can contribute to the further development of the branch of computing dealing with human use of interactive technology. It is my hypothesis that human-computer interaction can advance if redefined as an aesthetic discipline. More specifically, I look into Wartofsky's account on the history of perception, and the function of art in this. The potential of this account, in relation to human-computer interaction, is to place experience and culture as first-order aspects to be integrated with the traditional foci on cognition and work arrangement design.

Transparency

The concept of transparency and the current debate about it illustrate a dilemma in human-computer interaction. As recent critics (e.g., Bolter and Gromala 2003) point out, the concept is probably understood too literally or naively by some in the human-computer interaction community as just meaning the user does not notice the interface. I partly agree with this criticism, but at the same time it is important to maintain transparency as an indispensable feature of any computer-based artifact in the sense that the computer per se should not obscure the user's view. The problem, however, is a dichotomy between interfaces that are statically transparent and those that are reflective, artistic, or interesting in some other way. This is, I argue, a false dichotomy because the dynamics between computer applications interacting transparently with the object of work and those that are the object when one is learning to use the computer or when conditions for its use change, have been treated in human-computer interaction for the last 20 years. Thus, the concept of transparency as a feature of the dialectical cooperative relation between users, tools, and objects is still central to understanding computing technology based in human use.

It is, however, important for human-computer interaction to understand the technical substrate in which the digital interactive forms are constructed—the code, the gate, the algorithm, and so on—not primarily in technical terms but reflected artistically.

History

Two main tendencies are seen in human-computer interaction. In the first generation, focus was on individual users' perception and cognition in isolated interplay with the user interface; the aim was to minimize the cognitive load on the user by optimizing the interface to best fit the general human. In the second generation, it was realized that users couldn't be understood in isolation, and human-computer interaction should therefore take the whole work arrangement into account; the skilled workers' tool became the ideal. In both periods, transparency in some form has been the unspoken ideal.

An important factor in the evolution of the context-oriented second-generation perspective was politically engaged young researchers' experience in developing new technology for, the graphics industry, for example, with the workers in mind. They saw that many technology problems arose because the competencies of the workers were neglected. The tool perspective viewed the user not as an attachment to a computer-based system, but developed computer-based systems as transparent tools mediating the user's purposeful, skilled action on an object of work. The use aspects of a computer-based system was constituted in the situation of use, and therefore could not be deduced from the computer-based system in isolation. Thus, development in use became a key issue as computer-based systems were observed to be most often used in unanticipated ways (Ehn 1988; Kyng 1998).

Today, human-computer interaction seems to be caught in a dilemma between either decontextualized cognitivism or an exaggeratedly pragmatic focus on specific contexts. In both cases, the specifics of the technical substrate as such seem to be bracketed out. To advance this state, we need to understand how the second generation grew out of opposition to the first, and how its ideals are impossible by its own standards. Refusing central

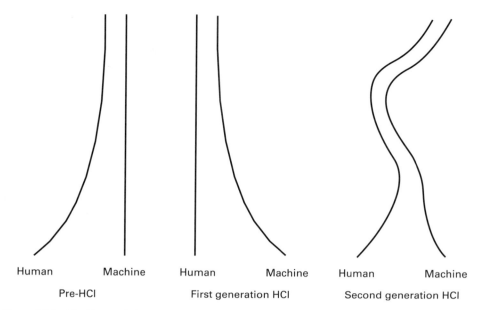

| Human | Machine | Human | Machine | Human | Machine |
| Pre-HCI | | First generation HCI | | Second generation HCI | |

Figure 18.1 The historical development of foci in human-computer interaction. In pre-HCI, the users were assumed to conform to the machine. In first-generation HCI, the aim was to fit the computer to the abilities of the general user. In the second generation, the aim was seen as supporting the continuing dialectical development of the human use of computer-based tools.

concepts such as transparency does not help the advancement of human-computer interaction; rather we need a nuanced understanding of the concept. The development of human-computer interaction is illustrated in figure 18.1. Pre-HCI, focus was on the machine alone. In first-generation HCI, focus changed to the "natural" affordances (Gibson 1986) of the interface, matching the invariable features of the human operator. In second-generation HCI, focus has been on the highly dialectical relationship between users and computers and the "canonical affordances" (Bærentsen and Trettvik 2002) of the interface. To account for the dialectics of the user-computer relation, however, human-computer interaction requires understanding of the aesthetics of computing technology—how computing technology is experienced and "experienceable." Input from aesthetic computing is greatly needed in human-computer interaction.

Activity

Human activity theory, adapted from psychology (Leontjev 1978) and developmental work research (Engeström 1987), has been useful in organizing the insights of the second generation of human-computer interaction. Its account of human-computer interaction in some ways negates the basic ideas of the earlier approaches (e.g., Bødker 1991; Kuutti 1991). First, it emphasizes that human action is purposeful and socially mediated, and consequently that use qualities of a computer-based system emerge in the context of use. Conscious human action, always part of motivated activity, is carried through by non-conscious operations triggered by conditions in the environment and the structure of the action. Second, it emphasizes that development is an ongoing aspect of the use situation. A behavioral pattern can be an action in one context but an operation through automatization; the reverse change, from operation to action, happens through conceptualization when operation conditions change.

To understand the features required for an interface to become transparent we can explore activity theory. Transparency is not a feature of the interface per se, but rather a quality of the user-artifact-object-context ensemble of the use situation. In activity theory terms, an application becomes transparent when the user is able to direct conscious actions to the object of work (e.g., the novel the writer is working on) whereas the computer application (the tool) is handled through nonconscious operations. In earlier work with Jakob Bardram (1995), we described how transparent interaction, from an activity theory view point (in particular, Gal'perin 1969), is achieved by either ensuring that the operations required to operate the application are already established with the user or that the interface can set conditions for the user's development of the relevant operations. We argued that the interface designer, mediated by the interface, sets conditions for the user to establish a zone of proximal development when it becomes relevant, that is, by placing nonintrusive clues that will appear for the user at the relevant moment. For this to happen, we emphasized development in use—that learning should be embedded in real, meaningful use situations, not as a separate activity. Further, the interface should strike a certain degree of initial familiarity for the user, and it should enable the user to establish an image of the future use. Finally, we emphasized the importance of setting conditions for the formation and automatization of actions, supporting mastery beyond sheer trial and error.

In our attempt to understand how to design for transparency, we bent the activity theoretical concept of the zone of proximal development (Bardram and Bertelsen 1995), considering the interface as a proper venue for social mediation between the designer acting as the adult and the user as the learning child, even though this "venue" was asynchronous and noncollocated. Indirectly, this use of the zone of proximal development concept points to the importance of including a cultural level of mediated development in understanding how the interface itself is a medium in which the designer's expressions can support the users' development with the application.

Olav W. Bertelsen

We did not, however, break with the idea of the zone of proximal development as a more or less universally well-defined path to progress. For the practical application of our approach, the designer must predict what the users need to do with the application. The dilemma is that the designer should predict the curriculum for the users' development but unanticipated use is a basic condition in IT design. When use emerges in use, it is impossible to write a curriculum beforehand. This dilemma is inherent in second-generation human-computer interaction because of its unilateral focus on purposeful action and development within the culture of a specific community of practice. While first-generation human-computer interaction was limited by the lack of focus on purpose and work context, the second generation is stigmatized by its focus on these issues, not least because they are in conflict with the widespread observation that applications almost always are used in unexpected ways.

Perception

To address the problem outlined here, I argue that it is necessary to understand use and design in a broader context than the community of work practice and immediate purposefulness. We need a perspective that not only understands use qualities retrospectively, in terms of natural affordance and canonical affordance crystallized in productive practice, but can account for how and why users' expectations, perceptions, and actions in context come about and change over time. Only within such a perspective will we be able to design computer applications that do not obstruct meaningful use.

Wartofsky's (1973) analysis of the history of perception is a fruitful basis for such a historical account of perception, and action should include a level of cultural and aesthetical analysis, but it has to incorporate the insights of second-generation human-computer interaction, including its understandings of reflection in transparency in tool-mediated action.

Wartofsky explains that human perception is not an invariant factor in interaction, and it is not independent of action. Consequently, in introducing an historical account of perception as an integral part of practice (not just a prelude to action), he says "I take perception itself to be a mode of outward action."

This breaks the sequential perception-decision-action loop that dominates large parts of human-computer interaction. Perception changes historically in the course of changed practice, and the historical change of perception influences the change of practice. Thus, Wartofsky suggests a perspective in which perception is understood as being historically variable: "the very forms of perceptual activity are now shaped to, and also help to shape an environment created by conscious human activity itself" (Wartofsky 1973).

In line with the activity theoretical account of the second-generation human-computer interaction, Wartofsky understands perception to be mediated by historically developed artifacts. The distinctive human form of activity is constituted by the creation and use of artifacts, in reproducing the species as well as producing the means of existence. Wartofsky identifies two types of artifacts mediating productive practice. Primary artifacts are used directly in productive acts. Secondary artifacts are representations used in preserving and transmitting the skills and modes of acting through which the productive practice is realized. Thus, secondary artifacts are representations of the modes of acting in production—not merely pictures of objects or environments relevant to production, but representations of modes of acting on and with these objects. A hammer is a primary artifact, a book about carpentry is a secondary artifact, as is a nursery school plate that pictures various situations in which carpenters work with their tools. A word processor is another example of a primary artifact, but integrated with word processors we often find fragments of secondary artifacts in help systems, and even in icons and other elements of the interface. Secondary artifacts shape human perception as they convey forms of action, thereby forming the action potentials we perceive. This is in line with what has been claimed by second-generation human-computer interaction.

Art

According to Wartofsky, however, human perception is not only shaped in productive practice. Wartofsky suggests another loop of imaginative construction mediated by another kind of representation, namely, tertiary artifacts. These tertiary artifacts are abstracted from their direct representational function: "[That] we see by way of our picturing, or our modes of representation, then, is to claim that perceptual activity is now mediated not only by the species-specific biologically evolved mechanisms of perception, but by the historically changing 'world' created by human practical and theoretical activity" (Wartofsky 1973).

Tertiary artifacts have origins in the productive practice but do not depend on it directly. They constitute an autonomous zone of free creation of visions that transcends the existing modes of perception and action in societal practice. Thus, tertiary artifacts reshape human perception, thereby influencing and changing productive practices. The representations Wartofsky points to with the concept of tertiary artifacts are those produced in the liberal arts, and the main point of his argument is the relation between art and societal practice in general. "The artist, in effect, re-educates us perceptually . . . as styles or canons of representation change, historically, the world has seen changes as well" (Wartofsky 1973).

Perception is shaped not only in our productive acts but just as strongly by our reception of artistic representations. Art and cultural expressions in general therefore constitute a zone of reconsideration and remediation, and these tertiary artifacts can be seen as probes into productive culture, as well as a melting pot in which new variations of productive activity take form.

Clusters

As argued elsewhere, mundane tools, including computer applications, exist in complex clusters of primary, secondary, and tertiary artifacts (Bertelsen 1998). The hammer is a primary artifact for driving nails. The hammer exists in a complex with secondary artifacts representing practices using hammers. Some of these secondary artifacts may be remembered from the plates and children's books in nursery school, represented later by the hammer itself. The tertiary artifacts coupled to the hammer are by definition harder to identify, but the hammer points to the artistic representations of hammers and hammering as the prototypical crafts activity, as well as the potential poetic meanings of the word "hammer." In this way, the hammer has a certain amount of tertiary artifactness attached.

In the original sense of the concept, a lot of computer-based works of art are tertiary artifacts that seem to have potentials for changing productive practice with computer applications. As Bolter and Gromala point out (in this volume), the majority of works in computer art explicitly address the new ways in which computer applications mediate our relation to our surroundings and ourselves.

Designing computer applications with built-in, but clearly distinguishable, tertiary artifacts might be an approach in some situations, creating a clear interface hybridity (Manovich 2001). However, as a general design approach I suggest focusing on elements of tertiary artifactness integrated with the tool interface, allowing for poetic openings into contingency and imagination, and supporting the development of transparent interaction without prescribing a specific curriculum.

With Wartofsky's concept of tertiary artifacts, reformulating human-computer interaction as an aesthetic discipline that will enable us to break out of the conceptual limitations of purpose and function and still focus on the dialectics of the use situation seems promising. In such a reformulation, based on the concept of tertiary artifacts (and clusters of artifactness), it will be possible to bridge the insights of second-generation human-computer interaction to the newer views that discard the concept of transparency and the tool perspective in general. Within such a new discipline, it will be possible to reconsider the dilemma of "curriculum for use" versus "unanticipated use" with which we were stuck in our earlier exploration of design for transparent interaction (Bardram and Bertelsen 1995).

Innovation

Distinguishing between the transfer of established modes of action mediated by secondary artifacts, integrated into day-to-day productive action, and the reformation of perception and expectation mediated by tertiary artifacts in an offline loop not directly integrated into productive action enables a more detailed analysis of the limits for development in use. The tertiary artifactness of mundane tools consequently defines a parallelism of various types of mediation in use; this parallelism may or may not be spatially and temporally intertwined in the course of purposeful action.

Because tertiary artifact is an aesthetic concept, Wartofsky's analysis leads to an extension of the concept of social mediation in activity theory beyond the confines of group interaction and the well-defined curriculum embedded into the interface. Development, including development in use, is culturally mediated. Consequently, a cultural unit of analysis can be introduced. The interface should also be understood as aesthetics and an art form. We should understand not only the functionality and the cognitive match, but also the cultural roots and impact, for example, by applying methods from the analysis of liberal arts in the analysis of computer applications (Bertelsen and Pold 2004). As the cultural formation becomes a basic unit of analysis, the aesthetic perspective offers an actual handle on the users expectations in the specific cultural formation. Thus, it may be possible, although complicated, to design for nonintrusive clues that become apparent right on time.

Dialectics

Currently, many writers emphasize the cultural and aesthetic dimensions of technology (e.g., Bolter and Gromala 2003, and in this volume; Dunne 1999; Djajadiningrat et al. 2000; Manovich 2001; Redström et al. 2000). These contributions indicate that technology today is important beyond the workplace, and they point to a general reorientation.

While writers such as Bolter and Gromala (2003) tend to interpret this reorientation as implying a break from the ideal of transparency, we have pointed out here that transparency and reflectivity are interdependent aspects of computer-mediated activity. Transparency at some level is a preconception for reflectivity at other levels, and reflectivity is needed to initiate the learning process, leading to transparency. More specifically, activity theory points to the importance of the dynamic alteration of the technical substrate or the tool being *in* and *outside* focus.

Bardram and Bertelsen's paper shows, however, there is a missing link between understanding that transparent interaction is developing in use, in unexpected ways, and understanding, in a design-oriented way, how this development takes place.

By introducing Wartofsky's concept of tertiary artifacts, mediating the historical development of perception as action, it is possible to integrate the transparent tool perspective through a theory of art as innovative practice. More generally, it becomes possible to integrate the work practice-oriented second generation with the current aesthetic reorientation, thereby reconstituting human-computer interaction as a new partly aesthetic discipline. I argue here that this new discipline can be based on dialectical materialism as expressed in activity theory and in Wartofsky's account on perception and aesthetics, particularly because such an approach seems to be both sufficiently pragmatic and sufficiently value driven. It is thus possible to avoid the idealisms and subjectivisms to which some of the current aesthetically oriented accounts of human-computer interaction tend to subscribe.

The dialectics between transparency and reflectivity in tools and in art are central to the further development of human-computer interaction into the third generation and to setting a new agenda for theories in digital aesthetics. Transparency is, in a way, already important in art. Even when "the medium is the message," artistic expression depends on moments of transparency, such as certain material features of the work; we do not just see canvas and paint when we look at a painting. To work with everyday artifacts, such as computer applications, will drive theoretical aesthetics, emphasizing the relation between transparency and reflectivity. It was realized within second-generation human-computer interaction that transparency was a developing feature of the use situation, but it was difficult to account for the dynamics behind its development, and how interface design could support it. In the future third-generation human-computer interaction, "the cultural," including digital art, will no longer be considered a stable backdrop for human-computer interaction, but will instead be understood as the level constituting the dynamics of human-computer interaction. The emergence of aesthetic computing as an intertwined field of science and liberal arts will become an important resource for basic research in human-computer interaction because it is concerned with the tertiary artifactness of computer-based representations.

Conclusion

This chapter discussed the program for aesthetic computing as highly relevant in addressing actual problems in human-computer interaction. When human-computer interaction has to transcend focus on individual cognition and specific workplace arrangements to understand such central issues as development in use, an aesthetic perspective is important. This should include the aesthetics of the computer-based substrates as such. In this sense, aesthetic computing contributes to an operational understanding of how computer-based mundane tools are clusters of primary, secondary, and tertiary artifactness. At the same time, the current issues in human-computer interaction discussed in this chapter are likely to inspire the adaptation of aesthetic theory in computing in the direction of emphasizing how aesthetic qualities are continuously reconstituted in human practice.

References

Bærentsen, K. B., and Trettvik, J. 2002. "An Activity Theory Approach to Affordance." *Proc NordiCHI 2002*, pp. 51–60.

Bardram, J. E., and Bertelsen, O. W. 1995. "Supporting the Development of Transparent Interaction." In *EWHCI '95, Selected Papers*. Blumenthal, Gornostaev, and Unger, eds. Pp. 79–90. Berlin: Springer Verlag.

Bertelsen, O. W. 1998. "Elements of a Theory of Design Artifact." PhD thesis. University of Aarhus.

Bertelsen, O. W., and Pold, S. 2004. "Criticism as an Approach to Interface Aesthetics." *Proc NordiCHI 2004*, pp. 23–32.

Bolter, J. D., and Gromala, D. 2003. *Windows and Mirrors: Interaction Design, Digital Art, and the Myth of Transparency*. Cambridge MA: MIT Press.

Bødker, S. 1991. *Through the Interface—A Human Activity Approach to User Interface Design*. Hillsdale, NJ: Lawrence Erlbaum Assoc.

Djajadiningrat, J. P., Gaver, W. W., and Frens, J. W. 2000. "Interaction Relabelling and Extreme Characters." *Proc DIS'00*. New York: ACM, pp. 66–72.

Dunne, A. 1999. *Hertzian Tales—Electronic Products, Aesthetic Experience and Critical Design*. London: Royal College of Art.

Ehn, P. 1988. *Work-oriented Design of Computer Artifacts*. Falköping: Arbejdslivscentrum.

Engeström, Y. 1987. *Learning by Expanding*. Helsinki: Orienta-Konsultit Oy.

Gal'perin, P. Y. 1969. "Stages in the Development of Mental Acts." In *A Handbook of Contemporary Soviet Psychology*. M. Cole and I. Maltzman, eds. New York: Basic Books.

Gibson, J. J. 1986. *The Ecological Approach to Visual Perception*. Hillsdale, NJ: Lawrence Erlbaum Associates.

Kuutti, K. 1991. "Activity Theory and Its Applications to Information Systems Research and Development." In *Information Systems Research: Contemporary Approaches & Emergent Traditions*. H.-E. Nissen, H. K. Klein, and R. Hirschheim, eds. Amsterdam: North-Holland, pp. 529–50.

Kyng, M. 1998. "Users and Computers." Dr Sci. dissertation. University of Aarhus. Aarhus, Denmark.

Leontjev, A. N. 1978. *Activity, Consciousness, and Personality.* Engelwood Cliffs, NJ: Prentice Hall.

Manovich, L. 2001. *The Language of New Media.* Cambridge, MA: The MIT Press.

Redström, J., Skog, T., and Hallnäs, L. 2000. "Informative Art: Using Amplified Artworks as Information Displays." *Proc. DARE 2000,* pp. 103–14.

Wartofsky, M. W. 1973. "Perception, Representation, and the Forms of Action: Toward an Historical Epistemology." In *Models.* Dordrecht: D. Reidel Publishing Company, 1979; pp. 188–210.

19

Transparency and Reflectivity: Digital Art and the Aesthetics of Interface Design

Jay David Bolter and Diane Gromala

In the introduction to this volume, Paul Fishwick defined aesthetic computing as "the application of the theory and practice of art to computing." Fishwick contrasts aesthetic computing as a critical practice with computer or digital art, whose goal is expressive and creative. In the spirit of this contrast, we focus on digital art—but not as art for art's sake. Instead, we consider digital art as a way of reflecting on the aesthetics of digital technology and design in general. Many, perhaps most, digital artists in the late twentieth and early twenty-first centuries are explicitly addressing digital technology as either the means or the subject of their art. We suggest that such art offers an important lesson for the design of computing systems in general.

In examining the aesthetics of computing, there are two places where one might begin: the "inside" or the "outside," that is, the code or the interface. For some, because the code itself is an aesthetic object, aesthetic computing is the study of the principles that make programming into an art form. Like traditional works of art, computer programs can be elegant and expressive. Programming and scripting languages can constitute the medium or material for expression, just as clay, stone, or oil on canvas are media that both constrain and make possible an artist's expressive power. This idea goes back ultimately to the much older notion that mathematics itself has an aesthetic dimension—for example, proofs can be beautiful and elegant. Ars Electronica, probably the best-known recurring exposition and conference on digital art, devoted its 2003 festival to exploring this view: its theme was "Code: The Language of Our Time" (see www.aec.at/en/festival/programm/index.asp).

The other approach is to consider the experience the program provides its users. Because ordinary users do not see the code, they do not have the opportunity to appreciate the aesthetics at that level. What the user sees and interacts with—by definition, the interface—is what defines her experience of the program. Whether or not she regards a program as aesthetically pleasing or significant depends almost entirely on its interface.

Those who favor the code view will develop a formalist aesthetics, because computer languages are rigorously formalized systems, and the aesthetic values of such systems seem to lie in the elegant manipulation of their syntax. It may be that only other programmers are in a position to appreciate the aesthetics of the code. Those who favor the interface view may adopt a more pragmatic or popular aesthetics, in which beauty is in the eye (or perhaps the eye and hand) of the user. The two approaches are complementary, and both are represented in this volume; for example, Lee (chapter 2) and Vickers and Alty (chapter 17) explore the code view, while Nake and Grabowski (chapter 4), Lowgren (chapter 20), and others examine the interface view. (The classification is not perfect, of course; some authors are interested in the aesthetics of both the code and the interface.)

This chapter takes the interface approach. Furthermore, we believe that applying aesthetic principles to interface design is not simply a matter of making the interface "prettier." Applying aesthetic principles does not necessarily make software more attractive to the user; instead, aesthetics should contribute to a more effective relationship between the user and the application. The work of many contemporary digital artists focuses on the way the viewer/user understands the visual and computational objects represented in the interface and the process of interaction with these objects. Such artists are exploring what the HCI community has called the user's "mental model" and the humanities community call the user's "epistemology"—her or his "way of knowing" what the interface is about.

Digital Art as Radical Interface Design

Digital art has been a facet of the contemporary art scene for many years, as we see from the Ars Electronica and Inter-Society for the Electronic Arts festivals (ISEA, www.isea-web.org) and the Zentrum für Kultur und Medien (ZKM, www.zkm.de) in Karlsruhe, Germany, all of which date back to the 1980s. The practice of digital art grew out of the performance and installation art traditions, which are themselves decades older. It has also developed in close association with computer technology and computer science, as indicated by the presence of art galleries at the SIGGRAPH conferences since the 1980s. SIGGRAPH is the largest and most important conference on research into computer graphics and new forms of interface design; it is also an important trade show for the digital entertainment industry. By including art at the SIGGRAPH conference, the computer graphics community is acknowledging the significance of artistic production (if not aesthetics) in their field of computing.

The presence of art at SIGGRAPH suggests a reciprocal relationship. Not only can interface design have an aesthetic dimension, but digital art can also be a form of interface design. Digital artists experiment with digital technology, creating prototypes to explore various design possibilities, new ways in which the user can interact with the digital artifact. Furthermore, the digital artist operates in an environment free of some of the constraints felt by the commercial digital designer or even the academic computer science (CS) researcher. Commercial designers are supposed to make a product that sells, often working directly for a client whom they must satisfy. CS researchers must often negotiate their projects' scope and plan with the agency that is funding the work. In both domains, the work must be relevant when judged by some appropriate standard of utility or usability. Even basic research must be justified as eventually having some applicability to real-world problems.

This is not to say that digital art is or should be "useless." However, its usefulness is measured by criteria other than those of the commercial world: first, by the artist's own aesthetic judgment and then by the response of the artist's viewers/users. Digital art is not pure expression—that romantic notion does not apply well to contemporary art in general or to digital art in particular. Most digital artists are concerned about the social and cultural contexts in which their work will be received and interpreted. Those contexts are represented by the user or group of users who constitute their audience. In this sense, a work of digital art is embedded in many of the same contexts that, for example, the HCI researcher Albert Badre has identified for the design of commercial Web sites (Badre 2002). Interactive digital art can be radical interface design. It can examine how digital technology presents itself to the user in its purest form, because the user comes to a work of art with only a few preconceptions about how the piece should "function" and without any practical (as opposed to aesthetic) needs the piece is expected to fulfill.

The SIGGRAPH 2000 Art Gallery (curated by a team including Diane Gromala) offered an excellent example of the range of such experiments. Thousands of visitors walked through a hall containing dozens of exhibits, including net art and screen-based pieces, digital video installations, and full-fledged interactive spaces whose interfaces involved the users' whole body (figure 19.1). We can regard the SIGGRAPH Gallery as a snapshot of digital art at the beginning of the new century.[1]

Wooden Mirror

One of the most compelling exhibits at SIGGRAPH 2000 was Wooden Mirror by Daniel Rozin. Wooden Mirror is an octagonal shaped from and composed of hundreds of wooden tiles, which look like Scrabble counters. Each tile is set on an individual electric motor, which can be commanded to tilt the tile forward (figure 19.2). In the center of the mirror, a tiny video camera records the image of anyone who comes to view the piece. A computer processes the image from the digital camera and sends appropriate signals to the tile

Figure 19.1 The Art Gallery of SIGGRAPH 2000.

Jay David Bolter and Diane Gromala

Figure 19.2   Wooden Mirror by Daniel Rozin (close-up view).

motors. The tiles are tilted to create a very coarse image of the person standing in front of the mirror (figure 19.3).

As Rozin explains,

the non-reflective surfaces of the wood are able to reflect an image because the computer manipulates them to cast back different amounts of light as they tilt toward or away from the light source.... The image reflected in the mirror is a very minimal one. It is, I believe, the least amount of information that is required to convey a picture.... It is amazing how little information this is for a computer and yet how much character it can have (and what an endeavor it is to create it in the physical world). (*SIGGRAPH 2000*, p. 68)

Wooden Mirror has the simplest possible interface, one that is grasped immediately by the viewer/user without any instructions. Viewers simply move into the field of view of the camera, and in a few seconds the tiles of the mirror begin to click as they rearrange themselves to reflect their image. If the viewer moves his or her head or raises an arm, the mirror readjusts itself in seconds. In the Gallery, those who passed by Wooden Mirror were easily pulled into its orbit. Watching others casting their image onto the wooden tiles,

Figure 19.3 Wooden Mirror by Daniel Rozin.

they then took their turn. A playful relationship instantly developed between the viewer/user and the interface.

As simple as it is in operation (from the user's perspective), Wooden Mirror is a multi-layered work of art. At one level it is a formal experiment in representation or even Gestalt psychology, as Rozin's previous statement suggests. It poses the question: How much information is needed to convey an intelligible image? At another level, the piece is a statement about digital technology and the construction of the (human) subject. For our purposes, what is most important is that Wooden Mirror can be taken as a playful exploration of the nature of the digital interface. The piece asks us to consider the interface as a mirror that reacts to and reflects its viewer. The reflection is not a clear and perfect illusion, as it is with a conventional silvered mirror. If the conventional mirror seems to be transparent, a window onto another world, Wooden Mirror suggests the irony of an opaque image, one that requires viewers/users to work to find themselves in the reflection. A conventional mirror has no moving parts and reflects instantly. Wooden Mirror, however, is a combination of the digital and the analog, the virtual and the physical, and makes the user conscious of the process by which the image is constituted.

Wooden Mirror, then, shows how a user interface can be reflective in at least two senses of the word. It reflects the user on its "screen." Instead of looking through the interface to something beyond, the user sees only a coarse image of him or herself. In addition, it causes the user to reflect on the process by which the digital and the analog come together and on his or her relationship to the interface. Wooden Mirror foregrounds an aesthetic contrast that is common to a great deal of digital art: the contrast between transparency and reflectivity.

Transparency and Reflectivity

When designers set out to define an interface for a application, they do not imagine they are creating a mirror. On the contrary, they usually assume that the interface should serve as a transparent window, presenting the user with an information workspace without interference or distortion. They expect the user to focus on the task, not the interface itself. If the application is a word processor, for example, the user should be concentrating on the document she or he is writing, not on the menus and toolbars. If the application calls attention to itself or intrudes into the user's conscious consideration, this is usually considered a design flaw.

Donald Norman provided a good example of the assumption of transparency a few years ago in *The Invisible Computer* (1998), in which he argued that the future of digital technology belongs not to general-purpose computers, but rather to information appliances, each of which will perform one or a few specialized tasks. Although each of these appliances will contain processors and memory, Norman claims, we will not regard them as computers but as phones or electronic calendars or Web browsers—in other words, in terms of the services they enable. Norman made the analogy to the development of electric motors in the twentieth century. At that time, consumers bought a motor with attachments that made it a vacuum cleaner or a drill, but soon the motors were hidden inside appliances. Today, we have electric motors in many household appliances, but they have become invisible, as Norman argues the computer will.

In many circumstances, Norman is certainly right. We do want computers to become invisible in the machines and devices in which they are embedded as control mechanisms. We need to question the argument more closely, however, particularly as to whether the computer will be regarded as an appliance. Appliances are devices used for tasks that, as the term suggests, apply force or energy to change our environment. Toasters and electric drills are appliances. But would we ever call a book or a film an appliance? Over the past several decades, our culture has come to regard the computer as a medium or a set of media forms. A computer with a color graphic screen, a high-speed Internet connection, and stereo speakers now has more in common with a book or television set than with a toaster.

The computer has not always been regarded as a medium. The foundational work of Douglas Engelbart (the inventor, in the late 1960s, of the mouse and word processing), the creators of the ARPANET and later networks, and Alan Kay and his colleagues at Xerox PARC in the 1970s showed how computers could serve as a medium for communication and representation (Hiltzik 1999). Kay and Adele Goldberg explicitly characterized the computer as an expressive medium in a 1977 article: "although digital computers were originally designed to do arithmetic computation, the ability to simulate the details of any descriptive model, means that the computer, viewed as a medium itself, can be *all other media* if the embedding and viewing methods are sufficiently well provided" (Kay and Goldberg 1999). In Kay's vision of the Dynabook, the user would be able to create, edit, and store texts; to draw and paint; and even to compose and score music. The Xerox Star, the Apple Macintosh, and eventually the Windows PC have put the computer as medium into the hands of millions of users around the world.

Now, according to one powerful traditional view, the ideal medium is transparent; it should be a frictionless pipe for transmitting information to or from the user. Following this view, designers of computer media have attempted to make the interface transparent. This was the explicit goal of the graphical user interface (GUI) pioneered by Engelbart and PARC and improved and commodified by Apple. The GUI is supposed to be intuitive, easy to use, and consistent. With its "Human Interface Guidelines," Apple tried to guarantee the same simple and legible icons, menus, and dialogues functioning consistently across all applications, so they would intrude as little as possible into the user's conscious consideration. This consistency would enable the user to focus on the information task, not on the operating system or application interface (Apple Guidelines 1987). The GUI's aesthetic of transparency is represented by its most prominent information and design element, the window: the framed rectangles that present the user with textual or graphic information. The name "window" is significant, suggesting that the user should have an unimpeded and undistorted view of the information that lies "beyond" the interface. The computer screen, or portions of it, should function as the user's window onto a world of data.

The GUI has been the dominant interface now for more than a decade, and its aesthetic of transparency has shaped most interface design. Even some designers who say the GUI needs to be replaced (usually with a 3D interface) have justified the change by claiming the GUI, with its menus and dialogue boxes, is not transparent or natural enough. They want the user to jump through the computer window into a 3D world (Walker 1990). Thus, designer Meredith Bricken (1991), in her article "No Interface to Design," claimed that with Virtual Reality (VR) the interface itself could disappear.

This is not to say that all HCI researchers have the same notion of what constitutes transparency. In fact, the effort to define transparency has led to a fruitful discussion in the literature. For example, Bardram and Bertelsen (1995) argue that transparency cannot be defined simply as a "static feature of the interface" but rather it emerges through the user's active engagement with the interface (see also Bødker 1991). Although they may unpack the notion of transparency in various ways, researchers and interface designers nevertheless seldom question that transparency itself is the goal.

We argue, however, that transparency is an aesthetic value, a choice made by designers and artists in some cultures at certain historical moments. Our contemporary North American and European cultures inherited their version of transparency from the Renaissance. More immediately, the designers of the Apple Macintosh derived their commitment to the aesthetics of legibility and clarity from the tradition of modernist graphic design, which dominated our design schools in the mid-twentieth century (Meggs 1998).

But modernist graphic design is, itself, a late reflection of a notion of seeing (and therefore knowing) that is grounded in the Renaissance invention of linear perspective as an artistic technique for representing the visible world (Sturken and Cartwright 2001, pp. 111–15). Linear perspective made the painter's canvas a "window on to the world"—a metaphor explicitly stated by the fifteenth-century painter Leon Battista Alberti, who wrote: "On the surface on which I am going to paint, I draw a rectangle of whatever size I want, which I regard as an open window through which the subject to be painted is seen" (Alberti 1972, p. 55).

We can trace the principle of transparency from the fifteenth century to the present, through many changes in the history of painting and the introduction of new mechanical, chemical, and electronic technologies of reproduction such as photography and television. Transparency was never the only strategy of representation during the past six centuries, but it has usually been the dominant one. It was more than a way of seeing; it also underlay a scientific and rational (Cartesian) way of knowing as well, becoming an epistemology as well as an aesthetic principle (Sturken and Cartwright 2001, p. 115). The contemporary GUI window is the latest version of Alberti's window. The GUI window is also paradigmatic of aesthetic computing as we define it in this volume: the influence of a longstanding aesthetic principle on the practice and theory of computing.[2]

Reflectivity

Although transparency has been the dominant principle in Western art since the Renaissance, challenges have often come from transparency's opposite number, which we can call "reflectivity." Those challenges have been strong throughout the twentieth century, particularly in works of digital art (along with other forms of installation and performance art) toward the end of the century. If the window is the emblem of transparency aesthetics, the mirror is the obvious emblem for its counterpart. The principle of transparency conceives the canvas, the photographic paper, or the computer screen as offering an objective view of what lies "on the other side." In the aesthetics of reflectivity, the surface is a mirror in which the viewer is invited to reflect on her or his relationship to the work of art or the process and various physical and cultural contexts of production.

Reflectivity is a necessary counterpart to transparency. Even in a productivity tool or industrial application, both aesthetics have a place. (Jonas Löwgren, in this volume, also recognizes the importance of reflectivity, which he terms "parafunctionality"). There are times when the user wants to be immersed in the data and to forget the interface, and other times when the user needs to step back and look *at* the interface rather than through it. The need to step back becomes apparent when the application fails, or indeed whenever the interface provides the user with information that is totally unexpected. If an airline pilot suddenly gets an alarm indicating a possible engine fire, he or she must (at least briefly) consider whether the problem lies with the engine or with the alarm circuit or interface itself. At that moment the pilot must look at the interface and not assume it is a transparent window showing the condition of the engine. In less urgently serious situations, when we are using a desktop computer, we must often be aware of the interface to be sure it is not misleading us. For every application there is an appropriate rhythm between transparency and reflectivity, between looking through the interface to the information task and looking back at one's relationship to the interface. The interplay of transparency and reflectivity should be the major aesthetic and practical consideration in digital design.

When Norman argues that computers will disappear into information appliances, he ignores the fact that these "information appliances" are media forms, and our culture typically does not want its media forms to disappear. We have only to look around our media-saturated environment to see that computers and various digital media devices are not becoming transparent, but often remain stylish objects their owners are proud to display. Apple Computer, which pioneered the transparent design of the GUI, also realizes the value of reflective design. For the past several years, for example, its desktops and laptops have been highly visible design statements, with bright colors and retro-futuristic forms. Apple's iMacs and Powerbooks are meant to define the owner as someone who does not settle for a "drab" PC. When the iPod delivers MP3 music, it does so in a pocket-sized device that reflects its user's contemporary sense of style. Apple realized that the "interface" is not only what the user sees on the screen, but rather the whole package. The device is part of the user's physical world, and what the device does (the information it presents to the user for interaction) cannot meaningfully be separated from that world.

Even though successful designs such as the Apple line are reflective as well as transparent, our scientific and technical culture in general remains dominated by the aesthetic and epistemology of transparency. For that reason, the work of digital artists has focused on exploring reflectivity. Their radical experiments in interface design are meant to balance and to critique the dominant paradigm. Wooden Mirror is a one good example of a major trend in digital art. Throughout the SIGGRAPH 2000 Art Gallery were pieces that foregrounded the themes of reflectivity and process—pieces calling into question, often playfully, the assumptions of traditional UI design.

Some of the most memorable works reflected their viewers in various digital mirrors. Like Wooden Mirror, they took digital images of the viewer, which they then integrated into a composite or collage and presented to the user on projection screens. Two such examples were Text Rain by Camille Utterback and Romy Archituv (SIGGRAPH 2000, p. 78) and Nosce Te Ipsum by Tiffany Holmes (p. 47). Other pieces constructed elaborate interfaces that refused to be transparent. Entering the space of Kathleen Brandt's Exclusion Zone, for example, the user was presented with microscopic slides printed with text in miniature. To read Brandt's story, the user had to place each slide under a microscope and focus. This laborious interface compelled the user to imitate, and reflect on, the scientific process of a biologist examining a specimen (p. 34). T-Garden by the artistic collective Sponge (p. 71) and Biotica by Richard Brown (p. 35) were two highly interactive experiences in which users navigated a physical-virtual space using their entire body.

With these pieces, the users' interaction with the interface constituted the experience. The applications were all interface.

Today, digital artists are, of course, not alone in exploring the reflective interface. An important trend in computing is the research into various forms of mixed reality (MR), including ubiquitous computing, wearable computing, augmented reality, and systems in which computer-generated information is projected onto physical surfaces. (In one sense, most contemporary digital art could be said to be versions of MR, the deploying of virtual information in physical space.) It is true that some researchers in ubiquitous computing are still pursuing transparency by trying to embed computers into the environment so as to render them invisible to users. This was part of Mark Weiser's original conception of ubicomp (1991).

But more often, MR applications adopt a reflective interface. Although the user receives digital information overlaid on or blended into the physical environment, he or she can still distinguish the physical from the virtual. The user needs to make this distinction to exploit the fluidity and responsiveness of the virtual information. Furthermore, MR applications are often reflective in the sense that they situate applications in the user's physical and social world. They encourage the user to reflect on the contexts and often to interact with colleagues while using the interface.

Rhythm of Transparency and Reflectivity

We have described two aesthetics, transparency and reflectivity, and argued that digital art explores the latter. We must emphasize that transparency is not a bad aesthetic or design strategy. Problems arise only when transparency is regarded as the exclusive goal of interface design, because in such cases the design may ignore the need for the user to be critically aware of the interface itself. Digital art promotes such critical awareness, as do a range of new design strategies in MR.

We conclude by returning to the two approaches to aesthetic computing: what we called the code view and the interface view. In the code view, the aesthetic experience is abstracted from the application's purpose. Code is elegant because of the way it exploits the features of the coding language or other formal system: what the application does and its social and cultural contexts are not relevant. To appreciate the code, a programmer or knowledgeable user must therefore look past the interface to the code itself. In that sense, the code view of aesthetic computing is not concerned with reflectivity: the viewers or audience and their contexts are irrelevant to the aesthetics of code, except perhaps in the sense that tastes may vary from viewer to viewer. The principle of reflectivity belongs to the realm of interface design. As students of aesthetic computing, and as application designers, we must learn to value both aesthetics.

Jay David Bolter and Diane Gromala

Notes

1. For a further examination of the lessons that the digital art of SIGGRAPH 2000 offers to digital design, see our book entitled *Windows and Mirrors: Interaction Design, Digital Art, and the Myth of Transparency*. Cambridge, MA: MIT Press, 2003.

2. For a thorough and theoretically sophisticated study of the computer screen and its relationship to the film, photography, and other forms of Western representation, see Lev Manovich, *The Language of New Media*. Cambridge, MA: MIT Press, 2001.

References

Alberti, Leon Battista. 1972. *On Painting and on Sculpture: The Latin Texts of De Pictura and De Statua*. Cecil Grayson, trans. and ed. London: Phaidon.

Apple Human Interface Guidelines: The Apple Desktop Interface. 1987. Reading, MA: Addison-Wesley.

Badre, Albert N. 2002. *Shaping Web Usability: Interaction Design in Context*. Boston: Addison-Wesley.

Bardram, Jakob E., and Bertelsen, Olav W. 1995. "Supporting the Development of Transparent Interaction." In *Human-Computer Interaction*. 5th International Conference, EWHCI '95 Moscow, Russia, July 1995. Selected Papers. Blumenthal, Gornostaev, and Unger, eds. Berlin: Springer-Verlag (LNCS 1015).

Bødker, S. 1991. *Through the Interface: A Human Activity Approach to User Interface Design*. Hillsdale, NJ: Lawrence Erlbaum Assoc.

Bricken, Meredith. 1991. "No Interface to Design." In *Cyberspace, First Steps*. Michael Benedikt, ed. Pp. 363–82. Cambridge, MA: MIT Press.

Hiltzik, Michael. 1999. *Dealers of Lightning: Xerox PARC and the Dawn of the Computer Age*. New York: Harperbusiness.

Kay, Alan, and Goldberg, Adele. 1999. "Personal Dynamic Media." In *Computer Media and Communication: A Reader*. Paul Mayer, ed. Oxford: Oxford University Press.

Meggs, Philip B. 1998. *A History of Graphic Design*, 3rd ed. New York: John Wiley & Sons.

Norman, Donald. 1998. *The Invisible Computer: Why Good Products Can Fail, the Personal Computer Is So Complex, and Information Appliances Are the Solution.* Cambridge, MA: MIT Press.

SIGGRAPH 2000: Electronic Art and Animation Catalog. 2000. Computer Graphics Annual Conference Series. New York: Association for Computing Machinery.

Sturken, Marita, and Cartwright, Lisa. 2001. *Practices of Looking: An Introduction to Visual Culture.* New York: Oxford University Press.

Walker, John. 1990. "Through the Looking Glass." In *The Art of Human-Computer Interface Design.* Brenda Laurel, ed. Pp. 437–44. Reading, MA: Addison-Wesley.

Weiser, Mark. 1991. "The Computer for the 21st Century." *Scientific American* 265(3): 94–104.

20

Articulating the Use Qualities of Digital Designs

Jonas Löwgren

Use of digital artifacts is fundamentally aesthetic, in the sense that it entails emotional and affective dimensions. The work of shaping digital materials to create conditions for good use is known as interaction design. In the field of interaction design, we need to articulate knowledge concerning what good use is, including its aesthetic dimensions, and how properties of digital designs relate to it. I aim at illustrating such articulation by introducing a set of nineteen *use qualities*—properties of digital designs that are experienced in use and the designer can influence at design time. The concepts I introduce exist on a level of abstraction somewhere between the universal and the particular, and I propose that the notion of digital design genres be used to help us understand their respective scope.

First, it is necessary to ask what the use qualities I introduce here have to do with aesthetic computing. The short answer is that every experience of using a digital design involves aesthetics, albeit frequently located in the realm of boredom and frustration. There is room for developers of digital designs to work more consciously with the fact that their users are whole people rather than cognitive automata.

A slightly longer answer starts with the observation that the nature of computing has changed over the last 20 or 30 years. More important, the use of computing has evolved accordingly. This is obvious, but still deserves pointing out now and again. Whereas computers used to be tools for well-defined business tasks, most people now use them for general knowledge work, social communication, entertainment, recreation, shopping, and creative expression. A crucial difference between then and now is that most use is discretionary. People choose to use a digital service or product if they want to; otherwise not. It is clear that the conditions for good use are no longer confined to efficient and error-free performance of tasks with set goals, but rather hinge on emotional and affective qualities of the use experience.

Interaction design is about shaping the digital materials to create conditions for good use. The knowledge needed to do a competent job, however, is hard to come by. Learning the conditions for good use, understanding the relations between design choices and resulting use, is still largely a matter of practice and apprenticeship. If design is viewed in the larger context of knowledge construction, it is evident that the articulation and dissemination of interaction design knowledge is a priority.

The approach introduced here is an attempt to collect and articulate knowledge of the "conditions for good use" in the form of *use qualities*. This refers to properties of digital designs that are experienced in use and the designer is in a position to influence at design time. Use qualities are not claimed to be completely general, but rather are typically related to a particular class or genre of digital designs. I introduce nineteen proposed use qualities, some abstracted from my own design work and some from other sources. The intention is to create a reasonably coherent statement for others to refute or elaborate in the ongoing knowledge construction process that is the theory of interaction design. Given the scope of the current volume, my main emphasis is on use qualities with strong aesthetic elements.

To illustrate what is meant by a use quality, consider the following example. In my own design work, I have been occupied at times with reasonably large sets of (somewhat) structured information. How could we imagine people drawing more value, benefit, and meaning from such information spaces? And what can I contribute as an interaction designer? A few examples are Sens-A-Patch and the post-hoc worknotes project (Löwgren 2001; Andersson et al. 2002; web-09).

As I developed concepts and prototypes, studied knowledge work in practice and the empirical research available around it, and explored the ideas of other designers working in the field, an abstraction—a certain use quality—started to emerge as highly relevant to good use. Following the Pliant research group (web-08), I call it the quality of *pliability*. A digital design, including the information it contains, is pliable if it feels to the user like a responsive material. Inquiry, exploration, and learning is a tight loop between senses, thought, and action. I make a move; the information, the material, shapes and responds; I notice something; I make another move; and so on.

Pliability is an example of a use quality that I propose as important for a certain class or genre of digital designs, namely, tools for managing reasonably large information sets (a field often referred to as information visualization). The point here is that the pliability concepts sits on a level of abstraction between the general and the particular; it has scope and relevance for a significant class of designs, yet it is specific enough to be of gen-

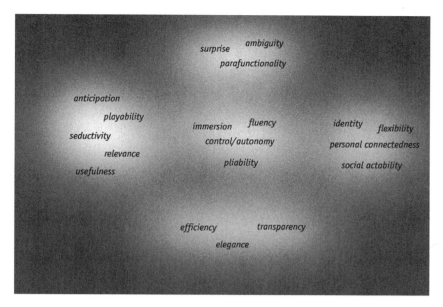

Figure 20.1 Nineteen proposed use qualities of digital designs.

erative value in a new design situation. I propose a number of use qualities on similar levels of abstraction and structure them loosely in a tentative map. The concluding discussion addresses the relevance and applicability of the approach, the issue of genre demarcation and the nature of the knowledge construction system surrounding interaction design.

Identifying Use Qualities of Digital Designs

In the following, I identify a few use qualities of digital designs that I find important and possibly fruitful. They are grouped together in five clusters as illustrated in figure 20.1. The map should be seen as a statement in an ongoing debate among designers, researchers, analysts, and critics on the conditions for good use of digital designs. Unfortunately, the debate itself is quite scattered throughout academic literature, the trade press, and the professional forums of interaction design. Part of my contribution, then, consists in pulling together and relating some of the threads to each other. This is in itself a statement on what I have chosen to include and omit, and what structure I have chosen. A small part of the map is based on my own firsthand design experience, primarily the notions of seductivity, pliability, and social actability. I also have a fairly solid background in mainstream HCI, which entails qualities such as relevance and usefulness, efficiency, and transparency. The rest of the concepts are drawn from publicly available material such as other designers' reflections, scientific use studies, and digital design critiques. I have invented some of the labels, whereas others come from the original sources. Löwgren and Stolterman (2004) include more details and elaborated examples.

Presenting each cluster separately, I discuss each proposed use quality in some detail. Emphasis is placed on the qualities that have significant aesthetic elements, in the sense that they concern emotional and affective use experiences. I then close with a more general discussion of my approach and its implications.

Qualities Having to Do with Motivation

Anticipation is a quality of use that has so far been connected mainly with dramatic structures and various forms of plot-driven interaction. Fujihata (2001) describes the interaction process as one of participation and imagination:

In an art of interactivity, one must be stimulated by interaction and enjoy having one's imagination activated. Interactivity is a stimulation of the power of imagination. By the power of imagination, one tries to see what will happen a few milliseconds ahead. This brings a future to the present. It is a bridge between a past and a future. Only interactivity can make such a jump, enabling us to escape from the chronological cage. I believe it is a real creation.

A game has high *playability* (or, as the trade press puts it, good gameplay) when the player says "Just one more time!" after game-over (Minter 1997). The notion of playability is quite elusive and obviously very attractive, given that computer games is one of the few areas in digital design in which the market "works" in the sense that consumer preferences have economic effects. What I mean is that computer games are assessed among players and reviewed in trade magazines. Their playability (in the sense used here) is a strong factor in the overall judgments players and critics form.

The literature on gaming suggests playability is connected to the balance of goals, resources, and obstacles in the game (see, e.g., Pearce 1997). If the player can acquire the resources needed to overcome the obstacles and reach the goals, but only after significant struggle, then the challenge is right to foster playability. A highly playable game should also not avoid risks. The playability of games based on character identification would presumably be less if there was no risk of failing. The struggle needed to reach the goals can certainly involve dying and starting over a few times.

I don't use the term goals in any ultimate sense. To the contrary, a highly playable game has a progression of goals with a new one introduced as the present one is reached. In adventure games, this progression is often connected with an unveiling or a new turn in the plot. Point-scoring games typically have the ever-progressing goal of beating the previous high score.

A related use quality is its *seductivity*. In the words of Khaslavsky and Shedroff (1999), seduction is a process of enticement (grabbing attention and making an emotional promise), relationship (making progress with small fulfillments and more promises, possibly ongoing for a long time), and fulfillment (fulfilling the final promises and ending the experience in a memorable and positive way).

Khaslavsky and Shedroff's example of a seductive digital design is the Visual Thesaurus by Plumb Design (web-10), a web application that adds new dimensions on the well-known contents of a traditional thesaurus by virtue of its interactive properties (see figure 20.2).

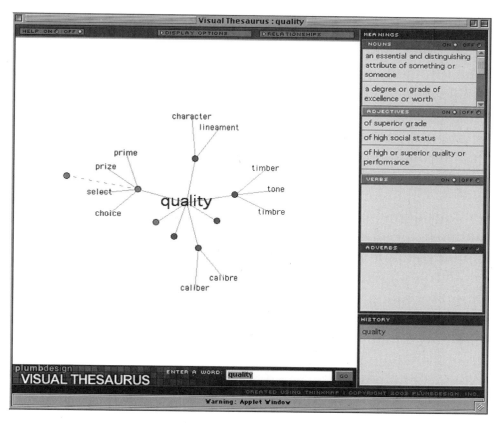

Figure 20.2   The Visual Thesaurus, visually redesigned in 2003, conceptually similar to the version analyzed by Khaslavsky and Shedroff.

- It delivers surprising novelty for most users.
- It goes beyond obvious needs and expectations. The traditional organization of a thesaurus is mainly an effect of the (paper) medium.
- It creates an emotional response due to its visual and interactional beauty.
- It connects to personal goals: the fascination of words and concepts (and, thus, mind and thought).
- It promises to fulfill those goals.
- It leads the casual viewer to discover deeper meanings of looking up a word: the multidimensional and dynamic relationships between concepts.

The heritage of work-oriented digital design has brought with it motivational use qualities such as *relevance* and *usefulness*. Something we call relevant, and even more what we call useful, always needs to be oriented to a purpose: useful for what? The traditional answer concerns work tasks. A system that offers the information and tools you need to perform a task is a useful and relevant system. The connections to modernist notions such as fitness for purpose should be obvious.

Though the concepts are typically used in reference to work tasks, the words in themselves do not preclude other applications. For instance, it seems quite sensible to talk about the relevance and usefulness of a web site dedicated to (hobby) fishing. But these and other purpose-related qualities certainly have some limits. As we move toward entertainment and aesthetic experiences, they seem to lose their significance. Is Tetris a relevant game? How useful is Osmose (see below)?

Qualities Concerning the Interaction in Itself and Surfaces Offered by Digital Artifacts for Handling and Perception

Digital media are increasingly infusing our environment, typically perceptible although not always demanding our attention. The growing peripheral presence of digital designs highlights the need for *fluency*. Use is not necessarily on or off, requiring full concentration or none at all. It is rather a fluent dance among multiple representations. Information streams move between center and periphery as we move through the shifting environments of everyday life and work. Transitions need to be graceful and nondisruptive.

As an example, consider Hazed Windows (web-05), a design concept presented by a group of interaction design students at the school of Arts and Communication in 2001. The topic of the project was Presence, and the group had concentrated on lightweight, peripheral social communication. The affective state they sought is somehow related to the thoughts of a child who draws a picture for grandmother without necessarily going through with the bigger commitment of actually talking her parents into mailing the drawing. The design is inspired by drawing in the mist on a window: you make marks on a digital surface that is connected to surfaces somewhere else (at the grandmother's house, for instance), and your marks show up on those other surfaces as well. The point is that the marks fade away gradually over time, disappearing completely after a few hours. This technically simple feature changes the whole communication situation, starting from a fresh set of assumptions regarding digital media, and creating conditions for fluent use.

The *autonomy* of a digital design has a strong influence on how it is handled and perceived. A strongly autonomous design, an agent, is an artifact that acts on its own in the world defined by the symbols accessible to it. It maintains its own goals, chooses its own means, and in some sense has a will of its own. To the user, an agent is an actor who can be more or less collaborative.

On the other end of the spectrum, purely nonautonomous designs are tool-like. The user wields the tool to process materials and refine them to work products. The tool is an extension of the hand or the eye; an instrument that facilitates or enables certain actions, strictly under user control.

The interesting parts of the spectrum are, of course, between the two extremes. Virtual spaces are increasingly being used as habitats for A life (artificial life) creatures where the user/visitor can affect the course of events to some extent. In some worlds, users construct their own creature and then return to learn how it has developed. An example is The bush soul by Rebecca Allen (web-03), and artists such as Christa Sommerer and Jane Prophet have presented similar works.

The genres of God-games and Sim-games can also be considered in terms of autonomy. An overall epic or a world simulation runs autonomously over a long-term time scale, whereas the player modifies local conditions and hopefully the general development of the gameworld by her or his actions. Are such virtual spaces and games autonomous or not? Clearly, they occupy places somewhere between the pure agent and the pure tool.

Autonomy and fluency interact in an interesting way in the installation Riding the Net (Sommerer et al. 2001), illustrated in figure 20.3. The idea is that a system captures and analyzes an ongoing face-to-face conversation. The system recognizes a word in the conversation, sends a request for a web image search based on the word, and then presents the returned images floating across a large display placed peripherally to the conversation participants. If the participants do nothing, the images simply float by and disappear. However, if a particular image catches a participant's eye, she or he can reach out and touch the display to hold the image still for a while. One may easily imagine providing a more detailed view and richer information, perhaps spawning a more focused search by, for example, a tap on the held image.

Figure 20.3   Riding the Net.

Apart from being an installation of digital art, Riding the Net can be seen as a concept for less intrusive collaboration support. In that perspective, the relative autonomy of the system in selecting search criteria and floating the images past the participants is significantly higher than for most collaboration support systems coming out of CSCW and HCI traditions. Riding the Net thus becomes more peripheral in a context of collaboration, and perhaps appropriately so.

At the focus of our attention, handling and perception can become *immersive*. Digital design offers possibilities for quasi-physical immersion by means of virtual reality technologies. The idea is to fill our sensory organs as much as possible with the "virtual world" and the canonical example is, of course, Osmose by Char Davies (web-07). In addition to visual and auditory immersion (see figure 20.4), the most powerful immersive effect in Osmose comes from exploiting our kinesthetic sense of body and motion. Moving around in the Osmose world is accomplished not by making contrived gestures with datagloves, but rather by breathing in and out and shifting your body weight. Technically speaking, a sensor around the chest is connected to your height above ground in the virtual world. You are standing on sensors connected to speed and direction of travel. The experience of navigating through the profoundly bodily function of breathing, however, is not reducible to simple technical understandings.

As we all know, immersion does not require expensive equipment for sensory surround-stimulation. Another kind of immersion comes from engaging so deeply in the task at

Figure 20.4 The oak tree by the pond in the Osmose world.

hand that the world around it ceases to exist. In terms of digital use experiences, it occurs sometimes when writing, drawing, or surfing the web. A slightly more passive but very real form of immersion comes from participating in or being told a captivating story. But perhaps the most immersive activity in the digital realm is programming, in which complex structures are built in the delicate balance between the programming language constructs and the limits of the programmer's mental capacity. Alex McLean's statement (web-04) should be familiar to many programmers, although the specific visualizations may differ widely:

Consider this mailing list post, part of a discussion about the "feel" of computer languages.

"I've always pictured programming as a dance of sorts, very slow and each gesture receives a great deal of attention, so that a limb or a step would not stray from a particular path. Loops look like pirouettes to me, I/O feels like delicate gestures with one's hands, no, just the fingertips drawing patterns in the air. Conditionals and cases are tumbles and jumps (into the air, that is). Arithmetic is kind of hazy, controlled slides with no traction (think 'slick moves'), things being pushed and brushed aside."

A program in execution is a program in motion. Control flows around the program, taking data with it. Data flows into the program, and is breathed out again. A hacker staring intently into her screen is probably turning somersaults in her mind.

A digital design and the information it contains is *pliable* to the user if it feels like a responsive material; a matter of inquiry that can be manipulated in an almost tactile sense; a highly involved process of exploration where the loop between senses, thought, and action is very tight and rapid. I make a move—the material shapes and responds—I notice something new—I make another move—and so on. Ahlberg and coworkers (1992) discuss a similar quality in relation to their design concept of dynamic queries, and call it tight coupling.

On a superficial level, I attempted to explore the notion of pliability in the design of the Sens-A-Patch (figure 20.5) interaction technique for navigation of moderately sized information spaces (Löwgren 2001). It is based on the idea of spatial constancy—information elements stay in the same place on the navigation surface through a session and across sessions. To fit many elements onto a small surface, the presentation is based on overlapping clusters, one of which is active at a time and the rest are visually faded into the back-

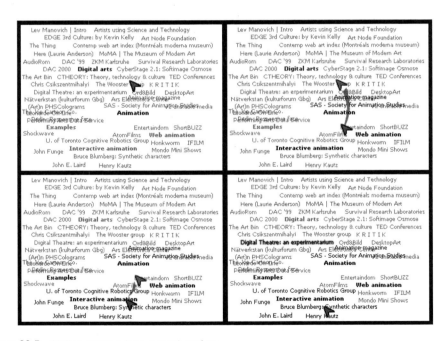

Figure 20.5 Sliding across a Sens-A-Patch surface.

ground (but still legible). The user experience indeed seems to create a certain amount of involvement, at least visual interest. In one case when Sens-A-Patch was used to present all the contents of a web site, users were observed to stay on the contents page longer than their information demands required, to play with the sensation of navigating the surface.

As we move beyond the surface, pliability as opposed to rigidity is a possible direction in many fields of administrative data processing (Henderson and Harris 2000; web-08). It is often the case that the use is unnecessarily constrained and structured merely because of the underlying database structures used for implementation. It is quite feasible to work in the direction of more free-form data, basing disambiguation and other technical needs instead on social mechanisms. A simple example is the rediscovery of the margins of paper forms, where annotations can be made and tied to the appropriate context (the form itself) for future interpretation. Most existing databases could easily be augmented with free-form fields similar to the margin.

Qualities Related to Actions and Their Outcomes on Social Levels

Constructing and maintaining *identity* is central in the use of digital designs, which possess symbolic use qualities like any other designed objects. The culture recently growing up around skins for accessory desktop applications demonstrates our common desire to project just the right image. Translucent covers in vaguely organic shapes have been fitted onto all available computing peripherals since the groundbreaking introduction of the iMac in 1998.

But the construction of identity runs deeper than merely picking the right skin (whether made of pixels or plastic). The software of Kai Krause and colleagues at Meta-Creations in the 1990s, the best-known examples perhaps being Kai's Power Tools and Bryce, were mostly discussed in terms of their innovative interfaces. However, the technical functions offered by the software were far more important (albeit perhaps less noticeable). Fairly sophisticated image manipulation, 3D modeling, and high-quality rendering were made accessible to a general audience and their desktop computers for the first time. The software focused on visual results, hiding much of the complexity behind a layer of skillfully designed abstraction. Users with no training or innate talent in the visual arts could produce stunning results quickly and with little effort—a significant contribution to the ongoing project of reconstructing your image of yourself.

There is a tendency, not the least among designers, to think of digital designs as something that is finalized in a development process and then deployed among the user community in its final shape. Many times this is adequate and not at all strange, given the heritage of mass-production and specialization of the industrial age. But at the same time, it is a case of underusing the potentials of the digital material. The use quality of *flexibility* is becoming increasingly relevant and deserves some consideration.

The canonical example here is, of course, the spreadsheet. Microsoft Excel and similar applications might seem like straightforward business tools for financial calculation, but in fact they are highly sophisticated programming environments. The programming paradigm is quite different from what is normally thought of as programming languages, and it is apparently easy for people without training in programming to learn and use. Millions of people are doing systems development every day when they construct Excel documents with calculation formulas, for personal use or for the use of colleagues in the group or department. Most of these system developers do not have formal training in systems development; many of the systems they develop continue to grow and evolve locally as the business needs change.

An increasing demand for flexibility can also be seen in the hacker communities and their public outlets in the form of open source projects, where design and use are closely linked in a neverending development process. The basic rules are that you are free to use any program you can find. If you don't like it, you don't file complaints. Instead, you modify it according to your needs and give your modifications back to the community. This aesthetic culture of freely sharing work and building on the work of others can be found not only among programmers but also in music, web design, and the digital arts, for example. The idea of extending it to mainstream application domains other than spreadsheet calculation is clearly appealing.

Personal connectedness is the quality of getting in touch, being in touch, and staying in touch in a personally meaningful way. Note the difference from technical connectivity or availability, which is rather about connections as such, with little regard for who is connecting to whom and why.

The most obvious example for a Scandinavian writer is the use among teenagers of the mobile phone Short Message Service (SMS). In spite of heavy limitations (messages no longer than 160 characters) and a text-entry interface that would never have passed the most elementary usability tests, the number of SMS messages sent in Scandinavia still outnumbers the number of placed calls by at least an order of magnitude. "Texting," as the SMS communication practice is known, serves many teenagers as the main vehicle for upholding connectedness throughout the day by means of frequent, brief, and often cryptic messages. An interesting variation is the Italian "drin" or "squillo," which lets you place a call, let it ring once, and then hang up. The receiver is aware of the protocol and never answers the first ring. Your call shows up on her phone as a missed call, the equivalent of sending a gentle thought without having to pay the fee typically associated with an SMS message.

These examples show how a rather crude communication technology can be appropriated for more subtle means of staying in touch. Interaction design research offers numerous examples of dedicated concepts for connectedness in an increasingly wired, wireless world. A seminal piece in the field of emotional communication is the Feather by Strong and Gaver (1996), in which a traveler sends a thought to the ones at home by lifting up an object similar to a picture frame. The transmission is visualized at home by a fan blowing a feather in a sculptural transparent tube. For the geographically distributed work context, early work in media spaces at Xerox Parc has inspired many experiments in the area of video- and audio-mediated connectedness.

The extent to which a digital design empowers you to act is called *(social) actability*. We may think of it as a space of possible courses of action, shaped by many factors including the digital tools and media involved. Classic examples include the ATM, redefining the bank in everyday life, and the possible uses of anonymous conference boards for open-hearted discussions as well as for vicious personal attacks.

In fiction and narrative settings, the corresponding use quality is typically called agency: the power to take actions that have effects in the dramatic universe (Murray 1997). A slightly more elaborate example is Avatopia (Gislén and Löwgren 2002; web-02), a recent attempt to create a forum for nonviolent societal action among young teenagers in Sweden. Our design work was driven mainly by the goal of creating adequate conditions for societal action. In other words, it was an example of design for social actability. Many important design decisions can be traced to this goal. For instance, broad visibility and credibility is needed for an impact on the public opinion, hence the forum consists of an avatar world (refer to figure 20.6) in close interplay with a short daily magazine on national public-service TV. The tools for action need to fit the medium of mass dissemination, hence the avatar world contains a rather innovative tool for collaborative creation of broadcast-quality animated film. Moreover, it was deemed necessary to have a set of community norms for societal action in place, socially speaking, at the time of public launch. Hence, a group of some thirty teenagers participated in the social and functional design of Avatopia, moving on to become a pioneer community and mentors for newcomers.

Qualities Mediating Structural Qualities to Engineering Ideals Reflected in Use Qualities

The *efficiency* of using a digital design is typically connected to performing tasks with external purposes. Efficient use is rapid and error-free. The interface stands between the users and their tasks; ideally, the interface is *transparent*, so that the required operations can be carried out without distractions. The field known as human-computer interaction (HCI) is mainly oriented toward improving the efficiency of computer-supported tasks.

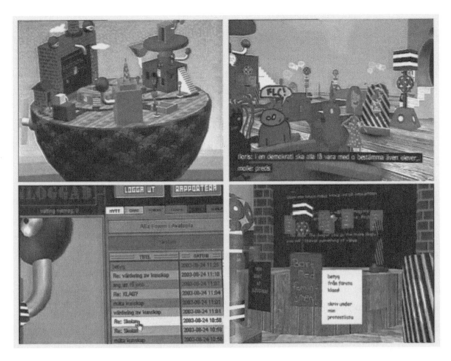

Figure 20.6 Snapshots from the Avatopia avatar world.

The *(technical) elegance* of a digital design is a combination of power and simplicity (Gelerntner 1998). As a general aesthetic principle for engineering, an artifact should perform as well as possible with as simple a construction as possible. For programming, this translates into creating elements (modules, objects, subroutines, programs) that compute rapidly in few lines of source code. Note that simplicity is not a simple concept—a highly efficient and compact program can be almost impossible to understand for all but a few experts, but still be considered an elegant piece of work.

The elegance = power + simplicity formula is often translated to the realm of use qualities, more or less consciously. The idea of functional minimalism can be seen as a reaction to the exploding number of features in many mainstream applications: provide tools that do their core functions well and nothing else. Shedroff (2001) presents the example of the Black Berry, a wireless PDA strictly limited to the functions of paging, e-mail, notepad, and personal organizer.

When the concept of Magic Lenses was introduced by Xerox Parc in 1993 (web-06), the combination of power and simplicity made the idea resonate with many people. A

Magic Lens is basically a semitransparent desktop tool that you can move over objects in a visual interface to get "behind the surface" of those objects. The first demos showed lenses that presented properties of graphics objects and made them available for editing; the concept has since been applied to various information visualization tasks. The power of the Magic Lens is in the generality of the concept and its ability to see all the way into the heart of the interface objects; the simplicity is its immediately recognizable operation.

Qualities Related to User's Meaning-Making in Relation to a Digital Design

Ambiguity is generally considered detrimental in HCI, and it certainly stands in opposition to the concepts of efficiency and transparency as they are commonly interpreted. However, as Gaver and colleagues (2003) argue, ambiguity can also be understood as a resource for encouraging close personal engagement with digital designs.

Gaver and coworkers identify three types of ambiguity—information, context, and relation ambiguity—and show how they are all used to good effect in digital arts and design. One of their examples, Desert Rain, is a mixed-reality installation on the subject of virtual warfare and the blurring of the boundaries between real and virtual worlds. The intention is to provoke participants to reexamine the boundaries between reality and fiction. To this end, the boundaries are deliberately ambiguous in the way they mix elements of theater, installation, and computer game; the content is a mix of 3D gamelike graphics and video clips describing real people's experiences of the Gulf War; rain curtains are used for projection, providing a continually shifting and blurred view of the virtual world.

Ambiguity makes easy interpretation impossible by creating situations in which people are forced to participate to make meaning of what they experience. The ambiguous design sets the scene for meaning-making but does not prescribe the interpretation. The task of making the ambiguous situation comprehensible befalls the human actor, which may lead to inherent pleasure as well as deeper conceptual appropriation of the design.

When you use a digital design, it is *surprising* if it challenges your assumptions. Auto-Illustrator by Adrian Ward (web-01) presents itself as a prototypical member of the productivity tool class, a vector drawing program that looks a lot like Adobe Illustrator and even has a similar name. Once you start using it for drawing, however, you are constantly surprised (refer to figure 20.7). The tools in the palette are not quite like the draftsman's tools you expect, but more playful and (perhaps) somewhat threatening. For example, there is a setting that distorts your shapes in such a way that when you try to draw a square it comes out as a children's drawing of a house. The color palette reacts to your choice of color by calling you a sissy and suggesting a really strong color instead. Little creatures called bugs walk around your drawing surface on their own, leaving trails of ink. Your assumptions with respect to the program's autonomy, its toolness, are challenged.

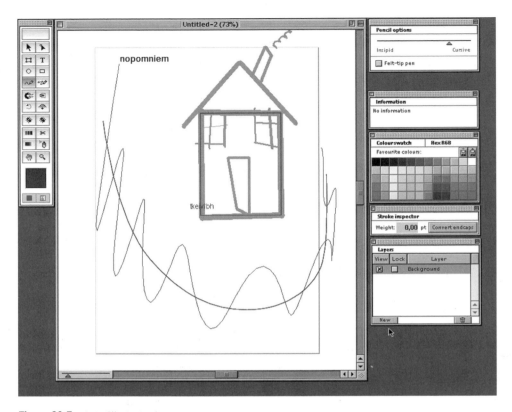

Figure 20.7 Auto-Illustrator in use.

Dunne (1999, p. 44) defines *parafunctionality* as a form of design in which function encourages reflection on our relation to technology, or "how electronic products condition our behavior." Using a parafunctional object creates a heightened sense of distance, mainly because it is conceptually difficult to assimilate into your view of reality. To acknowledge its usability is hence also to discover new ways of seeing (parts of) the world. It should be noted that some parafunctional designs cannot be (safely) used, such as the Intolerable Object by Philippe Ramette, whose lens focuses sunlight onto the top of your head. Modeling a use scenario in your mind is, in many cases, enough to achieve the estrangement motivating the parafunctional design.

An example of parafunctionality in digital design, striking in its simplicity, is the Jeff Kipnis's ATM competition proposal (cited in Dunne 1999): "People like to play lotto and people like to use the ATM. Why don't you make it an option in the ATM to say put your card in and say, I'll bet a little bit and see if I can get a little more out, so you ask for twenty dollars, and you push the button, and you could get twenty-five or you could get fifteen." I would expect that most readers have never before thought about combining lottery and the ATM, but once the idea is introduced, it gives rise to all kinds of thoughts, from ATM use to the role of money in society and everyday life.

Surprise and parafunctionality both have to do with distancing. As the preceding examples indicate, this is a design strategy found mainly in critical art, although there is the occasional attempt to use distancing qualities analytically to also understand work-oriented use. One example is Holmlid's (2002) discussion of surprise and confusion as a complementary pair of aspects found in professional IT use.

Conclusion

The presentation in this chapter aims to illustrate articulation of knowledge about good use of digital designs, specifically the aesthetic elements of good use appearing in various genres of digital designs. What, then, is the relevance of the approach I propose in interaction design: the shaping of digital materials to create conditions for good use? I claim there is at least three areas of potential: supporting upstream design work, facilitating communication with clients and other stakeholders, and structuring statements in the ongoing process of knowledge construction.

First, *a vocabulary of use qualities can be helpful to practicing designers in early phases of a development process.* In the initial contacts with a design situation, not very much is fixed and any road forward might be equally fruitful (or fruitless). If one or a few desirable use qualities can be identified, roughly on the level of abstraction illustrated here, the design process will more easily develop a sense of direction. As work proceeds through conceptual to more detailed phases, the desirable qualities can be gradually refined into more specific goals.

From an HCI point of view, the approach I hint at is a possible answer to the commonly observed shortcoming of usability engineering: that it is impossible in most cases to specify measurable usability goals as early in the development process as the typical methodologies would have it. Similar ideas of starting with more abstract goals, then gradually refining them into a usability specification, have been advanced. An example is the notion of user experience goals suggested in the recent textbook by Preece and others (2002). This work can be seen as a clarification and elaboration of such HCI notions.

The second area of potential is in *clarifying communication between designers and other stakeholders,* primarily the clients. Different techniques have been developed in the design disciplines to deal with this notoriously difficult area, including the graphic-design practice of collecting and discussing visual examples sharing a "tone" we also want to reach in the project at hand. Similarly, desirable use qualities can be communicated and clarified through examples early in a digital design process. My arguments here hint at a possible way of structuring such communication.

Finally, I claim that the articulation of use qualities is a potentially valuable approach *to the construction of actable interaction design knowledge.* This statement requires some substantiation.

My basic assumption is that research and, more generally, knowledge construction is a discursive rather than an additive process. Maps such as the one I presented here always carry a sense of finality, as though they were the last word on the subject. However, I want to strongly emphasize the tentative nature of the work. It should be seen as a statement in an ongoing debate, the goal of which is not to win the argument but rather the debate itself; to modify my proposal, question my choices and structures, and add new concepts is to contribute to the development of an amorphous body of knowledge that facilitates interaction design and supports better use of digital designs. Important actors in such a debate are designers and critics as well as researchers. These groups traditionally contribute through different forms of expression (artifacts, essays, scientific studies, and so on). Articulation work is essential in creating the necessary conditions for communication and growth of interpersonal knowledge.

A feature of the use qualities I propose here is that they are applicable to new design situations beyond the examples used to illustrate them, still not uncritically generalized. In fact, this feature points toward another important aspect of the knowledge construction of interaction design, namely, the notion of *genres*. In media theory, a genre is a category of "texts" socially co-constructed by producers and consumers that continually evolves and is distinguished by traits such as use expectations, narrative structure, format, and typical elements. Interaction design already has a fairly clear awareness of genres, albeit mostly implicit and manifested only in practice. For instance, a designer of productivity applications does not typically get commissions to work on broad-market game projects; a web user visiting a government site does not expect to buy music; and so on.

Use qualities may be part of what constitutes an interaction design genre. An example is Hult's (2003) work on digital encyclopaedias. Based on design work and empirical and analytical studies, he outlines the digital encyclopaedia genre by means of examples, use-oriented accounts, and a set of use qualities that he finds central for the genre. Among the fourteen qualities proposed are currency, authority, reliability, integration, and comprehensiveness. None of the qualities are unique in themselves, but their particular combination goes a long way in delineating digital encyclopaedias as a possible genre of digital designs.

To summarize, I view interaction design as a field in which there is potential for a knowledge-constructing design culture to evolve. Such a design culture requires the participation of designers, critics, and researchers in the ongoing construction and reconstruction of interpersonal design knowledge. Articulating use qualities of digital designs may be a step in that direction, provided the aesthetic dimensions of good use are also recognized outside the rather exclusive field of digital arts.

Acknowledgments

I am deeply indebted to my students and colleagues at the School of Arts and Communication for participating in our ongoing efforts to construct fruitful articulations of the qualities of digital designs. Olav Bertelsen, Jay Bolter, and Noam Tractinsky provided many valuable comments on an earlier draft of this chapter.

References

Ahlberg, Cristopher, Williamson, Craig, and Shneiderman, Ben. 1992. "Dynamic Queries for Information Exploration: An Implementation and Evaluation." In *Human Factors in Computing Systems (CHI '92 Proceedings)*. Pp. 619–26. New York: ACM Press.

Andersson, O., Cacciatore, E., Löwgren, J., and Lundin, T. 2002. "Post-hoc Worknotes: A Concept Demonstration of Video Content Management." *Proc. ACM Multimedia '02*. Video and short paper. New York: ACM Press.

Dunne, Anthony. 1999. *Hertzian Tales: Electronic Products, Aesthetic Experience and Critical Design*. London: Royal College of Art.

Fujihata, M. 2001. "Understanding the World." In *Cyberarts 2001*. H. Leopoldseder and C. Schopf, eds. Pp. 80–85. Vienna: Springer-Verlag.

Gaver, William, Beaver, Jacob, and Benford, Steve. 2003. "Ambiguity as a Resource for Design." In *Human Factors in Computing Systems (CHI '03 Proceedings)*. Pp. 233–40. New York: ACM Press.

Gelerntner, David. 1998. *Machine Beauty: Elegance and the Heart of Technology*. New York: Basic Books.

Gislén, Ylva, and Löwgren, Jonas. 2002. "Avatopia: Planning a Community for Non-violent Societal Action." *Digital Creativity* 13(1): 23–37.

Henderson, Austin, and Harris, Jed. 2000. "Beyond Formalism: The Art and Science of Designing Pliant Systems." In *Software Design and Usability*. K. Kaasgard, ed. Copenhagen: CBS Press.

Holmlid, Stefan. 2002. "Adapting Users: Towards a Theory of Use Quality." Linköping Studies in Science and Technology, dissertation no. 765. Linköping University, Sweden.

Hult, Lars. 2003. "Publika informationstjänster: En studie av den Internetbaserade encyklopedins bruksegenskaper." [Public information services.] Linköping Studies in Science and Technology, dissertation no. 785. Linköping University, Sweden. In Swedish.

Khaslavsky, Jane, and Shedroff, Nathan. 1999. "Understanding the Seductive Experience." *Communications of the ACM* 42(5): 45–9.

Löwgren, Jonas. 2001. "Sens-A-Patch: Interactive Visualization of Label Spaces." In *Proc. Fifth International Conference on Information Visualization (IV2001)*. E. Banissi et al., eds. Pp. 7–12. Los Alamitos, CA: IEEE Computer Society.

Löwgren, Jonas, and Stolterman, Erik. 2004. *Thoughtful Interaction Design: A Design Perspective on Information Technology*. Cambridge, MA: MIT Press.

Minter, Jerry. 1997. "Computer Gaming's New Worlds." *Computer Graphics* 31(1): 12–3.

Murray, Janet. 1997. *Hamlet on the Holodeck*. Cambridge, MA: MIT Press.

Pearce, Celia. 1997. *The Interactive Book*. Indianapolis: MacMillan.

Preece, Jenny, Rogers, Yvonne, and Sharp, Helen. 2002. *Interaction Design: Beyond Human-Computer Interaction*. New York: John Wiley & Sons.

Shedroff, Nathan. 2001. *Experience Design 1*. Indianapolis: New Rider.

Sommerer, Christa, Mignonneau, Laurent, and Lopez-Gulliver, Robert. 2001. "Riding the Net." *Proc. SIGGRAPH 2001 Conf. Abstracts and Applications*. P. 133. New York: ACM Press.

Strong, Rob, and Gaver, William. 1996. "Feather, Scent and Shaker: Supporting Simple Intimacy." *Videos, Demos and Short Papers of ACM Conf. Computer-Supported Cooperative Work (CSCW '96)*. Pp. 29–30. New York: ACM Press.

Web-01. Auto-Illustrator, created by Adrian Ward. Available at www.auto-illustrator.com. Last accessed February 16, 2004.

Web-02. Avatopia. Work in progress, 2000–03. Available at www.animationenshus.eksjo.se/Avatopia. Last accessed October 31, 2003.

Web-03. The bush soul, created by Rebecca Allen in 1997. Available at emergence.design.ucla .edu. Last accessed February 16, 2004.

Web-04. Hacking sound in context, by Alex McLean. Available at www.generative.net/papers/ hacking/index.html. Last accessed February 16, 2004.

Web-05. Hazed windows, design concept by Trine Freiesleben, Miska Knapek, and Henrik Moberg in 2001. Available at webzone.k3.mah.se/kid01016/projekt_forskningstema.htm. Last accessed February 16, 2004.

Web-06. The MLI Project. Collection of papers on Magic Lenses by Eric Bier, Ken Fishkin, Ken Pier, and Maureen Stone. Available at www2.parc.com/istl/projects/MagicLenses. Last accessed February 16, 2004.

Web-07. Osmose, created by Char Davies in 1995. Available at www.cyberstage.org/archive/ cstage21/osmose21.html. Last accessed February 16, 2004.

Web-08. The Pliant research group. Available at www.pliant.org. Last accessed February 16, 2004.

Web-09. Post-hoc worknotes. Project introduction and concept demo in Swedish, full reports in English, created in 2001–02. Available at www.animationenshus.eksjo.se/phwn. Last accessed February 16, 2004.

Web-10. Visual thesaurus, by Plumb Design. Available at www.plumbdesign.com/thesaurus. Last accessed October 31, 2003.

21

Exploring Attributes of Skins as Potential Antecedents of Emotion in HCI

Noam Tractinsky and Dror Zmiri

The role of computers in society has evolved and grown significantly from their use by a handful of experts in the early days of computing to support well-defined organizational goals or complex scientific problem-solving. Today's computers serve much broader purposes and are operated by a large and diverse user population. This course of development increases the importance of studying the various aspects of human-computer interaction (HCI). Traditionally, the field of HCI has concerned mainly the efficiency of accomplishing users' tasks, by improving the motor or cognitive efficacy of the interaction. Consequently, the HCI academic community has neglected other aspects of the interaction (e.g., Muller et al. 1997). One such aspect is emotion (Cockton 2002).

Users strive for a more complete and satisfying interactive experience; an experience that not only achieves certain well-defined goals, but also involves the senses and generates affective responses (Bly et al. 1998). The growing demand for personalized user interfaces seems to spring from this quest (Blom and Monk 2003). The desire expressed by users to tailor their applications' appearance according to their tastes is epitomized by the proliferation of skins—alternative interfaces to commonly used applications—that allow users to change the appearances of their applications while preserving their functionality. By the year 2000, more than 50 million skins had been downloaded from the major skin sites (Koeppel 2000). While some argue that skins represent a superficial manifestation of variety seeking, others suggest the desire is much deeper: "People get attached to their computers. . . . By customizing something that's important to you, you make the world your own" (Ian Lyman, cited in Koeppel 2000). Koeppel suggests the need to personalize our immediate environment is existential. "When you put personalized imagery in a user interface, the user's relationship to the technology becomes emotional rather than cognitive" (Eric Gould Bear, quoted in Koeppel 2000).

Blom and Monk (2003) propose that personalization of information technology devices affects users cognitively, socially, and emotionally. Indeed, recent trends in PC-based application design indicate that "skinnability" has become a common feature in many types of personal computing applications. Applications ranging from operating systems to media players and from Web browsers to computer games allow users to alter their original appearance, to better control the look of their computing environment. Moreover, this look can be changed easily and frequently. Thus, the skinning phenomenon appears to serve as a fertile ground for research on emotion in HCI.

Interest in the role of emotion in the interaction between humans and their surroundings, including various designed artifacts has been on the rise in recent decades. Examples range from the environment at large (Porteous 1996) to urban planning (Nasar 1994) and buildings (Maass et al. 2000); from stores (Russell and Pratt 1980) to consumer products and designed objects in general (Desmet and Hekkert 2002; Norman 2004). In the organizational context, researchers have emphasized the importance of physical artifacts in generating emotional response (Rafaeli and Vilnai-Yavetz 2003). Similar interest appears to have grown significantly in the field of HCI as well (Brave and Nass 2003). Thus, a special issue of *Interacting with Computers* has dealt with "affective computing" both theoretically and experimentally (e.g., Picard and Klein 2002).

Based on recent theorizing on physical artifacts and emotions (e.g., Rafaeli and Vilnai-Yavetz 2003; Norman 2004), we suggest that interactive applications are evaluated by users on three distinct categories, which elicit emotion toward the application. We then report about an exploratory study that was conducted to assess the viability of this model for the field of HCI, in the context of users' use of skins to personalize PC-based entertainment applications.

Research Framework

Emotion is a relatively short-term reaction to a particular object or event that is relevant to an individual's needs, goals, or concerns. Emotions are considered a main cause of choice and action (Frijda 2000; Norman 2002). This has been demonstrated in a variety of contexts, including those that involve profit making and goal accomplishment (Zajonc and Markus 1982; Rafaeli and Vilnai-Yavetz 2003). Recently, the case has been made for the importance of emotion in HCI as well (Cockton 2002; Brave and Nass 2003). It has been argued that emotional responses often precede cognitive ones in human judgment, and might have a lasting effect despite contradictory cognitive evidence (Lindgaard and Dudek 2003).

Recent research into the potential effects of emotions generated by artifacts has yielded several theoretical frameworks. Norman (2002; 2004) suggests a three-level theory of human behavior that integrates affective and cognitive processes. In each level, the world is evaluated (affect) and interpreted (cognition). The lowest level processes take place at the reaction (or visceral) level, which surveys the environment and rapidly communicates affective signals to the higher levels. The routine (or behavioral) level is where most of our learned behavior takes place. Finally, the reflection level is where the highest-level processes occur. The important role of affect in human behavior is that our thoughts normally occur *after* the affective system has transmitted its information.

Desmet (2003) maintains that emotions arise when an individual appraises how a product can influence (positively or negatively) his or her interests. Desmet identifies five classes of product emotions—instrumental, social, aesthetic, surprise, and interest—that can explain the nature of product emotions (Desmet 2003). Rafaeli and Vilnai-Yavetz (2003) propose a model in which physical artifacts in organizations are evaluated according to three dimensions: instrumentality, aesthetics, and symbolism. These three dimensions, in turn, evoke various, not necessarily intended, emotions. The three dimensions in Rafaeli and Vilnai-Yavetz's framework are quite similar to the five dimensions proposed by Desmet, especially if we consider that novelty and interest are highly associated with aesthetics (e.g., Berlyne 1974a). There are also interesting parallels between the framework suggested by Norman and that of Rafaeli and Vilnai-Yavetz. Instrumentality considerations are most likely to take place at the routine level. Considerations of the artifact's symbolism are likely to occur at the reflective level. Aesthetic evaluations may take place on all three levels, but there are some hints that first aesthetic impressions are formed immediately at a low level and precede cognitive processes (e.g., Berlyne 1974b; Zajonc and Markus 1982; Norman 2002; 2004). Those first impressions may linger and correlate highly with later evaluations of interactive systems (Tractinsky, Shoval-Katz, and Ikar 2000; Tractinsky, Cokhavi, and Kirschenbaum 2004; Fernandes et al. 2003). Thus, to a large extent, aesthetics sets the tone for the rest of the interaction.

We suggest that applying Rafaeli and Vilnai-Yavetz's model to the HCI context can contribute to developing a more comprehensive theory of emotion in HCI. We will now discuss each of the proposed artifact dimensions in the context of HCI. Interestingly, one of these constructs, usability, is a HCI cornerstone that has not been generally associated with emotion (Haughe-Nilsen and Galer Flyte 2002). A second construct, aesthetics, is the subject of a new awakening area of research (e.g., Tractinsky et al. 2000; Hassenzahl 2004). The third construct, symbolism, has seldom been investigated in the mainstream HCI literature. We suggest that each of these constructs deserve attention in the context of HCI. While Rafaeli and Vilnai-Yavetz suggest processes by which usability, aesthetics and symbolism affect emotion, our empirical investigation has a more modest objective, because of its exploratory nature. Our goal is to establish that users of interactive applications indeed perceive these constructs and are able to distinguish among them, and that these three aspects are associated with general measures of the user experience.

Usability

Rafaeli and Vilnai-Yavetz (2003) view instrumentality as the extent to which the artifact contributes to the organizational functioning or to promoting organizational goals. They speculate that instrumental aspects of an artifact can elicit only negative emotions when instrumentality is lacking, but they do not promote positive emotion when instrumentality is adequate.

Adapted to the context of HCI, "instrumentality" fits Nielsen's (1993) concept of "usefulness," which is composed of the system's utility (i.e., the degree to which its functions can potentially advance users' goals) and its usability (i.e., the extent to which the system enables users to achieve those goals). While the field of HCI has mainly stayed away from dealing with the utility aspect of interactive applications, it has warmly embraced the aspect of usability. HCI researchers and practitioners have traditionally emphasized supporting users' goals in terms of objective performance criteria, such as error rate and time to complete a task (Butler 1996). Usable products smooth the human-computer interaction, making it efficient and effortless. This, in turn, can potentially enrich the users' experience and improve their satisfaction. Products lacking in usability often prevent users from accomplishing their goals, frustrate them, and induce negative affect. In accordance with Rafaeli and Vilnai-Yavetz's theory, Zhang and von Dran (2000) found that usability-related aspects of websites were strongly associated with "hygiene" factors (Herzberg 1966), which caused user dissatisfaction. In line with the traditional notions of HCI design, some suggest that the use of skins might hamper usability because of the nonstandard, ornamental (at times cryptic) interfaces (Koeppel 2000). For example, it may be difficult to locate certain controls on certain skins or understand how to operate the application. The overwhelming demand for skins suggests that even if this is the case, users are willing to trade off the loss in usability for gains in other aspects of the interactive experience.

Aesthetics

Aesthetics plays an important role in our lives. Social scientists have shown that people associate physical appearance with personality attributes (Dion, Berscheid, and Walster 1972). Researchers in the area of marketing and consumer behavior came to a similar conclusion, namely, that the aesthetic quality of a product influences consumers' attitudes toward the product. For example, Bloch (1995) claimed that the "physical form or design of a product is an unquestioned determinant of its marketplace success" (p. 16). Economists suggest that physical appearance affects people's earnings (Hamermesh and Biddle 1994). Natural and manmade landscapes have been linked to emotion through aesthetic perceptions (e.g., Porteous 1996; Nasar 1988). Contrary to the indirect effect of instrumentality on emotion, Rafaeli and Vilnai-Yavetz (2003) and Lindgaard and Dudek (2003) suggest aesthetics is directly linked to emotion through the immediate impact of the artifact on the senses. Similarly, Norman (2004) notes that appearance may have a visceral effect on emotion. Recently, growing evidence has started to emerge supporting the importance of aesthetics in HCI. This evidence encompasses both hardware and software issues. For example, Apple's iMac was heralded as the "aesthetic revolution in computing" (e.g., Postrel 2001). HCI researchers have also begun studying the role of aesthetics in interaction design—its effects on the users and its relation to users' perceptions of other system attributes, including the seemingly orthogonal usability dimension (e.g., Karvonen 2000; Tractinsky 1997; Tractinsky et al. 2000). Recently, it was found that aesthetics plays an important role in users' evaluations of websites (Schenkman and Jonsson 2000; van der Heijden 2003) and of skins for a PC-based entertainment system (Tractinsky and Lavie 2002; Hassenzahl 2004).

Symbolism

A symbol is a "powerful vehicle for conveying deep-rooted meanings" (Hirschheim and Newman 1991, p. 32) or associations, that might evoke either positive or negative, intended or unintended, emotional response (Rafaeli and Vilnai-Yavetz 2003). While symbolism may be associated with complex and elaborate messages, it can also be communicated by mundane such things as chairs and tables (Rafaeli and Vilnai-Yavetz 2003). As opposed to aesthetics per se, effective symbolism depends on a cognitive process in which the individual recognizes a denotative meaning (the content of the formal structure) and infers its connotative meaning. Thus, for architecture, style represents an important symbolic variable (Nasar 1994). Interface skinning may be conceived by users as an opportunity to convey various meanings or associations regarding, for example, themselves, their reference groups, and their perceived or aspired status. Moreover, by creating or acquiring skins or by altering common interfaces, we make them part of ourselves (c.f. Belk 1988; Blom and Monk 2003). Thus, good skins, like successful self-gifts represent the owner's identity (Schultz Kleine et al. 1995). The symbolic role of artifacts relates to Desmet's social class of product emotion (Desmet 2003) and to some of Hassenzahl's hedonic product attributes (Hassenzahl 2003). Desmet suggests that objects can be associated with user groups or institutions, which are the objects of social appraisal. According to Hassenzahl, people can express their selves through products, and products can represent events, relationships, or thoughts that are important to the individual. Similarly, Blom and Monk (2003) suggest that personalization reflects users' personal and group identity.

Method

Despite its prevalence, the skins phenomenon has gained very little attention from HCI researchers (Tractinsky and Lavie 2002). This may have to do in no small part with the strong association of the skins' phenomenon with affect—a neglected aspect of HCI. We believe that studying emotions in the context of how users apply and use skins can enrich our understanding of both skinning and emotion in HCI. Because of the relatively unexplored nature of these two subjects, our aim in this study is quite modest. We would like to explore the viability of Rafaeli and Vilnai-Yavetz's framework to the field of HCI by concentrating on users' evaluations and choice of a skin for a popular type of application. We would like to find out whether the three artifact dimensions Rafaeli and Vilnai-Yavetz identify are meaningful within the HCI context. For this purpose, we extend the experimental procedure reported by Tractinsky and Lavie (2002), as described in the following sections.

Participants

Sixty undergraduate students (35 male, 25 female, average age of 23) who did not have previous coursework in HCI participated in this study for course credit.

Procedure, Stimuli, and Tasks

The participants were presented with 12 skins for Microsoft's Media Player (MP) Version 7. Among the skins used for this study was the default MP interface. Eleven additional skins were downloaded from Microsoft's Windows Media site (http://windowsmedia.com/mg/skins.asp). We chose the skins arbitrarily for the purpose of this study. We did not evaluate a priori any of the skins' attributes or overall appeal. In the first experimental stage, the participants were instructed to experiment with the available skins and to select the two skins (except for the default interface) they liked the most. In the next stage, the participants performed at least three tasks with each of three MP interfaces: the two skins that they chose in the previous stage and the default interface. The tasks included changing the speaker's volume, adjusting the MP's equalizer setting, and playing an audio track. The participants were allowed to experiment with these three skins further. After working with each of the three skins, the participants answered a questionnaire regarding each skin's attributes, and described in their own words the reasons that brought them to select that specific skin. The questionnaire was composed of 15 items, as described in the following sections. After evaluating the three skins, the participants chose the skin they preferred and explained the reasons for their choice.

Measures

Two types of measures were used in this study. The first type consisted of statements regarding the application's properties. The participants responded on a 7-point agreement scale with 1 indicating strong disagreement with the statement and 7 indicating strong agreement. Four usability statements were adopted from Tractinsky and Lavie (2002), and four aesthetic measures were a subset of the study's aesthetic measures. Based on Lavie and Tractinsky (2004), who found that Internet users' distinguish between two aesthetic dimensions, we chose to concentrate on one of the dimensions, which refers to the expressive aspect of aesthetics, as opposed to the other dimension centering on orderliness. Because the latter aesthetic dimension is strongly correlated with usability perceptions of the application (Lavie and Tractinsky 2004), we decided to exclude it from this study to facilitate clearer distinction among the three aspects of the user interface. Five additional items for symbolism were constructed for this study based on the characterization of this construct by Rafaeli and Vilnai-Yavetz. In addition, we measured two items that captured general traits of the user experience: satisfaction and pleasance of experience. These variables are highly associated with emotion (e.g., Westbrook and Oliver 1991).

In addition to the variables measured by the closed-format items, the participants responses to the open-format questionnaire were coded into four possible categories: usability, aesthetics, symbolism, and an "other" category for responses that were not interpretable or did not fit any other categories. A measure of the number of reasons given for the choice of a skin was then calculated for each of the three skin aspects.

Experimental Results

Of the 12 available skins, 11 were chosen by at least one of the participants in the study. Twelve participants (20 percent) chose the default skin design as their most preferred skin, while the other 48 participants chose a nondefault skin. The fact that some 80 percent of the participants chose to deviate from the default interface is comparable to the results obtained by Tractinsky and Lavie (2002), and suggests users have a viable need to personalize their application. The selection of 11 skins highlights yet another facet of personalization—multiplicity of tastes and preferences.

The extent to which the various skin attributes played a role in the users' selections of a preferred skin can be inferred from figure 21.1. This figure juxtaposes the participants' mean ratings of the attributes of the default MP style (which all of the participants evaluated) against the mean ratings of attributes of the two alternative skins chosen by each

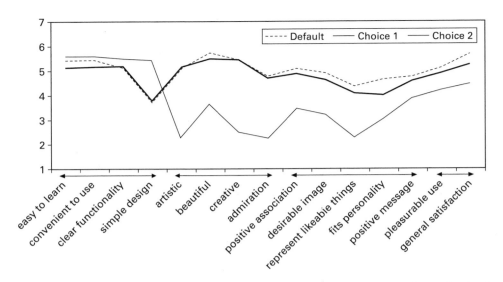

Figure 21.1 Average ratings of the default interface and the two preferred alternative skins on the closed-format items. From left to right, items represent three skin attributes (usability, aesthetics, and symbolism) and the overall user experience.

participant. (Recall that the specific chosen skins were not identical for all participants. Thus, in this analysis, "first choice" and "second choice" refer to the participants' ratings of the skin they chose first and second, respectively, regardless of which skins these actually were.) The attributes in figure 21.1 are organized from left to right according to the following categories: usability, aesthetics, symbolism, and overall experience. We conducted repeated measures ANOVA for differences between ratings of the default MP and the ratings of each of the alternative skins (as can clearly be seen in figure 21.1, ratings of the two alternative skins, "Choice 1" and "Choice 2," are nearly identical). There are statistically significant differences at the 0.001 level between the default design and each of the alternative skins for all of the items in figure 21.1 except for the three leftmost. Overall, the default style was slightly favored over the other skins in terms of the usability attributes. However, with the exception of the item regarding the skin's simple design, these differences were not statistically significant. On the other hand, significant differences existed between the default skin and the other two skins for all other attributes. These differences were most pronounced with respect to the aesthetics attributes. The alternative skins were significantly preferred in terms of specific aesthetic attributes such as creativity, originality, artistry, and impressiveness. At the same time, the alternative skins appear to have violated the Holy Grail of usability engineering: simple design. Yet 80

Table 21.1 Rotated factor matrix of responses to items reflecting usability, aesthetics, and symbolism

Items	Factor 1 Aesthetics	Factor 2 Symbolism	Factor 3 Usability
Artistic design	0.877	0.314	−0.036
Creative design	0.860	0.390	−0.031
Admirable design	0.819	0.445	−0.061
Beautiful design	0.727	0.462	0.129
Positive message about user	0.067	0.862	0.122
Communicates desirable image	0.433	0.828	0.069
Represents likeable things	0.525	0.757	0.020
Creates positive associations	0.319	0.747	0.282
Fits personality	0.423	0.743	0.113
Simple design	−0.747	−0.034	0.295
Convenient to use	−0.013	0.144	0.924
Easy to learn	−0.032	0.112	0.924
Clear functionality	−0.137	0.086	0.834

percent of our participants chose alternative skins, probably because these participants placed a premium on the aesthetic and the symbolic attributes of those skins.

Dimensionality of the Model

Our measures have to be assessed for two requirements. First, we need to demonstrate the reliability of the measurement scales of the various skin dimensions (i.e., aesthetics, usability, and symbolism). Second, we need to demonstrate the discriminant validity of the scales, that is, that each of the scales indeed measures a separate skin attribute.

To assess discriminant validity, the data gathered from the close-format items for the three skins (the two chosen alternatives and the default design) were subjected to principal component analysis.[1]

Three factors were extracted and rotated using the VARIMAX method (see table 21.1). Items belonging to each of the three dimensions explored in this study (usability, aesthetics, and symbolism) loaded consistently on their respective factor with one exception: the item concerning simple design, which was considered a priori a usability item, loaded (negatively) on the aesthetics factor. This item was not included in the composite variable scoring that ensued.

Based on the factor analysis results, composite scales were constructed for each of the three skin aspects. Table 21.2 presents scale reliabilities and interscale correlations. The

Table 21.2 Alpha reliabilities (on the diagonal) and intervariable correlations

	Usability	Aesthetics	Symbolism
Usability	(0.89)		
Aesthetics	0.03	(0.95)	
Symbolism	0.21*	0.72*	(0.92)
Number of Items	3	4	5

$*\, p < 0.01.$

Table 21.3 Results of regressing Satisfying Experience and Pleasant Experience on three skin attributes: usability, aesthetics, and symbolism

			Independent Variable		
Dependant Variable	R^2	Adj. R^2	Usability	Aesthetics	Symbolism
Satisfying Experience	0.68	0.68	0.56**	0.38**	0.23**
Pleasant Experience	0.59	0.58	0.43**	0.43**	0.22*

$*\, p < 0.01.$
$**\, p < 0.001.$

three scales exhibit high reliabilities. Also evident is a high correlation between the aesthetic and the symbolic aspects of the skin, perhaps reflecting an inevitable association between symbolism and aesthetics (Nasar 1994).

Table 21.3 shows the results of regression analyses with satisfying and pleasant experiences as dependent variables and usability, aesthetics, and symbolism as independent variables. Each of the three scales contributed significantly to the regression equations, eventually explaining 68 percent and 59 percent of the variance in satisfaction and pleasant experience, respectively.

Open-Format Responses

We examined the participants' responses to two free-form questions. The first was a general question, asking for the main considerations in choosing a PC-based entertainment system such as the MP. Overall, 151 statements were given by 57 participants (an average of 2.65 statements per person). The second question asked the participants why they chose their most preferred skin. In response to this question, 133 statements were supplied by 58 of the participants (an average of 2.29 statements per person). For both analyses, two independent judges (both PhD students) classified each statement as belonging to one

Table 21.4 Number (percentage) of reasons provided for the open-format questions, tabulated by aspect

	General Question (%)	Choice Question (%)
Usability	77 (57.4)	53 (45.3)
Aesthetics	19 (14.2)	46 (39.3)
Symbolism	19 (14.2)	6 (5.1)
Other	19 (14.2)	12 (10.3)
Overall	134 (100)	117 (100)

of four categories: usability, aesthetics, symbolism, and "other" (that is, either not interpretable or not belonging to any of the previous three categories). The agreement between the two judges, as measured by Cohen's *Kappa*, was considerably above chance level ($K = 0.815$ and 0.823 for the first and second questions, respectively). On reexamination of the disagreements between the two judges, it became clear that most of the disagreements stemmed from statements that were difficult to interpret. Therefore, we did not attempt to reconcile those differences. Consequently, the analyses hereby use only data for which the judges reached agreement (134 and 117 statements for the first and the second question, respectively).

For each of the two open questions, we tallied the number of reasons that were related to the design's usability (e.g., "clear functionality"), aesthetics (e.g., "attractive design"), and symbolism (e.g., "favorable image"). The results are presented in table 21.4. In response to the general question (i.e., the main considerations in choosing a PC-based entertainment system in general), 77 statements were usability-related, 19 were related to aesthetics, 19 to symbolism, and 19 categorized as belonging to none of the above categories. Regarding the reasons for choosing their most preferred skin, 53 statements were categorized as belonging to the usability dimension, 46 statements belonged to the aesthetic dimension, and 6 to the symbolism dimension.

Conclusion and Future Work

The purpose of this study was to assess the suitability to HCI of a model that considers three distinct properties of the artifact to study how it affects emotion. For this purpose, we have used both close- and open-format questions. In the context of selecting a skin to personalize one's PC-based entertainment application, the results indicate that all three aspects, namely, usability, aesthetics, and symbolism, can be semantically distinguished from each other and they all contribute to overall measures of the user experience related to emotion. The factor analysis and reliability results (tables 21.1 and 21.2, respectively) indicate that each of the three aspects can be captured and distinguished from each other. A notable exception is the loading pattern of the "simple design" item. This item, supposedly reflecting the usability dimension (Nielsen 1993), was not associated with the usability factor. Rather, it was loaded negatively on the aesthetics factor. Recall that we made conscious effort to distinguish between the usability and the aesthetic factors in this study. We accomplished this goal by concentrating on the expressive dimension of aesthetics because the dimension of aesthetics that deals with orderliness was found to be highly correlated with usability (Lavie and Tractinsky 2004). Yet, at least within the context of this study, simple design appears to be judged more in terms of its lack of creative aesthetics than in terms of its contribution to usability. That is, various design aspects can be consequential for both aesthetics and usability. Designers should therefore be aware of potential tradeoffs arising from this dependency. Given the innumerable contingencies that affect users' interactions with computers, however, there may be no better solution than to allow users to customize their interfaces in a way that optimizes contextual preferences.

Analysis of the closed-format items (see table 21.3) indicates that the three aspects of the skins accounted for a considerable portion of the variance in the overall measures of the user experience ($R^2 = 0.59$ and 0.68). The skins' usability had the strongest effect on overall satisfaction, followed by aesthetics and symbolism. The pleasantness of the interaction with the skin was affected equally by usability and aesthetics considerations, followed by the skin's symbolism.

The analysis of the open-format questions portrays a similar picture, in which all aspects of the model contribute to users' considerations. Usability aspects are considered paramount by far when in responses to the general question about the most important factors for choosing a PC-based entertainment system. However, when asked specifically about the reasons for choosing a preferred skin, users gave as many reasons relating to the aesthetics of the skin as to its usability.

Besides users' tendency to provide more aesthetic-, and symbolic-related reasons for choosing skins when actual choices are concerned, another interesting aspect of the results is the discrepancy between users' *answers* regarding which factors affect their preferences and their *actual* choice. While the open-ended responses indicate that usability, aesthetics, and symbolism affect choice in that order (table 21.4), analysis of users' choices (figure 21.1) indicates that they rated the alternative skins higher than the default skin on the aspects of aesthetic and symbolism but not usability. Since some 80 percent of the users eventually chose an alternative skin over the default, we tend to believe that their choices were based on aesthetic and symbolic considerations. These results are similar to those obtained by Tractinsky and Lavie (2002). One possible explanation for this is that there was no significant difference in users' estimation of the default skin's usability and the usability of alternative skins. Thus, the participants were able to choose a skin based on the second-, and third-most important aspects (namely, aesthetics and symbolism). Alternatively, users may have tried to provide rational (i.e., usability-related) justification for choices that were based on other grounds. For example, early aesthetic impressions may have subconsciously affected the choice of a skin (e.g., Bargh and Chartrand 1999). In any case, the disparity between users' explicit answers regarding the various aspects of the application and the implicit preferences revealed by their actual choice is intriguing and deserves attention in future research.

The results of this study, combined with those of Tractinsky and Lavie (2002), demonstrate the diversity of users' tastes. The results emphasize users' need to personalize their computing space, and the importance of this personalization for the overall user experience. It also brings attention to the possible discrepancy between what professionals or academicians consider "good design" and what users are looking for in their computing environment. The two may not always overlap: in other domains, lay evaluations of aesthetic objects were found to differ from those of experts and practitioners (e.g., Getzels and Csikszentmihalyi 1969; Hekkert and van Wieringen 1996). The presence of a skins "movement" ensures that, at least in terms of aesthetics and symbolism, users are no longer subjected to the tastes of a limited group of designers. As such, the movement represents many of the qualities of aesthetic computing (Fishwick 2003).

Limitations and Future Research

It is important to note the limitations of this study. First, the type of application being used here—an entertainment system used on a voluntary basis—stresses elements of aesthetics and symbolism. Thus, future research should examine users' reactions to other types of applications, to assess the generalizability of the three-aspect framework. Second, because of this study's experimental setting, users were exposed to only a limited set of possible skins. In the future, we intend to see whether an increased set of alternative skins might enhance the effect of symbolism and aesthetics on users' choices and their interactive experience. We suspect that, given a larger set of skins, users will be more likely to find a match for their tastes on the aesthetic and symbolic aspects. Third, while this study established the viability of the three aspects' model, we have not looked into the processes that relate these aspects to emotion. In addition, more refined views of usability, aesthetics, and symbolism can all enrich our understanding of the user experience. Thus, there is ample room for future research to build on this study's modest beginning. Finally, we have studied users' preferences given only a relatively short exposure to various skins. Future work should concentrate on how these preferences evolve over time.

Regardless of these limitations, this study demonstrates that the range of users' considerations and preferences when interacting with computers expands beyond the usable and the practical toward the aesthetic, the personal, and the affective. This is especially the case when we consider the emerging wave of personal, popular applications of the type examined in this study, and given the ease with which the computing environment can now be personalized. The "Aesthetic Computing Manifesto" (Fishwick 2003) lists the benefits of a cultural, personal, and customized set of aesthetics. This study provides evidence supporting the Manifesto's claims.

Note

1. Combining the results for all three skins may violate the assumption of independence of observations. We conducted similar factor analyses for each of the skins (i.e., the default skin and each user's first and second choice), and the results were very similar in all cases, and almost identical to those obtained by the combined dataset. In the interest of space, only the results of the combined dataset are presented here.

References

Bargh, J. A., and Chartrand, T. L. 1999. "The Unbearable Automaticity of Being." *American Psychologist* 54(7): 462–79.

Belk, R. W. 1988. "Possesions and the Extended Self." *Journal of Consumer Research* 15(2): 139–68.

Berlyne, D. E. 1974a. "Novelty, Complexity, and Interestingness." In *Studies in the New Experimental Aesthetics: Steps toward an Objective Psychology of Aesthetic Comparison*. D. E. Berlyne, ed. Washington, DC: Hemisphere.

———. 1974b. "The New Experimental Aesthetics." In *Studies in the New Experimental Aesthetics: Steps toward an Objective Psychology of Aesthetic Comparison*. D. E. Berlyne, ed. Washington, DC: Hemisphere.

Bloch, P. 1995. "Seeking the Ideal Form: Product Design and Consumer Response." *Journal of Marketing* 59: 16–29.

Blom, J. O., and Monk, A. F. 2003. "Theory of Personalization of Appearance: Why Users Personalize Their PCs and Mobile Phones." *Human-Computer Interaction* 18(3): 193–228.

Bly, S., Cook, L., Bickmore, T., et al. 1998. "The Rise of Personal Web Pages at Work." *Proceedings of the Conference on Human Factors in Computing Systems*. Los Angeles, CA, April 1998.

Brave, S., and Nass, C. 2003. "Emotion in Human-Computer Interaction." In *Handbook of Human-Computer Interaction*. J. Jacko and A. Sears, eds. Mahwah, NJ: Lawrence Erlbaum Associates.

Butler, K. A. 1996. "Usability Engineering Turns 10." *Interactions* 3(1): 59–75.

Cockton, G. 2002. "From Doing to Being: Bringing Emotion into Interaction." *Interacting with Computers* 14: 89–92.

Desmet, P. M. A. 2003. "A Multilayered Model of Product Emotions." *The Design Journal* 6(2): 4–13.

Desmet, P. M. A., and Hekkert, P. P. M. 2002. "The Basis of Product Emotions." In *Pleasure with Products: Beyond Usability*. W. S. Green and P. W. Jordan, eds. New York: Taylor and Francis.

Dion, K., Berscheid, E., and Walster, E. 1972. "What Is Beautiful Is Good." *Journal of Personality and Social Psychology* 24(3): 285–90.

Fernandes, G., Lindgaard, G., Dillon, R., and Wood, J. 2003. "Judging the Appeal of Web Sites." *Proceedings 4th World Congress on the Management of Electronic Commerce*. McMaster University, Hamilton, ON, 15–17 January, 2003.

Fishwick, Paul. 2003. "Aesthetic Computing Manifesto." *Leonardo* 36(4): 255–56.

Frijda, N. 2000. "Emotions." In *The International Handbook of Psychology*. K. Pawlik and M. R. Rosenzwieg, eds. Thousand Oaks, CA: Sage Publications.

Getzels, J. W., and Csikszentmihalyi, M. 1969. "Aesthetic Opinion: An Empirical Study." *Public Opinion Quarterly* 33(1): 34–45.

Hamermesh, D. S., and Biddle, J. E. 1994. "Beauty and the Labor Market." *The American Economic Review* 84(5): 1174–94.

Hassenzahl, M. 2003. "The Thing and I: Understanding the Relationship between User and Product." In *Funology: From Usability to Enjoyment*. M. Blythe, C. Overbeeke, A. F. Monk, and P. C. Wright, eds. Pp. 31–42. Dordrecht: Kluwer.

————. 2004. "The Interplay of Beauty, Goodness and Usability in Interactive Products." *Human-Computer Interaction* 19(4): 319–49.

Haughe-Nilsen, A. L., and Galer Flyte, M. 2002. "Understanding Attributes that Contribute to Pleasure in Product Use." In *Pleasure with Products: Beyond Usability*. W. S. Green and P. W. Jordan, eds. New York: Taylor and Francis.

Hekkert, P., and van Wieringen, P. C. W. 1996. "Beauty in the Eye of Expert and Nonexpert Beholders: A Study in Appraisal of Art." *American Journal of Psychology* 109(3): 389–407.

Hirschheim, R., and Newman, M. 1991. "Symbolism and Information Systems Development: Myth, Metaphor and Magic." *Information Systems Research* 2(1): 29–62.

Herzberg, F. 1966. *Work and the Nature of Man*. New York: World Publishing.

Karvonen, K. 2000. "The Beauty of Simplicity." In *Proceedings of the ACM Conference on Universal Usability*. Washington, DC. November 16–17, 2000.

Koeppel, D. 2000. "GUIs Just Want to Have Fun: The Faceless Interface Is Dead. Long Live Skins, the Hyper-Personal Edge of Desktop Computing." *Wired* [online]. Available at http://www.wired.com/wired/archive/8.10/skins.html. Cited August 10, 2000.

Lavie, T., and Tractinsky, N. 2004. "Assessing Dimensions of Perceived Visual Aesthetics of Web Sites." *International Journal of Human-Computer Studies* 60: 269–98.

Lindgaard, G., and Dudek, C. 2003. "What Is This Evasive Beast We Call User Satisfaction?" *Interacting with Computers* 15: 429–52.

Maass, A., Merici, I., Villafranca, E., et al. 2000. "Intimidating Buildings: Can Courthouse Architecture Affect Perceived Likelihood of Conviction?" *Environment and Behavior* 32(5): 674–83.

Muller, M. J., Wharton, C., McIver, W. J. Jr., and Laux, L. 1997. "Toward an HCI Research and Practice Agenda Based on Human Needs and Social Responsibility." In *Proceedings of the CHI '97*. Atlanta, GA. March 22–27, 1977. New York: ACM, pp. 155–61.

Nasar, J. L., ed. 1988. *Environmental Aesthetics: Theory, Research, and Applications*. New York: Cambridge University Press.

————. 1994. "Urban Design Aesthetics." *Environment and Behavior* 26(3): 377–401.

Nielsen, J. 1993. *Usability Engineering*. New York: Academic Press Professional.

Norman, D. A. 2002. "Emotion and Design: Attractive Things Work Better." *Interactions* 9(4): 36–42.

———. 2004. *Emotional Design: Why We Love (or Hate) Everyday Things*. New York: Basic Books.

Picard, R. W., and Klein, J. 2002. "Computers that Recognize and Respond to User Emotion: Theoretical and Practical Implications." *Interacting with Computers* 14: 141–69.

Porteous, J. D. 1996. *Environmental Aesthetics: Ideas, Politics and Planning*. London: Routledge.

Postrel, V. 2001. "Can Good Looks Really Guarantee a Product's Success?" *The New York Times*, July 12, Section C.

Rafaeli, A., and Vilnai-Yavetz, I. 2003. "Instrumentality, Aesthetics, and Symbolism of Physical Artifacts as Triggers of Emotion." *Theoretical Issues in Ergonomics Science (TIES). Special issue: Theories and Methods in Affective Human Factors Design* 5(1): 91–112.

Russell, J. A., and Pratt, G. A. 1980. "Description of the Affective Quality Attributed to Environments." *Journal of Personality and Social Psychology* 38(2): 311–22.

Schenkman, B. N., Jonsson, F. U. 2000. "Aesthetics and Preferences of Web Pages." *Behavior and Information Technology* 19(5): 367–77.

Schultz Kleine, S., Kleine, R. E., and Allen, C. T. 1995. "How Is a Possession 'Me' or 'Not Me'? Characterizing Types and an Antecedent of Material Possession Attachment." *Journal of Consumer Research* 22(3): 327–43.

Tractinsky, N. 1997. "Aesthetics and Apparent Usability: Empirically Assessing Cultural and Methodological Issues." In *Proceedings of the CHI '97*. Atlanta, GA, March 22–27, 1977. New York: ACM, pp. 115–22.

Tractinsky, N., Cokhavi, A., and Kirschenbaum, M. 2004. "Using Ratings and Response Latencies to Evaluate the Consistency of Immediate Aesthetic Perceptions of Web Pages." *Proceedings of the Third Annual Workshop on HCI Research in MIS*. Washington, DC, December 10–11, 2004.

Tractinsky, N., and Lavie, T. 2002. "Aesthetic and Usability Considerations in Users' Choice of Personal Media Players." *Proceedings Volume 2 of the 16th British HCI Conference*. London, September 2002, pp. 70–73.

Tractinsky, N., Shoval-Katz, A., and Ikar, D. 2000. "What Is Beautiful Is Usable." *Interacting with Computers* 13: 127–45.

van der Heijden, H. 2003. "Factors Influencing the Usage of Websites: The Case of a Generic Portal in the Netherlands." *Information and Management* 40: 541–49.

Westbrook, R. A., and Oliver, R. L. 1991. "The Dimensionality of Consumption Emotion Patterns and Consumer Satisfaction." *Journal of Consumer Research* 18(1): 84–91.

Zajonc, R. B., and Markus, H. 1982. "Affective and Cognitive Factors in Preferences." *Journal of Consumer Research* 9(2): 123–31.

Zhang, P., and von Dran, G. M. 2000. "Satisfiers and Dissatisfiers: A Two-Factor Model for Website Design and Evaluation." *Journal of the American Society for Information Science* 51(14): 1253–68.

About the Authors

James Alty received the PhD in Nuclear Physics at Liverpool University, and then worked with IBM(UK) Ltd for four years before becoming Director of the Computer Centre at Liverpool University. In 1982 he was appointed Professor of Computer Science at Strathclyde University, where he also was Executive Director of the Turing Institute in Glasgow. In 1990 he was appointed Professor of Computer Science at Loughborough University, where he was Head of Department and later Dean of Science. He is now an Emeritus Professor at Loughborough and also Professor of Human Computer Interaction at Middlesex University. Alty has published more than one hundred research papers and four books. He is also a composer of music, having had a number of works performed in public, and has carried out research into the use of music in human-computer interaction (HCI), for creating diagrams for the blind, using music in program debugging, and the sonification of algorithms.

Olav W. Bertelsen is an associate professor of human-computer interaction and systems development at the Department of Computer Science, University of Aarhus. He received his MSc in Computer Science and History of Ideas from the University of Aarhus, Denmark. After working on establishing the Danish National Centre for IT-research, he completed his PhD in informatics in 1998. He worked with the Danish Basic Research Foundation funded Centre for Human-Machine Interaction, and later joined the Department of Computer Science, University of Aarhus. Bertelsen has been teaching human-computer interaction at the interdisciplinary multimedia education center since 1998, and developed several courses in the intersection between human-computer interaction and digital aesthetics. His PhD thesis, "Elements of a Theory of Design Artifacts," was an attempt to give a systematic account, based on activity theory, on the tools, methods, techniques, and so on mediating the design of computer artifacts. Actual research interests include common information spaces; activity theory–based methods and techniques in human-computer interaction; and a reformation of human-computer interaction as an aesthetic discipline based in dialectical materialism.

Jay David Bolter is Co-Director of the New Media Center and Wesley Professor of New Media in the School of Literature, Communications, and Culture at the Georgia Institute of Technology. His work with computers led in 1984 to the publication of *Turing's Man: Western Culture in the Computer Age*, a book that was widely reviewed and translated into several foreign languages. Bolter's second book, *Writing Space: The Computer, Hypertext, and the History of Writing*, published in 1991, examines the computer as a new medium for symbolic communication. Together with Michael Joyce, Bolter is the author of Storyspace, a program for creating hypertexts for individual use and World Wide Web publication. Recent books include: *Remediation*, written in collaboration with Richard Grusin, which explores the ways in which new digital media, such as the World Wide Web and virtual reality, borrow from and seek to rival such earlier media as television, film, photography, and print; and *Windows and Mirrors, Interaction Design, Digital Art and the Myth of Transparency*, written in collaboration with Diane Gromala, which examine the impact of digital art on new media and computer interface design. Bolter is now working closely with Prof. Blair MacIntyre on the use of augmented reality to create new media experiences for informal education and entertainment.

Donna J. Cox is Professor in the School of Art and Design at the University of Illinois at Urbana-Champaign; and the Director for Visualization and Experimental Technologies at the National Center for Supercomputing Applications. Cox received the international Coler-Maxwell Award for Excellence granted by the Leonardo International Society in Arts Science and Technology for her seminal paper on "Renaissance Teams." Cox has written numerous publications on scientific and information visualization. She is an internationally recognized keynote speaker in countries including Australia, New Zealand, Brazil, Finland, Japan, and Switzerland. Inviting institutions include MIT, Kodak, Motorola, EDUCOM, T. J. Watson Research Center, and the National Library of Medicine. Her collaborative work has been cited, reviewed, or published in more than one hundred publications including *Newsweek*, *Time*, *National Geographic*, *Wall Street Journal*, *New York Times*, and *The Chronicle of Higher Education*. Cox has been featured in numerous television programs including "Good Morning America." She was Associate Producer for Scientific Visualization and Art Director for the PIXAR/NCSA segment of the IMAX movie, "Cosmic Voyage," nominated for 1997 Academy Award in documentary short subject category. Recent projects include two Hayden Planetarium digital space shows, at the American Museum of Natural History in New York City; The Discovery Channel's "Unfolding Universe"; and the NOVA HDTV "Runaway Universe," which received the 2002 Golden Camera Festival Award. She is juror on the NSF's Visualization Challenge and SIGGRAPH 2005 Emerging Technologies Chair. Cox is currently working on a PBS NOVA show and Denver Museum of Nature and Science Planetarium Show on Black Holes.

Mark d'Inverno is Professor and Director of the Centre for Agent Technology at the University of Westminster and has been one of the UK's leading researchers in the formal modeling of agent-based systems for the last ten years. He is best known for developing the SMART Agent Framework with Michael Luck using formal methods. Much of this research can be found in a book entitled *Understanding*

Agent Systems, which is now in its second edition. He has collaborated with a number of leading agent researchers such as Michael Luck, Michael Wooldridge, and Mike Georgeff and has published more than seventy papers in this area in the past ten years. In addition, he has co-authored a book published in 2004 on agent-based software development. He was one of the founding members of the UK's special interest group on MAS and was general co-chair of the fourth and fifth UK workshops (UKMAS 2000 and 2001), both supported by the EPSRC. He was the general co-chair of the *First European Conference on Multi-Agent Systems (EUMAS)* held at Oxford University in December 2001, which attracted more than 130 people. In addition, University of Westminster is a founding member of the EPSRC-funded project entitled AgentCities UK and is an original member of the European Network of Excellence for Agent-Based Computing (*AgentLink I, II, and III*). In the last year or so he has branched from his formal, theoretical work to more practical and cross-disciplinary projects such as a MAS approach to modeling stem cell behavior and using MAS techniques to build intelligent responsive *music installations*. Mark is also a well-established musician; his last album, entitled *Joy*, received widespread national acclaim.

Stephan Diehl   is a Professor for computer science at Catholic University Eichstätt. He studied computer science and computational linguistics at Saarland University, and is a Fulbright scholar at Worcester Polytechnic Institute, Massachusetts. He got his PhD from Saarland University as a scholar of the German Research Foundation (DFG) working in Prof. Reinhard Wilhelm's group. Stephan Diehl's research interests include programming languages and compiler design, web technologies, educational software and visualization, in particular software visualization.

Michele Emmer,   born in Milan on September 15, 1945, is full Professor of Mathematics at the University of Rome "La Sapienza," Dipartimento di Matematica, Piazzale A. Moro, Rome, Italy. He was previously Professor at the University of Ferrara, Trento, Viterbo, L'Aquila, Sassari, Venice, and Visiting Professor at Princeton, Paris Orsay, Campinas, Barcellona, and several Japanese universities. His areas of activity were PDE and minimal surfaces, computer graphics, mathematics and arts, mathematics and culture, and films and videos. He received in 1998 the Galileo award from the Italian Math Association for best popularization of Mathematics, and in 2004 the Pitagora award. He was President for three years of the Italian associations for scientific media, part of the European association Media in Science; member of the American Mathematical Society, of the American Association for Aesthetics, of the European Math Association, ISAMA, and ISAST; President of the electronic scientific journal *Galileo* (http://www.galileo.webzone.it); collaborator for the last twenty years on the cultural and scientific pages of the newspaper *L'Unità* and other magazines including *Diario, Telema, Sapere, Scientific American, Alliage*, and *FMR*; and a filmmaker. His series "Art and Math" has been broadcast on TV in Italy and many other countries. Emmer has organized several exhibitions and conferences on the topic of Art and Mathematics, including the annual conference on "Mathematics and Culture" at the University of Venice; the exhibitions and conferences on M. C. Escher (1985 and 1998) at the University of Rome; the section on Space at the Biennal of Venice (1986), the traveling exhibition "The Eye of Horus" (Roma, Bologna, Milano,

Parma, 1989); and the exhibition and congress on "Math & Art" in Bologna, 2000. He edited the series *Mathematics and Culture* (Springer Verlag), *The Visual Mind* (MIT Press), and the video series "Video Math" (Springer Verlag). He has been responsible for the math section of the Science Center in Naples and many other traveling exhibitions on math.

Paul A. Fishwick is Professor of Computer and Information Sciences and Engineering at the University of Florida. He received the BS in Mathematics from the Pennsylvania State University, MS in Applied Science from the College of William and Mary, and the PhD in Computer and Information Science from the University of Pennsylvania in 1986. He worked in industry, at Newport News Shipbuilding & Dry Dock Co. and NASA Langley Research Center doing computer-aided design for six years prior to his academic post. Fishwick is a Fellow of the Society for Modeling and Simulation International (SCSI), has given twelve international keynote addresses in modeling and simulation, and serves on numerous journal editorial boards, including ACM Transactions on Modeling and Simulation and the SCS Transactions on Modeling and Simulation. He has chaired or co-chaired five conferences, and served as General Chair of the 2000 Winter Simulation Conference (WSC). He has written more than 150 technical publications, including one textbook and six edited books. Fishwick co-chaired the *Aesthetic Computing* workshop in 2002 in Dagstuhl, Germany, along with his colleagues Roger Malina and Christa Sommerer. Fishwick's primary interests are in model representation, simulation, program visualization, and in the intersection between the arts and computing, especially as the arts can be applied to mathematics and computing, in reconsidering the role of aesthetics in these disciplines. His web page is at http://www.cise.ufl.edu/~fishwick.

Monika Fleischmann is a research artist and head of the MARS-Media Arts Research Science Department at Fraunhofer Institute for Media Communication. Previously, she founded and codirected Art+Com in Berlin. She studied visual arts, fashion design, drama and computer graphics in Zürich and Berlin. Her multidisciplinary background made her an expert in the world of art, computer science, and media technology. Her areas of expertise are Knowledge Arts & Knowledge Media, Interface Cultures, Interactive Systems, Virtual and Mixed Reality Environments. Fleischmann is the editor of the book *Digital Transformations*, and an editorial board member and reviewer for professional journals, conferences, and study courses. In 2000 *Time Fast Forward* magazine named her among the People to Watch. Her work—in partnership with Wolfgang Strauss—was awarded the Ars Electronica Golden Nica in Interactive Art in 1992. MARS is called one of the fifteen Media Art & Technology Labs with an international reputation. Since 1999 MARS has been developing an Internet platform for media art and digital culture, netzspannung.org, and knowledge discovery tools to explore this online archive.

Ben Fry recently completed his doctoral degree at the MIT Media Laboratory, where his research focused on methods of visualizing large amounts of data from dynamic information sources. His dissertation, "Computational Information Design," examines methods for combining the disparate fields of computer science, statistics, graphic design, and data visualization as a means of understanding complex data.

The research has been applied to understanding the human genome data. Fry's work has been shown at the Whitney Biennial in 2002 and the Cooper Hewitt Design Triennial in 2003, as well as the Museum of Modern Art in New York, Ars Electronica in Linz, Austria, and seen in the films *Minority Report* and *The Hulk*.

Carsten Görg   is working as a postdoctoral research fellow, funded by the German Academic Exchange Service (DAAD), at the College of Computing at the Georgia Institute of Technology in Atlanta. He studied computer science and mathematics as a double major at Saarland University in Germany, where he also received his PhD in computer science. His research interests include graph drawing, in particular dynamic graph drawing, information and software visualization, and also software engineering and software evolution.

Susanne Grabowski   began her work on the design of hypermedia as learning environments during her studies of social management and media education at the Fachhochschule Munich and the University of Augsburg, Germany. Since 1998, she has been a member of the Working Group on Computer Graphics and Interactive System, University of Bremen. Her obligations encompassed teaching and research in digital media. As a member of the compArt project she investigates the dialectics of algorithmics and aesthetics in the early history of computer art. She has authored several papers in this area. Her current interests include computer art, semiotics, aesthetics, didactics, critical theory, and digital media. In her PhD research, she applies Peircean semiotics and the metaphor of space to describe potentials of digital media as study environments.

Diane Gromala   is the founding Director of the BioMedia Lab and Associate Professor at the Georgia Institute of Technology. An artist, designer, theorist, and curator, Gromala's research explores the co-constituitive possibilities of embodiment and emerging technologies. Gromala's artwork in virtual reality, biomedical technologies, and pain has been exhibited worldwide and featured on the BBC, CNN and the Discovery Channel. Its technological innovation was recognized by American Institute of Graphic Arts, the American Institute of Architects, *Discover* magazine and the U.S. Congress. Since her work at Apple Computer in the 1980s, Gromala's design work has received numerous awards and is currently supported by the National Science Foundation and the United Nations Educational, Scientific and Cultural Organization (UNESCO). Gromala's extensive publications have appeared in numerous scholarly, scientific, art and design journals. Her recent book, *Windows and Mirrors, Interaction Design, Digital Art and the Myth of Transparency*, was coauthored with Jay Bolter and published by the MIT Press. She is currently collaborating with Dr. Tom Ettinger of Yale University on the development of systems for pain management, self-regulation, and sensory integration that combine immersive virtual reality and biofeedback technologies.

Kenneth A. Huff   is an independent fine artist working primarily in digital/new media. His three-dimensional organic constructions are presented as prints, sculptures, and time-based works and documented at http://www.kennethahuff.com/. He started showing his work in October 1997 and since has received over 110 visual arts awards. His work has been exhibited in seven consecutive ACM SIG-GRAPH art exhibitions (1998–2004) and is held in private, corporate, and public collections throughout the world. Huff has lectured about his work and demonstrated his techniques frequently. Venues include the School of Visual Arts (New York), the College for Creative Studies (Detroit, Michigan), and numerous SIGGRAPH conferences.

Frederic Fol Leymarie is a graduate of the Polytechnic School of Montreal (Electrical Engineering, honors in aeronautics, 1986), McGill University (MEng in biomedical imagery, 1990), and Brown University (PhD in 3D shape representation, 2003). He was Project Manager in the R&D group of the GIS activity of Thales (then Syseca) in Paris from 1994 until 1998. In 1999, he cofounded the SHAPE lab at Brown University. Since 2004 he has been Professor of Computing at the Goldsmiths College, University of London, in the UK, where he leads a new graduate program in Arts and Computing. His recent collaborations include working with archaeologists (site of Petra, Jordan), sculptors (from the Mid-Ocean studio in Rhode Island), textile specialists (at the Constance Howard Center, London), and applied mathematicians and engineers in computer-aided design and free-form shape understanding.

Michael Leyton's mathematical work on shape has been used by scientists in more than forty disciplines including radiology, meteorology, computer vision, chemical engineering, geology, computer-aided design, anatomy, botany, software engineering, architecture, linguistics, mechanical engineering, computer graphics, archaeology, and quantum mechanics. His work is widely applicable because Leyton has established new foundations for geometry that fundamentally oppose the standard foundations for geometry from Euclid to modern physics including Einstein. In Leyton's foundations, a geometric object acts as a memory store for action rather than a memoryless object (invariant) as in the standard foundations. His scientific contributions have received several prizes, such as a presidential award and a medal for scientific achievement. He is also a much exhibited artist. His paintings, sculptures, and architectural projects have been featured in international design journals and invited exhibitions. He is also a prolific composer, and the scores of his string quartets are currently being published. His artistic work exemplifies his new foundations for geometry. Leyton is a professor in the Center for Discrete Mathematics and Theoretical Computer Science at Rutgers, as well as the Psychology Department. He is President of the International Society for Mathematical and Computational Aesthetics and has been the keynote and plenary speaker at conferences in virtually every scientific and artistic discipline.

John Lee is deputy director of the Human Communication Research Centre at the University of Edinburgh, and also a senior lecturer in the School of Arts, Culture and Environment. He holds an MA in Philosophy and a PhD in Philosophy and Cognitive Science, both from Edinburgh. His time is divided between informatics and architecture, reflecting a longstanding interest in computing and cognition in design and learning, and in means of communication and external representation that are not narrowly linguistic, especially using graphics. He directs a master's degree program on Design and Digital Media, and has a long history of research on multimodal dialogue, including dialogue systems that seek to combine natural language with graphics and gesture, and on the roles of dialogue and representation in learning. He is also the coordinator of the Edinburgh-Stanford Link program of research and development into speech and language technology, funded by Scottish Enterprise.

Jonas Löwgren, born 1964, is Professor of Interaction Design in the School of Arts and Communication, Malmö University, Sweden. His work is partly about designing digital things, mainly in the fields of interactive visualization, mixed material-virtual media and at the intersection of mass media and interactive media. The other part of his work is to contribute to the design theory of digital materials. In terms of quantitative output, Jonas's work has led to two textbooks, around forty peer-reviewed publications and thirty portfolio items as well as fifty invited talks and fifty publications for general audiences and less rigorous scientific venues. More important, however, some of the work has turned out to be useful in professional applications and other parts have worked well as learning resources for interaction design students. More details can be found at webzone.k3.mah.se/k3jolo.

Roger Malina is an astronomer and space scientist. He was the Principal Investigator of NASA-EUVE Observatory, which carried out the first maps of the sky in the extreme ultraviolet portion of the spectrum. He is currently a coinvestigator in the Super Nova Acceleration Probe proposal to build a wide-field space telescope to map the large-scale structure and geometry of the universe; such mapping using supernovae as standard candles and mapping of gravitational lensing will allow the nature of dark energy and dark matter to be studied. Malina is a Directeur de Recheche of the CNRS at the Laboratoire d'Astrophysique de Marseille. He has also been, since 1982, Chairman of Leonardo/International Society for the Arts, Sciences and Technology; Leonardo/ISAST is the publisher of the Leonardo Journals and Books with MIT Press, awards a number of prizes and organizes workshops and other services to the art, science, and technology profession. A member of the International Academy of Astronautics and co-chair of the IAA Space and Society Commission, Malina leads the Leonardo Space Arts Working Group, which seeks to enable collaborations between artists and space scientists and engineers.

Laurent Mignonneau is an internationally renowned media artist working in the field of interactive computer installation. He holds a position as Professor for Interface Culture at the University of Art and Design in Linz Austria and at the IAMAS International Academy of Media Arts and Sciences in Gifu, Japan. He previously worked as researcher and Artistic Director at the ATR Advanced Telecommunications Research Lab in Kyoto, Japan. Mignonneau has been collaborating since 1992 with media artist Christa Sommerer, to create pioneering interactive computer installations such as "Interactive Plant Growing" (1992), "Anthroposcope" (1993), "A-Volve" (1994), "Trans Plant" (1995), "Intro Act" (1995), "MIC Exploration Space" (1995), "GENMA" (1996), "Life Spacies" (1997), "Life Spacies II" (1999), "HAZE Express" (1999), "VERBARIUM" (1999), "Industrial Evolution" (2000), "PICO_SCAN" (1999/2000), "Riding the Net" (2000), "The Living Room" (2001), "The Living Web" (2002), "Nano-Scape" (2002), "Mobile Feelings" (2003), and "Eau de Jardin" (2004). Their works have been shown in around 130 exhibitions worldwide and are permanently installed in media museums and media collections around the world, including the Media Museum of the ZKM in Karlsruhe, Germany, the NTT-ICC InterCommunication Center in Tokyo, the Cartier Foundation in Paris, the Millennium Dome in London, the Tokyo Metropolitan Museum of Photography in Japan, the AEC Ars Electronica Center in Linz, Austria, the NTT Plan-Net in Nagoya, Japan, Shiroishi Multimedia Art Center in Shiroishi, Japan, and the HOUSE-OF-SHISEIDO in Tokyo. Mignonneau and Sommerer have won major international media awards, for example, the Golden Nica Ars Electronica Award for Interactive Art 1994 (Linz, Austria), the Ovation Award of the Interactive Media Festival 1995 (Los Angeles), the Multi Media Award '95 of the Multimedia Association Japan, and the World Technology Award in London (2001). They have published numerous research papers on Artificial Life, interactivity, and interface design and lectured extensively at universities, international conferences, and symposia. In 1998, together with Christa Sommerer, Mignonneau edited a book on the collaboration of art and science called *Art@Science*, published by Springer Verlag.

Frieder Nake is a Professor of Graphic Data Processing and Interactive Systems at the Department of Computer Science, University of Bremen, Germany. He earned degrees in mathematics from the University of Stuttgart (Diplom in 1963, Dr.rer.nat. in 1967). He was a visiting researcher in computer art at the University of Toronto in 1968–69, and an Assistant Professor in Computer Science at the University of British Columbia, Vancouver, in 1970. In 1972, he went to Bremen as a full professor. His research interests are in computer graphics, digital media, computer art, computers in education, semiotics, and the theory of computing science. He began work in computer graphics and art in December 1963, and is recognized as one of the first to exhibit computer art (November 1965). He contributed to many art exhibitions, mainly between 1965 and 1972. Recently, he had one-man shows at the prestigious Kunsthalle Bremen and ZKM Karlsruhe, and has designed hypermedia installations for museums in Germany. He has published widely and taught on all levels of computer science, but also in the humanities and education. He won the First Prize of the Computer Art Contest of "Computers and Automation" in 1966. He has been a visiting professor to the University of Vienna, University of Oslo, University of Colorado at Boulder, and University of Aarhus, Denmark.

Ray Paton was Lecturer of Computer Science at the University of Liverpool, UK, and passed away during the editing of this book. The following text was taken from the Computer Science Department web page, and we include it here verbatim. Ray entered academia relatively late in life, after a spell as a teacher in a Liverpool high school. He joined the Department of Computer Science in 1989, initially as a research assistant in the area of knowledge-based systems. He became a Lecturer in 1991, and was promoted to Senior Lecturer in 2001, and then Reader in January 2004. Ray's main research interests were at the intersection of biology and computer science. He was an original, influential, and charismatic researcher, with collaborators across the world. Many computer scientists with an interest in biology are met with scepticism by researchers in the biology community, but Ray had the rare ability to win over researchers in both computer science and biology with his vision. Those who worked with him will readily attest to his enthusiasm and willingness to listen, and his skill at making connections between people and ideas. The author of innumerable research papers and books, Ray was also involved in founding and editing several journals. As well as being a successful academic, Ray was a dedicated and loving father and husband. He is survived by his wife Christine and two sons, Daniel and Andrew. Our thoughts are with them.

Jane Prophet is Co-Director of the Centre for Arts Research, Technology and Education (CARTE) and Professor of Visual Art and New Media at the University of Westminster, London. She graduated in Fine Art (Sheffield Hallam University 1987), completing her PhD at Warwick University in 1995. She is an artist whose work includes large-scale installations, digital print, websites and CD-ROMs. Her art reflects her interest in complexity theory, landscape, and artificial life. Among her past projects is the award-winning piece, TechnoSphere. Site-specific projects include Conductor (the inaugural installation at The Wapping Project, made using 74 tons of water and 120 electroluminescent cables), Decoy, and The Landscape Room, which combine images of real and computer-simulated landscapes. She works collaboratively across disciplines in a number of internationally acclaimed projects that have broken new ground in art, technology and science. In CELL (2002–) she collaborates with mathematician Mark d'Inverno and Neil Theise, a scientist whose ground-breaking research into stem cells behavior is changing the way we understand the body. She has just been awarded a National Endowment for Science Technology and the Arts Dream Time Fellowship to spend a year developing her interdisciplinary collaborations.

Aaron Quigley is a member of the systems research group and college lecturer in the University College Dublin, Ireland. He has previously held positions as a Senior Research Fellow in the University of Sydney, Australia, a visiting scientist in Mitsubishi Electric Research Labs, Massachusetts and an Associate Lecturer in the University of Newcastle, Australia. He was awarded his PhD in 2002 and has produced over thirty publications since 1998. These include three journal publications (two in submission); two edited volumes; one book chapter; eighteen international conferences and workshops; and twelve national conferences and workshops. He holds two international patents. His research interests fall broadly within the area of adaptive systems. In particular, his specific research interests include information visualization and ubiquitous computing. Along with this, he is a core member of the ARC Research Network in Enterprise Information Infrastructure in Australia and was recently appointed as a faculty fellow with the IBM Dublin Centre for Advanced Studies. He has previously collaborated with Motorola, MERL, Semantic Designs, NICTA, Smart Internet CRC, and Telstra on joint research projects. Dr. Quigley's supervision responsibilities currently include two PhD students and he has had two MSc and six honors (1st class) completions. He is a member of the Editorial Board of Journal of Pervasive Computing and Communications. He has taken a leading role in four international conference/workshops (Treasurer Chair, Co-Chair, Volunteer Chair, Proceedings Editor) and has been a member of eighteen other conference/workshop scientific/program/organizing committees.

Casey Reas is an artist and educator exploring process and abstraction through diverse digital media. Reas has exhibited and lectured in Europe, Asia, and the United States and his work has recently been shown at Ars Electronica (Linz), Kunstlerhaus (Vienna), Microwave (Hong Kong), ZKM (Karlsruhe), and the bitforms gallery (New York). Reas received his MS degree in Media Arts and Sciences from MIT, where he was a member of the Aesthetics and Computation Group. He is an Assistant Professor in UCLA's Design|Media Arts Department.

Christa Sommerer is an internationally renowned media artist working in the field of interactive computer installation. She holds a position as Professor for Interface Culture at the University of Art and Design in Linz, Austria, and at the IAMAS International Academy of Media Arts and Sciences in Gifu, Japan. He previously worked as a researcher and Artistic Director at the ATR Advanced Telecommunications Research Lab in Kyoto, Japan. Sommerer has been collaborating since 1992 with media artist Laurent Mignonneau, creating pioneering interactive computer installations such as "Interactive Plant Growing" (1992), "Anthroposcope" (1993), "A-Volve" (1994), "Trans Plant" (1995), "Intro Act" (1995), "MIC Exploration Space" (1995), "GENMA" (1996), "Life Spacies" (1997), "Life Spacies II" (1999), "HAZE Express" (1999), "VERBARIUM" (1999), "Industrial Evolution" (2000), "PICO_SCAN" (1999/2000), "Riding the Net" (2000), "The Living Room" (2001), "The Living Web" (2002), "Nano-Scape" (2002), "Mobile Feelings" (2003) and "Eau de Jardin" (2004). Their works have been shown in around 130 exhibitions worldwide and are permanently installed in media museums and media collections around the world, including the Media Museum of the ZKM in Karlsruhe, Germany, the NTT-ICC InterCommunication Center in Tokyo, the Cartier Foundation in Paris, the Millennium Dome in London, the Tokyo Metropolitan Museum of Photography in Japan, the AEC Ars Electronica Center in Linz, Austria, the NTT Plan-Net in Nagoya, Japan, Shiroishi Multimedia Art Center in Shiroishi, Japan and the HOUSE-OF-SHISEIDO in Tokyo. Sommerer and Mignonneau have won major international media awards, including the Golden Nica Ars Electronica Award for Interactive Art 1994 (Linz, Austria), the Ovation Award of the Interactive Media Festival 1995 (Los Angeles), the Multi Media Award '95 of the Multimedia Association Japan, and the World Technology Award in London (2001). They have published numerous research papers on Artificial Life, interactivity, and interface design and lectured extensively at universities, international conferences, and symposia. Sommerer is also an international coeditor of the *Leonardo Journal* (MIT Press). In 1998, together with Laurent Mignonneau, she edited a book on the collaboration of art and science called *Art@Science*, published by Springer Verlag.

Wolfgang Strauss is an architect, media artist, and Codirector of the MARS-Exploratory Media Lab at Fraunhofer Institute for Media Communication. He was a Visiting Professor in Kassel and Saarbrücken and a research scientist. He studied Architecture and Visual Communication at the Berlin University of the Arts. His areas of expertise are Interactive Media Art and Design. Currently he is working on interfaces connecting the human body and digital media space. His work, in partnership with Monika Fleischmann, was awarded the Ars Electronica Golden Nica in Interactive Art in 1992. MARS is one of the fifteen Media Art & Technology Labs with an international reputation that has been developing an Internet platform for media art and digital culture, netzspannung.org, since 1999, and knowledge discovery tools to explore this online archive.

Noam Tractinsky is a Senior Lecturer at the Department of Information Systems Engineering at Ben-Gurion University. He received his PhD in Information Systems from the University of Texas at Austin. His research appeared in journals such as *Behavior & Information Technology*, *Communications of the ACM*, *Human-Computer Interaction*, *Interacting with Computers*, *International Journal of Human-Computer Studies*, and *MIS Quarterly*. His recent research projects involved the study of consumer behavior in e-commerce and the effects of time pressure and time delays on decision making and user behavior. He is currently interested in the study of aesthetic and affective aspects of information technology.

Paul Vickers holds a BSc degree in Computer Studies from Liverpool Polytechnic and a PhD in Human-Computer Interaction from Loughborough University. He is currently Principal Lecturer in at Northumbria University, where he has been since 2001. Between 1989 and 2001 Vickers taught at Liverpool John Moores University, and before that worked in a software development team at Digital Equipment Co. Ltd. Vickers is a UK Chartered Engineer and a member of the Institution of Electrical Engineers as well as a registered practitioner in the UK's Higher Education Academy. His research centers on human-computer interaction (HCI) and auditory visualization, with a particular focus on the use of music as a medium for external representations. Vickers has presented at and been on the organizing committees for a number of international conferences and has been interviewed by international media about his work on auditory representations of programs. A keen musician, he is very interested in bringing together technologists, engineers, musicians, composers, sound artists, audio engineers, and programmers to build well-motivated and well-designed tools for exploring sound as a communication medium. He owns no cats.

Dror Zmiri is a graduate student at the Department of Information Systems Engineering at Ben-Gurion University. He has a BSc in Management & Industrial Engineering, specializing in Information Systems, and a BSc in Computer Science & Mathematics, both from the Ben-Gurion University.

Index

AbsInt, 231
Abstraction, 321
  and interface, 362
  and large-scale data, 321, 327, 329
  and minimalism, 16
Action spaces
  explorative space, 121 123
  image retrieval system, 175 179
  information space, 118 123, 126 129
  participation space, 123 126
Activity, 359–362, 364
Adams, D., 336, 337
Adams, L. S., 5
Administrative data, 393
Adobe, 222–225
Aesthetic computing
  appearance vs. behavior, 193
  code vs. interface, 369, 380
  computer role, 44
  definitions, 6, 54, 57, 305–310
  future directions, 215–225
  goals, 130–131
  institutional programs, 45–47
  methodologies, 47

  modality, 13
  novelty, 11
  process architecture, 7f, 9
  reusability, 310
  strong and weak claims, 47, 50
  teaching tools, 198–202
Aesthetic Computing Manifesto, 46, 54
Aesthetic diversity, 6
Aesthetic induction, 253
Aesthetics. *See also* Beauty
  of abstraction, 327
  and algorithmic art, 62
  and art, 12–13, 54, 57
  in auralization, 341–348
  and consumer attitudes, 408
  definitions, 4
  early impressions, 417
  emergence, 172–174, 190
  and emotions, 407, 409
  Goodman view, 31
  of graphs, 316–320, 324–327
  of interface, 66–69, 412, 415–417
  and mathematics, 9–11, 13–19, 246
  models, 13–19

Association for Computing Machinery, 5, 11, 54
Associativity, 296
Astronomy, 103, 104f, 106–108, 109f
Asymmetry principle, 301, 304
ATMs, 395, 398
Atom, 308
Audio, 341, 410–415. *See also* Auralization
Augmented reality, 13, 380
Auralization. *See also* Sound
  aesthetics of, 341–348
  early examples, 337–339
  and programming, 337, 340, 343, 348
Authorship, 190. *See also* Sharing
Auto-Illustrator, 397, 398f
Autonomy, 389
Avatars, 106, 389
Avatopia, 395, 396f

Badre, A. N., 371
Baecker, R. M., 338
Baerentsen, K. B., 359
Bagrow, L., 101
Ball, T., 230, 316, 317
Banff Center for the Arts, 46
Bar charts, 101
Bardram, J. E., 360, 363, 364, 377
Bargh, J. A., 417
Barnes, J., 319, 329
Baumgarten, A. G., 4
Bear, E. G., 406
Beautification, 193
Beauty, 229
  and communication, 229–235, 240
  defined, 241–243, 251, 252
  as judgment, 229, 247–249, 253
  in mathematics, 229, 240–246, 250–253
  and objectivity, 250
  and shape, 261–263
  in software, 234

time factors, 250, 252, 254
Behavior
  vs. appearance, 192–194
  drawing tool for, 209
  three-level theory, 407
Belk, R. W., 409
Benjamin, W., 69
Bense, M., 130
Berlin, B., 94
Berlyne, D. E., 407
Berners-Lee, T., 119, 121
Berscheid, E., 408
Bertelsen, O. W., 377
Betts, A., 96, 97
Biddle, J. E., 409
Bill, M., 249
Binary digits, 38
Binford, T., 268
Biology
  genetics, 173, 174f, 175f, 339
  stem cells, 185–194
  tissue slides, 187, 189
Birkhoff, G. D., 243
Bitangency, 266–269
Black, J., 101
Black, M., 90
Blackberry, 396
Blackwell, A. F., 10
Blascovich, J., 343
Bloch, P., 409
Blom, J. O., 405, 406, 409
Blum, H., 263, 268
Bly, S., 405
Boardman, D. B., 338
Bobick, A., 124
Bock, D. S., 338
Bødker, S., 360, 377
Bogaevsky, I., 277
Bohn, C., 116
Bolter, J., 44, 357, 363, 364

Explorative space, 121–123

Expression, 32

Expressionism, 16

FADE (Force Algorithms by Decomposed Estimation), 318, 327–331

Feather, 395

Ferguson, C., 9

Ferguson, H., 9

Fermat's Last Theorem, 247, 255

Fernandes, G., 407

Fiber, 299–305

Field, M., 241

Figa Talamanca, A., 249

Film-making, 45, 55

  IMAX, 104–107

Filter, 7, 8, 322

Financing, 46

Fingerprints, 143

Fishwick, P., 8, 13, 41, 46, 341, 417, 418

Flexibility, 393

Flow

  of information, 126–129, 217

  and 3D shape, 268

  and transfer, 295, 308

Flow geometry, 95–99, 102f, 108

Flusser, V., 125

Foley, J., 94, 95

Forceville, C., 91

Form, 282. *See also* Shape

Four Color Theorem, 240

Fowler, M., 232

Frames, 77, 79–81

Francioni, J. M., 338, 339

Fraunhofer Institute, 115

Freeland, C., 5

Frijda, N., 406

Fry, B., 9, 204

Fujihata, M., 386

Functionality, 398. *See also* Utility

Galer Flyte, M., 407

Galloway, A., 45

Galloway, E., 48

Galois's theory, 250

Gal'perin, P. Y., 360

Games

  autonomy, 389

  code examples, 223f, 224f

  and GUIs, 56

  Nintendo, 221, 222

  playability, 386

  Super Mario Brothers, 222

Gapenne, O., 283

Garden icons, 99–101, 104f, 109

Gardner, M., 72

Garland, K., 78

Gateways, 76t, 83

Gaver, W., 344, 395, 397

Gelerner, D., 10, 234

Gender, 44

Generative Art, 171

Genetics, 173, 174f, 175f, 187, 339

Genres, 400

Geometry

  and art, 12

  and causality, 309

  flow geometry, 95–99, 102f, 108

  and graph drawing, 324, 328

  and medial axis, 264

  and recoverability, 300–302

  and transfer, 296–300, 302–311

Geons, 232

Gestalt theory

  definition, 300

  and medial axis, 264

  original principles, 262

  shock scaffold, 277

  and transfer, 311

Getzels, J. W., 417

Giblin, P., 267–270, 277, 279, 282

Gibson, J. J., 359
Gilmore, M., 96, 97
Gislén, Y., 395
Giusti, E., 252
Glaser, D., 191
Glyphs, 95–98, 323, 327
God-games, 389
Gold, R., 46
Goldberg, A., 376
Goldberg, K., 49, 376
Gold trade, 316
Gombrich, E., 242
Goodman, Nelson
  implementation, 36–40
  (non)notational work, 33, 35, 40
  relevance, 40
  symbol systems, 29–33
Gorg, C., 241
Granularity, 230, 234
Graphic user interfaces (GUIs), 53, 56, 234, 376
Graphs. *See* Diagrammatic graphs
Grau, O, 8
Green, T. R. G., 36
Greenwold, S., 215
Gregory, R. L., 94
GRID method, 49
Gromala, D., 44, 357, 363, 364
Group identity, 410
Groups. *See also* Clusters
  and abstract representation, 327
  and symmetry-breaking, 301, 310–312
  and transfer, 296

Hackers, 394
Hadamard, J., 9
Hall, M., 96, 97
Hamermesh, D. S., 409
Hamiltonian mechanics, 294
Hansen, K., 222
Harmony, 9

Harré, R., 74
Harris, J., 393
Harry Potter, 56
Hass, U., 125
Hassenzahl, M., 407, 409
Haughe-Nilsen, A. L., 407
Hazed Windows, 388
Hekkert, P., 406, 417
Henderson, A., 393
Henderson, L., 12
Hermeneutics, 72–74, 194
Hershberger, J., 338
Herzberg, F., 408
Hierarchies
  and collections, 77
  elision techniques, 323
  and FADE, 328, 330
  hyperbolic view, 322f
  in prime factor encoding, 157–161
  and transfer, 292, 298, 307
Hiltzik, M., 376
Hirschheim, R., 409
Hirsh, H., 119
Hoffman, D., 240
Hoffman, J. T., 240
Holbein painting, 290, 305
Holmes, T., 379
Holmlid, S., 399
Hoofman, D., 241
Höök, K., 54
Hopkins, J., 14
Hult, L., 400
Human activity theory, 359–362, 364
Human beings. *See also* Cognition; Perception;
  Senses
  behavior, 398, 407
  brain, 171
  emotions, 6, 405–408
  identity, 117, 393, 409
  objectives, 62

awareness of (*see* Reflectivity)

challenges, 21

consistency, 377

cultural factors, 362

customization (*see* Skins)

desirable qualities, 384–401

dialectics, 364

efficiency, 395, 396

elegance, 396

evolution, 358

focus, 361, 364

future requirements, 9

GUIs, 53, 56, 234, 376

innovation, 363

music analogy, 44

objects in, 362–364

participation space, 123–126, 362

perception, 362

pliability, 9, 65–66, 384, 392

seductivity, 387

as sign, 65

and software design, 67

transparency (*see* Transparency)

usability, 408, 415–417

International Symposium on Electronic Arts
(ISEA), 44

Internet

and distant users, 124

image retrieval system, 174–179

individual requirements, 121

and Processing, 210–212

and visualization, 99, 100f, 175–179

Interpretation

in complex systems, 190

and computer programs, 38

of encoded objects, 153

meaning-making, 397–399

mouse/slider example, 64

of music, 346

of visualizations, 94, 99, 109

Inter-Society for the Electronic Arts (ISEA),
370

Interval Research Inc., 46

Intuition, 249

Invariance, 9, 302

Inverse, 296

Irani, P., 232

IRCAM, 46

Jackson, J. A., 338

James, J., 335

Jameson, D. H., 338

Java. *See also* Processing

audio, 215, 349

and Goodman, 35

for learners, 207–210

RUBE project, 14

stem cell project, 192, 193

Jerding, D. F., 317

Jitter by Cycling, 225

Johnson, M., 73, 90, 94

Jones, S., 175

Jonsson, F. U., 409

Journeys, 76t, 81, 83

Kaap, T., 103

Kahler, R., 107

Kandinsky, W., 248

Kanizsa, G., 262

Kannan, S., 233

Kant, I., 4, 13, 192, 242

Karvonen, K., 409

Kaufmann, W., III, 93

Kay, A., 376

Kay, P., 94

Keller, M. M., 95

Keller, P. R., 95

Kelly, M., 4, 6

Kemp, M., 12

Kepes, G., 45

Khaslavsky, J., 387
KidsRoom, 124
Kim, T., 14
Kimia, B., 265, 267–270, 277, 279, 282
Kinesthesia, 116, 390
King, J. P., 253, 254
King, R. D., 339, 347
Kinloch, D. P., 315
Kipnis, J., 398
Kirschenbaum, M., 407
Klein, J., 406
Kline, M., 239–240
Knowledge
  for design process, 400
  and diagrams, 73–75
  and discovery, 245
  space of, 117–123, 126–129
Knowledge discovery tools, 121–123
Knowledge Explorer, 121
Knuth, D., 10, 347
Koehler, W., 262
Koenderink, J., 282
Koeppel, D., 405, 408
Koffka, K., 259
Kohonen Map, 122
Kramer, G., 337, 338
Krauß, M., 58
Krause, K., 393
Kruja, E., 72
Kurzweil, R., 119
Kuutti, K., 360
Kyng, M., 358

Lakoff, G., 9, 73, 90, 94, 126
Lamping, J., 322
Language(s)
  of computing, 34–36 (*see also* Programming
    languages)
  for Goodman, 29–32
  in interactive space, 125
  in interdisciplinary project, 188

in knowledge space, 126
and metaphor, 90
visual encoding, 139, 148
Large-scale information
  cognitive load, 320, 322, 325
  distortion, 322
  emphasis techniques, 321–323
  FADE paradigm, 318, 327–331
  filtering, 322
  graphing, 316–320
  relationships, 321
Lavie, T., 409, 410, 416, 417
Laws, symmetry of, 294
Learning, 407
Learning tools, 198–210
Lee, J. R., 36
Lehman, F., 72
Leonard, L., 103
Leonardo, 3, 43–50
Leontjev, A. N., 359
Levoy, M., 260
Levy, S., 96, 97, 104, 107, 108
Leyton, M., 9, 263, 265
Lindgard, G., 406, 409
Literature. *See* Novels; Plays; Poetry
Livio, M., 229
Lloyd, B., 94
Loeffler, C., 48
LOGO, 225
Lopez-Gulliver, R., 174, 175, 179
Lorensen, W. E., 98
Lorenz attractor, 241
Löwgren, J., 8, 54, 66, 378
Lucas, P. A., 347
Lyman, I., 405
Lyman, P., 315

Maas, A., 406
Macintosh
  and aesthetics, 377, 409
  iMac, 56, 393, 409

groups of, 327
location, 325
Nonlinear equations, 241
Norman, D., 341, 375–376, 379, 406, 407, 409
Norman, M., 107, 108
Notation, 33, 35, 40
secondary, 36, 41
Novak, J., 71, 120, 121
Novels, 35, 36, 38
programming metaphor, 170
Numbers. *See also* Prime numbers
composite, 148, 152
Design By Numbers, 198–202
random, in ranges, 140–146
visually encoded, 139, 148
Nuñez, R. E., 9

Objectivity, 250, 252
Object-oriented programming, 348
Object-oriented structures, 35, 310–312
Objects
in algorithmic art, 62–65
definition, 282
deformations, 296, 299–305
encoded, 139, 148–150, 156
infinite encoded (*see* Prime factors)
interaction with, 13
in interface, 362–364
multiperspectivism, 6–7
parafunctionality, 398
similar but unique (*see* Prime factors)
of social appraisal, 409
and symmetry-breaking, 301, 310–312
Oliver, R. L., 411
OpenGL, 192, 206
Order, 242, 244
Ordinary differential equations, 241
Orthogonal drawing, 324
Osborne, H., 4

O'Shea, B., 108
Osmose, 390

Paal, S., 118, 119, 120
Pablo, 217
Pacioli, L., 239
Paintings, computer-generated, 57–60
Paint programs, 38
Papert, S. A., 249
Parafunctionality, 398
Parallelogram, 301
Pardoe, J. P., 347
Parker, D. H. H., 346
Parncutt, R., 345, 346
Parsimony, 6, 9, 13
Partial differential equations, 241
Participation space, 123–126
Paton, R., 72
Pattern notes, 79
Pattern recognition, 338
Patterns
in complex systems, 179
in prime factor encoding, 137. 145, 143, 156
unconscious, 249
Patterson, R., 96, 97, 104, 105, 107, 108
Paul, C., 129
Pearce, C., 386
Peer-review, 191
Peirce, C. S., 61, 64
Peitgen, H. O., 241
Penrose, R., 254
People tracking, 99, 102f, 108
Perceivability, 57, 62
Perception
and interface, 362
multiperspectivism, 6–7
and practice, 361
and senses, 54, 63, 116
of sign, 53, 66
in slider example, 64

Perception (cont.)

technology effect, 44, 50, 64, 116

trends, 116

Performance, 21, 36–40

Perlin noise algorithm, 211

Personal computers, 68. *See also* Apple
Computers

Personal connectedness, 394

Personalization

and identity, 410

and information space, 118

of interfaces, 405, 410–415

of technology devices, 406

and visualization, 11

Perspective, 6–8

shared, 74

Petre, M., 10, 36

Phillips, A., 192

Photography, 45

Photorealism, 193

Physics, 294, 301, 302, 304–310

Picard, R. W., 406

Picard's theorem, 250

Picasso, P., 75, 79, 321

Pictorial metaphors, 91

Pictures, for Goodman, 30–32

Pitaru, A., 215

PIXAR, 105

Pixel maps, 234

Pizer, S., 283, 284

Placement, 140

Planar drawing, 324

Planetariums, 104f, 106–108

Plato, 4, 9, 239, 241

Platonic solids, 250, 252

Plays, 33, 36–40

Pliability, 9, 65, 384, 392

Pliant research group, 384

Plurality, 6

Poetry, 35, 292–294

Poincaré, H., 248, 249

Pold, S., 364

Polyline drawing, 324

Porteous, J. D., 406, 409

Post-hoc worknotes, 384

Postrel, V., 409

PostScript, 206

Power, 396–397

Pratt, G. A., 406

Precision, 32. *See also* Vagueness

Preece, J., 399

Presence, 8, 116

Presentation, and content, 14

Prime factors

bracket elements, 149, 157

encoding schemes, 157–166

identity elements, 148–150, 153

reading spines, 149, 150, 154

used, 149, 150, 152, 157

Prime numbers

computation algorithm, 235

defined, 148, 150

early work, 142

and Nature, 137–139

and prime factor encoding, 144–146

skipped, 149, 157

Problem-solving, 9, 249

Process, of diagramming, 81

Processing, 9, 204–212, 213

project using, 219

Proebsting, T., 233

Programming languages

Boolean logic, 348

C++, 104, 192

for complex systems, 170–181

control, 170

and data, 220–222

deconstruction, 218, 223f, 224f

future trends, 217, 225

for learning, 198–210

Riding the Net, 389
Rigas, D. I., 340
Robbin, T., 12
Robbins, H., 252
Robertson, P. K., 94
Robotics, 312
Rockeby, D., 124
Rockefeller Foundation, 46
Rosch, E., 94
Rota, G. C., 250–251
Rotation, 244, 296, 299–304
Rotational symmetry, 295
Rovira, K., 283
Rozin, D., 371–375
RUBE project, 14
Rules
   and auralizations, 345
   conformity, and pleasure, 242
   and memory storage, 289, 309
   for shape construction, 306
   symmetry laws, 294
Runge-Kutta algorithm, 98
Run-time
   inheritance, 311
   and music, 340
Russell, J. A., 406

Sano, D., 53
Santoro-Brienza, L., 4
Saunders, R., 192
Scaffolding, 263–277, 278–281f
Scalable vector graphics, 15
Scale, 191–193
Schattschneider, D., 12
Schelhowe, H., 68
Schemata, 77t, 81
Schenkman, B. N., 409
Schiesser, G., 131
Schiffman, J., 215–216
Schlain, L., 12

Schmidt, K., 211
School for New Media, 45
Schroeder, W., 95
Schroedinger's equation, 308. *See also*
   Dynamical law
Schultz Kleine, S., 409
Science, 57, 294, 305–310. *See also* Physics
Screen space, 319, 326
Searching, 126–128, 179, 392
Sebastian, T., 277
Seductivity, 9, 387–388
SeeSoft, 230
Self-image, 393
Self-recognition, 117
Semantic density, 32
Semantic domains, 31, 35, 41
Semantic Map, 121–123
Semantic network, 126–129
Semiotics, 63–66
Sens-A-Patch, 384, 392–393
Senses. *See also* Auralization; Visualization
   and art perception, 116
   and concepts, 126
   and emotion, 409
   hearing and touch, 116, 390
   and perception, 54, 63, 116
   and the unobservable, 43, 49
   and virtual world, 390
September 11th, 116
Sequences
   in diagrammatic graphs, 80
   and prime factors, 145–154, 157–166
Serial numbers, 222–225
The Shamen, 339
Shape
   and beauty, 261–263
   complexity, 60
   computational model, 263–277
   cylinder, 299–303
   definition, 282

Sound-generating devices, 336
Sowa, J., 71–72
Space. *See* Action spaces; Screen space
Space shows, 104f, 106–108
Space-time, 308, 309. *See also* Time
Spatial organization, 123, 392
Speech, 175
Spell-checkers, 38
Spheres, 266–269
Spider diagrams, 79
Spreadsheets, 337, 394
Standardization, 13
Star graph, 79–81
Stasko, J., 11, 229, 317
Statistical functions, 104
Steadman, P., 12
Stem cells, 185–194
Stimulation, 386
Stolterman, E., 386
Storm, 96f, 97f
Storm (visualization), 96f
Strong, R., 395
Structure
  and Gestalt theory, 262–264
  in mathematics, 246
  object-orientation, 35
  in programs, 233
  transfer, 289–300, 303–305
Struppa, D., 254
Sturken, M., 377, 378
Subjectivism
  avoidance of, 365
  consequences, 13, 54
  and mathematics, 243, 247–250, 252
  and readability, 324
Subject/Medium filter, 7, 8
Supercomputing, 105
Super Mario Brothers, 222
Surface modeling, 329

Surfaces
  infinite minimal, 240
  information on, 380
Surprise, 397, 399
Surrealism, 16
Symbolic systems, 34–36
Symbolism
  and autonomous design, 389, 393
  and skins, 409, 413, 415, 416
Symbol systems, 29–32
Symmetry
  and aesthetics, 6
  asymmetry principle, 301, 304
  and curvature, 306
  and Gestalt theory, 262, 263
  in graph drawing, 326
  of laws, 294
  and mathematics, 9, 244
  and physics, 308
  and resemblance, 30
  translational, 295
Symmetry-breaking, 301–306
Syntax
  density, 32
  editing, 217
Synthesis, 6, 13
System dynamics, 13–19
Systems, 171–173, 175f, 179, 190, 192

Talamanca, A. F., 249
Taylor series, 20, 22f
Tek, H., 265, 277
Tele-presence, 116
Text
  cluster analysis, 122
  and diagrams, 76t, 83
  encoding scheme, 150
Theise, N., 185, 192, 194
Themes, 80

Theorems
  beauty in, 242–246, 250–254
  corollaries, 245
  of Fermat, 247, 255
  proofs, 240, 250, 253
Thickness, 140
Thiébaux, M., 105
3D. *See also* CAVE™; Shape
  and diagrammatic graphs, 259
  flow, 268
  geons, 232
  and glyphs, 95
  image retrieval, 175–178
  and IMAX movies, 104
  Internet visualization, 99, 100f, 175–179
  and mathematical beauty, 243
  Milky Way visualization, 104f
  and prime factor approach, 140–143, 154
  in RUBE project, 14–19
  scaffolding, 263–277, 278–281f
  screen space use, 326
  and sound, 215
  stem cell project, 193
  from 2D, 104
Time
  and auditory displays, 337
  and beauty, 250, 252, 254
  in code operation, 222
  real time, 116
  and recoverability, 303–309
  and skins preference, 417
Timeline, 121
Tissue slides, 187, 189
Tornado, 96f, 97f, 99
Touch, 116, 390
Touchscreen, 126
Tracking system, 99
Tracking systems, 99, 102f, 108–109
Tractinsky, N., 407, 409, 411, 416, 417

Trajectories, 95–99
Transdisciplinary projects, 185–194
Transfer, 289–311
  and Gestalt theory, 311
Transform structure, 311
Translation, 296, 299–302
Translational symmetry, 295
Transparency
  as aesthetic value, 377–378
  definition, 377
  discussion, 357–360
  and efficiency, 395
  and games, 193
  vs. reflectivity, 358, 361, 364, 375–380
  semi-transparency, 397
  and unanticipated use, 363–365
  Wooden Mirror, 371–375
Tree, 79–82, 322–323, 330f, 331
Treinish, L., 95
Trettvik, J., 359
Trigonometry, 104
Trogemann, G., 115, 130
Truth, 187
Tsunami, 116
Tufte, E., 101, 321
Tully, B., 104, 107
Turing, A., 216
Turkle, S., 129
2D
  and algorithmic art, 58
  geons, 232
  and sound, 20
  and stem cells, 193–194
  to 3D, 104

Ubiquitous computing, 380
unconscious mind, 249
UNESCO, 46
Unified Modeling Language (UML), 232